TAXING BLACKNESS

ATLANTIC CROSSINGS

Gabriel Paquette, Series Editor

TAXING BLACKNESS

Free Afromexican Tribute in Bourbon New Spain

Norah L. A. Gharala

THE UNIVERSITY OF ALABAMA PRESS
Tuscaloosa

The University of Alabama Press
Tuscaloosa, Alabama 35487-0380
uapress.ua.edu

Hardcover edition published 2019.
Paperback edition published 2025.
eBook edition published 2019.

Typeface: Garamond

Cover image: Miguel Cabrera, *De español y negra, mulata*, c. 1763; courtesy of Museo de Historia Mexicana, Monterrey, Mexico
Cover design: David Nees

Paperback ISBN: 978-0-8173-6227-0

A previous edition of this book has been cataloged by the Library of Congress.
ISBN: 978-0-8173-2007-2 (cloth)
E-ISBN: 978-0-8173-9220-8

Contents

Illustrations

MAPS

FIGURES

TABLES

Acknowledgments

This book resulted from a chance meeting about twelve years ago in a beautiful, provincial city in southern Mexico. While studying in Mérida, Yucatán, I saw Melchor Campos García's *Castas, feligresía y ciudadanía en Yucatán: Los afromestizos bajo el régimen constitucional español, 1750–1822* on the shelf of a university bookstore. This text served as my introduction to the history of a group of Afromexican militiamen and their families, who became the focus of my first archival visits. Ann Wightman fostered my interests in social history and advised my senior thesis, "Marriage Patterns among Afromestizos in Mérida and Campeche from 1789 to 1822," at Wesleyan University. Professor Wightman, known for her incredible dedication to her students and formidable classroom persona, brought out the best in me as a young historian.

My undergraduate project led me to my graduate adviser, Ben Vinson III, at Johns Hopkins University. My copy of *Bearing Arms for His Majesty: The Free-Colored Militia in Colonial Mexico* shows all the copious highlighting of a college student. I was thrilled to be accepted as Ben's student and to continue my study of colonial Afromexico with a historian whose work had influenced my early studies. Constantly opening doors for his students, Ben has been a mentor and friend for nearly a decade. Gabriel Paquette also began to direct my graduate research soon after he joined the faculty at Johns Hopkins and has generously supported my scholarship and career since. His professionalism, prolific research, and collaboration with academics from all over the world have inspired me and many other students besides. I thank both Ben and Gabe for their contributions to this book.

As I revised the manuscript, I often turned to comments from the members of the faculty at Johns Hopkins, including Franklin Knight, Sara Castro-Klarén, and María Portuondo. I had the good fortune of studying with Sara Berry, Richard Kagan, Philip Morgan, and A. J. R. Russell-Wood, whose nuanced Atlantic perspectives helped me lay the foundations for this book. Álvaro Caso Bello hosted me in Montevideo for my first conference presentation outside the United States and commented extensively on chapter 4. Joseph M. H. Clark and Sara Damiano thoroughly read multiple chapter drafts. Paige Glotzer offered a modernist take on my arguments and frequently bolstered my sense of the importance of my work. Amanda Mignonne Smith, Cathleen Carriss, Isaias Rojas-Perez, Gustavo Valdivia, and Túlio R. Zille (and other members of the "PLASeres") created a rich, interdisciplinary environment in which to exchange ideas. At the Milton S. Eisenhower Library, research librarians Chella Vaidyanathan and Stephanie Gamble assisted me as I revised the manuscript. Margaret Burri has been a wonderful friend and colleague over the years. Whether I was visiting her office or sitting at her kitchen table, she pointed me in the right direction.

I am grateful to a broader community of Latin Americanist historians who took an interest in my project. Presenting at the TePaske Seminar in Colonial Latin American History left me with a sense of affirmation and myriad directions to explore. At the Conference of the Rocky Mountain Council for Latin American Studies, I received excellent advice from Dana Velasco Murillo and Laurent Corbeil. Bianca Premo and Rachel O'Toole chaired panels at meetings of the American Historical Association and each offered detailed, thoughtful comments on pieces of what later would become chapters in this book. Brandi Waters offered insightful critiques of chapter 3. For their encouragement over the years, I thank Robinson Herrera, Marcela Echeverri, and David Sartorius.

My archival research in Mexico and Spain would not have been possible without funding from the Andrew W. Mellon Foundation in the form of a fellowship through the Council on Library and Information Resources. I thank Amy Lucko for her assistance while I was a fellow from 2010 to 2011. Ryan Kashanipour has graciously helped me in a range of capacities since my time as a Mellon Fellow. I thank him for his many suggestions throughout the course of this book project.

I owe a debt of gratitude to numerous people and institutions in Mexico and Spain. My correspondence and meetings with colonial specialists like Ricardo A. Fagoaga Hernández and Rafael Castañeda led me in many important historiographical directions. Groundbreaking Mexicanist research on colonial Afromexico has shaped my own work. I thank María Elisa Velázquez Gutiérrez and Adriana Rodríguez Delgado for their early support of the project. Purely by chance, I stayed in a boarding house in Coyoacán with future colleagues Trenton Barnes and Natalí Alcalá Moreno, whose talent and friendship were amazing outcomes of an internet apartment rental. I must also acknowledge the archivists at the Archivo General de la Nación in Mexico City. Angélica Pérez Nava and Alina Argüelles González, among many others, helped me consult and identify the materials I needed. Access to the public resources at the Instituto de Investigaciones José María Luis Mora is much appreciated. For their assistance at the Biblioteca Ernesto de la Torre Villar, I thank Ramón Aureliano Alarcón and Germán

Mejía Estrada. In Seville, I thank the dedicated archivists at the Archivo General de Indias as well as the staff at the Escuela de Estudios Hispano-Americanos.

My time at Northern Arizona University as visiting assistant professor in Latin American history was everything I could have asked for in a first job. I thank the entire History Department for giving me a space to develop as a scholar-teacher. Specifically, Heather Martel acted as my faculty mentor, a role that facilitated our collaboration as Atlanticists in the classroom as well as many fruitful discussions. Always willing to read materials and talk through whatever was concerning me, Heather was an ideal mentor. Chris Jocks (Kahnawake Mohawk) and I had neighboring offices during my first year, where I often shared ideas about history, teaching, and learning with a truly remarkable person and a great friend. I was also fortunate at NAU to have two successive department chairs who took a genuine interest in me. Eric Meeks welcomed me when he was chair and has continued to support my career. John Leung became chair in my second year at NAU; I thank him and Janet for the many rides to church and the humor and peace they brought to those Sunday mornings. While in Arizona, I was given the chance to work with a group of professors who showed me great generosity. For leading me by example, I thank Sanjam Ahluwalia, Alexandra Carpino, Leilah Danielson, and Ana Varela. For their advice on teaching and writing (and reminding me to drink water at high altitudes), I would like to recognize my friends Jeremy LaBuff, Cristi Wilson, Camarin Porter, Kendra Moore, and Roman Chacon. I owe a special debt of gratitude to my students in my first semesters of teaching. I had the pleasure of designing topical courses that drew undergraduates interested in Latin American studies whose ideas brought me along new paths. Among them were Caleb Endfield (White Mountain Apache), Brittany Erwin, Eli Keeling, and Alejandro E. Silva, who studied with me in seminar or independent study. I thank the incomparable Susan M. Deeds, who offered comments on parts of chapters 3 and 4 at the Southwest Seminar and opened her home in Mexico City.

As the book was in progress, I started an assistant professor position in world history at Georgian Court University (GCU). A summer grant following my first year at GCU allowed me to revisit some archival materials and acquire important new books in Mexico City. My colleagues have engaged enthusiastically with my research, especially members of the multidisciplinary Latin American Studies Working Group Kathryn Quinn-Sánchez, Marny Requa, and Jaime Rivera. Jaime's friendship has kept me on an even keel as I revised the manuscript.

For the publication of this book, I sincerely thank the University of Alabama Press and Wendi Schnaufer, who walked me through the process of creating this book. I greatly appreciate all her advice throughout the process. I am grateful to be part of the Atlantic Crossings book series and to work with series editor Gabriel Paquette. The two anonymous reviewers who read my manuscript gave an excellent balance of praise and criticism, showing me important findings to highlight and offering invaluable suggestions for how to improve.

I published much of chapter 6 as "*Calidad*, Genealogy, and Disputed Free-Colored Tributary Status in New Spain," *The Americas* 73, no. 2 (April 2016): 139–70. This material has been reprinted with permission from Cambridge University Press.

One of the aims of this book is to elucidate the genealogies and family histories that ordinary people drew on to improve their futures. In a way, I was raised on the stories people tell about themselves. My father's lifelong study of autobiography, slavery and freedom, and black intellectual history has been an inexhaustible source of information. As I have grown, so has my appreciation for his wisdom and the impact of his many books. My mother has always demonstrated to me the value of compassion for others, especially when expressed through creative endeavor. My brother's willingness to offer me new perspectives as a fellow history educator has sustained me. I thank my extended family, the Gharalas and Singhs, for the many home-cooked foods that kept me going. Finally, my spouse dedicated many hours to this book, all while filling our home with laughter and jokes. Our life together has challenged me to see past barriers and boundaries, to explore new ideas and tell new stories.

Map 0.1. Mexico/New Spain in the eighteenth century (Norah Gharala)

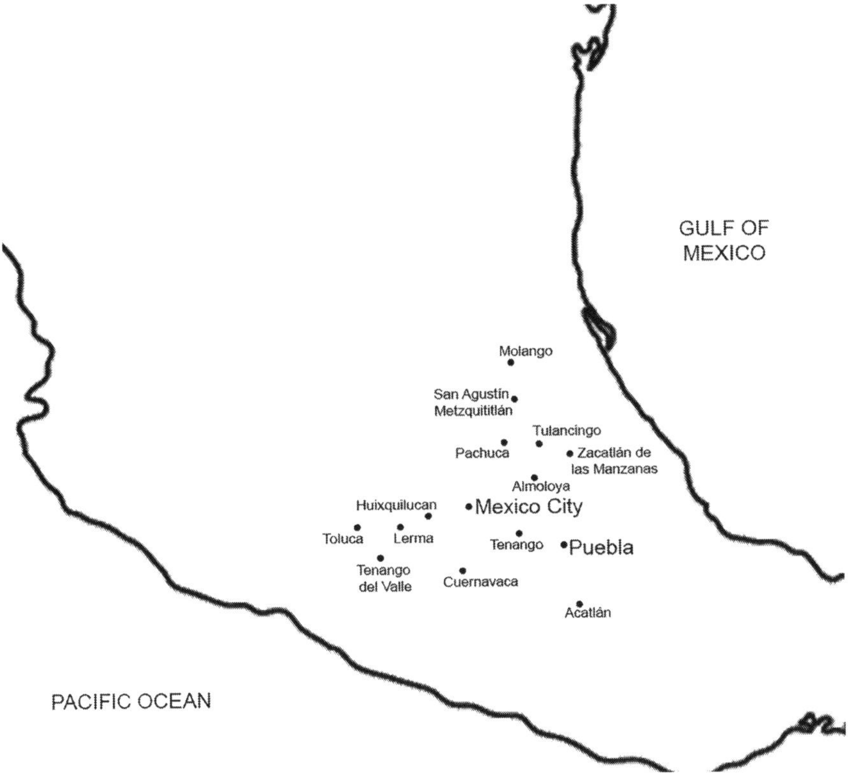

Map 0.2. Locations of regional case studies (Norah Gharala)

TAXING BLACKNESS

Introduction

Accused of fraud in 1782, Josef Francisco Chavira, a young man from Guanajuato, Mexico, apologized for posing as an Indian to save himself three reales in royal taxes.[1] The son of a Spanish woman and a free man of African descent, Chavira confessed that he was a *mulato* with no indigenous ancestry. Royal authorities later confirmed this admission based on their evaluations of his appearance (*presencia*). Chavira gave no hint that earlier a government official had recorded him as an Indian. Yet according to a local tax collector, Chavira and other *mulatos* who tried to save money by posing as Indians represented a much bigger problem. Examples of people who "say they are Indians when it suits them, and when it does not, they claim to be of another status" were rife among potential taxpayers.[2] Such behavior was, at best, criminal and, at worst, potentially treasonous. The theft of a few coins from the royal treasury by one man may have been negligible, but it was the specter of an entire group of mutinous subjects that haunted royal and local officials. For them, Chavira's refusal to submit to colonial categories represented a rejection of the king's right to collect taxes and the duty of his vassals to demonstrate their loyalty through the payment of royal tribute.

The tribute tax served social and economic purposes from its beginnings in the immediate aftermath of Spanish conquest of New Spain until the fall of the colonial regime. Spanish monarchs and jurists believed that tribute was a natural part of a wide array of societies that had noble and commoner elements. Castilian rulers extracted resources from their *pecheros*, peasants who paid tribute, a term later used to designate tributaries in Spanish America and the Philippines.[3] Conquistadors encountered stratified societies in the Valley of Mexico, where Indian commoners became tributaries of the Spanish crown, and exemptions from royal tribute were eventually granted to Indian nobility. Enslaved Africans, already a salient part of the colonial social fabric in the sixteenth century, were not expected to pay tributes because they were not free vassals. But their descendants sought freedom through self-purchase and marital unions with free people, thereby obtaining freedom for their children. The growth of a population of mixed ancestry in the sixteenth century caused the crown to reassess and expand the *pechero* designation. A 1574 law that placed free people of African descent squarely within the tributary population did so by equating them with manumitted slaves, in that free people of color had "acquired their freedom, and have a livelihood and property."[4] Spanish King Philip II believed that Africans, like Indians, had historically been accustomed to paying hefty tributes to their leaders "in their native lands."[5] While tribute did exist in Mesoamerican and West and West-Central African societies, Spanish royal tribute imposed social markers that would create a new language of obligation and privilege.[6] These newly established tributary vassals quickly became entrenched through the idea of genealogy, "the foundation of multiple practices and identities that helped mold historical memory at both the individual and collective levels" in the Ibero-Atlantic world.[7]

Many *mulatos* paid their taxes without incident as vassals of the Spanish crown, but Josef Francisco Chavira and tens of thousands like him chose to exploit their ambiguous appearance and fluid status. They invented genealogies and peddled their own "genealogical fictions" to tribute officials, thereby defrauding the royal treasury, or Real Hacienda as it was known in New Spain.[8] The rapid expansion of the Real Hacienda, one of the achievements of the political and economic reforms undertaken during the Bourbon dynasty (1700–1808), required obedient colonial subjects. If the colonial bureaucracy could not assign and control tributary status, then the right of the king and his bureaucrats to categorize, regulate, and rule the diverse free populations of late colonial Mexico would be seriously compromised. *Taxing Blackness* explains the attitudes and practices of colonial authorities regarding taxation of people of African and Indian descent in colonial Mexico. More importantly, this book reveals how free people of African descent perceived and represented themselves within a colonial system bent on defining and controlling them for the benefit of the crown. I explore the institutional effects of tribute, its logics and its dependence on formulations of the concept of "*calidad*" (literally, "quality," but better understood as "status") posited by bureaucrats and officials. The reactions of free people of African descent to tribute indicate what they thought of *calidad* and (often through subtle means) who they believed themselves to be. The questions I raise in this book about how free people of color dealt with the imposition of tribute shed new light on stimulating developments in recent research. Among the questions I explore are, In the minds of potential Afromexican tributaries, what were the obligations of blackness within colonialism? What were the stakes in individual or familial decisions to pay tribute to the crown or to contest one's registration as a tributary? What were the meanings of genealogy and family, and how did they influence one's *calidad*? *Taxing Blackness* shows how free people of color in colonial Mexico tried to redefine freedom, subjecthood, and blackness on their terms, often negotiating the effects of the tribute regime using the bureaucracy's own apparatus.

The confusion tax collectors experienced in Guanajuato with the likes of Chavira demonstrates some of the key differences between eighteenth-century Mexico and much of North America today. Late colonial Mexican society relied on visible signs and social signals that indicated specific categories based on a concept of *calidad. Calidad* incorporated multiple levels of knowledge that included physical appearance, written proofs of lineage, local reputation, and taxpayer status, among others. Many Americans living in the United States today can describe a set of widely understood physical signs and cultural signals that allow individuals to place others into racial or ethnic categories. Yet, a system of exclusively racial classification did not exist in colonial New Spain. A method of categorization based entirely on bodily features could be "very fallible," to use the words of bureaucrats in the colonial treasury.[9] To determine *calidad* reliably, one would need the assistance of neighbors, priests, friends, family, colonial officials, and the individual in question in addition to an evaluation of physical aspect. Modes of dress, language, occupation, color, religiosity, place of residence—these and other qualities of personhood had significant bearing on judgments of a person's *calidad*. A point of interlocking characteristics and reputations, a person's *calidad* could change over time depending on an individual's choices and the unpredictable influences of gossip, rumor, or fortune.

Between 1572 and 1810, the Spanish colonial regime required all free people of African descent in colonial Mexico to pay a tax based on their African ancestry. The royal tribute that colonial authorities collected from free people of African descent formed an important part of an expanding and sophisticated tax structure in the eighteenth century. This group of more than 300,000 people dwarfed the population of free blacks in the United States, who numbered 59,000 on the 1790 census.[10] In colonial Mexico, also called New Spain, tributary obligations applied to Indians and free Afromexicans alike. The royal justification for this tax was rooted in the transition from slavery to freedom, for which colonial rulers believed payment was due to compensate the monarch for his largesse.[11] Long after the general decline of African slavery in New Spain, the tribute regime continued to track Afromexican individuals and families as potential sources of colonial wealth.[12] Where tributary categories crystallized, colonial administrators identified free people of color based on their social and genealogical ties. Free people of color, in turn, defined themselves in relation to tribute, either as taxpayers or as exempt by virtue of their service or privilege. By the late eighteenth century, colonial authorities and ordinary people had begun to rely on markers of tributary status to help determine Afromexican social positions and, more broadly, the obligations of colonial subjecthood. Tributary status became a ground of contestation where, ultimately, the significance of blackness itself was alternately attested and challenged in colonial courts and tribunals.

The millions of Indians and hundreds of thousands of free people of African descent who lived in what is now Mexico represented a tax base unrivaled in eighteenth-century North America. Some of the most prominent Bourbon reformers in the Spanish Empire, such as *visitador general* (general inspector) José de Gálvez, viewed the colony as a source of wealth mismanaged under Spanish Habsburg rule (1516–1700). Although Afromexican tribute never challenged the primacy of Indian tribute, Afromexican tribute did grow substantially over the course of the colonial period. Eager to capitalize on late colonial demographic upturn, bureaucrats sought untapped wealth for the Real Hacienda, the powerful agency based in Mexico City that managed the monarch's revenue from public and private sources.[13] These aggressive attempts to increase the number of taxpayers, or tributaries, surpassed actual population growth among free people of color. The result was a widening category of tributary that included male and female, rural and urban colonial subjects. By enforcing tribute on Afromexican and Indian families, the crown lumped Africans and Indians into a common vassalage.

The multitude of taxes required of residents of New Spain was a relatively great economic imposition for ordinary people. At the turn of the nineteenth century, a four-member family in New Spain paid an estimated eight pesos in various taxes per year out of an income of about sixty pesos.[14] The process of registering as tributaries placed an additional burden on free people of color. Although there was great variation among the practices of local districts, potential Afromexican tributaries were required to appear before a magistrate and declare themselves, returning three times a year to pay their royal tributes. Taxpayers might have to travel to another town or borrow money to stay current with commissioners of the tribute regime. Failing to do so could result in a home visit from a collector or being taken into custody at a jail or private residence. Given the crushing costs of tribute for struggling families, why did so many free people of color engage with the regime rather than flee? Certainly many tributaries hid or absented themselves when the time came for registration or collection. Tribute registers created in the latter half of the eighteenth century contain a column for any eligible adults who were "absent" and with whom they shared a home. In 1622, all free *negros* and *mulatos*, men and women, were required to come before the comptroller (*contador general*) in Mexico City to be "listed and charged tribute." However, it was clear that many had "sought the protection of some people who assist them."[15] Some colonial subjects were willing to support Afromexican attempts to avoid the tax.

As data from this book show, many families who allowed themselves to be recorded on tribute registers were farmers or workers on a ranch or hacienda. Others practiced skilled or semiskilled trades and participated in commerce in the vibrant cities of New Spain. Rather than abandon their hard-won positions, livelihoods, and roots in their communities, many free people of color chose to bear the brunt of discriminatory taxation. Perhaps they understood that such was the price of participation in colonial society, and their few opportunities were not worth squandering in favor of a life of separation from their friends and families. These were people deeply integrated into surrounding networks of other tributaries—Afromexican and Indian—who developed reputations that reflected those of their kin and loved ones. In the vibrant and populous cities of colonial Mexico, especially in the capital, Africans and their descendants changed the cultural landscape both as a cohesive group and through their ties to people of other *calidades* with whom they worked or formed social bonds.[16] The choice to cut ties with these people, thereby denying their own blackness and searching for a new life as a mestizo of Indian and Spanish ancestry or even an Indian, was impossible for many, though not unheard of. Hundreds of thousands of free people of color kept their *calidad* and its associated tributary obligations while continuing to dedicate themselves to improving the economic prospects of their families through their labor.

Payment and registration as tributaries could act as a "path to political personhood and belonging," which allowed free people of color a "loyal subjectivity" available to them as an individual who usually occupied the lower strata of a dense and hierarchical colonial society.[17] Being closer, rather than farther, from monarchical power could protect free people of color from the myriad abuses of colonial officials and elites. By using alternate terms for tribute such as "*vasallaje*," free people of African descent claimed a measure of dignity through relationships of royal paternalism and protection, duty and loyalty. Juan Francisco Ferrete, who called himself in official documents a free *mulato* and *vecino* of San Luis Potosí, positioned himself as an authority on the creation of tribute registers, or records of "vassalage" (*vasallaje*) in 1712. He observed that local registers were flawed because of the presence of many "*forasteros* whose names could not be obtained."[18] This migrant category (*forastero*) among Indians implied an outsider status, as opposed to *originarios* (those born in the community) but could mean integration into economic and social structures.[19] At the same time, more transitory migrants who did not belong to the community, through tribute payments or kinship, were often associated with a lack of permanent residence or vagabondage. Such were the unknown free people of African descent Ferrete described who had "fled" registration,[20] thus failing to meet their obligations as colonial subjects and community members. This testimony upheld the belief by officials in tributary communities that fulfilling community obligations could yield belonging in Indian towns, even for migrants born elsewhere.[21] Although *forastero* was much more closely associated with Indians, Ferrete employed the term to denote transience, duplicity, and vagabondage—traits often associated with free people of African descent by those wishing to discredit them as disruptive or deviant. Ferrete's testimony separated him and other Afromexican *vecinos* from migrant outsiders not to be associated with the law-abiding tributaries who understood the symbolism of their tribute payments to the crown. Ferrete used the term to elevate some free people of color as truly belonging, thereby undermining prevalent negative understandings of Afromexicans as permanent outsiders in the colonial world, unable to put down roots anywhere.

Despite the advantages that could accrue to those who accepted their bureaucratically assigned tributary status, family, friendship, and love motivated many to contest their status rather than submit to the onerous economic burden and invidious *calidad* that accompanied tributary status. Legal means intended to improve the social standing, opportunities, and lives of future descendants included not only tribute exemption but also petitions filed by *mulatos* and *pardos* of good social standing to remove their *calidad* from official records (*gracias al sacar*), court cases of enslaved people suing for their freedom, and requests to obtain positions and professional licenses.[22] Many of these petitions and complaints addressed the issue of children and descendants as well as the petitioners. Afromexican tributaries who sought official tribute exemptions nearly always mentioned the detrimental effects of tributary status on the lives of their children and future descendants. Not all petitioners explicitly rejected an Afromexican *calidad*, believing that blackness and tribute exemptions could coexist, provided a lineage that included an illustrious ancestor with proven loyalty to the crown was officially recognized. For centuries, free people of color had occupied a complex position as both the target of "restrictive legislation" and the recipients of individual considerations and privileges.[23] However, the aggressive expansion of tribute registers in the latter half of the century led to protests from many families who understood such registration to be a grave error, if not a threat, fraught with damaging long-term consequences. Those who sought exemption from tribute acted out of profound concerns for the *calidad* of their ancestors and descendants, as well as themselves. Such resistance to tributary status, but not to colonialism itself, signified a growing conviction among some free people of color that they and their descendants deserved a better life and a more respectable reputation within the empire. Expressing their distaste for the negative effects of the tributary category, whether by throwing stones at a tax collector, hiding in a nontributary friend's home, or petitioning for justice in colonial courts, demonstrated the varying lengths that free people of color would go to create a space within the complex hierarchy of *calidad* that could serve the interests of tributaries themselves.

Afromexican *Calidad* and Tributary Status

Paying royal tribute reinforced a "sliding scale of inferiority" among Spanish imperial subjects that divided colonial society between tributaries, who were Indian commoners and free people of color, and those who were exempt because they were Spaniards or the children of Spaniards and Indians.[24] Although Afromexican tribute brought little financial gain to the crown, levying tribute maintained the distinctions between growing populations of free people of African descent and Indians, distinguishing them from people of Spanish descent and tribute-exempt mestizos. Bureaucrats and rulers envisioned a tribute regime that would maintain categories of genealogy and *calidad* while yielding monetary gains and massive amounts of demographic information.

The tribute Spanish rulers and their agents forced Indians to pay served as the foundation for a tribute tax from free people of African descent implemented decades later. An established literature has discussed the effects of and motivations behind Indian tribute to individual Spaniards, called *encomenderos*, and to the monarch. Classic studies have weighed the effects of tribute on Indians' corporate structures, finding that burdensome taxation also contributed to the development of communal resources.[25] Others have followed the trajectory of pre-Columbian tributes to the system imposed by Spanish colonial rulers.[26] Scholars have used data related to this tax to follow trends in demography, prices, movements of people, and natural disasters.[27] The sixteenth century has received particular attention as a transitional moment when the establishment of tribute also demonstrated the political thought and economic motivations of Spanish imperialism.[28] Integral to the connections between tribute and *calidad* were ideas about gender and reproduction, which played a pivotal role in the history of tribute in Spanish America.[29]

Two recent overviews of the legal basis and social implications of Afromexican tribute suggest a protracted and regionalized legal history that never fully pinned down the parameters of the institution or those subject to it.[30] Older studies have analyzed the perspective of colonial militias and their role in obtaining tribute exemptions for militia companies and surrounding communities.[31] *Taxing Blackness* differentiates individual and familial petitions for tribute exemption from those of militias made up of free men of African descent, which used fundamentally different rhetoric in exemption requests and have been treated in scholarship in detail. Studies of the *mulato* and *pardo* militias have not focused on the genealogies and family histories free people of African descent employed in petitions for tribute relief outside corporate settings. Groundbreaking studies of demography and geography by Sherwin F. Cook and Woodrow W. Borah, as well as Peter Gerhard, used tribute summaries to describe the distribution and size of Afromexican populations broadly. These summaries have also informed regional studies and provided detail for microhistories.[32] Especially in New Spain, tribute summaries and data have provided evidence of the presence of free people of African descent, their networks, occupations, and integration into the colonial regime through tax payments. Beyond the numbers themselves, *Taxing Blackness* shows how the practices of collecting, counting, and categorizing that produced these data affected the lives of free people of African descent.

Placing the lives of Afromexicans within an institutional framework allows us to understand their experiences of the bureaucratic changes in New Spain and the Ibero-Atlantic on a more personal as well as political basis. Previous scholars have noted the central roles of free people of color and how their varied understandings of blackness affected colonial institutions in New Spain, such as Catholic lay brotherhoods, militias, and the Inquisition.[33] Africans and their descendants often suffered terribly under a harsh colonial regime that dehumanized them and dispossessed them of any material and social gains. Recent scholarship has asked how people of African descent formed communities, maintained an interior sense of personhood and worth, and undertook the difficult task of finding aspects of the colonial regime that could better their lives.[34] In the process, enslaved and free Afro-descendants altered the political, social, and cultural meanings of colonialism by using its categories and institutions. Their actions placed powerful ideas of freedom, loyalty, and morality within the reach of black imperial subjects.[35] *Taxing Blackness* takes the position that even as they were forced to submit to an oppressive tax regime, free people of color used their engagement with a colonial institution to push the limits of their status as some of the lowliest vassals of the Spanish monarch. *Taxing Blackness* uses an institutional framework to reveal how free people of color perceived their social status, their connections to a far-flung colonial system, and their beliefs about their own blackness.

Understanding a nuanced and historically informed concept of *calidad*, "an inclusive impression reflecting one's reputation as a whole" used in New Spain and the Ibero-Atlantic is crucial to *Taxing Blackness*.[36] Influenced by reputation, lineage, and physical features, *calidad* mapped social differences using terms like "*mulato*," "Indian," "black," or "Spanish." Already in use in the seventeenth century,[37] *calidad* would become widespread in documents produced under Bourbon rule. As colonial authorities and ordinary people began to use this term to describe appearance, reputation, and occupation in the same phrase, this approach to classification combined elements of class (*clase*) and caste (*casta*).[38] Although *calidad* encompassed a colonial "lexicon of purity of blood increasingly merged with 'bourgeois' concepts of diligence, work . . . and the public good," it retained its long-standing connections to lineage.[39] Beyond physical appearance, *calidad* also indicated a person's behavior and judgment.[40] Adopting behaviors that were associated with Spaniards or mestizos, such as wearing Spanish clothing or performing Catholic rituals, could allow individuals to change their *calidad*, though this was by no means guaranteed.[41] Based on *calidad* and other aspects of public reputation, families and individuals could amass or lose honor, an "elastic commodity" in colonial Spanish America.[42] In urban areas, free people of color could seek occupations or purchase property to alter their *calidad* to that of mestizo or Indian. Although *calidad* had its roots in genealogical thinking, caste and *calidad* had both heritable and performative aspects.[43] These perceived behaviors and innate qualities of personhood passed from parents to offspring reinforced widespread beliefs about blackness and its connections to behavior and lineage. Finally, as *Taxing Blackness* will demonstrate, *calidad* and tributary status were mutually influential and worked to situate free people of African descent in colonial hierarchies. These different qualities of personhood hung in a sort of balance in which "disadvantages in one scale of evaluation could be offset by advantages in another."[44]

Color, caste, and other qualities of personhood could change based on social or institutional context. Tributary status joined other social markers that described people of mixed ancestry, or *castas*, in bureaucratic, legal, religious, occupational, and artistic documents.[45] In the late eighteenth century, bureaucrats in Mexico City debated, and ultimately upheld, the early modern belief that "bodily differences were real, but by no means permanent."[46] Divisions of society by caste and blood purity were widespread in the seventeenth century, although both categories were subject to local interpretations and the personal evaluations of the beholder. Caste and *calidad* were, in some parts of the Spanish Empire, so sporadically enforced that ordinary people could improve their standing by "avoiding the use of racial labels in most situations."[47] For ordinary people, "self-identification seemed to hinge on who was doing the asking, and why,"[48] though the potential for self-definition had its limits. People used the word *calidad* widely and toward a variety of legal and social goals, some of which concerned the meanings of African ancestry, dark skin color, family ties, occupation, ritual and religious practices, and certain caste categories—a group of ideas and identifications that can be collectively applied to the concept of blackness. While people undoubtedly used modes of seeing to identify others, they were using a wide range of clues to determine a person's status.[49] What people did might influence *calidad* as much as how they appeared. Occupational categories sometimes mapped onto *calidad*, though in late colonial New Spain, free people of African descent benefited from economic expansion and found work in agriculture, mining, transport, and as particular types of urban artisans.[50] These complex modes of seeing applied to officials as well as to ordinary people, as both groups possessed knowledge necessary to determining categories of caste and *calidad*.[51] People of African descent brought their own interpretations of genealogy, *calidad*, and the colonial obligations of blackness to the tribute regime.

This book generally avoids the term "identity" in favor of perhaps equally contested but not quite so nebulous concepts of *calidad*, blackness, and tributary status.[52] These terms served as a kind of "cluster," influencing one another and working in concert to determine a person's status or that of their family and future lineage.[53] However, ideas about social difference did not take on a "coherent ideology of race" that would operate in the Spanish Atlantic.[54] Recently, scholars across disciplines have made compelling cases for taking a long view of the development of race as an idea and organizing principle that developed in conjunction with other understandings of social difference, from conversion to humoralism. A variety of early modern and colonial racisms forces historians to think beyond modern conceptions of what race is.[55] For the purposes of this study, I find the concept of *calidad* most useful to describe understandings of social difference so deeply entrenched in the tribute regime. Certainly systems of racial classification share commonalities with the discourses of *calidad*, physiognomy, *casta*, genealogy, and subjecthood that arose in petitions and procedures related to tribute. They preserve debates that formed in fits and starts, conforming not to a progression toward entirely racial thinking but a series of proposals and conjectures that did not always follow a coherent path. Most strikingly, free people of African descent or those registered as tributaries avoided designations that could be interpreted today as racial or phenotypical, preferring those that were genealogical, reputational, and familial. Although the term *race* in colonial scholarship often stretches to encompass all kinds of physical, cultural, and social differences, ideas about "race" in this context become too elastic and historically ill fitting unless *calidad*'s relationship to "race" is understood. *Calidad* was a status marker that encompassed more than phenotype or color. In this book, I unpack the uses of *calidad* to show how the colonial regime applied the term to consign *mulatos* and *negros* to inferior status and how free people of African descent struggled to reclaim the term so as to qualify themselves for a status of dignity and respect.

Ordinary people represented their tributary status and *calidad* using a variety of idioms, but the one that was most prevalent was that of genealogy. Using this tool, free people of color sought to avoid or alter a tributary status. These genealogies are preserved in witness testimony, self-descriptions, and dispensations families acquired from royal authorities. The genealogies petitioners sought to construct, confirm, and control were tenuous. People described their ancestry using phrases common in tribute petitions such as, "it is publicly known," "it is notorious," or "it is heard said," all of which reinforced a family's lineage.[56] One historian has recently pointed to this phenomenon as an explanation for why caste could be based on genealogy, while remaining somewhat flexible.[57] Caste and *calidad* could change over time, as people migrated and joined communities in which they were a minority.[58] To what extent, then, were genealogies elite constructions and, for most Afromexican tributaries, simply out of reach? The answer depends on the period as well as the institutional venue. The relative importance of lineage, color, and caste in the seventeenth century depended on recording practices, which sometimes privileged physical appearance in the absence of genealogical information.[59] In other institutional settings, free people of color were at a "lineage disadvantage" and were not given the chance to produce genealogies at all.[60] R. Douglas Cope asserts that many ordinary people "were uninterested in the complexities of the *sistema de castas*."[61] Petitions for tribute exemption suggest that even if they did not care about the intricacies of caste terms, some free people of color did express a deep interest in their genealogies.

In the eighteenth century, free people of color petitioned authorities for tribute exemption on genealogical grounds following a set of increasingly codified practices. These petitions could include baptismal, marriage, and death certificates; testimony from neighbors and friends; copies of tribute registers; and tales of ancient family histories dating back to the conquest. The proofs these petitioners provided usually rested on some nontributary *calidad* and were not always exact with respect to caste. What petitioners sought was a genealogy of people who were "publicly known" as nontributaries, mestizos, *castizos* (usually the children of a mestiza and a Spaniard), caciques, or Spaniards. This public knowledge and community confirmation of truths resonated beyond tribute and allowed people of African descent to exert some influence over the preservation of their status in written documents.[62] While they often could not construct family trees of unquestioned *calidad*, the importance of genealogy and privilege nevertheless became especially apparent in petitions and lawsuits seeking tribute exemption. Within these legal contests, high-ranking bureaucrats, local officials, and ordinary people used a shared vocabulary of genealogy and kinship tied to tributary status. One historian has argued that creole elites descended from Spaniards could not "imagine their kingdom without recourse to ideas of lineage and purity."[63] Deploying genealogy as a way to confirm and valorize an individual's or family's status was not a strategy limited to the two communities—Indian elites and Spaniards—that recent historiography of colonial Mexico has recognized.[64] A full accounting of the cases for tribute exemption shows how much genealogy meant to a minority of nonelites attempting to avoid the detrimental effects of blackness in colonial society.[65] Although simply "casting off markers as tribute payers erased a symbol of inferior status," alone it could never "attach privileges of whiteness" to *mulatos*.[66] Particularly for those who sought to avoid tributary status even if they could not formally pass into the Spanish category, nontributary lineage was a social prize and an economic asset in very real terms.

The case studies brought to light in this book show the many ways that free people of color conceived of their genealogies and described the familial bonds they formed over the course of their lives. Throughout the Atlantic world, people of African descent counterbalanced "unavoidable stigmatizing labels" by bringing "into being paper that could surround these words with other signs of continuity and recognition." If free people of African descent could access "their specific ancestry," they stood a better chance of tempering the effects of negative colonial categories associated with blackness using official colonial channels.[67] In the process of reconstructing their genealogies, Afromexican petitioners also revealed their "lateral relationships" of friendship and kinship.[68] Some free and enslaved people of African descent in the Ibero-Atlantic formed families that accommodated ideas of Catholic morality, chastity, and marriage, while others either could not do so or saw family from a more complex perspective.[69] Adoption and guardianship, child-rearing and tender care often surfaced in petitions for tribute relief that involved genealogy as well. The imposition of taxation and the construction of genealogies were interrelated processes. As they sought relief from royal tributary status and collection, free people of African descent constructed and testified to genealogies that featured complex constellations of social ties that coexisted with lines of descent.

Taxing Blackness: Slavery, Subjecthood, and Vagrancy

Tribute was an imposition of empire shouldered by millions of people throughout the Spanish Atlantic world, and the part free people of African descent played in this empire-making process fundamentally marked their position in colonial society. From the perspective of the colonial regime, blackness represented a host of obligations tempered by the possibilities of gaining privileged status through service to the regime. Some documents related to tribute offer us a window into how free people of African descent understood their own blackness, a topic related to a rich body of scholarship on Afromexicans' sense of community.[70] This is one of the most intimate and complex issues that arose from the many petitions sent on behalf of families accused of being tributaries. Petitioners voiced a variety of opinions about tribute, but not all Afromexican petitioners denied their blackness. Black tributary status was, for thousands of free Afromexicans, an inescapable fact of life in the colonial regime. However, a few contested these demands and created notably individual ways of representing blackness, sometimes as a stain on the family genealogy but at other times as an integral aspect of their honor and their personhood.

At its core, tributary status preserved the legacy and presence of blackness in late colonial New Spain. Tribute registers and, indeed, the name of tribute itself, were directed at *negros y mulatos libres*. Black and brown people shared this obligation, and this aspect of *calidad* united them under the tributary label in the eyes of the Real Hacienda. In practice, very few individuals actually appear as *negros* or *negras* on tribute registers in the eighteenth century, their preference being for labels like *pardo*, *mulato*, or none at all. The term *negro* was long associated with enslavement, African ancestry or ethnicity, and dark color in New Spain. Few free people of African descent called themselves *negros* in the late eighteenth century, preferring designations that distanced them from slavery and rooted them in New Spain itself. Accompanying demographic changes, coupled with the decline of the slave trade to New Spain, facilitated this transition away from the *negro* category in the late colonial period.

Tribute retained the same name given it by Philip II in the sixteenth century.

It was a tax on blackness, freedom, vassalage, belonging, family. It was never called a tax exclusively on *mulatos* or other labels prominent in the eighteenth century that denoted some amount of African ancestry. In the final decades of the eighteenth century, the printed grid used for tallying non-Indian tributaries was the register of "Negros y Mulatos libres." This was the official procedure, but the practices of local and regional authorities remained heterogeneous as a rule.[71] Some local officials included *indio laborío* and *vago* tributaries alongside *mulatos* or placed *mulatos* on lists of *indios de pueblo*. *Negros* themselves do not appear in any significant numbers on the registers examined in this book. Despite these variations, I argue that the legacy of blackness remained the reasoning and justification behind the tax. By the end of the eighteenth century, a few bureaucrats in the Real Hacienda argued that this tribute was actually due from plebeians, rather than as the direct result of manumission from slavery. By this and other convoluted logics, administrators and accountants implied that tributary status was not equivalent to a modern notion of race. Still, the tax persisted until the end of the colonial period under the same name but with myriad interpretations from bureaucrats and ordinary people. The royal tribute paid by free people of African descent was an obligation dependent on their genealogies and enduring colonial connections to the legacies of slavery in the Ibero-Atlantic.

Imperial and local authorities throughout the Americas used exclusion from institutions and professions, restrictions on movement, and punishing taxation to further structure free people of African descent into roles of inferiority.[72] The institution of African slavery was central to the economic, genealogical, and social justifications for tribute and other limitations on the lives of free people of African descent. The deep connection between African slavery and tribute was distinctive in eighteenth-century New Spain, a place where pockets of slavery persisted while the vast majority of people were free. Between 1521 and 1639, an estimated 110,525 enslaved Africans were shipped to colonial Mexico.[73] After 1640, New Spain was eclipsed by other North American societies in its importation of enslaved Africans. The key to the massive influx of enslaved people in British America lay in sugar production, a "veritable destroyer of life" for one in four Africans who died within three years of their arrival.[74] A majority of Afromexicans had never experienced slavery directly, long before the end of the colonial period, but the tribute regime attempted to ensure that they would not wander freely without masters. The laws that established this royal tribute rested on the idea that these subjects had not always been free, nor could they be fully loyal if they failed to pay the tax.

Taxing Blackness analyzes one of the methods by which the crown both profited from Afromexican labor and designated free people of African descent as inferior elements of the colonial hierarchy of New Spain. Spaniards and their descendants continued to demand labor from Indians and free people of African descent, and tribute registers provided a means to track and enforce residence on these groups. The inclusion of logics of manumission in the laws applying tribute to free people of African descent decades after the establishment of Indian tribute further points to the enduring association between tribute and the labor of freed slaves. At the level of the household, "manumission as a means to recompense slave workers, and ultimately negotiate access to their labor, illustrates the continuous struggle of the terms of this work relationship."[75] Some parallels exist between the labor demands of Spanish colonial authorities and the struggle for dominance between individual masters and enslaved workers. The Spanish crown and colonial authorities frequently sought free laborers of African descent to fulfill vital colonial labor in the mining industry as well as urban environments. These demands were justified in laws demanding tribute and fixed residence from a population that had, according to the law, experienced slavery and been rewarded with freedom. As an act of gratitude and loyalty, these vassals were obligated to pay royal tribute and make their whereabouts known to authorities. Thus, slavery remained a justification for the centuries-old imposition of tribute on Afromexican families.

Tribute registration was a mode of continued "indexing bodies to territories" reminiscent of enslavement and its role in sovereignty.[76] Officials repeatedly advocated for forcing free people of color into a designated place or under the supervision of a Spaniard, mirroring the preoccupation with flight from captivity. Throughout the empire, elites warned that without a master's control and armed with their own independence, formerly enslaved people as well as fugitive slaves would prove a growing unstable element in society.[77] Heavy taxation among free blacks, or a "freedom tax," in the United States was intended more to curb the success and growth of free black populations than to generate revenue in slave states. Poll and other taxes aimed at free blacks were common in the late eighteenth and nineteenth centuries, though some free blacks objected to these taxes based on their lack of representation in government.[78] Another tax on manumission, or freedom tax, was practiced in the French Caribbean, where it weighed heavily on enslaved Africans attempting to buy their freedom.[79] Bourbon bureaucrats in New Spain were inclined to articulate the need for tribute as a combination of regulation of unruly subjects and a means to revenue expansion, what they saw as the right of the crown to profit from the labor of black bodies.

Tributary and enslaved status were tied to gender and reproduction through genealogy and *calidad*. Because both statuses were passed on at birth, registers of tributaries contain the names and ages of hundreds of thousands of women and their children. Some *negra* and *mulata* women paid tributes regardless of marital status or children in the seventeenth and eighteenth centuries, though there was notable variation across geography.[80] Despite these regional variations, unmarried sisters who lived alone, young servant girls, and elderly widows appear scattered across multiple tribute registers. Women of African descent would eventually be exempted from payment in 1786, but they were still registered in many jurisdictions included in this book.[81] Even when this exemption came from the highest levels of authority, the importance of local custom prevented a single gendered interpretation of tribute from taking hold across New Spain. Officials were more likely to record only tributary men in coastal areas where the *pardo* militia presence reduced tribute registration, but there were exceptions to this pattern. In general, tributary status was an expression of family and required relationships of reproduction and kinship to reassert itself. Many colonial authorities in local districts and in Mexico City associated tributary status with slavery, believing that blackness and reproduction were the basis of both.

From the bureaucratic data that ballooned in the second half of the eighteenth century, we can better understand the attributes of Afromexican taxpayers as Bourbon reformers tried to quantify them. Although these data do not describe the population as a whole, they provide snapshots of families headed by married couples or by single adults, orphans, unmarried men, and other kinds of family arrangements. Because bureaucrats were keenly aware of the value of this information, we can infer that not only were Afromexican communities tightly knit, they were also distinguishable from the rest of the population. Far from a few dispersed individuals, Africans and their descendants, especially rural farmers, formed important and interconnected populations in the Spanish Atlantic world.[82] Agents of the Bourbon regime recognized these groups and attempted to convert their interconnectedness into a cash nexus, a profit ledger in the service of the colonial enterprise. But the names, occupations, and family connections of free people of color recorded by regime bureaucrats testify nonetheless to the kinships, friendships, and communities that free people of color created and maintained in many regions across what is now Mexico.

Tribute officials expanded the tributary populace on paper by attempting to draw segments of the population into the tax base and establishing fewer exceptions. These trends toward a tributary subject with general, standardized characteristics had more in keeping with modern taxation than with their medieval Castilian foundations. The increase in tributary numbers indicates a concerted effort to augment the tributary population on a basis other than natural increase. In their effort to invent new tributaries, officials fused new categories with older ones: caste with purity of blood, color with caste, and *calidad* with all of the above. The following chapters show how the intertwined concepts of *calidad* and tributary status influenced collection and understanding of local registers. Although some families, individuals, and towns pushed back against the ever-growing category of Afromexican tributary, data from the last decades of the colonial period show the limited scope and number of such petitions and complaints. With fewer privileges and greater obligations, free people of color entered the national period as subjects expected to display loyalty to a regime that provided little in return.

Using qualitative and quantitative sources, this book addresses one of the most enduring negative representations of free people of African descent in the Ibero-Atlantic world: the vagabond. Although not a term exclusively applied to free people of color, the vagabond as an uncontrolled, filthy, dangerous, and slothful individual frequently entered the record when officials discussed *mulatos* and *negros*.[83] As early as the 1550s, Spanish officials believed free people of color to be "inherently rootless" and a direct threat to both Indian conversion efforts and the fantasy of the "dual sociopolitical order" embodied in the two republics.[84] Rampaging through Indian villages and swindling decent citizens, the figure of the free *mulato* vagabond circulated endlessly in documents pertaining to tribute. Some tribute registers placed free people of color alongside "*vagos*," or people without association with a specific place.[85] Yet, a "double image" of free people of African descent also circulates through official documents in New Spain, some of which actively contradicted each other in their portrayals of the same population as hardworking and industrious.[86] The collection of tribute implied that they did have access to cash and were part of the labor force. The data that tribute administrators and local officials collected, particularly from the second half of the century, undermine the very arguments that tribute officials promoted about the innate transience of free people of color, their lack of commitment to forming families or communities, and their continued resistance to their obligations as vassals. We must read many of these statements as anxieties refracted through the concerns of collectors and local officials as well as bureaucrats in the capital. First, local officials struggled to collect tribute, a shortcoming they often sought to blame on free Afromexicans' behavior and inherent mobility. Second, by constantly referring to free people of color as people in need of supervision and discipline through work, authorities pointed to tribute registration as a means to reducing the constant shortage of labor. Yet, if free people of color were so incorrigible and lawless, how could thousands of them also be paying regular tributes to the king? My analysis of vagabonds in relation to tribute shows the contradictory nature of these discourses and their utility to different actors in the colonial regime.

The people who made decisions about taxation, from bureaucrats in Mexico to local Indian governors, created a web of tributary characteristics that drew on legal status, residence, reputation, gender, and lineage. Exemption petitions were the exception to the normal pattern in which commissioners registered Afromexican heads of household, along with others living in the home or associated with the family. Using qualitative data from petitions for exemption and tribute registers, *Taxing Blackness* argues that blackness and tributary status became increasingly synonymous in the second half of the eighteenth century. The Bourbon regime sought out communities of Afromexican tributaries related by marriage, labor arrangements, adoption, birth, and place of residence. Hundreds of thousands of people registered as tributaries, thus confirming their blackness and accepting its obligations to the colonial regime. Even these great leaps in administration for the Bourbon regime could not transform *calidad* and tributary status into a universal indicator that colonial subjects accepted at face value.

SCOPE OF THE STUDY: BOURBON NEW SPAIN

This book elucidates eighteenth-century tribute disputes and questions that also encompassed concerns of the seventeenth-century Habsburg tribute administrations. The history of the Bourbon reforms has recently been written as one of Enlightened ideas developed in Atlantic intellectual circles and the colonial subjects who modified and collaborated in reform projects, as well as those who ignored or interfered with reformers.[87] This work focuses on Bourbon Reforms through a specific lens to ask how changes within the Real Hacienda shaped bureaucratic understandings of blackness as well as the impact *calidad* and tributary status had on the lives of Afromexican people. The Afromexican tribute tax is not, for the purposes of this book, examined as a barometer of the overall success of the reforms, though the increase in revenues discussed in chapter 4 and in a broader historiography constitutes a positive outcome for colonial and imperial finance.[88] Instead, I use tribute as a site of negotiation between taxpayers, local elites, and royal bureaucrats on which would be determined the nature of Afromexican subjecthood. Tribute reforms exemplify the tendency of Bourbon reformers to consider a wide variety of ideas and debate their merits toward the end goal of producing greater yields for the treasury, upholding the rights of the king, and maintaining order and public happiness. While tribute taxes were, from a historian's perspective and that of free people of color, intrusive and overwhelming, the Real Hacienda viewed its mission as one that was sound and inherently tied to the prosperity of the empire. It sought to maintain justice and a centralized system of knowledge to make fair decisions based on data and the principle that colonial vassals demonstrated their loyalty through tribute. Just as access to the courts in Castile promoted loyalty,[89] the implications were similar among tributary and Afromexican subjects.

Enlightenment ideas, mixed with older concepts like blood purity, underpinned a series of reforms, legal decisions, and bureaucratic practices that show how the colonial regime identified and categorized free people of color. The nature and implantation of tributary reform in the late eighteenth century indicated Bourbon attitudes toward free people of African descent that were often quite suspicious. In 1770, the *fiscal* of the high court in Mexico City, José Antonio de

Areche, complained that "a Mulatto, for instance, whose color helps him somewhat to hide in another '*casta*,' says, according to his whims, that he is an Indian to enjoy privileges as such and pay less tribute."[90] The impetus behind Bourbon classification was to control and contain this population to the benefit of royal coffers, often drained by war, as part of a century-long period of reform. These reforms were not spontaneous but instead "emerged from a long and complicated political process in which foreign and domestic interest groups with very different political agendas contested for power."[91] The change in structure of colonial government to an intendancy system ushered in a period of unprecedented data collection and tax payments.[92] The tribute regime showed both hallmarks of Bourbon centralization and the internal disputes and conflicts with local elites that prevented most radical changes. Not all reformers believed in the wisdom of tribute, perhaps most famously José del Campillo y Cossío, a minister of finance, of the navy, of war, of the Indies, and of the state during the reign of Philip V (1700–1746) who advocated for easing tribute burdens and encouraging Indians to become active consumers of Spanish manufactures.[93] Yet, as tribute reforms gained momentum through the introduction of new instruments and procedures, officials and tributaries perceived the increasing trends toward standardization of the regime. New procedures facilitated the collection and transmission of data and ideas along with tribute payments.

The tribute regime was deeply invested in questions of law and colonial administration, making documents related to tribute fruitful for the study of the relationships of free people of color to the colonial state. Royal tribute was part of a vast bureaucratic machine that grew to remarkable complexity in the eighteenth century. A new cadre of royal officials bent on the expansion of mining, excise, and personal taxes brought the Real Hacienda increased revenue. In itself not very lucrative, Afromexican tribute was an administrative quandary that brought to the fore problems of geographical diversity. At the same time, questions of legal status for Afromexican families formulated arguments dependent on local administration and customary law. The importance of geography for administration has long been apparent in Latin American history, and tribute was subject to the local circumstances and resources that commissioners and local officials encountered. Even in the second half of the eighteenth century, the tribute regime faced obstacles both in the Valley of Mexico and on frontiers. Overlapping jurisdictions, muddled local customs, and disease crippled the tribute administration of Mexico City until the end of the century.[94] Far from the capital in the mining centers of the near north, officials were unable or unwilling to enforce standards either inapplicable to local realities or impossible to enforce.[95] Following the formula "I obey but do not execute" ("*obedezco pero no cumplo*"), local officials rejected or postponed the implementation of disruptive or inconvenient decrees from centers of imperial power.[96]

Tributary status was a legal category, dependent on reputation and genealogy, which developed connections to ideas about colonial "classes." Drawing on Iberian models, administrators conceived of the tributary class as one of *pecheros* who were defined by their lineage, removing all Spaniards and their descendants from this category in the Americas. By *real cédula* in 1803, adopted orphans lacking knowledge of their birth parents (*expósitos*) had been removed from the tributary group and placed in the "class of good men" with "other honorable vassals" who were not blacks, Indians, or *mulatos*.[97] Tributaries of multiple castes were often funneled into a similar tributary status, because commissioners and bureaucrats saw Afromexican workers and *indios laboríos* as a kind of "floating population."[98] Where possible, bureaucrats in the late eighteenth century simplified the distinctions between castes and grouped people together based on other unifying characteristics. Tributary categories were labels with the potential to totalize all free people of African descent, *moreno*, *pardo*, and *negro* alike. Thus the regime ensured that free people of African descent experienced their tributary status as a social marker encompassing many forms of distinction into a single category.

ORGANIZATION OF THE BOOK

This book is structured in such a way as to explain Bourbon motivations, policies, and degrees of success related to tribute collection followed by chapters examining the actions, experiences, and networks of free people of African descent and potential tributaries. Chapter 1 traces the development of the royal tribute tax on free people of African descent in Bourbon New Spain and its connections to various methods of defining social difference. Tributary status and *calidad* became interrelated modes of defining social position that allowed bureaucrats to bring free people of color into periodic contact with the colonial regime. This tax had distinct meanings of privilege, obligation, and loyalty for the crown and Afromexican subjects. Although a small part of New Spain's tax regime, Afromexican tribute was a significant burden on taxpayers, who paid some of the highest rates of taxation in the Atlantic world. The economic burden of Afromexican tribute was heavy, and social stigmas attached to blackness only compounded its weight.

Chapter 2 explores the relationships between tributary subjects, property owners, local officials, and royal bureaucrats that fostered regional variability in early Bourbon tribute registration and collection. Prior to the reforms of the 1760s, tribute collection was sporadic, plagued by uncertainties of *calidad* and vague documentation. Bureaucrats in Mexico City could not impose *calidad* or Afromexican tribute without obtaining the valuable local knowledge of officials, elites, and ordinary people. The chapter uses a case study from the mining region of San Luis Potosí to illustrate how Afromexican tribute initiated early

Bourbon debates about the stability of *calidad*. I compare the difficulties of collecting tribute in San Luis Potosí to highly regularized and successful collection elsewhere. Using a series of tribute registers from a central salt-producing region, Acatlán and Piastla, I analyze what we learn when local authorities were cooperative and effective. These records of registration and payments from 1739 to 1743 attest to the efficacy of *calidad* for registration of the same individuals multiple times. But imposing tribute on Afromexican subjects was a laborious process that could only function with some degree of cooperation from local actors.

In response to Bourbon attempts to reestablish and reinvigorate tribute, Afromexican families in central Mexico sought legal means to prove a nontributary genealogy in the first half of the eighteenth century. Chapter 3 analyzes how the arguments free people of color and local officials made characterized them as pernicious outsiders, cherished sons, or abandoned daughters. The cases in which the protagonists are men show complex genealogical and personal ties to Spaniards that bolstered arguments for exemption. These petitioners did not deny their established or implied genealogical connections to blackness. Instead, they positioned themselves as privileged by virtue of a prestigious ancestor. A comparative case involves two orphaned sisters who were punished for failing to pay tribute and their resulting struggle to define themselves as young girls in need of paternal protection. Their initial complaint eventually became a criminal case, demonstrating the fragility of their claims to virtuous femininity in the face of an expanding colonial tax regime. These Afromexican petitioners did not view their own *calidad* as an insurmountable obstacle to obtaining tribute exemption. Some free people of color used genealogical understandings of family to support their petitions for exemption, while others viewed family as a necessary support for paying tributes.

The second half of *Taxing Blackness* is devoted to the period of the Caroline Reforms. Chapter 4 evaluates the efficacy of Afromexican tribute as a method of gathering information and revenue. I place the new instruments used for gathering data in the context of Bourbon developments in scientific administration and Enlightened reform. These reforms affected the lives of free people of color and local officials through processes of registration and collection, which I discuss in detail using local examples of successful implementation as well as spectacular failures. Evidence for local amounts of tribute collection derives from the accounts in the Archivo General de Indias, from 1768 to 1800 and builds on the foundational work of John J. TePaske and Herbert S. Klein. Because of reforms in counting and registration, tribute collection and registration rose dramatically in a few jurisdictions where Afromexican populations were substantial. Using collection figures from 1768 to 1788, the chapter shows that Afromexican payments fluctuated at the local level but, as a result of new methods of collection and registration, increased overall along with other sources of income for the Real Hacienda.

Tribute mapped local and imperial belonging through payment and registration. Drawing on more than 7,500 records of Afromexican tributary individuals and families from across colonial Mexico, chapter 5 identifies the characteristics that defined the Afromexican tributary. The tribute institution existed within a colonial regime that clung to stereotypes of Afromexicans as itinerants lacking family ties, but many tribute registers contradicted these prevalent conceptions. The typical tributary family was made up of married Afromexican couples with children who maintained social and genealogical ties within their communities. I then argue that tribute officials focused on the familial and social connections between free people of color to establish a community of tributaries. The registers show what bureaucrats and officials knew (or wanted to know) about Afromexican family life across geography and how they intended to locate and fix these subjects in a place. Examining practices of record keeping on Afromexican tribute registers as Bourbon officials revised and expanded tributary categories, I show that tracking these Afromexican tributaries over time was a difficult and complex process that did not always yield results in urban areas.

As collection became much more systematized, ordinary people contested their new, unwanted status using strategies tailored to the late Bourbon period. Chapter 6 samples exemption cases from individuals and families from the 1780s to the early nineteenth century. In these cases, the coexistence of the terms "tributary class," "tributary caste," and "tributary quality" shows conflicting Bourbon attitudes regarding tributary status, appearance, and genealogy. By far the most important determinant of success in a tribute exemption case during this time was the strength of a family's genealogy, which could be based solely on *calidad* or on a public reputation of exemption. Slowly, ideas about heredity and race also emerged in tribute, but they were unconvincing to the highest courts and unattractive to the petitioners. Each side preferred to define a tributary not by race but by centuries-old notions of genealogy and privilege, and newer concepts of *calidad* and economic status.

This book tells three interlocking stories: (1) the development of the institutional frameworks surrounding Afromexican tribute, (2) their social and economic effects on free Afromexicans, and (3) the differing interpretations of blackness that free people of color and bureaucrats marshaled as they argued over who was subject to tributary status. Ordinary people believed that their petitions or lawsuits could result in justice, or at least an improvement in their circumstances. As royal bureaucrats and ordinary people confronted each other, each side struggled to define blackness in ways that sometimes invoked and at other times rejected status determinants such as genealogy and *calidad*. Tributary status and *calidad* illustrate Ann Laura Stoler's contention that colonially imposed categories were "binding," but they were often "unbound by those within them."[99] Bourbon interest in Afromexican families as objects of royal taxation indicated a continuing preoccupation with reproduction and revenue and the desire to contain and define Afromexican social relationships within bureaucratic structures. In spite of the energy bureaucrats devoted to this tax, the sparse attention to Afromexican tribute in historical inquiry derives, in part, from the absence of this topic in traditional national narratives of the Mexican past as a story of Indians, Spaniards, and mestizos. Yet, as *Taxing Blackness* shows, Bourbon bureaucrats intent on raising tribute gave explicit recognition to another population in New Spain, free Afromexicans. Alternately contesting and acquiescing to Bourbon attempts to categorize and define them, free people of color asserted their presence and consequence in New Spain as active participants in the regime's attempts to maximize taxation for the crown. Social and economic recognition for the purpose of taxation spurred free people of color into debates with royal authorities over who could be identified as tributary and to what degree blackness would constitute that status.

1

Tribute and *Calidad* in the Spanish Empire

In the name of expanding revenue and demanding loyalty to the crown, late colonial officials and bureaucrats sought new families and individuals in New Spain who could be subjected to tributary status. These actions infringed on ordinary people's lives in ways that tested marriages, depleted meager incomes, and ruined reputations. In 1793, a woman named Lugarda de Jesús was arrested for failing to pay royal tribute in the jurisdiction of Tenango del Valle, now in the state of Mexico. Although Tenango del Valle was home to thousands of Indian tributaries, she had been registered as a *mulata*.[1] Concerned about the fate of Lugarda de Jesús, her husband Agustín Antonio, an Indian, sought an investigation into the matter by royal authorities. In response to his entreaties, Viceroy Juan Vicente de Güemes Pacheco de Padilla, second count of Revillagigedo, requested more information on the matter from the local subdelegate, Juan Antonio Flores. He informed the viceroy that "it is true that [Lugarda de Jesús] is a *mulata*."[2] Who recorded her as a *mulata* and why are questions unanswered in the short, formal document. Living with her Indian husband, Lugarda de Jesús may have eventually run afoul of someone who sought to discredit her, prevent her from engaging in commercial activities, or even remove her from her home. Frictions between Indians and free people of African descent in Tenango del Valle arose over property ownership and belonging, as well as tribute payments.[3] To confirm Lugarda de Jesús's reputation, the subdelegate cited her inclusion on the *padrón de pardos*, or Afromexican tribute register. He seemed uninterested in pursuing the matter of a single tributary any further, considering it a waste of time and a strain on the already stretched resources of the tribute regime. The couple pressed for a resolution to the situation, leading to Lugarda de Jesús's release without explicitly changing her tributary status or her monetary obligations to the Spanish monarch.

Characterizing the matter as unworthy of the viceroy's continued attention, the subdelegate quipped that "if they were loyal vassals, it would be better to pay what they owed his majesty than to spend so much on impertinent journeys and complaints."[4] The connections between loyalty, vassalage, and tribute were not lost on officials with local or regional jurisdictions, who saw a refusal to pay tribute as tantamount to an insult to the colonial order. The "impertinence" of these members of the tributary class, Indian and *mulata* alike, seemed to question the looming social divide between the tributary and nontributary groups. This divide was critical to understanding the lives of ordinary people in colonial New Spain as well as their relationships with agents of the colonial regime. These men had the power to apply labels like "*mulata*" or "Indian" and thus change the economic lives of individuals and families for generations to come.

Tribute had two major outcomes for the lives of ordinary people and authorities. First, tribute was a principal institutional channel through which free people of color interacted directly with agents of the colonial regime. Second, the process of registering for and paying tribute reinforced and reinscribed colonial categories of caste, gender, and reputation. As these categories changed, the tribute regime adjusted to reflect changing social realities. When tribute officials did not accurately assess social relationships of kinship and genealogy, reputation and status, or color and caste, potential tributaries petitioned authorities using legal channels. Tribute offers a lens through which to view the process of fiscal reform in the Bourbon period as well as a chance to understand the impact of free people of color on those processes and how members of this group—or those attempting to distance themselves from the group—understood their positions within colonial society. As an institution that both occasionally rewarded loyalty and routinely levied burdensome taxes on families because of their African ancestry, tribute demonstrated the complex relationship between blackness and the colonial regime. Changing categories of taxation and social markers existed within the tribute regime over the course of the colonial period, and the relative flexibility or lack thereof was crucial to the success of royal tribute.

This chapter explores the development of social and economic categories related to the tribute regime and their meanings in Atlantic, colonial, and imperial contexts. Although a small part of the overall treasury, Afromexican tribute appeared to Bourbon bureaucrats as an untapped potential source of revenue with the means to control a segment of the masses that bureaucrats often characterized as untrustworthy, unruly, or simply dangerous. Tributary status joined other social markers in the colonial context that informed the vocabularies of bureaucrats and ordinary people as they described colonial hierarchies as well as their own families. A primary determinant of tributary status was *calidad*, a term used to describe an individual status, but what kind of people were obligated to pay tribute was a question that ordinary people and bureaucrats struggled to answer over the course of the colonial period. Within the tributary category, distinctions remained important, for bureaucrats able to apply rates of royal tribute and for ordinary people who found that the categories within this tributary class also influenced their daily lives, abilities to conduct business, personal relationships, and understanding of themselves within a colonial regime.

AMERICAN TAXATION AND IMPERIAL WEALTH

The fiscal systems of early modern Spain and its empire contained distinct tax statuses based on social groups or geography, producing a wide range of information, institutions, and government agents.[5] The fundamental distinction in taxation in the New World was between Indians and non-Indians. Indians were the first to pay tributes to *encomenderos* and the Spanish crown as part of a severe ecclesiastical and civil tax regime.[6] Indian tribute in labor built churches and public works, while goods such as blankets and foodstuffs sustained holders of encomiendas, grants of Indian labor and tribute. These Indian tributes in goods and labor reflected pre-Columbian practices, though Spanish colonial taxes were undoubtedly much more exploitative.[7] Indian tributes were especially abundant in what became the Kingdom of New Spain and were not to be found on the same scale elsewhere in North America.[8] Even as the larger unit of the Viceroyalty of New Spain grew to the north, income from tribute remained comparable to that of the Andean zone, partly owing to the loss of potential tributaries into the mestizo category in the mid and late colonial periods.[9] To alleviate some of the strain on Indian communities, the crown excused them from paying sales taxes. This tax status kept rural Indian economies under the protection of the crown, which reserved for itself a set rate of tribute based on population and production.

Non-Indians were subject to sales and customs taxes such as the *alcabala* and *almojarifazgo* applied to trading in local economies and larger commercial networks. The Castilian crown created the innovative *alcabala*, a sales tax, in the fourteenth century. Prior to the establishment of the *alcabala* in the Americas, the principal income from American treasuries to Spain was made up of the *quinto* and *diezmo* taxes on silver followed by Indian tribute. Together, these accounted for more than 75 percent of the income from the Americas at the beginning of Philip II's reign (1556–98).[10] Of these taxes, the *quinto* mining tax would bring the most annual income to Spain.[11] Taxation from non-Indians and the commercial activities they controlled was, from an early stage, the fiscal underpinning of the colonial project.

Only free people of African descent were required to pay both sales taxes and royal tributes, among other taxes. This special status grew out of the legacies of slavery and conquest in New Spain, the uncertain place free people of African descent occupied in the colonial legal regime, and the assertion of early colonial monarchs that free people of color were vassals with fiscal obligations to their lord. More than three hundred thousand free people of color, as well as ten thousand slaves, formed vital labor forces in the urban centers and mining communities of New Spain.[12] They grew during the eighteenth century from just 1 percent to about 10 percent of the population.[13] With this demographic shift, free people of color and their economic activities occupied an increasingly important place in the minds of policy makers in the eighteenth century. Thousands of free people of color paid tribute, with a remarkable surge in registration and collection following the visitation of José de Gálvez (1765–72), who placed an emphasis in his report on the need to incorporate free people of African descent into the tribute regime more effectively.[14] Although many of Gálvez's suggestions would never be implemented, new registrations of free people of color eventually occurred because of more streamlined administrative methods and aggressive attempts to maximize the tributary population.

A degree of flexibility continued to flourish within this modernizing tax regime, allowing local administrators to control revenue in ways that were beneficial to the continued survival of the Spanish Empire. Individual jurisdictions often maintained local tax privileges based on geopolitical factors such as proximity to hostile Indian groups. Subjects throughout the Spanish Empire expected to be able to reject taxes they saw as unfair or unlawfully extracted.[15] In the far-reaching Viceroyalty of New Spain, tributary status became complex, and even broke down, where powerful rivals challenged the Spanish for economic and political control.[16] Distance allowed officials and subjects to assert their needs while creating multiple nodes of authority throughout New Spain. This tension between control and variety would become a hallmark of taxation across Spanish America, allowing the tax regime to reflect locally and regionally specific histories, economies, and demographic patterns.

The tax structure of late colonial New Spain reflected the growth of Indian and *casta* populations, the colony's expected prosperity, and its compliance with imperial demands. As the centerpiece of Spanish Atlantic trade and effective colonial taxation, Mexico became the "tax jewel" of the Spanish Empire, especially after 1780.[17] Mexico City was the capital of the vast Viceroyalty of New Spain, which included the Philippines, the Spanish Caribbean islands, Florida, what is now the western United States, and Central America, with the exception of Panama. Within the viceroyalty, the Kingdom of New Spain contained most of the population. Its capital city was the largest city in North America in the late eighteenth century with more than 112,000 residents.[18] As a center of colonial administration and taxation, the Kingdom of New Spain was the key to fiscal success in the Americas.

The sheer size of the Real Hacienda in New Spain meant that sources of income like royal tributes, which made up relatively small percentages of the overall income, remained fiscally significant. Prussian naturalist Alexander von Humboldt, in his extensively researched *Political Essay on the Kingdom of New Spain* of 1811, estimated that New Spain produced more than a third of all the bullion in the Spanish and Portuguese Americas during the course of three centuries; subsequent historians have placed the figure closer to 45 percent.[19] Royal tribute registration among Indians was actively expanding at a rate of between 13 and 25 percent at the end of the century, reaching 1.1 million pesos in net income to the royal treasuries between 1795 and 1799.[20] This accounted for a little less than 8 percent of the total revenue collected in the royal treasuries of New Spain, which exceeded 15.3 million pesos after collection costs.[21] An 1805 summary showed Indians paid more than 1.3 million pesos in tribute, compared to about 200,000 pesos collected from free people of African descent.[22] Royal tributes paid by free people of African descent, then, amounted to only 19 percent of what Indians paid for the same tax. Just as significant are the experiences of taxpayers who found themselves, often unwillingly or unexpectedly, subject to tax increases at the core of Bourbon colonialism. The outcome of the rapid growth of Afromexican tribute in New Spain was a tax base that was more integrated into the colonial regime and increasingly burdened by discriminatory laws and practices, including taxation.

The Rise of Tribute in the Spanish Atlantic

Iberian taxes transplanted to the New World solidified the relationship between the Spanish monarch and Indian subjects in the Castilian tradition of inclusion through taxation. Taxes were already in place on Jews and Muslims resident in medieval Castile, incorporating them within Castilian society but marking them as subjects for royal financial gain.[23] Indian tribute grew out of medieval and early modern predecessors from Castile as well, including the *pecho* peasants paid.[24] Supplemental taxes called "*servicios*" of variable amounts were charged according to the needs of the crown. The *servicios* defined the status of *pecheros*, who were the only members of society required to make the contribution. The *pechero* designation was somewhat nebulous, being defined by inclusion on a register rather than belonging to a particular social status or an assessment of income.[25] In contrast, free blacks in Portugal paid taxes based on categories pertaining to the sizes of their estates, which were usually meager in both Lisbon and rural areas.[26] Many formerly enslaved Africans in Iberia lived in poverty, and their economic circumstances depended in part on behavior and decisions of former masters.[27] This population was not subject to a special tax based on blackness. While there were some similarities between the *pecho* and the tax paid by free people of African descent in Spanish America, the tax statuses were distinct.[28] Indeed, officials in the Real Hacienda at the end of the eighteenth century characterized the tax as "original and unique to the Americas."[29]

Attaining the status of the minor nobility, the hidalgos, led to important tax exemptions in the early modern period. Lexicographer Sebastián de Covarrubias derived "hidalgo" from the root "*itálico*," denoting one who did not pay any tributes.[30] In Spanish America, all Spaniards received exemption from royal tribute, signifying their nobility over all other caste groups.[31] Tax breaks of various kinds were regularly granted to European colonists in North America.[32] The Cámara de Indias extended the practice of granting patents of nobility to peasants through *cartas de hidalguía* comparable to those used in Castile, with the consequence that these titles were also available to members of the Indian nobility who held the title of cacique.[33] Originally associated with nobility, by the eighteenth century this term came to refer to members of a family of status whose members held offices in local Indian governments.[34] For Indians and Spaniards, tribute became another method of recognizing privileged status in the new society.

In the New World, the monarch experienced fewer barriers to taxation, unlike in Castile where consultation with the Cortes of Castile, or Castilian parliament, could stall tax reforms. Members of the aristocracy who enjoyed privileges in the area of taxation understood themselves to be bound by a contract that, to be broken, required the agreement of nobles and monarch alike. In contrast, the Indies provided the Spanish crown with revenue in the form of the *quinto real* and Indian tribute, both justified by the act of conquest and subsequent ownership over the land.[35] Charging royal tributes was a means, throughout Spanish America, of formalizing an economy based on conquest and plunder.[36]

Indian tribute in New Spain was originally conceived as a tax in kind, by which Indian residents would produce goods for collection by caciques. These goods would eventually benefit individual *encomenderos* or the Spanish monarch.[37] As well as being the most economically significant tax levied on Indians in the early colonial period, the administration of this tax required the first integrated aspect of governance involving both Spaniards and Indians.[38] For royal tribute, Indian local officials collected the funds or goods and handed them off to district magistrates (*alcaldes mayores* or *corregidores*) or their agents.[39] These officials were notoriously corrupt in both New Spain and Peru. From its earliest implantation, tribute collection could easily lead to abuses, such as graft and physical violence, by provincial officials.[40]

Not long after it was established, the tribute regime underwent sweeping reforms in New Spain and Peru. The process of *tasación* was initiated by royal decree in 1536. Viceroy Antonio de Mendoza oversaw the implementation of this decree in New Spain, which required him either to visit or send an emissary to survey tributary communities.[41] Throughout Spanish America, implanting a rate of taxation assessed by crown agents had the effect of diminishing the authority of the *encomendero*, who was no longer in charge of extracting any tributes he or she saw fit to levy.[42] A price was set at half a *fanega* (around one and one-half bushels) of corn and eight reales per Indian tributary couple; the schedule of payment switched to the *tercio*, a four-month cycle customary in Castilian debt payments; and the crown reasserted its right to control tribute monies and goods.[43] In 1559, Philip II decreed that his representatives in Peru also "appraise and declare justly the tributes, rents, and other fees that the Indians have to pay, so that this can be done with greater justice and a more sound basis."[44] These investigations and reforms were crucial to addressing the heavy burden of taxation on Indian subjects, thousands of whom agitated throughout the colonial period for relief from tribute or reductions in amounts charged.

Early reforms limited tribute to silver payments and a reduced number of local products. After midcentury, goods exacted for tribute were sold at public auction based on prices that included the cost of transport.[45] Indeed, a major difference between Aztec and Spanish colonial tribute concerned transportation: Aztec tributaries absorbed the expense of transporting tribute goods, rendering it a kind of bonus for Aztec rulers. Spanish colonial authorities extracted tribute from members of the political unit over which they ruled, meaning that transportation constituted either a higher tax or an expense the colonial regime was forced to absorb.[46] Mendoza's 1536 decision to convert tribute into gold or silver might have proved more economical for Indians, who would not be burdened with transportation costs. Historians of the Real Hacienda in the nineteenth century posited that allowing Indians to pay tribute exclusively in money discouraged them from producing staple crops, prompting the king to continue to allow diversity in tributary goods and money.[47]

The names of tributary subjects were recorded on a tribute register, which, by definition, did not describe the entire population. Its purpose was to target a segment of the populace for a specific purpose. A *padrón* was the "list that is made in cities, villages, or other place in order to know by name the number of contributing residents (*vecinos*) for tributes and royal taxes (*pechos reales*)."[48] In a similar vein, a *matrícula* was a "list or catalog of the names of people who are chosen and recognized toward a determined purpose."[49] The *padrón* or *matrícula* was a list or register of names of people and their families, as well as, ideally, their places of work.[50] Unlike a general census, a tribute register included only the details relevant to tribute collection and the identification of future tributaries.

From the mid-sixteenth to the mid-eighteenth century, the basic unit of tribute was a family made up of a male tributary, a wife, and children.[51] Bourbon reformers later attempted to convert royal tribute to a simple head tax to be charged of adult men ages eighteen to fifty.[52] For free people of African descent, the tax did have some characteristics of a capitation tax charged "without attention to capital, rents, or other products of industry."[53] Yet, family was central to counting methods in the tribute regime, a long-standing practice and set of attitudes that remained influential. Tribute retained its associations with lineage, reproduction, and family ties, even as reformers pushed for a single rate of pay based on age and gender. For much of the colonial period, royal tributaries consisted of units of married "whole tributaries," who paid a greater rate of tribute. "Half tributaries" included unmarried people and those married to exempt individuals, such as Spaniards or mestizos. Colonial authorities understood the centrality of women's and minors' labor for producing tribute monies and goods.[54]

When Philip II established the tribute tax for free people of African descent in 1572, he addressed the case of intermarriage between Indians and African slaves or free people of color.[55] The following year the crown issued a law stating that any offspring from such marriages "should pay tribute like the other Indians, even if they say they are not."[56] This law acknowledged the already prevalent mixture between Indian and African ancestry and closed a loophole many potential tributaries had exploited to shield their children from the tax.[57] The king attempted to prevent any future assertions that only Indian lineage justified tributary status with a 1574 decree establishing the formal inclusion of men and women of African descent as royal tributaries.[58] The use of the terms "*mulatos*" and "*mulatas*" grouped together people with African ancestry, whether they were also the children of Spaniards or Indians.[59] Each was to pay two pesos if married to either a free or enslaved person. Half the rate would be applied to unmarried men or women who lacked a trade.[60]

Attempts to create a graduated tax applicable to free people of color failed. Under a qualification to the 1574 law, viceroys, high courts and their judicial advisory bodies (*audiencias*), and governors could decide tribute payments of "the quantity . . . that seems best,"[61] depending on yearly income and property. This graduated rate would disproportionately burden any men and women who had prospered despite oppression.[62] Colonial officials were given a considerable amount of leeway in their decisions regarding not only the amount of tribute but also who exactly would be charged. Under this law, those without property or income would supposedly be taxed at a reduced rate.[63] Even in the sixteenth century, free people of color were not systematically subjected to a graduated tax in any generalized way.[64] Officials already found it extremely difficult at times to locate and identify free people of color, and the additional assessment of their wealth would have imposed even greater strains on a system that was barely functional in many areas of New Spain.

The Uneven Enforcement of Tribute among Free People of Color

Across large swaths of Spanish America, royal tribute from free *mulatos* was enforced sporadically if at all. Royal decrees of the seventeenth century suggest that free people of color in South and Central America paid tribute, though in small amounts and with little reliability. In the Caribbean islands, no examples of royal tribute from free people of African descent have yet been found, but in the circum-Caribbean, large free black populations attracted attention from Habsburg bureaucrats and rulers. Royal tribute from free people of color was already present in areas of Guatemala by 1603, where adult men paid four *tostones* annually (where two *tostones* were equal to one peso), adult unmarried women paid two *tostones*, and married women were exempt.[65] Receipts showed payments from free black residents, property owners who paid on behalf of their employees, and possibly even a slave.[66] Tribute had already become a bargaining chip for free blacks and former maroons in Panama by the end of the sixteenth century.[67] New Granada also implemented the tax in the seventeenth and eighteenth centuries.[68] Despite being home to a free black population, royal tribute from Afroperuvians was inefficient when implemented at all.[69] In the mid-seventeenth century, jurist Juan de Solórzano y Pereira (1565–1655) wrote that tribute in specie and labor from free people of color in Peru had been "put into practice in some provinces, though with a small yield. As for putting them [free people of color] in the mines and to other services, I have not seen it practiced anywhere."[70] In Alto Peru, free *mulatos* paid royal tribute between 1619 and 1635.[71] As far afield as Chile, in 1703 the "free *negros* and *mulatos* and the *negras* and *mulatas* and their sons and daughters" were required to pay.[72] They did pay small sums to the *caja* in Santiago de Chile between 1695 and 1706.[73] In the early eighteenth century, colonial authorities in Paraguay attempted to extract the tax, which may have had the effect of driving men to seek their fortunes elsewhere.[74]

Attempts to intensify tribute among free people of African descent met with severe resistance outside New Spain. By the mid-eighteenth century, bureaucrats in Quito had considered extending tribute, though the decision was made not to enforce the tax for fear of violent resistance.[75] The 1764 "Rule for the Declaration of Mestizos" exempted illegitimate children of Spanish women in all cases in New Granada,[76] a practice whose end result was a decline in potential tributaries. The extraction of tribute from non-Indian groups was an issue of great concern among bureaucrats in Lima and Buenos Aires during the era of intensifying Bourbon reform under the reigns of Charles III (1759–88) and Charles IV (1788–1808). Yet, authorities feared uprisings in response to drastic changes in the tributary status of various groups. Payments from *negros*, *mulatos*, or *zambaigos* lacked standardization in Peru and were not collected at all in Buenos Aires and Montevideo.[77] Bourbon reformers were forced to abandon the tax in Nicaragua in 1788 because of resistance as well.[78] Yet, New Spain's tribute regime was so profitable that its practices were exported throughout the empire. Starting in the 1770s, royal inspector (*visitador general*) José Antonio de Areche undertook reforms of the Peruvian tribute regime that would make it similar to that of New Spain.[79] There, tribute reformers had managed to more than double the number of free black and *mulato* tributaries in many key regions of the kingdom. But tribute inspired violent resistance among militiamen in Peru, who rejected tribute on the grounds that it demeaned their status.[80]

Only the Kingdom of New Spain possessed the necessary combination of administrative institutions, legal tradition of taxation, and a large, Afromexican tax base that would yield reliable tribute revenue in the late eighteenth century. At the time, in all of mainland Spanish America there were 650,000 free people of African descent;[81] perhaps half of them resided in what is now Mexico. For every enslaved person who lived in New Spain at the end of the eighteenth century, there were at least thirty free people of color. The Peruvian population, in contrast, included 40,000 enslaved people and 41,000 free people of color.[82] In many regions of mainland Spanish America, free people of color outnumbered those who were enslaved by the eighteenth century.[83] New Spain had experienced a decline in slavery since 1640, though enslaved labor remained important in certain industries well into the eighteenth century.[84] The replacement of slavery with free labor led to a large population of Afromexican subjects required to pay royal tributes. In New Spain, this population had been growing for centuries by the time of the resurgence of tribute and taxation in the late eighteenth century.

The Viceroyalty of New Spain was a patchwork of local taxation practices and varied demographic landscapes. Free people of African descent had consistently paid tribute in central Mexico in the sixteenth and seventeenth centuries, but amounts collected fluctuated dramatically.[85] In the first half of the eighteenth century, tributes dropped from their late Habsburg levels, in part due to regional episodes of disease and famine.[86] While some areas suffered disasters, other wealthy regions registered population shifts in favor of free people. In Guanajuato, where tribute was highly infrequent and contested, free people of African descent provided a vital labor source in mining and represented more than two-thirds of the population by the 1750s.[87] To the far north, the mines at Rosario also had a majority-*mulato* tributary population in the same decade.[88] These areas of population concentration were well known to bureaucrats in Mexico City, who saw an opportunity in the eighteenth century to increase revenue through an established tax with direct implications for vassalage.

Meanings of Tribute for the Crown, Administrators, and Free Subjects

Tribute was, for the Spanish crown, a sign of lordship and a right exercised in the colonies as well as on the peninsula. From the earliest implementation of royal tribute in New Spain, this tax cemented the privileges and obligations of crown and subject.[89] Royal tribute from Indians and free people of African descent was justified by the relationship between the monarch and his subjects.

Far from onerous, in the eyes of Philip II, such tribute constituted a privilege of the descendants of Africans and Indians to continue "living in peace and justice, having passed through slavery."[90] The reference implied that subjects owed their sovereigns a grateful allegiance and was part of a larger current of European political thought regarding taxation in the medieval and early modern periods.[91] Scholars and jurists in the Ibero-Atlantic world saw Indian tribute as a sign of the power of the monarch as well as the necessary contribution of subjects who received services from the Church and colonial government.[92] This right of the ruler to exact tribute emerged in discussions of tribute, in which bureaucrats and ordinary people referred to the right of tribute, sometimes called "*vasallaje*," as the king's legitimate dues from his subjects.

Demonstrating proper loyalty and vassalage through Indian tribute began in the sixteenth century. The Spanish state was driven by an evangelizing and civilizing mission carried out by ecclesiastics and bureaucrats intent on imposing behaviors that conformed to Catholic morality and would benefit the treasury.[93] The Indians' will was not only fundamental to their religious indoctrination, it was also widely discussed as a barrier to the implantation of Spanish political control. A variety of contemporary authors discussed whether the will of the Indians to become tributary vassals should influence policy in the Americas. An anonymous author in 1554 proposed to the king that "all the Indians or the majority of them, at their will, want to become your vassals . . . and in this way Your Majesty is the natural ruler over them as well as the Spaniards, and in good conscience you will receive fair tributes, sustaining [the Indians] in justice and Christianity."[94] This idealized description of the relationship between willing vassals and a paternal king was the justification behind royal tribute for both Indians and, later, free people of African descent in the sixteenth century.

Tribute was tied to the transition from bondage and enslavement, usually to individual Spaniards, to freedom and fealty to the Spanish crown. Recent estimates suggest that more than 650,000 Indians were enslaved and then forcibly moved within the Americas and Ibero-Atlantic world in the sixteenth century.[95] Enslaved Indians were part of tribute in a variety of goods to powerful Spaniards, including Hernan Cortés, in the decade following the conquest.[96] This practice was unpalatable to multiple monarchs, who preferred Indians as free vassals rather than the property of conquistadors. The papal bull *Sublimis Deus* of 1537 further asserted the humanity of Indians and condemned their enslavement. The Council of the Indies, a governing council in Spain with extensive authority over colonial matters, went on to support Dominican efforts to abolish Indian slavery and resettle free communities in the 1540s and 1550s.[97] As many as three thousand people used legal means to demand their freedom at the high court in Mexico City following the issuance of the New Laws in 1542 against Indian slavery.[98] Indians who had been slaves in Guatemala found themselves distributed among Spaniards under the obligation of *servicio personal* labor justified by the fact that they did not pay tribute. These Indians petitioned the king, who, in 1559, banned the practice of forcing emancipated Indians to provide labor for public or private demands. Instead, the crown created a payment schedule for such Indians to become future tributaries. Again in 1568 the crown affirmed its position on this issue and reasserted the status of these Indians as the king's vassals.[99]

The early presence of African slavery in Spanish America, and narratives of a transition to freedom, provided further justification for royal tribute. In New Spain, blacks numbered more than 150,000 people by 1640; the minority were born in Africa.[100] Many of these Afromexicans successfully sought avenues to freedom for themselves and their children, and the ratio of enslaved people to free people shifted. As these American-born people gained their freedom or were born free, they would become vassals and free subjects of the Spanish crown. This population encompassed *negros*, who were mostly or entirely of African lineage, born in Africa, the Americas, Iberia, or elsewhere; *mulatos*, who had some African ancestry, but could also have European or Indian ancestry; *morenos* and *pardos* who were "brown" or "dark"; and less common castes of partial African ancestry like *lobos*, *moriscos*, *chinos*, *coyotes*, and *zambaigos*.[101] Tribute laws incorporated these complex categories to contain the growing free population and retain its ideological connections to slavery. Rulers and tribute officials seized on what they saw as the fitness of Afromexican individuals to be grouped and economically exploited, if not as slaves, then as tributary units.

Colonial authorities created and consulted tribute registers to continue to extract taxes from this free labor force. Toward this end, Philip II had decreed that all free *negros* or *mulatos* live with *amos*, masters or labor bosses who were obliged to pay tribute on behalf of their charges. In the event that workers ran out on their *amos*, these tributaries were to be captured, jailed, and then returned, a practice reminiscent of the treatment of runaway slaves. The dual purpose of such a practice would be to enrich the treasury as well as provide local elites with much-needed labor.[102] Although this additional stipulation that free people of African descent be barred from moving proved unenforceable, the king also called for the implementation of a "*padrón* of all of them, with their names and people with whom they live."[103] In the early colonial period, the *padrón* traced workers back to the locations of their masters, meaning the crown had some recourse in the event of resistance to payment. The right of authorities to construct *padrones* periodically would be met with complaints from residents of all castes who saw this document as a symbol of dishonor assigned by zealous administrators to collect more taxes.

For administrators, the tribute regime provided a convenient method of organizing colonial subjects into categories and annually reinforcing tributary status using *padrones*. This practice could create a cycle of registering and re-registering individuals based on their past identification as tributaries, effectively maintaining a social order built from family histories of tribute. In 1618, Philip III had decreed that tribute registers include the names and ages of children of tributaries. The registers "should be orderly, in order to avoid arguments" and prevent individual protests on registration as adults.[104] Keeping a close watch on who enjoyed which tribute privileges, and for which reasons, was of critical importance to maintaining the local knowledge that set certain families apart by blood or by service to the crown.

Registration among free people of color could be conducted entirely separately from Indians, but this was not always the case. Free people of African descent and Indians might appear on the same list, provided the latter worked and lived outside special Indian communities. These *indios laboríos* lacked the corporate privileges and obligations of Indians in townships (*indios de pueblo*). The term *laborío* took on nuanced meaning dependent on changing usage over time, as well as local labor conditions and understandings of caste.[105] Sometimes *indios laboríos* were listed alongside free people of African descent in the early eighteenth century, preserving earlier precedent across the Spanish empire.[106] Because both were tributary but did not contribute to or benefit from the community coffers of *indios de pueblo*, free people of color and *indios laboríos* had legal commonalities that were not defined by color or caste. As vassals, both groups had similar obligations that characterized their relationships to the crown and eroded the fixity of caste categories in Spanish America.[107]

Habsburg authorities had called for orderly registers that would define tributary status for free people of African descent. Under the Bourbon dynasty, registration and collection would become more standardized, but the basis of the tributary category remained a matter of interpretation. Bourbon bureaucrats themselves did not always agree on the nature of tributary status. The lively debates between bureaucrats regarding the privileges and obligations of a tributary class at the turn of the nineteenth century offer new insight into *calidad* and its effects on colonial subjecthood, as it was understood by bureaucrats. The historical record preserves a few particularly vociferous advocates of phenotypic "signs" or "aspect," a physiognomic term that originated long before caste. Other accountants and bureaucrats favored arguments about genealogy and did not give opinions on the possible impact of physical features on tributary status. Internal debate within the tribute regime reveals an institution torn between a social order based on documented genealogies and one determined visually and therefore subject to individual interpretation. As bureaucrats were well aware, these procedural and often philosophical debates had fiscal consequences for the Real Hacienda.

Despite remarkable gains in collection and registration in the second half of the century, a chorus of critics continued to question the efficacy of tribute. Attempts to change the tribute regime were cautious and reflected the gravity, symbolism, and history of the tax. According to contemporary observers of the development of the Real Hacienda, tribute collection remained dysfunctional, becoming "day by day more worthless to the treasury, more damaging to the administrators and taxpayers, and more odious to the public." Much of the resulting damage and the "innumerable difficulties" impeding the creation of tribute registers could be traced to the legal and extralegal methods of Indians and *castas* to avoid the tax.[108] These strategies became more commonplace and notable as new regulations and registers took effect. Ordinary residents complained of the seemingly unending and illogical attempts by royal officials to create more tributaries. One group of annoyed residents from Tula claimed in 1804 that officials wanted "to make amphibious men who would be Indians for tribute and Spaniards to pay everything else."[109] Colonial subjects frequently sought relief from their tributary burdens, which they found increasingly intrusive. For these ordinary people, the extension of tributary status reflected the overreach of royal officials more than the reputations of the petitioners.

In times of extreme need, communities could request a temporary exemption from tribute payments or a delayed payment schedule from the Real Hacienda. Poverty was a common theme in such requests filed on behalf of Indian towns, but a few similar petitions could come from families of *castas* as well.[110] When epidemics struck Indian pueblos, officials might argue that free people of color also deserved tribute relief. In 1764, a magistrate (alcalde) from the jurisdiction of Temascaltepec and Zultepec, now in the state of Mexico, explained to an accountant from the Real Hacienda in Mexico City that he had not charged tribute from Indians or free people of color "because the epidemic also included the *negros* and *mulatos*."[111] Indian communities were able to retain access to some of their taxes and tributes, as some of the funds would go back to the town government and clergy for local expenses.[112] Royal recognition of community land and legal privileges reinforced Indians' obligation to pay tribute. Although paying tribute was an important way to put down roots in a rural community, Afromexican tribute offered little economic benefit, since these communities in New Spain were not, in the majority, distinct corporate entities, nor did they hold communal property as did *pueblos de indios*. A few recognized black towns dotted the landscape, including former settlements of Afromexicans who had escaped slavery in seventeenth-century Veracruz, but most tributaries lived far beyond the reach of a possible "República de Negros."[113] Whereas Indians paid tribute that went to the Real Hacienda as well as to community coffers, free people of African descent did not have their own settlements that could reap any benefits from taxes.

Both Indians and free people of African descent were obliged to show their loyalty to their monarch by paying tribute. By becoming tributaries, Indians performed a recognizable sign of deference and political incorporation.[114] The categories of *indio* (Indian), *tributario* (tributary), and *natural* (native) formed the basis for Indian constructions of loyalty and vassalage.[115] When free people of African descent engaged with the tributary regime, they too became part of a community of taxpayers. Where enslaved Africans were numerous, free *mulatos* may have seen tribute payment as a representation of their freedom and status, which distinguished them from other subordinated groups.[116] One of a few benefits from these payments was the symbol of legitimacy it afforded to maroon communities that became colonial towns like San Lorenzo de Cerralvo, now named for the maroon leader Yanga, who agreed to put down their arms and pay tributes to the crown "like all the other free blacks and *mulatos* of the Indies."[117] Such communities agreed to pay tribute as a gesture of loyalty and, perhaps more importantly for colonial officials, to hunt down and capture maroons and defend the realm from all other enemies.[118] But the demonstrations of loyalty and vassalage expected of Afromexican tributaries were not generally reciprocated as they were for the much more common Indian pueblos. Most free people of African descent did not receive communal property or fiscal benefits in exchange for their tributary status, yet they were still expected to act as loyal vassals by cooperating with payment and registration. A loyal tributary subject could be the descendant of Indians or Africans (or both), male or female, rural or urban, born into slavery or freedom, as long as he or she provided income to the Spanish crown.

Although there was no overarching practice of a graduated tax, the burden of tribute fell heavier on members of certain occupations. In cities, tributaries were likely to be artisans, apprentices, or part of the working poor, for whom tribute was a great imposition.[119] Miners fared better, because they were often exempt from tribute or had easy access to specie, yet their work was as low paying as that of their counterparts in cities and rural agricultural regions.[120] Among the tributary families examined in this book, farmers outnumbered members of all other occupations.[121] They may have been targeted as the result of their connection to property, either as renters or owners, but their rates of tribute were not tied directly to earnings or the value of a family estate.

For some families, tribute was a brief moment of contact with the state and its agents; for others, tribute meant public humiliation and dishonor. Tribute disputes provided an arena in which ordinary people voiced their interpretations of their own tributary obligations. Although paying tribute supposedly symbolized the faithful loyalty of Indian or Afromexican vassals, people claiming Spanish descent disputed tributary status based on the past loyalty of their ancestors. One such individual claimed in 1804 that not only was paying tribute detrimental to him financially, but also the comparison to Indians negated the "privileges acquired by his ancestors with their virtue, their valor, and their blood spilled for their king."[122] Intricate cases appeared in local courts, petitions to the viceroy, and even as far as Spain, on behalf of residents who refused to be counted as tributaries. For these families, tribute was a grave insult to their lineage and social standing, and they would not stand by silently while their names were neatly inscribed between the columns of the new registers.

The labels plebeians chose in legal documents allow glimpses of ordinary people's understandings and perceptions of self and others.[123] Afromexican tributaries employed a language of *calidad* within the tribute regime that was not explicitly tied to physical features. The language of color and aspect was unpopular among tribute complainants in New Spain. Instead, magistrates in eighteenth-century Mexico City heard hundreds of arguments for exemption based on complex articulations of genealogy under the rubric of *calidad*. With the exception of some *pardo* militiamen, individuals and families did not use color, phenotype, or appearance as indicators of their tributary status. The preference for genealogical arguments and reputational reasoning demonstrated the enduring importance of family histories, lineage, and marriage as determinants of status.

Through registration and payment as tributaries, or by contesting their tributary status, free people of African descent actively engaged with the colonial regime.[124] Tribute exemption symbolized the prestige of militias, which, as they accumulated tribute privileges through their military service, defined themselves as both *pardo* and nontributary.[125] People in communities that did not have prominent militias with tribute privileges probably paid tribute in part to preserve their livelihoods and maintain their homes. Scholars have argued that tax-paying colonial subjects "expected a return on their investment in the colonial state."[126] For free people of color, these returns would have been limited when compared with those of Indian communities; still, free people of color could expect that paying royal tribute would allow them to remain where they were without further molestation from crown authorities. Finally, tributary status was a symbol of freedom from slavery, a complicated construction that allowed the regime continually to tax manumission and place free people of color in contexts of loyalty and vassalage.

Calidad and Terminologies of Difference in the Spanish Atlantic World

The eighteenth-century tribute regime built on widely used vocabularies of caste and *calidad* in tribute registers as well as petitions and investigations.[127] Over time, the social markers that accompanied and defined tributary status in New Spain changed to accommodate shifts in terminology. The complex distinctions of caste and status that so preoccupied elites in the Atlantic world were also linked to tribute, and thus had economic as well as social implications for ordinary people. A sixteenth-century description of different types of people, or *géneros de gente*, began a centuries-long process of creating categories that "linked moral and social stereotypes to particular categorizations associated with lineage, culture, and phenotype," but not specifically with race.[128] Later, caste would describe lineage and the results of sexual reproduction. The growing usage of *casta* terms indicated both the presence of a range of people of mixed ancestry, the so-called *castas*, and an elite concern that such populations should submit to the crown and the colonial regime.[129] Tribute provided one avenue toward controlling this population and forcing it into a series of social categories that maintained the divide between Spaniards and those they deemed inferior. As colonial authorities sought to redefine the social identities and economic obligations of men and women subject to tribute, individuals and communities increasingly contested their assigned tributary status. Although many people had only sporadic interaction with the tribute regime, they knew that their tributary status could have a severe social and economic impact on themselves and their families. Tribute became a marker of identity not only for people forced to pay taxes but also for those whom the colonial regime decided to differentiate socially as people of African ancestry.

Before the notion of caste had fully developed, the genealogical underpinnings of tribute were taking root in the courts and in the popular imagination. The early structure of tribute and its theoretical basis in distinctions of blood and lineage reflected the Iberian concern with *limpieza de sangre* (purity of blood). The genealogical concept of *limpieza de sangre* was used widely to define difference in Iberian societies, and the dichotomy between tributary and nontributary echoed the distinctions between categories of Old and New Christians.[130] Privileging certain bloodlines above others—those of *españoles*, as Spaniards and their descendants were known, and mestizos, the children of Spaniards and Indians—was fundamental to the processes of differentiation that defined Spanish royal tribute. As early as the sixteenth century, African ancestry became associated with impurity, with few if any limitations on how far back this genealogy could be traced for the purposes of demonstrating proof of *limpieza*.[131] The issue of Indian purity would occupy the Inquisition until Charles II finally decided in the late seventeenth century to grant all Indians a pure status and caciques' legal equality with Spanish hidalgos.[132] The preoccupation with blood purity evident in a variety of institutional settings also influenced tributary status, though genealogies of blood did not supersede genealogies of privilege and reputation.

Genealogical markers of difference coexisted with visibly identifiable characteristics like color. In 1582, Juan Portugués, "brown in color," and his children gained tribute exemption. Despite having served in the conquest of central Mexico, Portugués was initially charged tribute because of his color.[133] Local bureaucrats may have associated blackness with servitude and obligation because Portugués and his family resided in Ocuituco, a town whose surrounding region was already marked by early African slavery and sugar production.[134] This was also an early community of rural blacks and *mulatos*.[135] Portugués may have known that viceroys had already begun to grant privileges, in the form of arms licenses, based on masculine honor rather than color.[136] As a result of this petition, the local magistrate received an order from Mexico City barring him from charging tribute from Juan Portugués and his family. How exactly Portugués managed to secure the status he desired as a nontributary is unclear from the short resolution. By 1590, however, he had become a property owner described as a "*negro libre*." The properties he possessed, in the form of a ranch and land in Tememilcingo, had previously belonged to none other than Martín Cortés y Zúñiga, second marquis of the Valley of Oaxaca and son of conquistador Hernan Cortés.[137] By consolidating his nontributary status and wealth—and perhaps by some political maneuvering—Portugués transferred his own status through a lineage of privilege for his children. Color never disappeared as a marker of difference; it became a modifier of caste.[138] A register from Texcoco, in the Valley of Mexico, listed individuals like Juan Antonio Mendoza, a man of Spanish and mestiza parentage (*castizo*) "of very dark color" and his wife Josefa Flores Miranda, a "Spaniard of very dark color."[139] The continuing use of these terms showed the importance of phenotype as a contributing factor to determining both caste and tributary status.

The rise of the *castas* was the most influential social development of the seventeenth century for tribute. By the late seventeenth century, the language of caste had become a widespread staple for tributary classification, forming the foremost indicator of tributary status. The idea of *casta* began as a descriptor of good animal breeding, though these associations weakened as elites developed a vocabulary that demeaned certain elements of the population based on lineage and phenotype.[140] Caste was somewhat fluid and subjective, which could lead to local disputes over self-identifications that clashed with the perceptions of others as well as debates across the Atlantic concerning caste terminology.[141] As one historian has put it, "in everyday experience casta was not a fixed location within a rigid hierarchy."[142] Terms of caste could be, by the end of the century, assigned to anyone, not just the people of mixed ancestry. Spaniards, Indians, and enslaved Africans could be of a certain caste.[143] The concept of caste throughout the Spanish Empire showed inherent instability and flexibility, although negotiations of this system of classification had limits dependent on reputation, tributary obligations, enslaved status, or physical appearance, among other factors.

Terms that assigned *casta* could be imposed or adopted actively by individuals and families toward specific ends and to give multiple meanings to their standing in communities and colonial hierarchies writ large. Across Spanish America, free people of African descent adopted and deployed caste terminologies that established favorable status, cemented social networks, and defined family ties.[144] Some attempted to use the flexibility of caste and its tributary associations to the advantage of their families. In 1671, a free *mulata* named Mariana de Ochoa lobbied for her children's exemption from tribute because she was a widow of Hernando Bravo de Lagunas, a Spaniard belonging to a prominent mining family in Pachuca. Claiming that the public "opinion and reputation" of her legitimate children was at stake, Ochoa focused on the status of her deceased husband rather than her own connection to the family, which would have given her children a lineage marked by blackness.[145] In this case, the petitioner attempted to associate exempt caste, the honor of being reputed as "*caballeros españoles*," legitimacy, and paternal lineage with her children, understanding that a *mulato* caste would burden her children with tributary obligations. The words "*casta*" and "*calidad*" are not used in this petition and witness testimony, but Ochoa repeatedly calls herself a free *mulata* and her children the legitimate children of herself and a Spaniard, her deceased husband. Paternal Spanish lineage, along with legitimacy and honor, provided a justification for nontributary status. The widespread use of caste terms to increase one's own or one's familial status, or to discredit that of others, ensured the influence of caste in daily life and colonial institutions.[146]

The word "*calidad*" was connected to tributary status in the Spanish Atlantic world as early as the sixteenth century. Early instances of *calidad* as a term within the tribute regime appear in assessments of the economic capacity of Indian communities. The written records of in-person evaluation or inspection (*visita*), population calculation (*cuenta*), and price determination (*tasación*) described the ability of tributary communities to produce tribute in goods or in specie, based on their properties and population size. In 1536, a *real cédula* instructed men designated by the *audiencia* and viceroy to "see the number of settlers (*pobladores*) and native inhabitants (*naturales*) of each town, the *calidad* of the land where they live, and inform yourselves regarding what they paid to their caciques and other people who ruled over them."[147] Because Afromexican communities lacked the legal corporate structure of Indian towns, free people of color were not evaluated as a group based on their pooled resources. The *calidad* of individuals and families, rather than their goods and properties, determined the rate of tribute. The New Laws issued by Charles V in 1542 also refer to the "*calidad* of the Indians and the land."[148] A foundational group of laws compiled under Viceroy Gaspar de Zúñiga Acevedo y Fonseca, fifth count of Monterrey, used the term *calidad* to describe the nature of tributaries and their access to resources. These printed instructions sent out from the capital called on local magistrates to compile lists of free people of color of "any *calidad* of the aforementioned and know with whom they live and with what they support themselves."[149] Here the term describes free people of color but also references the extent to which such people might be able to pay high tributes in cash by making reference to places of residence and occupation. In subsequent centuries, referencing *calidad* as a social category often allowed those who evaluated local tribute registers to count numbers of people with less regard for an accurate and thorough assessment of their regional economic resources.

An important social marker beginning in the seventeenth century, *calidad* as a descriptor of free people of color was inescapable by the mid-eighteenth century.[150] The primary entry from the *Diccionario de Autoridades*, an official dictionary published between 1726 and 1739, defined "*calidad*" as "the property of the natural body, naturally (except by the Power of Divine Omnipotence) inseparable from substance."[151] Properties or qualities of the body were not, therefore, independent of an individual's morality, family, or beliefs and practices. Magali Carrera has argued that "the *calidad* of mulatto was not solely associated with darker skin or other physical characteristics; it also aligned a person to certain diagnostics, such as debased social and moral traits."[152] This interpretation of *calidad* was widely understood in the Atlantic world. In sixteenth-century Castile, *calidad* as an organizing principle of social difference had roots in physiognomic thinking that posited that an observer could use external signs to assess the inner nature of another person.[153] Thus, tributaries possessed inherent "qualities" that were linked with caste but were not equivalent to physical markers, and these qualities defined them as part of a tributary group. The prominence of *calidad* as a social marker in tribute documents points to the growing importance of economic status and *clase* (class) in addition to caste in the eighteenth century.[154] Tributaries repeatedly used the word to describe a social status that was based on a mixture of genealogy, caste, and economic standing. An elderly Indian noble from Texcoco named Luis Sánchez requested an exemption from tribute based on his "*calidad* as a cacique and a *principal*," but he also stressed his crushing poverty.[155] The presence of multiple castes, qualities, and classes within the tribute regime allowed for divergent and conflicting interpretations of the tax and the status it conferred on subjects.

Like earlier markers of social difference, *calidad* depended on community and public perceptions. Reputations rested on the opinions of neighbors, the parish priest, local scribes, and others who participated in the quotidian social performance and communal interactions. These community members often served as witnesses in petitions, and their beliefs and understandings of community, *calidad*, and appearance fundamentally drove the process of social categorization for free people of color.[156] The resulting *calidad* and caste were frequently recorded on baptismal records, marriage licenses, and other ecclesiastical documents. Beyond the written record, people witnessed everyday indicators of *calidad* related to phenotype, dress, place of residence, and language. Religious devotion, in the form of attending church or participating in lay Catholic organizations, contributed to how people understood *calidad* and could offer Afromexicans an opportunity to claim honor based on gendered performances of piety.[157] How a person occupied public and private spaces affected daily power struggles that reflected on gender and honor.[158] How people acted could change their *calidad* in their communities, which was determined by public behavior and family ties as well as appearance. Based on gendered expectations and behaviors, individuals could gain or lose their honor, and damage that of their families, in colonial societies. As such, certain aspects of *calidad* were publicly identifiable and known in the community; however, these characteristics of *calidad* were not exclusively based on an individual's appearance.

Caste and genealogy were important determinants of *calidad*, but ordinary people turned also to other aspects of their personhood to define themselves, including tributary status, social circles, and occupation.[159] In 1788 in the city of Querétaro, José Miguel Núñez sought to bar his daughter María Guadalupe from marrying a man he believed to be a *lobo*, although he was "unaware of his *calidad*." Despite his uncertainty, Núñez claimed that *lobo* José Joaquín Morales was publicly reputed to have African ancestry and was otherwise a dishonorable, lazy drunkard who worked as a weaver in a textile workshop (*obraje*). In contrast to these many vices, Núñez positioned himself as the descendant of Spaniards who had never paid tribute or been recorded on the register of the tributary castes. Without complete knowledge of *calidad*, the complainant put together a series of insults and negative behaviors he and other members of the community associated with blackness, contrasting them with nontributary status and blood purity.[160] Tributary status mirrored complex constructions of *calidad* built simultaneously on an individual's physical features, genealogies both public and official, family ties, gender, political loyalty, and place of residence.

By incorporating Bourbon ideas about the qualities of being poor or wealthy, Spanish or *casta*, *calidad* was flexible and became intertwined with other terms. In 1802, a man called José María Zendrera y Villanis, a registered tributary, sought exemption based on his *calidad*, though he and his representatives also referred in his petition to "tributary castes," being "free of any bad race," as well as his legitimacy and *limpieza de sangre*.[161] Beyond the tribute regime, recent scholarship has noted that notaries used caste, *calidad*, class, *condición* (condition or status, often in reference to slavery), and even markers of ethnicity such as *nación* interchangeably in the seventeenth and eighteenth centuries. The use of these terms rendered caste terminologies increasingly unstable.[162] *Calidad* could combine with categories of caste (*calidad de mulato*); ethnicity (*calidad de Angola*); labor and class, in particular to denote master status (*calidad de maestro*); nobility (*calidad de cacique*); and tribute (*calidad de tributario*). In disputes of tributary status, the word also designated official capacities. An official could act as a judge in a case and take on the "quality," or capacity, of that position, giving him the *calidad* of a judge. Another phrase that surfaced in petitions for tribute exemption concerned temporality (*calidad de por ahora*) and often explained that privileges or protections would be granted "for the time being." In the tribute regime, *casta* and *calidad* both appeared in the eighteenth century on tribute counts and in petitions. By subsuming labels of caste and *calidad*, tributary status became a hybrid of characteristics from many social and legal categories, much like *calidad* itself.

Conclusion

Royal tribute from free blacks and *mulatos* in the Spanish Atlantic was not an economic success overall and only became profitable in a few regions at the end of the eighteenth century. Yet as a symbol of colonial subjecthood, this tax tied free people of African descent directly to the crown and colonial regime by regulating their movement and residence, profiting from their labor, and demanding their loyalty. Although Indians always made up the majority of the tributary population, the amount of tribute free Afromexicans could produce continued to entice bureaucrats and monarchs. New Spain would become the most prosperous and fiscally robust colony in the North Atlantic, and identifying potential taxpayers was of the utmost concern to Bourbon officials in Mexico City. The intersection between fiscal organization and the late colonial concept of *calidad* reveals how ordinary people became part of the colonial project. The development of Afromexican tribute would involve piecemeal legislation that often arose out of specific situations and individual reputations. Laws regulating tribute still depended on local custom and foundational decrees from the sixteenth century, but Afromexican tribute demonstrated a degree of ambiguity matched only by the confusion surrounding the status of free people of African descent themselves. Tributary registration and collection represented local points of contact between people of color, residents of other castes, and agents of the colonial regime. Like marriage and baptism, tribute recorded and reinforced caste categories and burgeoning ideas about *calidad* in the early eighteenth century.

The concept of *calidad* translated community reputation into words or phrases that bureaucrats in Mexico City or Madrid could recognize. Terms related to both *calidad* and caste could be found in petitions for tribute exemption and on registers of thousands of Afromexican tributaries. I assert that *calidad* and tributary status were deeply interconnected through a process of bureaucratic knowledge-making and a shared vocabulary of social difference intelligible to state and subject alike. Recorded on tribute registers, the *calidad* of a family member or head of household signaled the social standing of an entire lineage when viewed from the perspectives of bureaucrats in Mexico City. Tributary status also contributed to an individual's or family's *calidad* through public channels, such as gossip or publicly known associations with tributaries. Neighbors, friends, and family all were aware of who paid tribute, since names were called publicly and tribute payments were announced by a town crier. In evidence offered with petitions and on tribute registers, one word could reflect public perceptions of an individual's behaviors, social ties, and personal reputation. Although it inspired doubts, confusion, and resistance, *calidad* provided the bureaucracy of New Spain a standard flexible enough to define people of Spanish, African, and Indian descent according to a communally based social identity that could then be converted into a marker of economic responsibility to the crown. Afromexican tributaries did not exist on their own but rather in relationship to their ancestors, friends, families, colonial authorities, and the crown itself.

2

Revitalization and Reaction

Afromexican Tribute before 1763

In the early eighteenth century, free people of color in New Spain felt the burden of tribute to varying extents based on the region in which they lived and with whom they associated. As the town crier announced a new royal demand for tribute payment and registration, some free Afromexicans might remain in the homes where they served elite Spaniards and their families. Other Afromexicans shunned an association with any master and instead lived independently, according to some local officials. Records from the early eighteenth century show that free people of African descent did pay tribute in growing numbers in some parts of New Spain, and this phenomenon was linked to the practices of certain officials and their agents. Thus early Bourbon attempts at reassessing and revitalizing Afromexican tribute met with opposition in some communities but were successful elsewhere. These gains and losses resulted in an unsteady flow of Afromexican tribute to the regional treasuries, the *reales cajas*, in the first half of the eighteenth century. Targeting laborers with ready access to cash, such as those integrated into mining regions through their economic activities and places of residence, Bourbon bureaucrats attempted to impose tribute and enhance the treasury. Paying tribute represented loyal vassalage and membership in an orderly society, meanings that were not lost on local officials or fiscal bureaucrats who worked in the centers of colonial administration in Mexico City. Under Bourbon rule (1700–1808), free people of color saw renewed bureaucratic enthusiasm for tribute and often experienced direct contact with the colonial regime by way of this tax. Many free Afromexicans responded by participating in the regime and demonstrating their subjecthood through payment and registration. The documentation of tributaries that local officials created allows us to glimpse the connections free people of color made. Equally telling are the decisions officials made in their categorizations of tributaries based on *calidad*.

The official project of "reestablishment" of Afromexican and Indian tribute in parts of the kingdom proved time consuming and difficult at the turn of the eighteenth century. First, wealthy mining jurisdictions such as Zacatecas,

San Luis Potosí, and Guanajuato—full of potential tributaries—yielded little to no royal tributes, as authorities observed in the first decades of the eighteenth century.[1] Since the late sixteenth century, the crown had used exemption from tribute as an incentive to Indians to move to mining regions where they would alleviate chronic labor shortages.[2] Free people of color could also gain exemptions awarded to entire regions by way of their participation in militias on the coasts or as frontiersmen in territories dominated by hostile nations of indigenous people beyond Spanish colonial control. Second, this transitional period proved an inopportune time to intensify taxation in some potentially profitable regions of New Spain. Environmental factors depleted tax monies as Indians and free people of African descent were unable to pay. Social unrest and food shortages sparked a riot in the capital itself in 1692.[3] Between 1712 and 1714, the Bajío experienced severe droughts, poor harvests, and epidemics.[4] Lastly, widely accepted negative visions of free people of African descent as vagabonds allowed tribute collectors to attribute their failures to the inherent lack of families or stable places of residence. Despite these environmental and social constraints, bureaucrats in Mexico City pressed local officials for information in an attempt to investigate and reinvigorate taxation at the local level, thereby further integrating communities into larger fiscal, administrative, and social structures.

This chapter treats the problems of registration and documentation for tribute administrators as they sought greater knowledge of the lives of free people of color and their family, friends, associates, and employers. To explore the functioning of Afromexican tribute before the 1760s, I use registers and letters pertaining to tribute collection in the regions of San Luis Potosí, where free people of color worked in silver mining, and Acatlán and Piastla, a salt-producing region in what is now the state of Puebla. The two regional case studies show that vocabularies of *calidad* and caste had the potential to fuel doubts about the tributary status of individuals or families, while these same terms could serve as a method of stabilizing tributary populations and facilitate registration. These terminologies became tightly linked to tributary status through the processes of reinstituting, recording, and collecting that authorities undertook prior to the 1760s. Free people of color in the two case studies in question represented a diverse labor force engaged in the extraction of minerals and metals, making this tributary population doubly profitable for the economic health of the colonial project.

When Bourbon bureaucrats undertook the task of changing taxation at the local level, their decisions affected provincial governors and alcaldes, clergy, property owners, and tributaries themselves. Increasing taxes was often odious, but so was dragging new taxpayers into contact with a zealous fiscal regime. A gradual expansion of tributary obligations was preferable to any sudden change, noted early eighteenth-century officials wary of revolt.[5] Their concern was founded: the creation of a census by royal officials and its potential threat to local privileges led to rebellions in the southern Andes in 1730.[6] New Spain produced unmatched revenue for the Spanish Empire with relative compliance throughout the eighteenth century, although anger at local authorities did manifest periodically in uprisings generally confined to community boundaries and grievances.[7] The local population of Indians and free people of African descent, whose resources were already stretched thin in a time of food scarcity, reacted quickly to the arrival of royal collectors in San Luis Potosí in 1710. The possibilities for resistance among tributaries reawakened fears of hostile Indians, further discouraging local elites from wanting to participate in the tribute regime.[8]

When free people of African descent and Indians showed signs of conspiring to rise up against what they saw as unfair or dishonest behavior by officials, elites became particularly wary. Such alliances represented a disturbance to the peace, officials claimed in a description of the potentially "strange brotherhood of blacks and *mulatos* with [the Indians]" in San Luis Potosí.[9] Indians or free people of African descent who refused to pay royal tribute, *alcabala*, or *servicio personal* could be accused of denying the rights of the king by failing to pay the price of their obligation.[10] Similar complaints might be made about both Indians and free people of African descent who refused to pay tribute on other grounds as well. Bureaucrats and officials frequently portrayed those who did not pay the tax as ungrateful and unwilling colonial subjects, disloyal vassals, crafty and selfish loafers, or a threat to public order. In contrast, Afromexican tributaries who failed to pay, some of whom were subsequently jailed, represented themselves in petitions as a diverse lot with distinct reasons for nonpayment. Such individuals might be impoverished or unable to meet the many economic demands of family or a trade, mistakenly registered into the wrong *calidad*, or possess special privileges by way of militia service or frontier residence. Predictably, the image of the dangerous, conniving, and wandering *mulato* refusing the rights of the king was much more popular with bureaucrats than that of the hard-working, cash-strapped family.

Indians and free people of African descent frequently fled their communities when the time came to pay tribute or, according to officials, had no fixed residences whatsoever. The notion that free people of African descent were vagabonds continually intermingled with other tropes elites and officials used to categorize tributaries and laborers. Depending on the documentary or cultural context, free people of color might be deemed aimless wanderers, migrant laborers, or shifty strangers. The Real Audiencia advised that free people of color "be compelled to fix a residence, that they not roam, and that they practice their trades or find service with known masters."[11] The long-standing interest in *amos*, who could be masters or labor bosses, reflected the purpose of tribute as a control on the mobility and prosperity of free people of color. As early as 1590, Viceroy Álvaro Manrique de Zúñiga, first marquis of Villamanrique, advised the incoming viceroy that "pernicious free Africans and mulattos . . . are only capable of living as vagabonds." He recommended the death penalty for any person who "avoids [tribute] by not registering" or by leaving their place of registration. The first purpose of this action would be that "his Majesty collects the tribute that must be paid to him. The other intent, more central to the security and well-being of the country, is to command them to gather together for registration and then to apportion each one among all the mines, so they can serve there with miners, who will pay them."[12] In 1612, the local government of San Luis Potosí imprisoned *vagos*, among them free people of color, in a mine, forcing them to work in exchange for food.[13] Closely tied were labor demands, tribute, and perceptions of public order in mining communities where the tax could be levied. The ubiquitous image of the vagabond allowed collectors a well-worn excuse should they be unable to extract tribute and served the dual purpose of further demonizing free people of African descent as suspicious outsiders lacking community.

Afromexican tribute depended on the attitudes of local officials and their willingness to participate on the terms of Mexico City bureaucrats. The sentiments of local elites were varied, and the mechanisms for imperial revenue collection allowed local communities some control over how and when money would be collected. Still, multiple court orders mandated that owners of haciendas and other properties, as well as Indian officials, would provide lists of servants and Indians for the formation of *padrones*.[14] Bourbon bureaucrats saw potential gains for the Real Hacienda as well as the necessity to control the flow of specie. Examining the many and diverse regions of New Spain, bureaucrats in the capital attempted to harness and understand taxation through a lens of *calidad*. Officials in San Luis Potosí could not (or would not) use *calidad* as bureaucrats instructed. In contrast, an alcalde of Acatlán and Piastla provided more than a dozen lists of tributaries during his tenure between 1739 and 1743, while following many of the guidelines issued from Mexico City. Disputes and discussions—or a lack thereof—about tribute represented a larger process of incorporation of free people of African descent and their communities into the colonial regime, using terms based on *calidad*.

The application of *calidad* and the distinction between free people of African descent, *indios laboríos* (Indians who worked for wages on estates), and *indios de pueblo* (Indians who lived in legally defined towns) affected the livelihoods of local elites as well as tributaries. Afromexican tribute could have a more direct impact on elites who employed potential tributaries, who often resided on their properties or in their homes. The same was true of urban Indian tributaries, while the tribute of *indios de pueblo* was directly related to the administration and functioning of the Indian towns. The divide between free people of African descent and *indios laboríos* on one hand, and *indios de pueblos* on the other, can be understood through rates of tribute and their justification. Although regional variations existed, the generalized rate for tributary Indians was one peso and one-half a *fanega* of maize, which could be commuted to 4.5 reales.[15] *Indios laboríos* did not pay the additional reales from the maize. Tributaries who were *indios de pueblo* were understood to gain more from their agricultural labor on communal lands while the *indios laboríos* working on haciendas or other estates lived by their wages alone.[16] Eventually, tribute registers were standardized to reflect this divide visually by linking the lists of free people of African descent and *indios laboríos*. Keeping the groups apart facilitated tributary collection and also established important precedents that could affect access to land and water later, as occurred in the barrio of San Cristóbal del Montecillo of San Luis Potosí in 1753. In that year it was officially recognized as a *pueblo de indios*, giving its residents corporate access to lands, although other residents claimed the Indians were actually mestizos and *mulatos* unentitled to such a status.[17] Free people of African descent shared commonalities with *indios laboríos*, having no communal properties derived from their *calidad* or legal status and living from their wages. In the second half of the seventeenth century, free people of African descent in San Luis Potosí paid roughly the same rates of tribute as *indios laboríos*.

Collectors held a crucial position within the tribute regime that was at once powerful and precarious. Their compliance with a system of collection designed and implemented by far-off administrators was important for collecting data and money. But they often voiced common complaints about the difficulty of their work and its thanklessness. *Mulato* residences were frequently listed as "unknown" or "uncertain,"[18] in some cases perhaps because local officials had no desire to search for them. Even known residences of small populations would yield little for a commissioner's efforts. Many officials had little incentive to participate in tribute in the early eighteenth century, as it was underpaid, arduous, and, sometimes, dangerous work. Salaries for royal bureaucrats were subject to reduction during wartime. In 1704 and 1709, Philip V reduced salaries by 5 percent and later by 10 percent to cover war expenses until as late as 1727. In addition, creole, peninsular, and Indian collectors and officials risked becoming mired in debt.[19] As a result, by the time of the War of Spanish Succession (1702–13), officials and residents of some of the most lucrative areas of New Spain had grown used to not participating in Afromexican tribute.

A tribute register was often the product of discussion and disagreement, rather than an indicator of tacit acceptance or total control. As specified since the sixteenth century, the preferred form of documentation of tributary numbers was a list created by a mayor or magistrate.[20] Residents of a town could be deemed Afromexican tributaries with or without their knowledge. To facilitate the process and retain a record of families, the register could draw from prior lists following genealogical and marital ties. When no such list existed, the mayor called on a community member or local authority, perhaps an Indian governor or a clergyman, to compile the information. Ideally, registering individuals as free people of African descent required comparison with ecclesiastical records like baptismal certificates. Periodic instructions from Mexico City might require that the alcalde create an entirely new list using his knowledge of local social connections. Prior to the Caroline Reforms, Bourbon reformers sought to improve counting and extracting methods in part by drawing on interpersonal relationships, especially in areas with a high potential for yielding revenues.

The outcome of collection in the first half of the century was unpredictable. In the two cases presented in this chapter, local conditions and attitudes dictated the extent to which tribute collection was possible. In general, figures available from the first half of the century suggest a small amount of specie reaching royal coffers from communities with free Afromexican populations. In 1701, a list of municipal seats of administration in the Audiencia of Mexico shows that the amounts collected from subject towns and neighborhoods varied widely. *Mulatos* seem to have been charged disproportionately high levels of tribute, given the small numbers of Afromexican tributaries in many of the towns and cities surveyed.[21] In 1756, authorities reasserted that tribute would be collected on a standard *tercio* cycle, which could mean more frequent contact with the tribute regime for collectors and tributaries.[22] Officials in the capital frequently imagined free black and *mulato* subjects as potentially profitable and capable of shouldering a disproportionate amount of royal tribute. These attitudes and practices diverged from those held by some local leaders, who were decidedly more skeptical about the tribute regime and its effects on their interests.

Fiscal bureaucrats began reviewing tributary practice at the regional level early in the eighteenth century. The tribute regime was a nexus of institutions, motivations, and vocabularies that created documents as multivalent as the system propelling their creation. Case studies in this chapter illuminate the attitudes of local officials and high-ranking bureaucrats toward tribute as a means of gathering knowledge and extracting wealth. Bourbon bureaucrats set about evaluating the efficacy of tribute with the intention of regularizing and augmenting payments. Seen from Mexico City, regions like San Luis Potosí seemed to have populations that could be subject to taxation. Yet, the tribute regime was only lightly enforced and flexibly met the needs of local officials with little interest in implanting a complex and expensive tribute tax. Central New Spain posed its own challenges in the wake of widespread famine and rioting in Mexico City. In spite of the setbacks experienced in many tributary communities, some local officials streamlined the use of tribute registers and consistently extracted Afromexican tribute. These procedures foreshadowed the growth of tribute that would occur after the 1760s. Bureaucrats in Mexico City attempted to extend their authority within the tributary regime, though sometimes in the face of reluctance from local officials. During this period, compliant officials made lists similar to those found in the late eighteenth century. These would become the rational modes of knowledge-gathering that defined tributary community.

Ambiguous Tributary Status and *Calidad* in San Luis Potosí

In 1716, local officials in the city of San Luis Potosí scrambled to compile a list of Afromexican tributaries in accordance with instructions from Mexico City. According to clergymen, administrators, and local elites, free people of color who could pay royal tribute were simply nowhere to be found. Furthermore, the imposition of this tribute and its attendant connections of *calidad* on the terms of Mexico City bureaucrats hardly elicited an enthusiastic response. On one property near San Luis Potosí, there was apparently "just one" possible tributary of African descent, Marcos, which prompted a local friar to explain, "I do not know if he is *mulato* or mestizo, and in case he is a *mulato*, then he is the only one there."[23] On receiving this lackluster evidence, authorities in the Real Hacienda may have wondered why no one could confirm that Marcos was a *mulato*. Individual reputations often fluctuated over time and depending on the venue, requiring local authorities to look at multiple written records to determine the tributary status of a single individual. These explanations and their tone imply a local frustration with the demands of Mexico City and its expanding tribute regime based on categories of *calidad*.

A series of petitions and investigations into the tribute practices of San Luis Potosí in the early eighteenth century exemplify the necessity for cooperation among bureaucrats, local authorities, and elites for tribute to function. Mexico City officials often read explanations using the phrase "I don't know" and "it is not known" when dealing with local authorities attempting to assess the nature of *calidad* and tributary status in a given region. In the process of compiling lists, local officials met with resistance from miners, shopkeepers, governors, and other elites with free people of color in their households or laboring on their properties. Other nontributaries simply refused to take responsibility for paying tributes, a problem that began almost immediately after Afromexican tribute was established and continued to the end of the colonial period.[24] The statements about Marcos demonstrate the reluctance people felt, in San Luis Potosí and beyond, to use the categories of *negro* or *mulato* when registering tributaries. Characterizing their own servants or laborers as free *mulatos* or *morenos* would pull local elites into an orbit of Afromexican tribute registration and payment many wished to avoid.

Reluctance on the part of elites and local officials to register and collect from Afromexican tributaries manifested across jurisdictions, and the following case from San Luis Potosí provides an example from the first part of the eighteenth century. Founded in 1592 near the Cerro de San Pedro, silver mining was so successful that the site was named for its Andean predecessor.[25] The Indian population included local Guachichil people as well as Otomís, Tarascans, Nahuas (including Tlaxcalans), and other immigrants who formed a close-knit society across ethnic lines in the sixteenth and seventeenth centuries.[26] These categories were being eroded bit by bit as the colonial regime attempted to form a unified "*indio*" category, and San Luis Potosí was no exception.[27] The population of free and enslaved Afromexicans grew steadily, owing to favorable fertility rates in the seventeenth and early eighteenth centuries.[28] By the eighteenth century, the non-Indian population of San Luis Potosí had grown significantly. The 1743–44 census showed 4,955 Indian families in this jurisdiction, compared with 4,560 non-Indian families, which included Spaniards, mestizos, and free people of African descent.[29] Yet, the jurisdiction was not producing substantial amounts of Afromexican tribute, which drew attention from the capital between 1702 and 1720. In the first decades of the eighteenth century, officials in Mexico City undertook an extensive invigoration of royal tribute from Indians and free people of African descent.

A proclamation announced in 1680 had already decried the failure of free people of African descent in San Luis Potosí to meet their obligations to the crown. According to the document, there was an apparent "abundance" of men and women living in the city and its surrounding jurisdiction who were "independent of the service of miners, who are vagrants and without a trade and who live on their own without paying tribute." All unregistered Indian and Afromexican tributaries were to appear before authorities and be added to the list, allowing officials to "come to know who these individuals are, where they live, and to charge all that to Your Majesty is owed." Any potential tributary who did not follow this course of action would face ten days in jail as "disobedient and rebellious."[30] The difficulties facing officials in San Luis Potosí were multifaceted: a mass exodus of tributaries from the mines would deplete royal taxes, while a lack of tribute would likewise deprive the crown of much-needed revenue.

Bureaucrats, judges, and accountants in the capital instructed officials in the jurisdiction of San Luis Potosí to produce more tributaries of African descent, but local elites viewed this task as onerous because of the nature of the people in question. The perceived unruliness of the local population was a point of widespread frustration that served the interests of elites unwilling to pursue tributaries. Miners complained that their workers could not be obligated by force to labor in the mines; employees of the Real Hacienda worried that families did not pay taxes; clergy bemoaned the migratory practices of Indian and Afromexican populations. To transform these communities, local officials and bureaucrats in Mexico City attempted to create Afromexican tributary subjects who would be model vassals to the Spanish crown. In return for their participation, free Afromexicans could live in Spanish society and form sanctioned networks related to their commercial, familial, and religious affairs. However, the process of making tributaries through registration and collection had long been abandoned as an impossible task with little financial reward for the local elites involved.

Increasing and harnessing the wealth of New Spain was one of the most pressing issues for tribute bureaucrats as well as for the very survival of the Bourbon regime. At the turn of the seventeenth century, silver output from New Spain was increasing rapidly to match Chinese demand, and it continued to grow during the destructive War of Spanish Succession.[31] In 1710, the first *visitador* of the new regime, Francisco de Pagave, set out for the mines at Guanajuato, San Luis Potosí, Pachuca, and other locations to recuperate imperial finances following the war. On his *visita* to the *caja* at San Luis Potosí in 1712, Pagave discovered the notorious corruption perpetrated by Manuel Díaz de Llanos, accountant, and Pedro de Ibarra, treasurer.[32] Perhaps to cover up their own malfeasance, these two officials had denounced the behavior of men and women of color who had achieved a small measure of independence. According to the oversight at the *real caja*, these potential tributaries, instead of laboring in mines, chose to become vendors of foodstuffs and supplies.[33] In this light, the absence of monies in the *caja* would have resulted from the refusal of "free *mulatos*, *mulatas*, *negros* and *negras*" to "subject themselves to serve in any task."[34] Díaz de Llanos also blamed the behavior of local Spaniards, noting that free people of color supplied fuel and other goods, "which are constantly bought by the miners and *vecinos* of the city."[35] These services were vital to the working of any mine, and presumably local businessmen and women did not wish to drive away the peddlers and vendors by taxing them. And so, despite their publicly known source of income, these free people of color did not fulfill the right of the king to receive tribute from his vassals.

Local elites deployed a series of conflicting stereotypes and images to justify the lack of tribute collection. Díaz de Llanos and Ibarra referenced a trope of the devious and disloyal *mulato* familiar to local officials and administrators in the capital.[36] The failure to collect Afromexican tribute in the seventeenth century stemmed from the insubordinate nature of the people. Administrators were inculcated with narratives in which free people of color harassed Indian communities, questioned Spanish authority, and practiced dangerous magic.[37] At the same time, elites depended on Afromexican residents for labor and commerce, and these local activities could suffer if free people of color were deterred by tribute payments. These varied and sometimes conflicting arguments did not convince bureaucrats that free people of color should remain entirely exempt from tribute in San Luis Potosí. Instead, accountants, *oidores*, and other bureaucrats in Mexico City sought information about the collection and registration processes that were in place, regardless of their potential to disrupt labor relationships or strain local resources.

Table 2.1. Afromexican tribute payments in San Luis Potosí for 1653–54, 1689–90, and 1692–93

Tributary categories	Individuals	Tributes paid in pesos	Tributes paid in reales	Total Afromexican tribute payments[a]
Married couples	8[b]	6.0	24	72
Unmarried men	8	1.5	84	96
Other half-tributary men	11	7.5	108	168
Unmarried women	3	1.5	12	24
Other half-tributary women	11	9.0	60	132
Totals	41	25.5	288	492

Source: Data from Archivo General de Indias, Audiencia de México leg. 1043, cuaderno 1.
[a]Converted to reales, where one peso is eight reales.
[b]Includes one *mulata* slave.

Habsburg rule left behind numerous legal and procedural questions for the new regime. The effects of gender and *calidad* were particularly difficult to parse out in regions whose methods of implementing Afromexican tribute were unclear. Mexico City bureaucrats discovered that a previous group of officials in San Luis Potosí had collected tribute between 1650 and 1693 but had stopped without any warning, leaving eighteenth-century officials with an uncertain guide to traditional tribute rates.[38] How exactly authorities identified these tributaries and why they paid is unclear from the list, which simply gives names and rates of payment. During the second half of the seventeenth century, more than 250 families of *indios laboríos* and free people of African descent paid in San Luis Potosí (table 2.1). Most of the people discovered on these registers of payment were *laborío* Indians who worked in a variety of occupations in mines, private homes, bakeries, and shops. Another seventy-nine records do not contain caste categories and simply refer to the families as "tributaries." At least forty-one free people of African descent were also recorded, some of them making payments multiple times over the seventeenth century. These free people of African descent included people born in San Luis Potosí and others from Querétaro, Guadalajara, and León who came to work among *mulato* shoemakers, hatters, bakers, and makers of charcoal. A handful of these people married other Afromexicans (n = 8) or were widowed or unmarried (n = 11). The rest paid half-tributary rates, but the reasons for this are unclear from the list. It is possible that some of these individuals were married to people of other castes, though their spouses' names are not present. In this investigation by fiscal bureaucrats, however, the most important information was the rate and amount of payment as well as the names of the individuals. Other details, such as the *calidad* of spouses and the place of residence, are inconsistent. This small amount of data would be insufficient to produce a comprehensive tributary list, but it did begin to answer the question at hand concerning rates and schedules of payment among *indios laboríos* and free people of African descent.

At midcentury, Afromexican men and women paid tribute, but payments from male tributaries were more common.[39] Both were paying at similar rates of twelve reales per year, a similar rate to the tributaries in the *indio laborío* category as well as couples that included an *indio laborío* married to an *india*. Women paid as half-tributaries whose marital status was unspecified or in groups with their sisters or daughters. This was the case for two sisters, both *mulatas*, called Catalina and Petrona Lazerda, who paid three pesos between them as a full tributary unit in 1654. Officials may have adhered to laws and instructions from the sixteenth century, some of which stipulated that free women and men would pay equal rates of tribute. Women like the Lazerda sisters paid at the same rate that unmarried men would be charged in subsequent decades. Francisco de Espinal, a free *mulato*, paid four and a half pesos in 1690 to account for the years 1678–80. A man named Pedro Hernández, described as a *mulato libre criollo* from Guadalajara, also paid "three pesos in reales for the tribute that he owed for two years."[40] In 1654, Mathias López paid twelve reales on behalf of himself and his wife, an unnamed *mulata* slave and therefore exempt from tribute. After 1654, only María de Ortega, a *mulata libre*, paid tribute in 1689 as a single woman. The trend toward payment from men suggests a gendered meaning of tribute at the century's end.

These short descriptions of people who paid tribute from this time demonstrate a transition toward a tributary subject who was more likely to be male and less likely to be *negro*. This pattern in caste terminology follows general trends in the growth of the free and American-born population as the colonial period progressed. In 1654, a total of four *negras* and two *negros* appeared on the San Luis Potosí list of people who had paid. By the late seventeenth century, just one *negra* and one *negro* were recorded, and they were a married couple. The preference for terms like "*mulato*," "*pardo*," and even "*moreno*" reflects the predominance of *mulato* slaves and free people, who formed the majority of Afromexicans in the region by midcentury.[41] Between 1696 and 1700, forty *mulatas* and forty-six *mulatos* married in the city's main parish, compared with just four *negros* and one *negra*.[42] While authorities requested lists of all the *mulatos* and *negros* who could be registered or had paid, most of these people appear in documents as *mulatos*.

The late seventeenth-century records suggest that caste and *calidad* fluctuated in the tributary population, especially among those who were not *mulatos*. While the overall preference was for the term "*mulato*," some commissioners applied other labels to individuals, without much consistency. Changes in labels denoting

Afromexican status became evident when local authorities in San Luis Potosí managed to repeatedly register and extract tribute from the same individuals for several years. In 1689, *negra libre* María de la Cruz from San Lorenzo and her husband Juan de Dios, a free *moreno*, paid twelve reales. The following year, the couple paid the full three pesos, but this time Juan de Dios shifted from being a *moreno libre* to a *negro*. An unmarried man, Joseph García de Zeuda, changed on the register from being simply a *pardo* to being a *pardo de color*, a distinction that emphasized his appearance rather than his genealogy. In the city of San Luis Potosí, he paid twelve reales from his trade as a shoemaker in both 1692 and 1693.[43]

The officials who registered and charged tribute of Juan de Dios and Joseph García de Zeuda did not offer much evidence of why these different terms were applicable to the same people. It is clear from these examples that the rate of tribute did not necessarily depend on color, since Joseph García de Zeuda's rate remained constant in both years he was registered. The two cases show that labels denoting freedom, color, or caste might be added or removed, depending on commissioner preferences and individual reputation or physical appearance. These records imply that the two men may have appeared differently to the authorities who collected tribute in 1689 and 1690. These tributaries might have had darker skin or a close relationship with a *negro* or *negra*. In the case of Juan de Dios, his association with a *negra libre* through marriage may have prompted an official to realign his caste to mirror that of his spouse, regardless of his own appearance or reputation. This practice has been documented in other mining communities later in the eighteenth century.[44] The handful of married couples registered in the seventeenth century show a diversity of marital choices, some of them uncommon ones, such as a partnership between enslaved women and free men, that would have drawn the attention of commissioners. These patterns underscore the powerful role of commissioners who registered individuals and families based on their perceived reputations as well as their interpersonal associations.

With the knowledge of what had been collected and from whom over the past half century, officials in Mexico City looked for other instructions that would guide local collectors. One such document was a printed instruction from Viceroy Monterrey that had circulated to magistrates across New Spain in 1598. Local officials as well as bureaucrats in the capital consulted this circular for more than a century, and it was included in the San Luis Potosí investigations to decide the legitimacy of local privileges. Monterrey's instructions compiled laws from the late sixteenth century to codify the procedures of collection and registration of tribute, focusing on labor and reproduction. Tributaries would pay "one gold *peso* each year, being an unmarried man or woman without a trade (*oficio*) and married couples two *pesos* each year even if there are some married to a male or female slave."[45] Unmarried "craftsmen of any trade" would pay the same rate as a married couple: two pesos in tribute and four reales in *servicio real*. The same annual rate applied to unmarried men connected to Spaniards through "trade, work, or livelihood."[46] Thus, early forms of Afromexican tribute were based on financial resources and the knowledge local officials held regarding the livelihoods of free people of color.

The rise of *calidad* and its relationship to the category of the Afromexican tributary necessitated modifications to Monterrey's circular. Officials were concerned with the tributary status of servants and how they were to be counted based on their *calidad*. Judges at the Real Hacienda determined in 1710 that, in San Luis Potosí, lists should be kept based on "distinctions of the *calidad de las personas* of such servants and that of those to whom they are married."[47] The language of *calidad* was not completely fixed, and the Real Hacienda was careful to specify some approach that would approximate this social marker. The use of the phrase "qualities of the persons" suggested that *calidad* was to be an expression of caste categories, which themselves were not obvious. For this reason, these lists were only to "express [*calidades*] of those who are notoriously *negros*, *mulatos*, or *indios*, but not that of those for whom it is doubtful if they are or not, and much less that of their wives, without knowing them or their names." Doubts were to be assuaged through the process of "soliciting, searching out, and copying the baptismal certificates" for such people.[48] These instructions showed an emerging tension between a rationalizing central bureaucracy that sought to classify subjects using *calidad*, and the acknowledgment on behalf of the same officials that discovering the *calidad* of people who lived and worked in elite households would be complicated. The tributary unit was based on the married couple, and the wives of servants and laborers might remain anonymous in the eyes of elite employers. The status of unmarried women was also dubious, leading to a number of layers of confusion for local officials as they sought out the *calidad* and tributary status of hundreds of potential new tributaries.

Under pressure from Mexico City, some local officials and elites aided in the registration of *indios laboríos* and free people of African descent and confirmed their associations with elite households and properties. This undertaking represented a cross section of the population who could not claim a connection to a mining operation, either real or invented, for the sake of avoiding tribute payment.[49] General don Alonso Muñoz Castelblanco, himself a local miner, would become instrumental to the Pagave *visita*.[50] In 1711, Castelblanco affirmed that Indians and free people of African descent understood "the great obligation they have to contribute to Your Majesty."[51] Captain don Francisco Fernández de Herrera, *alcalde ordinario*, undertook the task of creating a *padrón* in 1711 for the city as well as any towns, barrios, haciendas, ranches, farms, or forges where tributaries lived. Authorities located nearly three thousand individuals subject to tribute, including 296 married couples of African descent and another sixty-seven unmarried free men of African descent.[52] The lists of the *indios laboríos* and free people of African descent of the jurisdiction were followed by a list of properties and their residents between 1715 and 1716. Tristán Manuel de Rivadeneira, an *oidor* who spearheaded the investigations into tribute in San Luis Potosí, claimed that "all *mulatos* and *negros* from this jurisdiction are in the same good state" of registration by 1711.[53]

The 1711 *padrón* was to contain all *negros*, *mulatos*, or *zambaigos*, along with "women in case the Viceroy Fernando de Alencastre Norofia y Silva, duque de Linares, decided that they should pay."[54] As mentioned, the use of *negro* had dropped, but as many as five *negros*, married and *solteros*, were recorded in 1711. The year 1716 also contained *negros*, like Pasqual Hernández, who was married and worked on a hacienda belonging to the Fathers of San Agustín. In addition, *mulatos*, *pardos*, *lobos*, *coyotes*, and *moriscos* all appeared on the *padrones* of San Luis Potosí during this period. Both tribute registers list adults and children, three of whom were called "*mulatillos*" who was registered on a hacienda in 1711. Describing a young person of indeterminate age, "*mulatillos*" could designate anyone of African descent who was not yet an adult.[55] This hacienda registered eleven married *mulato* couples, along with five other unmarried people, giving it the highest concentration of free people of African descent among the sixty-five ranches, haciendas, mines, and towns surveyed for that year. The term "*mulato*" could absorb both African and Indian ancestry, as was common across New Spain. On a *rancho* in San Miguel de Tequesquite, among five *mulato* children recorded was eight-year-old Bernardo, the child of Miguel Lopes, a *mulato* slave, and María Rosa, an Indian.

Local officials and ordinary people submitted their opinions regarding the flawed *padrón* to the judges in the Real Hacienda. The starkest shortcoming of the list was its lack of individuals, according to accountants. The paltry number of tributaries prompted local officials to defend themselves and their methods. Magistrate Josef Espinosa, formerly an alcalde, claimed that the free people of African descent registered in San Luis Potosí were "very few" and that "other vassals have not been found in this city" despite diligent efforts on the part of himself and his fellow officials.[56] To make matters worse, the past register was of little use for creating a new one. Some who had been recorded in the recent past were actually deceased, such as Francisco Xavier de los Reyes, a *mulato forastero* and *vecino* of the Real de los Porros. He was unmarried and had no family, which compounded his status as an outsider, a *forastero*. Mistakes like this one rendered older registers useless and impeded normal processes by which authorities would "discover" the location and *calidad* of tributary subjects.[57]

Juan Francisco Ferrete, a middle-aged free *mulato* and *vecino* of San Luis Potosí, testified to the flawed state of the tribute register. Ferrete presumably had witnessed past tribute collection efforts and knew about their outcomes among families. At the time of the last collection of "*vasallaje*" (another term for "tribute"[58]), Ferrete declared, free *mulatos* were registered twice, or mistakenly placed in towns, barrios, or on mining haciendas. He explained that "many were *forasteros* whose names could not be obtained," and "not even a third of them have been registered."[59] The presence of large numbers of tributary immigrants was plausible. Tributaries on the registers of the late seventeenth century hailed from other economic centers like Querétaro, León, and Guadalajara. Miners were mobile in the early eighteenth century and, in some cases, migrated from the near north to seek work in places like Chihuahua.[60] Ferrete's description of a dislocated cohort of mobile *forasteros* with confusing tribute obligations offered multiple reasons for the low tributary numbers. Previous officials had created unsatisfactory *padrones*, but these free people of color themselves also "fled" registration,[61] failing to meet their obligations as subjects. Ferrete distinguished himself, and other *vecinos*, from the flighty *forasteros* who were outsiders and not to be associated with the law-abiding tributaries who actually lived in San Luis Potosí. Obtaining testimony from an Afromexican *vecino* may have been a strategic attempt on the part of local officials to demonstrate that they had consulted relevant community leaders, thus doing everything possible to extract tribute. The task was simply impossible because of the lack of credible information as well as the lack of honor and loyalty of certain itinerant Afromexican subjects to their king.

To revise the register, officials needed not only to find the tributaries but also to determine or discover *calidad*. Commissioners seeking tributary *indios de pueblo* could label individuals and families based on their belonging to a particular town, but Afromexican *calidad* required a different set of descriptors based on more than residence. For colonial authorities in San Luis Potosí and, by extension, in Mexico City, these data collection projects required the knowledge of local property owners. Authorities believed that property owners and local free people of color were the best sources of information regarding the adults and children of varied castes who worked in the mines or in related industries. When the tribute registers were renewed in 1716, property owners and local officials were frustrated with the demands of tribute collection and registration. The responsibility of local officials, according to Viceroy Monterrey's instructions of 1598, was to collect Afromexican tribute from families and individuals or to "notify their *amos* that they should pay for them."[62] The onus of locating tributaries passed between collectors, magistrates, and disgruntled property owners. The owner of an unnamed hacienda near a mine declared that the handful of tributary miners on his property were "masters of their own will who work when they wish . . . which is why I am not obliged to pay on behalf of any of them."[63] Where tributaries were scarce, or where individuals earned their pay independently, some designated *amos* were unwilling to shoulder the tributary burden.

Despite these protests, at least fifteen property owners did submit to evaluation in 1711 and 1715–16. This number may be higher, because place-names were unstable over the years surveyed. Other descriptions of property and people are too vague to draw conclusions, such as the "workers who belong to Captain Ignacio Lambarri," who numbered fifteen in 1712. Of those that can be identified, not all appear to be Spanish. One Diego Ruiz, whose ranch registered two married *mulatos* and a *soltero* in both 1711 and 1716, appears to have been the father of the four *mulato* children registered on the property in 1711. A wealthier man who employed cattle ranchers and farmers, Captain Pedro Estrada Altamirano, registered his hacienda residents and workers in 1712 and 1716.[64] Between 1712 and 1715, a property belonging to Francisco Guerrero, attorney of the Real Audiencia, grew slightly, perhaps under greater scrutiny and pressure to increase tribute. The population of this property increased from six *mulato* married couples to eight, and twenty-three total children to twenty-five, all in all yielding ten pesos in total tribute from *indios laboríos* and *mulatos* (table 2.2).[65] Larger properties were more likely to attract the attention of officials, who targeted them for tribute registration and collection.

The continuities in registration and payments from property owners and laborers demonstrate the importance of tribute for maintaining local economies of both money and prestige. Wealthy men and women in San Luis Potosí who refused to pay faced scrutiny from the Real Hacienda—in the form of fines or prosecution—even as they tried to deny the application of rules to their mines, haciendas, and ranches. Although property owners reported small numbers, qualitative accounts speak to the mobility of the population. Mine operators enjoyed tribute privileges because officials could not afford to lose valuable revenue caused by worker flight. Throughout the San Luis Potosí investigation, *operarios* in the mines had "completely refused to pay anything under any terms," regardless of their *calidad*.[66] Less influential workers who trafficked in coal and firewood, or who labored underground, did face registration. Tribute officials extracted as much money as they deemed appropriate without driving away laborers. At the same time, if they wished to live in the city of San Luis Potosí or practice a trade, free people of color would leave documentary evidence of their sedentary lifestyle. The payment of tribute, from free people of color or on their behalf, allowed workers, tradesmen, merchants, and property owners alike to build a reputation of legitimacy and loyalty to the crown.

Many local elites saw the task of registering and charging Afromexican tributaries as cumbersome and unnecessary. These property owners and local elites claimed that small numbers of free people of color did not justify an overhaul in the local tax registers. These voices of resistance to royal demands blamed free people of African descent for living outside the bounds of the law or beyond the control of their employers. For their part, free people of African descent claimed that the lists made by local officials were insufficient and plainly wrong. The use

Table 2.2. Locations of Afromexican tributary registration in San Luis Potosí, 1712–16

Year	Property	Owner	Married *mulatos*	Other married people	Unmarried *mulatos*	Other unmarried people	*Mulato* children	*Lobo* children	All other children	Reserved from payment	Total individuals
1712	Rancho of Diego Ruiz	Diego Ruiz	4	6	1	0	4	0	9	0	24
1716	Paraje of Diego Ruiz	Diego Ruiz	4	0	1	0	0	0	0	0	5
1712	Rancho San Cristóbal del Palmar	Esteban Uribe and Cristóbal de Reyna	8	2	1	1	9	0	12	0	33
1715	Rancho San Cristóbal del Palmar	Esteban Uribe	4	2	0	0	0	0	5	0	11
1712	Estancia Tepetate	Francisco Guerrero	12	10	5	0	0	0	23	6	56
1715	Hacienda Tepetate	Francisco Guerrero	16	14	5	2	0		25	0	62
1712	Hacienda San Miguel	Lázaro de Yrriegas	6	52	2	3	1	1	38	3	106
1715	Hacienda San Miguel	Lázaro de Yrriegas	2	42	0	2	0	0	31	3	80
1715	Residents near Hacienda San Miguel	Lázaro de Yrriegas	6	10	0	4	0	10	0	0	30
1712	Hacienda La Ciénaga	Pedro Altamirano	14	12	3	0	0	0	0	0	29
1712	Hacienda San Diego	Pedro Altamirano	10	2	1	0	0	0	0	0	13
1712	Hacienda El Potrero	Pedro Altamirano	8	12	0	0	0	0	0	0	20
1712	Haciendas of Pedro Altamirano	Pedro Altamirano	12	26	2	3	0	0	0	0	43
1716	Haciendas La Ciénaga, San Diego, Nuestra Señora de Guadalupe	Pedro Altamirano	22	22	1	1	0	0	15	0	61

1712	Puesto Las Tortugas	Pedro Altamirano	6	0	0	0	2	0	6	0	14
1716	Puesto Las Tortugas	Pedro Altamirano	2	8	0	1	0	0	0	0	11
1712	Hacienda Guadalupe	Convent of San Agustín	0	84	1	19	0	0	35	4	143
1715	Hacienda Guadalupe	Convent of San Agustín	2	80	1	3	0	0	42	0	128
1712	Hacienda San Juan	Ignacio Lambarri	4	50	1	5	1	0	31	0	92
1716	Hacienda San Juan	Ignacio Lambarri	2	66	0	6	0	0	33	14	121
Totals			144	500	25	50	17	11	305	30	1082

Source: Archivo General de Indias, Audiencia de México leg. 1043, cuadernos 15 and 16.

of the term "*vasallaje*" as a substitute for "tribute" suggests that ordinary people were aware of the connections between royal tribute and loyalty. People like Juan Francisco Ferrete gave a variety of explanations for the failed tributary registration of 1711, but many of these explanations pointed to poor administration by local officials. Throughout these investigations, depictions of free people of African descent as willing participants in a colonial regime, whose allegiance was fiscally beneficial, competed with those of greedy, untrustworthy *negros* and *mulatos* who refused to comply with any official decree. At the local level, these documents bring into focus the many reasons for local elite resistance to charging tribute, which would occupy officials and compromise economic relationships as bureaucrats in the Real Hacienda sought to expand imperial revenue at the expense of local practice.

Stable Registration and Collection in Acatlán and Piastla

Local conditions made tributary status uneven and nebulous in the first half of the eighteenth century, but Bourbon reforms also began to influence tribute practices in the 1730s and 1740s. San Luis Potosí and its surroundings presented, according to local officials, significant challenges to collection, while officials in other regions viewed tribute as a more viable project. In the following decades, there were pockets of effective collection owing to the locally and regionally specific procedures, customs, politics, and interpersonal relationships that could facilitate the collection of tribute. Beyond this, some local officials were aware of the rationalizing and fiscally minded reforms of government that were underway in the capital. Through practices of record keeping, some officials were able to maintain standardized tribute practices that reflected and reinforced a stable tributary community (figure 2.1). Families might span generations and become publicly known in their communities as tributaries because of official interest in keeping knowledge of these families up to date. In a case from the jurisdiction of Acatlán and Piastla, sustained registration in the 1730s and 1740s demonstrated the relative manageability of Afromexican tribute (and the strategies the alcalde employed to make it manageable) and the compliance of a local leader in its collection. The cases of Acatlán and Piastla and San Luis Potosí show that Afromexican tribute was highly variable in the early decades of Bourbon rule. Some of this variation was due to diversity and breadth of the Kingdom of New Spain; however, local alcaldes, property owners, clergy, and other elites played a prominent role in the success or failure of collection and registration.

In Acatlán and Piastla, an area with a large and economically integrated free Afromexican population at midcentury, collection and registration were highly predictable. Officials in the jurisdiction charged free people of African descent

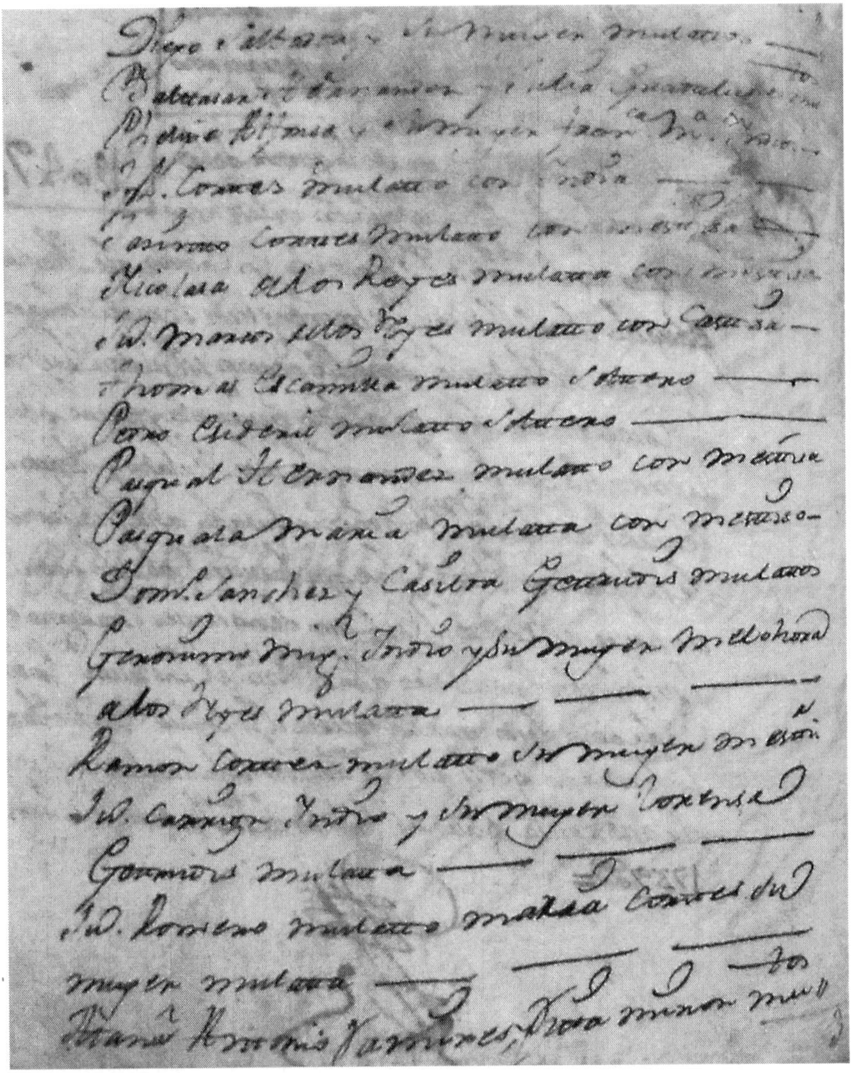

Figure 2.1. Page from an orderly tribute list made in 1739 in Acatlán (Archivo General de la Nación de México, Tributos vol. 46, exp. 28)

and *indios laboríos* a steady rate of tribute between 1739 and 1743. The information was not extensive, but it was consistent and organized using a readily legible system. Although it was collected during a lull in the imperial reforms during the War of Jenkins' Ear (1739–48), the systematized information from this jurisdiction shows the continuities and longer-term effects of fiscal reforms that weathered Atlantic events at the local level. In the 1740s, two major collections of place-specific information were undertaken in New Spain: the *Relaciones geográficas del Arzobispado de México* of 1743 and the expansive *Theatro americano: Descripción general de los reynos y provincias de la Nueva España y sus jurisdicciones* printed in 1746 and 1748.[67] *Theatro americano* described Acatlán as a productive area of salt production, haciendas and ranches, and Indian, Spanish, and mestizo families.[68] The lack of free people of African descent mentioned in this description underscores the importance of tributary registers as sources of data for colonial administrators. Their impressions of the many towns and cities of New Spain, mapped and described in the *relaciones* or in other works, also came from tribute accounts. In Acatlán and Piastla, the registers and receipts relayed the amount collected from the previous year from an individual or couple. The five lists from 1739 to 1743 also contain the names, marital statuses, and rates of payment among free people of African descent and *indios laboríos* working on estates. The compilation preserves the methods administrators used to monitor the payments and registration of individuals in a single area over a continuous period of years. Changes or consistencies in payments, population, and caste categories at the local level are valuable pieces of information not often available in the first half of the century. These documents established *calidad* and tributary status as stable categories among free people of African descent.

The tribute drawn from this region was made possible largely by its integration into local mining economies. The jurisdiction of Acatlán y Piastla was located about eighty miles south of the city of Puebla, in what is now the state of the same name. Salt mines at Chiautla and Acatlán and Piastla were closely tied to silver mining operations at Huautla.[69] Salt production eventually became one of the principal occupations in the region.[70] In the first half of the century, the jurisdiction of Acatlán and Piastla experienced a dramatic recovery of its previously decimated Mixtec- and Nahuatl-speaking Indian populations. In 1701, no *mulato* tributaries had been reported, but Indians had paid more than a thousand pesos in tribute.[71] In 1735, Acatlán had just ten Afromexican tributaries and about 1,800 Indian tributaries.[72] By 1743, over two thousand Indian families occupied the jurisdiction.[73] *Mulatos*, blacks, and Spaniards also moved to the area, especially in neighboring Chiautla, where they were involved in cattle and mining operations.[74] Population recovery showed periodic drops; this area also experienced the epidemic of *matlazahuatl* (typhus), which was demolishing populations in Puebla and Mexico City as well as smaller towns.[75] Tributary numbers dropped in 1741, perhaps due to the temporary relief from payment for some couples during this year.[76]

In spite of recent and ongoing epidemics, rates of payment were consistent and stable among *indios laboríos* and free people of African descent in Acatlán and Piastla. In 1739, Manuel de Orendain, the *alcalde mayor* of the jurisdiction, sent a brief tally to Mexico City of the Afromexican tributary population and associ-

Table 2.3. Combined Afromexican and *indio laborío* tribute collected in Acatlán and Piastla, 1739–43

Year	Afromexican and *indio laborío* whole tributaries[a]	Total paid in pesos	Avg. pesos per whole tributary
1739	47.0	117.50	2.5
1740	52.0	130.00	2.5
1741	42.0	105.00	2.5
1742	56.0	140.00	2.5
1743	61.5	153.75	2.5
Totals	258.5	646.25	2.5

Source: Data from Archivo General de la Nación de México, Tributos vol. 46, exp. 28.
[a]Includes all married couples (whole tributaries) as well as unmarried men or men married to women of an exempt caste (half tributaries).

ated payments in his jurisdiction, in compliance with a royal order from 1737. In that year, the nineteen and one-half tributaries registered as "free *negros* and *mulatos*" were required to pay a total of forty-nine pesos.[77] That rate of payment was just slightly over 2.5 pesos.[78] Between 1739 and 1743, the rate of payment held at 2.5 pesos per tributary (table 2.3). Exogamous couples paid the same 2.5 pesos if the couple contained an Indian and a *mulato* partner. Those who married exempt individuals would pay one peso and two *tomines*, the equivalent of 1.25 pesos. When an *indio laborío* or a *mulato* married an *india de pueblo*, rates of payment remained at 2.5, although this combination was exceptionally rare in the sample.

Following the 1737 assessment, local officials compiled and certified five lists for the years 1739 to 1743, comprising 340 entries. A total of 230 records contain one or more free people of color, many of whom were registered and paid for multiple years. Another fifty-six records do not mention free people of color but pertain to *indios laboríos*. For the remaining fifty-four records, castes are rendered partially or totally illegible by water damage, though rates of payment were discernible or possible to approximate. Allowing for expected errors due to illegible entries, these lists contain more than six hundred individuals of Afromexican, Indian, and exempt castes.

In this period, Afromexican tribute was a steady tax base for local officials. Free people of color paid an average of fifty pesos every year as a group, though amounts went up across all castes in 1743. In this year, tribute from endogamous and unmarried free Afromexicans did become a greater portion of the overall tribute paid, but the small increase can also be attributed to higher numbers of unknown tributaries in 1740, 1741, and 1742. Overall, Afromexican tributaries proved a dependable source of income. In fact, payments from Afromexicans

Table 2.4. Afromexican tribute in Acatlán and Piastla, 1737–43

Year	Afromexican whole tributaries[a]	Tribute paid by Afromexican tributaries[b]	% of all payments from Afromexican and *indio laborío* tributaries
1737	19.5	49.00	—
1739	20.0	50.00	42.6
1740	20.0	50.00	38.5
1741	15.5	38.75	36.9
1742	19.0	47.50	33.9
1743	27.0	67.50	43.9
Totals	121.0	302.75	46.8

Source: See table 2.3.

[a]Totals are the sum of all unmarried men counted as half tributaries and endogamous married couples counted as whole tributaries.

[b]Calculated in pesos, where one peso is eight reales.

amounted to a greater portion of the tax monies still. The numbers in table 2.4, which follow those compiled by the alcalde, do not count free people of color who married exogamously. Couples that included an Afromexican spouse added 37.5 pesos in 1739, 31.25 pesos in 1740, 27.5 pesos in 1741, 36.25 pesos in 1742, and the same amount in 1743. When combined, all tributaries containing free people of color paid more than 70 percent of the total *indio laborío* and Afromexican tribute over the five years.

Afromexican individuals made up about half of the sample (table 2.5). However, little information is given about these people beyond a first name or caste. Carlos de la Cruz and Paula Gerónima, both *mulatos*, were married before 1739 and remained together through 1743, paying their joint tribute of two pesos and four *tomines* each year. References to free or enslaved status were rare: A *soltero*, Pedro Martín, was listed as a *mulato libre* in 1743, and an unnamed woman was referred to as "a slave" without a caste label. All free people of African descent on the register were called *mulatos*, even though the alcalde's description of the register referenced "*negros* and *mulatos*." Depending on the year, 14 to 26 percent of the sample was Indian, and 13 to 15 percent exempt. Among these, none were Spanish, though the unnamed wife of a *mulato* called Juan Marcos de los Reyes was described as a *castiza*, a person of Spanish and mestizo parentage. Finally, *indios de pueblo* are conspicuously absent. Only in 1743 did *mulato* Matteo Antonio register with his unnamed Indian wife who was "recorded in her place,"[79] a phrase implying she was also recorded on the list of *indios de pueblo*. All other Indians lacked any evidence of being *indios de pueblo*. The language on the reg-

Table 2.5. Castes of individuals on the tribute register of *mulatos* and *indios laboríos* in Acatlán and Piastla, 1739–43

Year	All individuals	*Mulatos*	Indians	Exempt individuals	% *Mulato*	% Indian	% Exempt
1739	110	62	29	16	56.4	26.4	14.5
1740	121	60	19	17	49.6	15.7	14.0
1741	97	48	14	13	49.5	14.4	13.4
1742	129	60	28	17	46.5	21.7	13.2
1743	145	78	35	22	53.8	24.1	15.2
Total	602	308	125	85	51.2	20.8	14.1

Source: See table 2.3

ister shows a lack of specificity regarding both Indians and free people of African descent, because officials thought these distinctions unimportant for their purposes of collection. *Indios de pueblo*, *indios laboríos*, and free people of African descent all paid royal tribute, and their identities were of less concern than was their money.

To maximize efficiency and collection, officials in Acatlán and Piastla sought out married couples of legal majority with the ability to present payment. Married people, once located, represented greater returns. At the same time, married couples may have had fewer chances to avoid payment. Children and property restricted mobility, and artisans maintained other relationships that they did not want to jeopardize through refusal to pay. Although free people of African descent had begun to marry at steady rates, decreasing illegitimacy in the eighteenth century,[80] figures from this region favor married couples disproportionately (table 2.6). Of the 517 tributary individuals in the sample, 230 were married men and another 209 were married women. These lists were not explicitly concerned with future tributaries, concentrating instead on actual amounts of tribute received year to year. This subpopulation, as local officials defined it in Acatlán and Piastla, did not include children and adolescents, married minors, or anyone absent from home. Anyone unable to pay was of little interest to alcalde Manuel de Orendain, but tributary status was not restricted by caste or gender.

General trends in the tributary population on these registers do not reveal an obvious preference for recording male names before 1743 (see table 2.6). Only about half of the individual names recorded on the selected tribute registers were male. Another 45.5 percent were female and the rest indeterminate. The high rate of marriage contributed to the gender parity, and so too did the relative absence of unmarried men, especially in 1739–42. It is unlikely that these low numbers were accurate, given the opportunities for work in ranching or mining. Unmar-

Table 2.6. Marital status and gender on the tribute register of *mulatos* and *indios laboríos* in Acatlán and Piastla, 1739–43

Year	Married men of tributary caste	Married women of tributary caste	Unmarried men of tributary caste	Unmarried women of tributary caste	Unknown[a]	Men of exempt caste	Women of exempt caste	Total individuals
1739	45	39	6	1	3	7	9	110
1740	45	42	7	3	7	7	10	121
1741	38	37	6	1	2	6	7	97
1742	46	45	7	4	10	8	9	129
1743	56	46	14	5	2	6	16	145
Total	230	209	40	14	24	34	51	602

Source: See table 2.3.
[a]Includes half tributaries whose caste was not listed on the register.

ried men may also have been more mobile, rendering them less desirable as tributaries than their married peers. Although unmarried people were more difficult to locate and also yielded smaller payments, they would fall under increased scrutiny across New Spain as reform efforts gathered support in the capital.

The demography of this tributary population showed efforts on the part of officials to maintain their tributary numbers and to increase them by a little less than one-third from 1739 to 1743 (table 2.7). To accomplish this, the alcalde and his collectors focused on unmarried individuals and men whose wives were not tributaries. Because of these efforts, the tributary population of unmarried males more than doubled among the combined group of free people of African descent and *indios laboríos* (see table 2.7). This population was targeted periodically for registration at mines and haciendas. The handful of unmarried women also increased in this period, from just one *soltera* to an additional *soltera* and a widow, plus others of unspecified marital status. None of these women were Indians, echoing the laws, customs, and opinions of other jurisdictions. Perhaps Manuel de Orendain believed, like others of his time, that Indian women were fundamentally different from *mulatas*, who possessed tributary qualities tying them to the crown as former slaves who had become free vassals.

Why exactly the tributary numbers fluctuated when they did is unclear, but the year 1743 was one of concerted, notable expansion by Orendain and his agents. Excluding the anomalous year of 1741 allows us to see the overall trend more clearly. The year 1743 showed marked gender differences in the expansion of tributaries from the previous four years. Collection increased significantly among all

Table 2.7. Percentage rates of population change on the tribute register of *mulatos* and *indios laboríos* in Acatlán and Piastla, 1739–43

Year	Married men of tributary caste	Married women of tributary caste	Unmarried men of tributary caste	Unmarried women of tributary caste	Men of exempt caste	Women of exempt caste	Total
1739–42	2.2	15.4	16.7	300.0	14.3	0.0	17.3
1742–43	21.7	2.2	100.0	25.0	–25.0	77.8	12.4
1739–43	24.4	17.9	133.3	400.0	–14.3	77.8	31.8

Source: See table 2.3.

men. Men who married exempt women also increased in number at a rate of more than 75 percent (see table 2.6). Previously shielded from tributary status by their wives' *calidad*, free Afromexican and *indio laborío* husbands of mestizas were no longer excused from payment. In contrast, the number of tributary women who had exempt husbands dropped. For example, Agustina María, an Indian, and her mestizo husband paid a half rate every year between 1739 and 1742, then withdrew from the 1743 register. Populations of tributary women expanded at slower rates or not at all from 1742 to 1743, indicating that officials either began to take a more gender-specific view of collection or that this group was more difficult to track and charge.

This gradual accumulation evident in the previous three tables relied on collection from the same individuals over a period of successive years. Officials who compiled lists of tributaries were unlikely to start from scratch each time they did so, meaning that an initial point of contact between tributary and officials might determine tributary status for years to come. The repetition of names from the 1739 register across all five lists illustrates this practice. Almost two-thirds of all the records, more than two hundred, appear on multiple lists (table 2.8). And 85 percent of the records made in 1739 were repeated in subsequent years. In essence, the alcalde instructed his collectors to charge the same individuals who were tributaries in 1739 in subsequent years. Illegible names prevent a totally accurate reading, and it is possible that even more people were registered more than once. Of the 269 names that are discernible on all the lists, more than half are made up by names from 1739 that were recorded four or five times. These patterns confirm the preference to charge the same people each year and the overall goal of stability and maintenance on the part of officials.

Information from the 1739 list was often transposed directly onto other lists, even when the entries were incomplete. Some entries named only one spouse, as

Table 2.8. Repeated registration of tributary *mulatos* and *indios laboríos* in Acatlán and Piastla, 1739–43

Year	Total records	Repeated records	% of total
1739	60	51	85.0
1740	69	44	63.8
1741	53	36	67.9
1742	75	42	56.0
1743	83	50	60.2
Totals	340	223	65.6

Source: See table 2.3.

was the case of free *mulato* Diego Salbador who was recorded alongside a *mulata* referred to five times as simply "his wife." Antonio Martín appeared with his wife, "a slave," whose specific caste is not defined nor is her name given. Narcisa María, a *mulata*, was recorded four times as the wife of a mestizo whose name never appears. The absence of these names points to multiple possibilities. First, the spousal name was absent on the 1739 register, and no one undertook the responsibility to find these names out later. Alternatively, these names may have seemed irrelevant because some of the individuals were not subject to tribute, owing to their exempt caste or their enslaved status. In any case, these lists prioritized information that would lead directly to payment and the expansion of the registered tributary population. The presence, as well as the absence, of particular details helped to portray free Afromexicans as tributary subjects with specific characteristics that defined their status as taxpayers.

Individuals who were recorded multiple times were more likely to be married, reflecting the general trend of the tributary population and the construction of the free Afromexican tributary subject. Most married couples appeared multiple times on the registers, reflecting their repeated contact with local agents of the crown. Unmarried people experienced these interactions more sporadically and were usually charged only once (table 2.9). This pattern accounts for some of the variability discussed earlier between the years 1742 and 1743, when officials likely sought to expand tributary numbers by registering and charging *solteros*. Repeated records of unmarried women were even less common. The only single woman recorded on all lists was María Rosa, a *mulata* and a *soltera*. Another *mulata*, Josepha Escamilla, was widowed by 1742 from her Indian husband Juan de la Cruz. She was the only individual identifiable in this set whose marital status changed over the course of the three years.

Repetition brings into focus both the extent of payment compliance and the links free people of color and *indios laboríos* formed through marriage. The to-

Table 2.9. Repeated records as a percentage of total endogamous and exogamous couples of *mulatos* and *indios laboríos* in Acatlán and Piastla, 1739–43

Year	Repeated endogamous	Total endogamous	% of total endogamous	Repeated exogamous	Total exogamous	% of total exogamous
1739	23	25	92	21	24	88
1740	19	21	90	17	22	77
1741	13	16	81	17	18	94
1742	20	23	87	17	24	71
1743	25	31	81	17	27	63
Total	100	116	86	89	115	77

Source: See table 2.3.

tal numbers of repeated records of marriages between castes (exogamous) and within castes (endogamous) were remarkably similar (see table 2.9). Officials had a better chance of charging the same endogamous couples multiple times. These results can be discerned by comparing the mean number of records that appeared each year for different subpopulations. On average, twenty-three exogamous couples appeared on a register per year. In comparison, an average of 17.8 records contained exogamous couples who paid in multiple years. This mean of repeated records (17.8) was significantly lower than the expected mean (23) for this subpopulation ($p < 0.01$). This was true among marriages between free people of color and Indians as well as mestizos.

The case was different for repeated endogamous records, whose yearly average was statistically comparable to the mean number of endogamous records each year. These distinct phenomena demonstrate that, though the total numbers of exogamous and endogamous records were nearly equal, the exogamous couples avoided payment on other occasions. The behavior of the data points to the benefits of exogamous marriage for tributaries who wanted to avoid registration and collection. Exogamous couples either refused to pay their taxes or they went unnoticed or unaccounted for by tribute collectors.

Changes to caste over time were unlikely in this sample, in contrast to other regions of New Spain.[81] Such changes presented challenges and benefits to free people of color who chose or were forced to take on a new caste identification. The tribute registers of Acatlán and Piastla at midcentury offer just a few identifiable instances of caste changes among the tributary population. *Mulatos* and Indians who married exogamously could experience changes to their own identities based on a partner's caste, whether that was tributary or nontributary. Such couples sometimes left the list, but, very rarely, they became an endogamous couple. This was the case for the three couples in the sample whose caste fluctu-

Table 2.10. Caste fluctuation in three married couples from Acatlán and Piastla, 1739–43

Year	Juan Carrión	Lorenza Gertrudis	Diego Felipe	Manuela María	Gerónimo Miguel	Melchora
1739	*Indio*	*Mulata*	*Mulato*	*India*	*Indio*	*Mulata*
1740	*Indio*	*Mulata*	(None)	(None)	*Indio*	*India*
1741	*Indio*	*Mulata*	*Mulato*	*India*	*Indio*	*India*
1742	*Mulato*	*Mulata*	*Mulato*	*India*	*Indio*	*India*
1743	*Mulato*	*Mulata*	*Indio*	*India*	*Indio*	*India*

Source: See table 2.3.

ated over the five years (table 2.10). When Juan Carrión first paid royal tribute for 1739 along with his wife, a *mulata* named Lorena Gertrudis, he was an *indio laborío*. By 1742, though he paid the same 2.5 pesos in annual tribute, Juan became a *mulato*. This move did not affect the overall number of tributaries or the amount collected in that year. It was either the will of Juan Carrión to alter his tributary and caste status or the preference of an official or scribe for endogamy. These changes were not exclusive to any year, caste, or gender. In 1740, Melchora changed from a *mulata* tributary to an Indian, matching the caste of her husband, Gerónimo Miguel. These examples of caste movement suggest a tendency toward endogamy within tribute. Tributaries or officials could have any number of reasons for maintaining endogamy, though they would not have hinged on rates of payment. Although irrelevant for counting or collecting, endogamy maintained a social order of caste that assuaged elite anxieties. At the same time, tributaries had their own reasons to preserve their personal, genealogical, and community caste identities. Based on these motivations, the shift from exogamous to endogamous couple was possible for individuals of both genders and tributary castes.

Despite this handful of cases, the norm was caste constancy in this population. Endogamy and exogamy were both popular; exogamous marriages reached at least forty-seven and endogamous numbered at least forty-one (table 2.11). Another thirty-three castes were illegible or absent. The rate of endogamy among *mulatas*, in this case at least 69 percent, suggests that for these women, caste was an important, but not completely dominant, factor in marriage choice.[82] Among the *laborío* tributary group, however, women were less exclusive at just over 40 percent. The most endogamous group was Indian men, who chose Indian partners more than 70 percent of the time. Finally, *mulato* men showed nearly the same numbers of exogamous (n = 31) and endogamous (n = 29) marriages. The only exempt partners available were mestizos, mestizas, and one *castiza*. The most common combination of exempt women and tributary men was that of *mulato*

Table 2.11. Marriage patterns among tributary married couples with no caste fluctuations in Acatlán and Piastla, 1739–43

Caste	*Mulata*[a]	Mestiza[b]	*India*	Unknown[c]	Totals
Mulato	29	19	12	0	60
Mestizo	9	0	3	0	12
Indio	3	1	12	1	17
Unknown	1	0	2	30	33
Totals	42	20	29	31	122

Source: See table 2.3.

[a]Includes one slave of unknown caste.

[b]Includes one *castiza*.

[c]Includes one woman of unknown caste temporarily excused from payment.

and mestiza, reflecting the sustained contacts between *mulatos* and mestizos in New Spain.[83] The balance between endogamous and exogamous marriage choices does little to suggest a general attitude toward exogamy as a strategy for avoiding the tribute regime. In short, this population does not show any general efforts to drive tributary numbers up or down through marriage choices.

The result of the efforts and decisions of local officials was the maintenance of a profitable and stable tax base determined by caste. Many Afromexican and Indian tributaries met these predictable tax demands, perhaps to maintain their business, family, residence, or social standing. These decisions and compromises joined those of local officials, whose assessments of individual identities cemented caste and tributary categories year after year. Each official act of creating and maintaining, or changing and removing, various records culminated in the establishment of a snapshot of a local tributary community. Tributary labels often remained unchanged in this five-year period. Officials preferred to leave things as they had been since 1739, making less work for themselves and allowing tribute to have a tolerable impact on the local population.

Another striking feature that would contribute to the stability of tributary numbers was the lack of marriage partners or patrons who were Spanish men and women. Without the influence of their genealogy or status, current tributaries would produce offspring who were also tributary. The tributary population would thus grow without the potential disruption of exempt children. The absence of people who possessed a Spanish *calidad* distinguished these tribute registers and the networks they described from their counterparts in San Luis Potosí. These lists were a record of the stability and predictability of the tributary population of Acatlán and Piastla, where free people of color regularly paid taxes and assumed tributary identities.

The impact of these local ideas about tributary status and caste can be traced through the submission of these lists to Mexico City as well as the movement of local bureaucrats into other posts. Following his tenure as alcalde of this jurisdiction, Manuel de Orendain continued his career in the capital working for the royal mint. As a bureaucrat in the royal mint for more than three decades, Orendain verified periodic accounts of the gold, silver, and copper arriving there.[84] He would later become a member of the Real Sociedad Bascongada de los Amigos del País, an economic society founded in 1764.[85] His contact with high levels of the colonial bureaucracy, his participation in the Amigos del País, and his pedestrian interactions with local residents of Acatlán and Piastla connected a wide array of individuals and institutions. His career provides an example of the networks of power in taxation that were central in the collection of taxes in Puebla.[86] Orendain became an expert in the evaluation of accounts at the royal mint, where he also brought along his personal notions about free people of African descent and their obligations to the crown. The movements of varied functionaries throughout the bureaucracy meant that ideas about tribute and *calidad* permeated multiple levels of government. Officials like Orendain formed part of a Bourbon movement toward administrative and fiscal efficiency that culminated at the end of the century.

Conclusions

Assessing tribute in this period was an early part of a larger process of consolidation and review of taxation across New Spain. By creating tribute registers, officials could identify who tributaries were, through their social relationships and *calidad*; where tributaries were, through the residences kept by their *amos*; and what tributaries were, through conceptions of vassalage. All of these factors were controlled, in part, within communities and could not be imposed from the capital. Free people of African descent knew one another and could direct a commissioner to erase or inflate the numbers of deceased or absent people in a given area. When a bureaucrat in Mexico City wanted a list of tributaries from a jurisdiction, the people who had to comply included not only officials and ordinary people but also property owners, whose economic relationships to tributaries resulted in a kind of responsibility some tried to avoid. In these ways and others described in the chapter, the capital compromised and conversed with its provinces in order to revise the meanings of tributary status.

Bureaucrats and jurists constructed their own notions and drew on historic ideals of what a tributary subject should be.[87] These ideas began to feature *calidad* as a major factor in determining tributary status. In theory, a tributary was a person whose *calidad* was obvious, who worked in a designated trade, who belonged to a family, and who performed his or her duties to the crown. An abundance of Afromexican individuals, especially when economies were healthy, seemed to have access to cash and to work but served no *amo*. Others were prestigious and respected in their communities but refused to submit to the duties of tributary status. Still other individuals were itinerant or interacted with multiple social groups so as to maintain a variety of reputations and statuses. Although tributes made up nearly a quarter of the income of the *real caja* of Mexico at midcentury, these and other problems led to only modest increases in tribute collection in central New Spain between 1744 and 1748.[88]

Whether these characterizations accurately reflected people's lives or were the invention of frustrated provincial officials and elites is information to which bureaucrats did not have access. They simply had to trust the observations of a local agent or send a *visitador* hundreds of miles into what could amount to a bureaucratic wilderness. The particularly slippery nature of *calidad* only complicated matters. Within these disputes between local officials and bureaucrats in the capital, Afromexican subjects "found plenty of room to maneuver."[89] The tribute regime depended on the cooperation of local elites and officials to determine *calidad*.

Why did free people of African descent acquiesce to the imposition of tribute in the first decades of Bourbon rule? It is possible that some ordinary people chose to participate in order to maintain their families and social circles within the communities they valued. Much of the time, payment of taxes was a sign of vassalage and duty that free people of color saw little point in rejecting, as they did not wish to leave their homes or incur fines. Instead, some Afromexicans sought to negotiate the meanings of tributary status using the flexibilities of *calidad*. Unlike the focus in later decades on the singular insult of tribute,[90] the early uses of *calidad* within the tributary regime appear to have been more diverse. The onerous payments signified the stain of African ancestry on blood purity, but tribute also legitimated the status of free people of color as vassals of the Spanish monarch. Rather than perpetual outsiders or dangerous vagrants, free people of color used the tributary regime as a space in which to articulate positive narratives of service or historically privileged lineage. In San Luis Potosí, tributary status was at once a marker of blackness, obligation, residence, *calidad*, and loyalty. All of these pieces of information could be difficult to obtain for local officials, who frequently preferred to avoid the conundrum of tributary status among free people of color. A contrasting case from Acatlán and Piastla shows the streamlining of *calidad* and tributary status that would erode these multifaceted meanings as the eighteenth century progressed.

3

Sons of Hidalgos or Ringleaders of the Indians?

Defining Tributary Genealogies

Calidad, caste, and tributary status were interrelated, though not equivalent, concepts in eighteenth-century New Spain, leaving many to wonder whether people could simultaneously possess a lineage of blackness and a nontributary status. As bureaucrats and petitioners debated the nature of tribute and tributary status, a series of important questions remained unanswered. First and foremost was the persistent question of blackness and tributary status being one and the same. In the seventeenth century, free people of African descent had demonstrated that being a free *negro* or a free *mulata* was not necessarily an indicator of tributary status. Through their connections to Spaniards, involvement in conquest and settlement, lack of resources, or otherness and outsider status, free people of African descent repeatedly put forward the argument that they could be both people of African descent and individuals with the privilege to not pay royal tribute. Second, it remained unclear how free people of color would go about establishing family ties and lineage as a basis for avoiding tribute without simultaneously denying that they had African ancestry in the first place. A related third issue was that of belonging and community, which often was at stake in petitions that determined residence, freedom of movement, and protection from abuse. Outsiders who behaved badly featured prominently in the descriptions officials and bureaucrats gave as justifications for driving free people of color from their residences or subjecting them to onerous tributary obligations. Seen from the perspectives of families and their legal representatives, these same actors were far from outsiders preying on colonial subjects while flouting rules and hierarchies. Afromexican petitioners sought to root themselves in illustrious Spanish genealogies or, alternatively, beg the largesse of the crown in the absence of family ties and supports. Both of these tactics presumed the importance of family and belonging to a colonial society that undermined the ongoing vision of free people of color as vagabonds, ringleaders, and criminals devoid of value to the colonial regime.

During the transitional period to Bourbon rule, a handful of rulings and petitions confirmed the possible outcomes for free Afromexicans who pursued greater privileges. In 1708 Viceroy Francisco Fernández de la Cueva, Tenth Duke of Alburquerque, granted tribute privileges to a family using a definition of *calidad* that did not hinge solely on caste. Brothers Luis and Pablo de la Estrella y Mendoza of San Juan del Río lobbied for their temporary tribute relief (*reserva*) on the basis of their valor in the defense against the Indians of the Sierra Gorda, a region whose stability secured nearby mining operations. Their successful petition rested on "the *calidad* of the supplicants," which was determined by their service "as officials to their caste," as well as their "valor and performance."[1] This notion of *calidad* was older and more peninsular. Lexicographer Sebastián de Covarrubias understood *calidad* to mean a "person of quality, man of authority, and of good traits."[2] Referring to Luis and Pablo de la Estrella y Mendoza as free *mulatos*, the decision used *calidad* to indicate the high quality of their honor and service, which defined these men as much as did their caste. As loyal vassals dedicated to maintaining settlements, these men distinguished themselves through participation in government and defense. The decision validated claims that free people of color could rise above tributary status through their commitment to the colonial project and their indispensable services to the crown. Yet, this *reserva* was, by its name, an exemption that was not meant to defy the tribute tax or deny that Luis and Pablo de la Estrella y Mendoza were and would remain, along with their future descendants, people of African descent. As the eighteenth century wore on and Bourbon reformers took control of the Real Hacienda, the royal treasury in Mexico City, the strength and durability of these kinds of dispensations would be tested and broken.

This chapter explores the avenues toward tribute exemption that free people of color sought, beyond simple calculations of caste that denied African ancestry. For some potential tributaries, establishing their place in a lineage or community was, or became during the course of the petition or proceedings, more important than denying their blackness. These remarkable undertakings, in which petitioners questioned the deep associations between blackness and the stigma of tribute, demonstrate the limits of colonial impositions on the internal dynamics of Afromexican families. Colonial administrators could not change the family memories of a decorated ancestor who crossed the Atlantic or fought for his king. To explore these individual and interpersonal elements of *calidad*, I focus on five cases between 1700 and 1750 that addressed the integration of free people of color into towns and cities in central Mexico, the reputations of their ancestors, and the qualities of their ties to relatives. The core cases in the chapter are three petitions and subsequent lawsuits from settlements near the city of Toluca: the town of Huizquilucan, the city of Lerma, and the *cabecera* of Tenango del Valle. Two more comparative cases come from Cuernavaca and Actopan. All the cases in this chapter underscore the importance of family ties, sometimes across boundaries of caste, for free people of African descent navigating the tribute regime.

Affinities or familial connections between free people of color and Spaniards became resources that free people of color used to defy the profoundly negative aspects of the tribute regime. In two cases, from Huizquilucan and Lerma, men of color fought to retain the honors and privileges attained by a Spanish ancestor and passed on to future descendants of any *calidad.* Claiming genealogical and familial ties to Spanish men allowed *mulato* and *pardo* men to seek opportunities for social prestige, property inheritance, or legal privileges within late colonial societies.[3] Free people of African descent also used a lack of family ties as a reason for poverty and inability to pay tribute. A case from Tenango del Valle from the perspective of two orphaned *mulata* girls, along with a local official, describes the gendered vulnerability and isolation of the petitioners, who lacked the financial and familial resources to pay the tax. Petitions and other documents related to tribute in the early eighteenth century relied on concepts of community belonging, inheritance of Spanish or Indian privileges, and family. In analyzing these petitions, I identify some of the attitudes that free *mulatos,* tribute collectors, and local officials expressed in the early decades of the eighteenth century. These genealogical, familial, and spatial connections shaped tribute registration and community formation. What these documents do not contain is a deliberate, sustained denial of blackness on the part of people who contested tributary status as the basis of tribute exemption.

Afromexican Tributaries as Disquieting Outsiders or Honorable Subjects

Petitions and *padrones* that address tribute and *calidad* in the early to mid-eighteenth century show the basis of Afromexican tribute in interpersonal relationships and articulations of family and belonging. Petitioners used evidence of enduring familial relationships or exempt genealogies to bolster their claims to exemption from tribute, often by associating themselves with a powerful family member or honorable male ancestor of Spanish descent. Other petitioners argued that without family support, tribute payment was an impossible burden. Family, a building block of colonial society, was an expression not only of social and economic resources, it was also the ultimate arbiter of genealogy. Distinct from late colonial petitions in their arguments, some of these cases used interpretations of genealogy not to deny blackness but to affirm family honor and privileges.

Tributary identity had conflicting and complex meanings for tributaries and for those who taxed them. The cases addressed in this chapter deal with the kinds of discussions and insults, impositions and concessions, and friends and families that were documented as a result of tribute collection and registration. Local officials viewed gender and family through lenses of patriarchy, paternalism, and prejudice. Many believed that free people of African descent inherently did not belong in colonial society, making them perpetual outsiders without meaningful family or community ties. Alcaldes often knew tributaries personally and struggled with their own beliefs about who had the resources to pay and what charging tribute would mean for the livelihoods of their neighbors. Free Afromexicans actively pushed back against assertions by tribute officials that the descendants of Africans had no claims to colonial subjecthood or were unwilling to accept the terms of tribute because of their supposed disdain for colonial norms like family and taxation. Against this institutional and interpersonal backdrop, petitions display the social ties free people of African descent sustained among themselves and across *calidad* and how they characterized these relationships as familial and genealogical.

Free people of color had multiple, if limited, opportunities within colonial institutions to document and construct their local networks and reputations. Such avenues for participation in colonial institutions that would establish a reputation of belonging to a community and colonial society were divided by gender within the Afromexican category. To strengthen a family's reputation and regard, some people could more easily attain personal honor than could others in colonial societies. Chances to obtain honor were limited for people who were not mestizos or Spaniards, but people of African descent pursued more honorable reputations through a variety of institutional and personal means. Studies of lay Catholic brotherhoods show the many roles Afromexicans took on to support their communities, participate in public religious displays, and exercise power within their organizations. In the seventeenth century, these confraternities had "thwarted Spanish patriarchy" and served as spaces for women in New Spain to play central roles in a community organization.[4] Despite institutional and social obstacles, women of African descent used notarial practices to advance their own status and those of their families, sometimes by acquiring wealth and accessing wider social networks.[5] For women of African descent, honor and virtue could be associated with Catholic piety, while others who gained notoriety as healers were vulnerable to accusations of witchcraft.[6] Yet throughout the colonial period, Afromexican women faced prevalent and dehumanizing stereotypes of their perceived immoral sexuality, ritual practices, commercial dealings, and legacy of enslavement. Colonial authorities targeted free women of African descent and attempted to bar them from making economic or political gains. Often associated with undesirable behaviors and customs, women struggled to build reputations within a regime hostile to their presence.[7]

Afromexican men who sought to bolster their honor and create more favorable reputations for their descendants had gendered opportunities within colonial institutions to do so. In petitions to obtain the privilege to carry weapons, *mulato* men pointed to their honor and positive personal qualities, such as trustworthiness, as traits that qualified them for privileges.[8] Afromexican men accumulated honor by participating in militias and thereby avoiding tributary payments. Similar tax exemptions were granted in medieval Iberia in exchange for military service and in recognition of elevated social status.[9] Militiamen were particularly successful in establishing an alternative discourse to the negative ideas promoted among colonial bureaucrats and elites, and some men eventually made petitions that conflated militia privileges with caste by the late eighteenth century.[10] The fact that people often predicated their arguments for tribute exemption on gendered honor and service to the crown reinforced relationships of vassalage between ordinary people and their ruler. These performances of belonging and serving the colonial project offered Afromexican men greater integration into colonial structures, despite the severe restrictions against people of their *calidad*.

The notion of the free Afromexican as outsider had tributary implications at the same time that it undermined the legal fiction of exclusively Indian pueblos. Across the empire, early eighteenth-century towns that supposedly were only home to Indians also had *casta* residents, and some Indians also married enslaved Africans. These families and their descendants pushed the limits of colonial categories like "*indio*" and threatened the abilities of officials to keep separate records of free people of African descent and Indians.[11] By this time in Peru, it had become clear that idealized Indian towns, where Andeans could be protected from harassment by Afroperuvians and Spaniards, had broken down under pressure of colonial labor markets.[12] Even when Indians accused free and enslaved blacks of committing crimes, subsequent inquiries might suggest that the alleged criminal took refuge in the home of an Indian who was most likely an acquaintance, friend, or family member.[13] Who was Indian also had to do with who performed the duties of indigeneity, one of which was tribute, a strategy that Filipino immigrants used to integrate themselves into Indian towns and form relationships with indigenous women.[14]

The following case from Cuernavaca treats tributary status as a sign of community belonging, one of the central features of tribute, and explores the problem of tributary status produced by genealogies that crossed boundaries of *calidad* as well as the supposed geographic barriers between free people of African descent and Indians. Local officials used tribute as leverage for forcing free people of African descent out of their homes. They reasoned that free people of African descent could not belong to colonial communities if they willingly evaded their responsibilities as tributaries and loyal vassals. From Mexico City, attorneys (*fiscales*) pored over such cases with an eye toward privilege—whether Afro-Indians were deserving of royal leniency compared with those mestizos of Spanish descent. Residents shored up both genealogical connections and immediate spatial and familial ties within their communities to certify their place in local networks of family and friends.

In 1725, the Indian governor of the town of Cuernavaca asked the General Indian Court in Mexico City for increased authority to control his unruly residents.[15] His problems stemmed from the fact that free people of African descent and Indian immigrants were living among his Indian constituents and encouraging them to neglect their tribute responsibilities. In central New Spain, denser populations created higher stakes for tribute collection, and local officials depended on cooperative tributaries. The governor claimed that some of the people he had jailed had already appealed to the courts for their release, slandering him in the process.[16] The "disquieting" behavior of the "ringleaders of the Indians" threatened local finance and the labor draft to the mines at Taxco,[17] showing that free people of African descent did not belong in the tributary community.

The solution, according to the petition, would be to evict all *mulatos* and *lobos* (people of mixed Indian and African ancestry), along with immigrant Indian workers, from Coyoacán.[18] These people had attracted the attention of the governor not simply because they were outsiders, but because they disrupted his implementation of royal tribute. The governor wanted to arrest all offending parties, regardless of *calidad*, but he also made arguments that associated delinquency with not belonging genealogically. In response, Viceroy Juan de Acuña y Bejarano, second marquis of Casa Fuerte, confirmed that those Indians who owed tribute should be arrested, but only by their elected Indian officials. Indian tributary activities thus asserted the cohesion of local Indian government, punishment, finances, and community. The Indian governor also mobilized Indian *calidad*, coupled with the importance of place, to identify those who had sparked the resistance to the formation of a tributary community.

The decision from Mexico City demonstrates that the conflation of Afromexican *calidad* and immigrant status was not uniform in the early eighteenth century. In this instance, birthplace overshadowed caste. As the case implies, free people of African descent and Indians could coexist without incident, provided they met tribute demands and belonged to families.[19] According to the consulting *fiscal* (most likely experienced administrator Prudencio Antonio de Palacios),[20] those Spaniards, *negros*, mestizos, and *mulatos* who were immigrants were known to treat Indians poorly and expose them to "bad customs." These "*mulatos*, mestizos, and others of mixed color (*color quebrado*)" in the barrios were to return to their towns of origin to pay their taxes.[21]

According to the decision, some free people of color—especially those who had Indian ancestry—did not display the negative tendencies common in outsiders. The *fiscal* then distinguished unwanted intruders from a group of mestizos and *zambaigos* who were "children of Indian women, born among them and heirs to their houses and properties."[22] These subjects had Spanish or African fathers, but their maternal lineage and property ownership solidified their community membership. Although limited by the seventeenth century, Indian women in central New Spain inherited property and dispensed with it based on Spanish and pre-Columbian traditions.[23] Such connections among property, maternal lineage, and tributary status confirmed, for bureaucrats, that these mestizos and *zambaigos* belonged in Cuernavaca. Ideas about family determined the outcome of the Indian governor's complaint. "Because it seems a harsh thing to separate them from their parents,"[24] administrators reasoned, those Afro-Indians who were "natives" (*nativos*) could stay. Such a paternalistic argument speaks to the value placed on nuclear family and Indian femininity, as well as maintaining order and local customs.

Tribute payments were a record of an individual's place in his or her community and an asserted connection with the place itself. The repeated use of the word "native" to distinguish between those who belonged and those who did not drew clear distinctions of geography and community through acts of tribute. As one historian has argued of early modern people, "by enacting the role of citizen or native they created a public image that they were citizens or natives."[25] In early Bourbon New Spain, paying tribute was part of such a role among Indians and Afromexicans; a person could become "native" in the eyes of authorities and other subjects. Without seeing baptismal certificates, the viceroy's legal counsel believed that certain free people of African descent could be "natives," provided they resided with their parents, were heirs to property, and paid tribute. By the end of the eighteenth century, free people of color had become residents of many Indian towns and lived harmoniously with their neighbors. They were accepted as they married into Indian families and adopted their ways over time.[26] This piece-by-piece construction of tributary status gradually became entwined with *calidad*. Yet, as the Cuernavaca case makes clear, the *calidad* an individual established through tributary status was not immutable or beyond doubt. The characteristics that indicated tributary status and *calidad* were not stable, nor was there much agreement about what they meant or how closely connected they were.

Officials and ordinary people drew on competing interpretations of *calidad* and tributary status, hashing out concepts and theories of genealogy and gender as they went. The spread of vocabularies of *calidad* was, as one historian writes, "the result of ordinary people in everyday life pushing, expanding, and testing the categories by grading themselves up and others down."[27] For free people of color, one way to "grade themselves up" without denying their connections to blackness was to eschew tributary status, thereby changing the associations of *calidad* and the onerous tax. Confusion and confrontation over the obligations of blackness or Indianness in local contexts brought questions about *calidad* as a social category to the fiscal bureaucracy. When tributaries paid, registered, resisted, or complained, local interpretations met bureaucratic discourse on *calidad*, promoting a vocabulary of *calidad* linked to tributary status. In some cases, this shared language allowed local disputes to blossom into problems of concern to the highest levels of government. Some petitions and inquiries in the early eighteenth century reveal that individuals did not necessarily associate their blackness with tributary status. Such people sought to decouple their *calidad* from tributary status without dismantling their reputations as free people of African descent.

"He Raised and Educated Him as a Son": Family and Spanish Lineage in Exemption Petitions

The centrality of family in the tribute regime allowed potential tributaries to articulate arguments against tributary status based on lineage and reputation, rather than caste and *calidad* alone. Spanish ancestry and family ties were valuable assets for free *mulatos* and *pardos* in legal documents concerning tributary status in central New Spain. The following case studies from the Toluca region show distinct motivations on the part of men and women of African descent, ranging from immediate economic need to long-term projections of honor and genealogy for future generations. What the cases had in common, in the minds of officials and petitioners, was the importance of family as the organizing principle of the tribute regime. The extent to which family implied tributary status or could shelter an individual from tribute depended on the officials interpreting the petition as well as the nature of the familial connections. Later tribute petitions sent to bureaucrats in the capital usually highlighted the dissatisfaction of petitioners on learning of their registration as *mulatos* and their subsequent denial of any African ancestry. These earlier cases show the narratives free people of African descent created using their interpersonal connections, family relationships, and popular ideas about family honor to avoid paying tribute.

Some petitions for tribute exemption showed free people of African descent integrated into towns and cities, surrounded by friends and family, and familiar with local officials. Unlike some free Afromexicans who lived in "attached subordination" to Spanish elites or employers,[28] the petitioners of color in central New Spain portrayed themselves as the cherished children of individual Spanish men, meant to enjoy the same privileges as other members of the lineage or household. These petitioners lived in proximity to Mexico City and had greater access to the legal system, but they were also a target for tribute officials intent on making central New Spain as profitable as possible for the crown. The cases come from neighboring jurisdictions of Tenango del Valle, Lerma, Tacuba, and Metepec, all of which were close to the city of Toluca. Tributaries in this region were agricultural laborers, though many were forced to work in *obrajes* or in mines at Taxco or Zacualpan.[29] Although predominantly an Indian community, Tenango del Valle had been part of the regional slave trade surrounding Toluca.[30] A handful of families and associates made detailed petitions questioning their tributary status during the period between 1700 and 1760 that are now housed in the national archive in Mexico City; only one such dispute appears to have reached the Archive of the Indies in Seville. These cases were not the norm. Most tributaries did not have the documentation or social clout necessary to sustain a petition that would reach the high court in Mexico City or the Council of the Indies. However, if petitioners lived in a jurisdiction where tribute collection was haphazard or under investigation by the Real Hacienda, their concerns might be more readily heard.

Afromexican individuals in the periods of the War of Spanish Succession (1702–13) and the beginning of the Bourbon reforms used genealogical logic to promote their own privileges. Perhaps the most extensive and inventive case for tribute exemption from New Spain at this time spanned hundreds of folios and claimed a conquistador as part of the family tree. In 1705, a tribute dispute between a family from Tacuba and a *fiscal* from the Real Hacienda stalled in a second round of appeals. Gabriel Fernández de Cabrera had offered a proof of his conquistador lineage through his paternal and maternal lines as the basis for a petition for tribute exemption, though case records identified him both a free *pardo* or a free *mulato* (figure 3.1). The petitioner claimed in 1695 that he and his brothers and sisters were descendants of Gonzalo Fernández de Cabrera, a conquistador of Mexico, and others including Gabriel Pie de Hierro, who served "in the conquest and discovery of the province of Constancia [Nicaragua] with his arms and horses and servants and all at his own cost."[31] The far-flung family now included siblings who resided in Guanajuato as well as Huizquilucan, a town in Tacuba with a significant non-Indian population that included free and enslaved Afromexicans.[32] One brother, Antonio, had even left for the Philippines with the intention of becoming a soldier. No one in this large family had, according to witnesses, paid tribute "or been registered in any tribute list." Using family history and reputation, the petitioner and his siblings sought to prove their own status and those of their ancestors as "people understood to be honorable."[33] Fernández de Cabrera and his siblings were descendants of "hidalgos, gentlemen," who never paid the *pecho*.[34] Such an honorable connection to a line of conquistadors elevated the petitioner and his family above others required to pay this tribute tax.

The petitioner eventually had to explicitly address the issue of his caste and *calidad*, as multiple parties throughout the case had labeled him and his siblings as free people of color. Documents related to the petition referred to some family members as free *pardos* or *mulatos* multiple times. To contest these insinuations, Fernández de Cabrera had to prove an absence of *calidad* in the marriage records of his ancestors. In the words of a priest named Alonso Alberto de Velasco who was called on to evaluate the *calidad* of Gabriel Fernández de Cabrera's father,

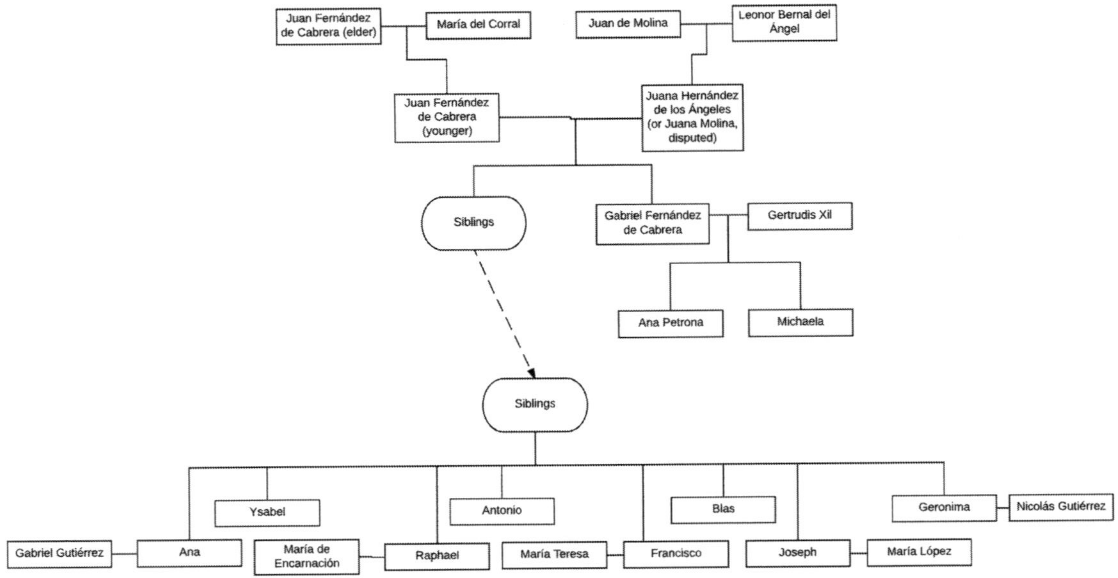

Figure 3.1. Family tree of Gabriel Fernández de Cabrera (Norah Gharala)

"*calidad* is not added beside names for banns and marriage certificates of Spaniards." Among "*mulatos*, *negros*, and mestizos," the opposite was true. When information related to caste or *calidad* was absent from such records, the priest asserted that "it [was] understood that they are Spaniards."[35] The absence of information was to serve as proof of a lack of tributary *calidad*. Gabriel Fernández de Cabrera and his legal representation played on this lack of information as well as witness testimony affirming their lack of family history of paying tribute.

Despite witness testimony affirming the public reputation of the petitioner's father as a Spaniard, local collectors again attempted to intimidate the family during the course of the proceedings. Under threat of imprisonment, Gabriel Fernández de Cabrera's brothers, their wives, and their children fled the jurisdiction as they hoped for a favorable decision that never came. Witnesses and family members began to attest to the "extreme poverty" of the Fernández de Cabrera family as they attempted to secure their status as nontributaries.[36] Unable to sustain themselves, let alone pay tributes to the crown, the family appealed to the mercy of their ruler. This layer of the petition now painted the Fernández de Cabrera family as a dispossessed clan of conquistador descendants who, though honorable and committed to serving the crown, were not reaping the benefits of their ancestors' loyalty.

In 1701, Gabriel Fernández de Cabrera, on behalf of his children and siblings, appealed his case before the Council of the Indies. Complaining that community members and officials had made baseless accusations against his reputation, Fernández de Cabrera rejected assertions that the family had some *mulato* members of questionable lineage. However, other statements he made in the case suggest that some people in the family were not Spanish. He claimed that tribute would constitute an "irreparable prejudice threatening children and descendants, since some of them are married to Spaniards," a statement that could have implied that some family members had married partners who were not Spanish. Yet, in the arguments of the appeal, the presence of non-Spanish lineage did not negate the privileges the family sought. Fernández de Cabrera argued that the spirit of the law allowed his ancestors to "enjoy all the honors . . . and grace and privilege" that the king had "conceded amply to those pobladores and discoverers without limitation or restriction of *calidad*." The honor of these male ancestors outweighed the status of his blood purity, since "not even blood mixture could have made them unworthy" of the privileges granted conquistadors.[37] Fernández de Cabrera did deny that his family possessed a *mulato* caste, but his more intriguing assertions, and the ones that dominated much of the case, pertained to his alleged conquistador ancestry.

The case was not, for Fernández de Cabrera, strictly about caste or *calidad* but about family history and genealogy. If he could establish a genealogical link

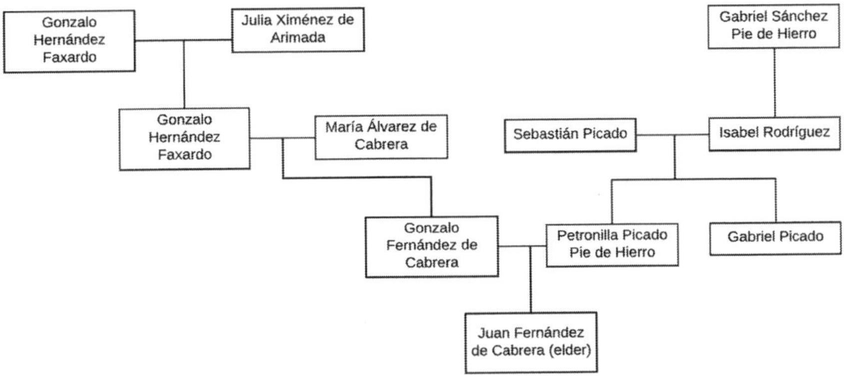

Figure 3.2. Family tree of Juan Fernández de Cabrera (Norah Gharala)

to a conquistador ancestor, then he and his kin were entitled to privileges, regardless of their current reputation or the presence of an African ancestor. He did not directly argue that African blood was a positive aspect of his genealogy, but he questioned whether it should compromise an otherwise noble lineage.[38] Furthermore, African ancestry could, for the petitioner, coexist with conquistador lineage. If anything, it was only to be expected, as the conquest occurred at a time when there were, in his words, "so few or no women equal in *calidad*" available for marriage in the new American possessions.[39] Authorities had also used the argument that many descendants of conquistadors were *mulatos*, although this assertion was meant to block their eligibility for favors.[40] Fernández de Cabrera acknowledged the presence of a possible ancestor who was not of Spanish descent but focused on the royal service and honor of his paternal ancestors instead.

These honorable, male ancestors mattered most in the arguments of the Fernández de Cabrera family. Bound separately in leather and included in the case were documents providing proof (*probanza*) of the nobility and ancestors of the petitioner's grandfather Juan Fernández de Cabrera, compiled in 1635 and notarized at his request (figure 3.2). Spanning the sixteenth and seventeenth centuries, these documents chronicle the multiple attempts of Juan Fernández de Cabrera's extended family to obtain conquistador privileges, buttress male honor, and prove their lines of descent. Included is a copy of a petition from 1587 originating in Nicaragua intended to establish, through witness testimony, that the conquistador Gonzalo Fernández de Cabrera remained an "honorable man" in his community, who owned horses with which he was able to serve the crown.[41] Demonstrating the importance of legitimacy and genealogy, Juan Fernández de Cabrera presented witnesses who confirmed his parents "conceived during their marriage and fed, raised, and recognized [him] as such." The ancestors included in the *probanza* were all "of good conduct and customs," and their Spanish ancestry is rarely mentioned.[42]

Non-Spanish ancestry was not directly opposed to conquistador lineage, but officials did not share the petitioner's disregard for the centrality of blood purity and *calidad* in determining tributary status. While the Fernández de Cabrera family sought protection and privilege in their Spanish conquistador ancestry, skeptical bureaucrats insisted on the importance of the present for determining the veracity of these claims. *Fiscal* Francisco Blanco del Castillo from the *audiencia* in Mexico was "convinced of the *mulato calidad*" of Fernández de Cabrera because he had been named as such throughout the length of the case. The *fiscal* also observed that his "appearance evidently qualifies him" as a person with African ancestry; therefore, "the reputation which he should have is as a *mulato*."[43] The attention to "appearance" rather than *calidad* predates this case and would continue to influence bureaucrats who focused on physiognomic traits in the tribute regime. To distract from what he believed were visible signs of social difference, the *fiscal* accused the family of Fernández de Cabrera of attempting to mislead officials. For Blanco del Castillo, the case showed evidence of multiple people deliberately obfuscating the *calidad* of family members to disguise their *mulato* identity. The arguments Blanco del Castillo made focused on the present, rather than Fernández de Cabrera's construction of a distant, honorable past.

The strategies taken demonstrate the intersections of lineage, blood purity, *calidad*, physiognomy, and privilege within tribute. The case was reviewed by Philip V in 1703, though further instructions and decisions are now separated from the case. Neither *fiscal* Blanco del Castillo nor the Fernández de Cabrera family denied the importance of genealogy for tributary status; they simply disagreed on which genealogy would prevail. These genealogies were wrapped up in reputation as well. Was this petition brought by conniving, self-serving *mulatos* intent on shirking their duty to their ruler and undermining the colonial order? This was certainly the perspective of Blanco del Castillo. Or was this case about long-suffering descendants of valiant conquistadors whose honorable lineage would be sullied with tributary status? Gabriel Fernández de Cabrera's appeal to honorable male lineage asserted that tributary status was unfit for descendants of conquistadors, regardless of African ancestry.

A common thread throughout these early tribute petitions and complaints is that of participation in establishing Spanish control through conquest, especially into territories occupied by hostile Indian groups. As the Spanish Empire increased taxation in New Spain, subjects contested tributary demands using narratives of loyalty, masculinity, and privilege, and were sometimes successful, as shown at the start of the chapter. Afromexican tributaries couched their dis-

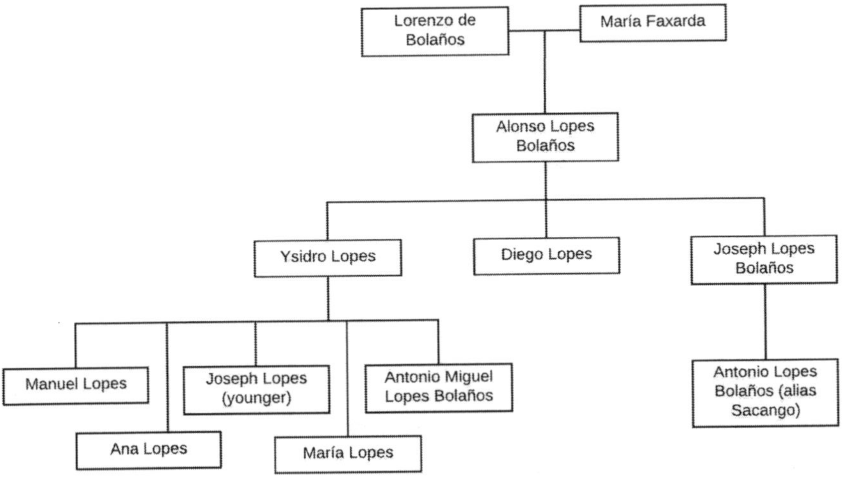

Figure 3.3. Descendants of Alonso Lopes Bolaños (Norah Gharala)

cussions of color, caste, and *calidad* within a rubric of territorial expansion. At the same time, *calidad* itself could be used to justify or detract from privileges at the turn of the eighteenth century. Bureaucrats, officials, and ordinary people used petitions and the courts to discuss what exactly *calidad* meant, how it could be manipulated, and its relationship to tributary status. These discussions reinforced genealogy, gender, and family as fundamental indicators of status in colonial society.

The following decades showed the enduring importance of *calidad*, genealogy, and family as key modes of expression for free people of color seeking privileges. As Bourbon bureaucrats continued to assert control over the disjointed tribute regime, families and communities contested their obligations to pay the tax. Privilege and lineage remained mutually dependent for a family of free people of color who disputed their tributary status in the small city of Lerma, where many families were reputed to have a *calidad* that was neither Spanish nor Indian.[44] In the spring of 1744, Antonio Lopes Bolaños (alias "Sacango") and his brother Antonio Miguel Lopes Bolaños presented evidence demonstrating that all of their grandfather's "ancestors and descendants" were exempt from tribute.[45] These included the men making the claims as well as the brothers and sisters of Antonio Miguel, Joseph, Manuel, Ana, and María (figure 3.3). Based on previous assessments, this claim rejecting tributary status fits a pattern. In 1735, Lerma had only five Afromexican tributaries and 1,001 Indian tributaries.[46] Census data from 1743 suggested that more potential Afromexican tributaries lived in Lerma, judging from the 133 families of *mulatos* and mestizos who were registered there.[47] The six grandchildren of Alonso Lopes Bolaños were part of a potential tributary population that officials were attempting to rein in as they addressed unorthodox practices and unclear definitions of tributary *calidad.*

The complainants based their claims to exemption on the status of their grandfather and a document he had procured more than a century earlier. Alonso Lopes Bolaños was an immigrant from Fuente del Maestre in Extremadura and the son of a hidalgo, or member of the minor nobility. His father was Lorenzo de Bolaños, a *vecino* of Fuente del Maestre, and his mother was a *negra* named María Farxada whose place of origin is not given. Although Alonso was born out of wedlock, he and his legal representatives stressed that both parents were "free and unwed and not subject to any imposition to wed at the time." Owing to his birth, Alonso could expect the same "exceptions and privileges" accorded to his father. Alonso began a lawsuit accusing the comptroller of royal tributes of attempting to charge tribute solely on the basis of his "being of *mulato* color." In June 1621, the magistrates of the high court in Mexico City decided in favor of Alonso Lopes Bolaños and granted his exemption from tribute, "freeing him from it and as such may he be crossed out and erased from the register where the other *negros* and *mulatos* who pay are noted."[48] This outcome was not unique in the region in the seventeenth century, though such dispensations were rare. A 1652 decree granted Nicolás de Trejo, a free *mulato* and *vecino* from neighboring Toluca, freedom from tribute because he was the grandson of a hidalgo and a free *mulata.*[49] In the far south of the viceroyalty, even the children of an enslaved African woman might request such privileges, as illustrated by the case of Guatemalan-born Antonio Meléndez de Valdés, son of a former colonial governor from Asturias.[50] These legal documents presented *mulatos* who were honorable *vecinos* with direct ties to peninsular Spaniards, the most powerful group in colonial society.

The descendants of Alonso Lopes Bolaños found witnesses in the surrounding community who had personally known him and could confirm that he was a gentleman and a hidalgo; that he had three legitimate sons, Ysidro, Diego, and Joseph; that these men had direct relationships with the petitioners; and that all of the people discussed "have been free and exempt from paying tribute." One mestizo who had met Alonso in Istlaguaca in neighboring Metepec had maintained a "close friendship" with him over the years and had heard him "say many times that he had a royal dispensation for himself and his descendants," proving that he was a gentleman and a hidalgo. Other witnesses described Antonio Miguel, Joseph, Manuel, Ana, and María as legitimate children and Antonio as an *hijo natural.* Men in the community declared that they had seen various acts of parenting, including raising the children and maintaining them financially. Joseph treated his natural son Antonio "Sacango" with great care, "raising him and educating him as a son." Multiple people remarked that Joseph carried his son in his arms with "great tenderness" and "as his own."[51] The image of a baby cradled in his father's arms not only legitimated the brothers' claims to family but also distinguished them from negative images of *mulatos* as rowdy, socially marginal, and without meaningful ties that would bolster his honor and family lineage.[52] As the sons of Spaniards, *mulatos* from this family may have been publicly recognizable by their use of finer clothing and styles distinct from Indians and poorer free people of color.[53] In spite of the great love Joseph had for his natural son, it was Ysidro who was able to provide his children with basic literacy; Antonio "Sacango" did not have these abilities. Antonio Miguel, a legitimate child, learned to sign his name, which he did in official documents. His status as a literate man with noble lineage, regardless of his possible Afromexican *calidad*, justified his tribute exemption.

In September 1744, local officials and authorities in Mexico City were continuing to examine the problem of the "pending removal of free *negros* and *mulatos* registered" in and around Lerma, Istlaguaca, and Metepec, where significant increases in Afromexican tributaries occurred.[54] In addition to the petition of the Lopes Bolaños family, there was an ongoing dilemma of local registers that were useless and troublesome. Previously, local officials had not created separate registers that would allow outsiders to distinguish between "mestizos and *castizos*" and "*negros, mulatos, lobos, coyotes, moriscos*." Rather, the *calidades* had been mixed together on the same register, causing an inflation of the number of individuals registered as Afromexican tributaries to 187, whom the alcalde was required to charge "as if they were all *mulatos*." The increased amount of tribute expected from the *alcalde mayor* would now be 477 pesos and four *tomines*, a hefty sum. In 1745, Pedro Vedoya y Ossorio, *fiscal* of the high court, wondered whether the previous official had done this because he believed mestizos to be "of infected blood, as are *mulatos, lobos, coyotes, moriscos*, and others like them." Vedoya recommended that an investigation (*visita*) proceed into the "type (*clase*)" of mestizos who had been registered "among the *negros* and *mulatos*." This concern with the intricacies of tributary *calidad* was much more in keeping with Bourbon thinking. If the mestizos in question were the children of Spanish men and Indian women, they could claim tribute exemption. Vedoya also noted that these types of questions had also arisen in the city of Celaya and "other jurisdictions," where tributary *calidad* had multiple local interpretations.[55]

The Real Audiencia, or high court in the capital, carefully consulted the materials over a period of more than five years while investigations were underway. In 1748, it remained unclear how many tributaries would actually need to pay and, therefore, how much money the *alcalde mayor* would have to remit to the Real Hacienda. The previous *alcalde mayor* had deserted his post and fled the jurisdiction under suspicion of concealment of assets. New registers needed to be made and additional officials appointed and consulted. The *visita* eventually uncovered the inclusion of "129.5 *castizos* and mestizos, 31.5 *mulatos*, and 26 *coyotes*, *lobos*, and *moriscos*" as tributaries on the register of *negros* and *mulatos* in 1744.[56] The presence of these less common *casta* categories may point to the connections between Afromexicans, Indians, and Spaniards. Although they had technical definitions, terms like *morisco* (one Spanish grandparent and three African grandparents) and *lobo* (one Indian parent and one African parent) were relatively rare in tribute disputes and records when compared with *mulato* or mestizo. If these tributaries presented themselves using these terms, they may have had close ties to the region's Spanish or Indian populations. Over the next two decades, the number of free people of color dwindled in Metepec, as perhaps more families changed their *calidad* to mestizo or *castizo* without petitioning the high court.[57]

The Lopes Bolaños family then lost the privileges of which their *mulato* ancestor was so proud. The comptroller was to compare "similar situations" with the case at hand to determine whether "the children of Spanish *hidalgos* and black women and their descendants should pay tribute or not." This decision was not given nearly as much weight as the overall fate of nearly two hundred people in nearby Metepec. Instead, the definition of a tributary seemed much simpler when the hidalgo designation was removed altogether. The *oidores* determined that "the children of a Spanish man and a black woman should pay tribute" with little explanation beyond this cut-and-dried definition. In 1752, they confirmed that they would only grant exemptions to those who were "purely mestizos and *castizos*."[58] While the *oidores* dropped the earlier presumption of privileges for peninsular hidalgos in favor of caste, they also turned to the notion of pure bloodlines, an Iberian concept that predated caste categories. Interestingly, mestizos and *castizos* were, by definition, *castas* descended from a mixture of Spaniards and Indians. This decision demonstrated the continual reevaluation of what *calidad* and tributary status meant and how closely tied to caste they should be. Among these conundrums of *calidad*, the Lopes Bolaños case was distinctive in its claim to a genealogy of privileges without exempt *calidad*. The family hoped to bypass the primary site of tribute negotiation—the local register—using a royal dispensation and defining their linage based on a male Spanish ancestor. Without conforming to the pure tributary categories, the grandchildren of Alonso Lopes Bolaños, a *mulato* and a noble, could not claim exemption.

In the decades of early Bourbon reform, entire communities protested the imposition of new tribute registers, causing some potential Afromexican tributaries to shore up connections to Spanish genealogies or family members. In 1727, a group of individuals and families comprising five men and six women from the jurisdiction of Actopan, now in the state of Hidalgo, petitioned to be removed from the tribute list of *mulatos* where they and "others of [their] *calidad*" had recently found themselves. None of the petitioners listed a spouse, and the identities of mothers are virtually ignored all together. Instead, Juan Simón Gómez and

Antonia de Barba, as well as two young women named María Teresa and Phelipa Victoriana, all asserted that they were the illegitimate children of Spanish men of publicly known and accepted *calidad*. Spaniard Agustín Gómez had taken in three foundlings of completely unknown parentage called Gertrudis, Agustina, and Phelipe Gómez, and a final petitioner, Joseph Moreno, also claimed to be a foundling, or *expósito*. Testimony by men from Actopan confirmed the aforementioned claims, but witnesses saw more uncertainty in the families of three other petitioners who were part of the complaint. Isabel Gómez Castellano was reputed to be a *morisca* of Spanish and African descent, and she was also publicly known to be the illegitimate daughter of don Pedro Gómez Castellano, a Spaniard. The presence of some African ancestry in her lineage would have made her subject to royal tribute, although she clearly hoped her association with her father would carry more weight in the determination of her tributary status. Asked whether the final two petitioners, brothers Andrés and Joseph Benegas, were of Spanish ancestry, a witness recalled that twenty years previously Juan Benegas of Castile "said on multiple occasions that he had two sons by a *mulata* called Pascuala Pacheco, who is the mother of Joseph and Andrés Benegas." Despite these claims, the witness could not be sure whether Juan Benegas had publicly recognized his sons.[59] Such recognition might have allowed his children the privileges that had been accorded throughout the seventeenth century to the offspring of a peninsular father.

Although these petitioners could cite tenuous ties to living or deceased Spanish men, none could claim the kind of airtight lineage that would satisfy stringent Bourbon definitions of tributary status. Being raised by a Spanish man as orphans in his home, Gertrudis, Agustina, and Phelipe Gómez argued that they could have been Spaniards on the basis that no one could prove the *calidad* of their unknown parents. This logic had a legal basis from the sixteenth century onward, although it was hotly debated and never fully accepted throughout the imperial bureaucracy.[60] This strategy was already popular in the early eighteenth century, as men claiming to be foundlings managed to remove themselves from tribute registers comprising Indians, free people of color, and even some technically exempt categories like mestizos, across the empire.[61] Attached to this and other petitions from panicked residents was a list detailing individuals who had proven their exempt *calidad* and an adjacent list of individuals who had failed in their attempts to define themselves officially as caciques, mestizos, *coyotes*, or Spaniards. The names of ten of the natural sons, orphans, and foundlings who made this petition are absent from these lists. The only name present under the list of those who could not "justify" their *calidad* is Phelipe Gómez, whose presence on this list suggests that the other complainants may have been unsuccessful as well.[62]

The petitioners from Actopan used the more immediate past as well as their current connections to important Spanish men in the community to attempt to shield themselves from tribute without delving too deeply into their individual genealogies. In contrast, the Lopes Bolaños sons echoed the claims to honor and Spanish privileges cited in the case of Gabriel Fernández de Cabrera and his siblings. These cases used genealogical connections to Spaniards to claim Habsburg tribute privileges. For these families, some combination of blood, reputation, honor, *calidad*, and upbringing defined tributary status. The attempts by free men of color to maintain identifications with both blackness and tributary exemption met with resistance in Mexico City. While residents of Actopan could draw on rumors and reputations in living memory, the Lopes Bolaños brothers relied on—or rebuilt—a more tenuous connection to a Spanish ancestor who lived a century prior to their petition. The combination of the passage of time and the demands of the Lopes Bolaños family to live as privileged *mulatos* did not receive the sympathy of authorities concerned with enforcing tributary categories rather than honoring distant family memories.

Orphanhood, Poverty, and the Contested Tributary Status of *Mulata* Girls

Without connections to family, regardless of its history and reputation, women became increasingly vulnerable to tribute and its justifications based on *calidad*. The previous cases demonstrated the possibilities of family connections to shield potential tributaries, particularly those who could show their ties to a Spanish man of considerable importance. Juana de la Encarnación and Sebastiana María became the focus of scrutiny because they were financially insecure, without family, and, therefore, unable to pay the tribute they owed as *mulatas*. Instead of creating a genealogy that showed their privileges, these individuals attempted to document their poverty and isolation. Their case contains a microcosm of the shifting categories, prejudices, laws, and customs that constituted Afromexican tribute in Tenango del Valle.

Free people of African descent living in the town of Tenango del Valle and surrounding communities failed to make tribute payments throughout the 1720s. When local officials attempted to change this custom, residents of African descent resisted using legal channels. A resulting case in which the court-appointed representative for the poor (*procurador de pobres*) depicted his *mulata* clients as young women needing protection from a local tyrant quickly became embroiled in the caste- and gender-based confusion of the piecemeal Habsburg tribute regime. State relief was already highly dependent on caste, underpinning the prejudices authorities held against the non-Spanish poor.[63] The court case was built on competing articulations of gendered power, or "patriarchy as contest,"[64] entangled with legal minority, caste, and poverty. The language used exposes long-standing suspicions in society toward free persons of color, orphans, unmarried women, people without defined trades or employment, and disobedient subjects. Bureaucrats folded those concerns into their uneasy relationship with local customs and authority.

Rather than side with two poor, young women lacking community ties, the Bourbon regime attempted to strengthen hierarchies of *calidad*. Officials at multiple levels of government reasoned that *mulatas* should not enjoy privileges denied women "superior" in *calidad*, such as those of Indian or Spanish descent. Such distinctions continued to serve specific purposes in the tribute regime, especially when they allowed administrators to extract additional tributes, even as they began to fade away elsewhere in the empire.[65] As a result, the petitioners were relayed from the civil to the criminal courts.[66] The outcome of the case and its attendant rhetoric confirmed the fundamentally different standing of Afromexican women and Indian women vis-à-vis the colonial regime. Afromexican young women were unworthy of gendered privileges, while Indian girls necessitated protection and care from their communities.

In the summer of 1728, sisters Juana de la Encarnación and Sebastiana María of Tenango del Valle found themselves in a desperate situation. More than two months prior they had failed to pay their ten reales in royal tribute, forcing authorities to take Juana into custody (*depósito*). Under *depósito*, women were either punished or protected away from prying eyes and loose tongues in what was often the rural equivalent of a jail.[67] This scenario usually implied work for those women who found themselves in *depósito* as a form of punishment.[68] Rural patriarchy and paternalism loomed large in this case and in local ideas about government in Tenango and the surrounding Toluca Valley.[69] Having lost both of their parents, the two young women had few resources and were "suffering without having anyone to support or maintain them."[70] Frequently described as unmarried girls (*doncellas*) in documents pertaining to their case, Juana and Sebastiana drew on a vocabulary used by many eighteenth-century *mulatas* as they attempted to portray themselves as young, virtuous, and honorable, in spite of the many negative associations attached to their *calidad*.[71] According to their lawyer, Francisco Manuel Chirlín, the *alcalde mayor* had charged the girls without having the right to do so. This petition sparked a discussion specific to a region in which free people of African descent were scarce and their ties to Indians tenuous. Here, privileges or obligations were not articulated through service or belonging; this petition focused on the meanings of female gender and blackness.

The case piqued the interest of the Real Audiencia in Mexico City once its members realized that this nearby jurisdiction had not charged Afromexican tribute for ten consecutive years. Experts in the capital reviewed the case for its legal content, citing the ongoing debate about women's status in the tribute regime. Accountant for tribute Joseph Luis de los Ríos deduced from laws more than a century old that the architects of Afromexican tribute had not intended for girls under eighteen to become tributaries, reserving this status for married couples, widows and widowers, and unmarried men and women. No girls had appeared on the registers the accountant had in his possession.[72]

The beleaguered *alcalde mayor* of Tenango del Valle, Captain Juan Antonio Navarres, admitted his ignorance of the subject. His testimony typified a fatherly concern for residents of his jurisdiction, coupled with frustration at their disobedience. Far from the crazed official described by Sebastiana and Juana's lawyer, the alcalde was initially reluctant to charge female minors of any caste. He knew of fewer than twenty *mulato* tributaries, but no one among them was a young, orphaned girl. The few free people of African descent who lived in the jurisdiction formed bonds among themselves, as evidenced by a marriage contracted in 1722 between Agustín Pérez, an eighteen-year-old *mulato*, and a *morisca* named María Antonia de la Piedra. The bride-to-be was sixteen and had come to Tenango del Valle via the town of Coyoacán. The witnesses to the marriage all represented traditionally Afromexican occupations: a weaver, a coachman, and a blacksmith.[73] In contrast, Juana and Sebastiana were on their own. In this unusual situation, the alcalde had been "unable to attain any reliable evidence that there was at that time any *mulata* girl of that age, nor if she paid tribute or not." These layers of doubt and ambiguity, which so often characterized the implementation of Afromexican tribute at the local level, appear to have created some discomfort for the alcalde. He claimed that he remembered only that "with some repugnance, I charged ten reales of Salbadora María, *mulata doncella* which she says she is, for tribute in the year of [17]26 and another ten reales for the tribute in said year of the aforementioned Sebastiana María."[74]

His competing motivations lay in the balance of payments within local structures of tribute collection. Captain Navarres had to juggle his paternalistic sensibilities with his financial responsibilities to tribute creditors. He had assumed his post as *alcalde mayor* only to be served with a petition from Felipe del Barrio, a miner at Zacualpan. To pay the treasury the tributes from both Indian and free people of African descent, the alcalde borrowed from one or more guarantors (*fiadores*), who could provide funds until all tributaries had remitted their payments. Labor bosses, guild leaders, masters of servants, and even clergy could collect tribute on behalf of an official. Alcaldes then solicited certificates from Mexico City stating that payment had been made in full. Navarres found himself in a difficult position that pitted his ideology against his financial obligations. Navarres's predecessor had died without paying his tribute debts. Don Felipe del Barrio provided Navarres with a list made by the deceased mayor that detailed "the free *mulatos* and *negros* of this town who had owed him tribute, some of them for five years." Armed with this information, don Felipe approached the new mayor, "asking [him] to compel the debtors that they pay what they still owed." Discovering Sebastiana María and Juana de la Encarnación on the list of five-year delinquents, Capitan Navarres had little choice. The girls stood firm, responding that "they did not have any [receipt] nor had they paid anything."[75]

Capitan Navarres had to pay his debts, and "many times" he solicited payment from the sisters.[76] He began to feel personally attacked and maligned as the accusations against him multiplied. He resorted to the act of *depósito* so that "by this means the payment could be secured," but it is also clear that he could no longer abide the sisters' public protest. He agreed to allow twenty days during which he would let Sebastiana María try to come up with the money. "For this reason," he explained, "I only locked up said Juana in a house where she is very well, and not, as it is supposed, suffering." According to Navarres, the girls also claimed that he was attempting to overcharge them or sell them into slavery, a story they devised "with great maliciousness which is how they normally behave."[77] In the eyes of their mayor, these free people of African descent were an unwelcome presence in the town and a source of disturbance and defiance that undermined his authority.

Presenting himself as a "loyal vassal" of the crown, Navarres offered his interpretations of age, gender, *calidad*, and tributary status. He cited a decree from 1726 stating that "the Indians who were under the care (*patria potestad*) of their parents did not in the past pay tribute."[78] He went on to quote an earlier decree from Philip II that condemned such exemptions, which discouraged marriage until age twenty-five or thirty.[79] Before they were evangelized, Navarres had heard that the same people would have married as early as age twelve. Some aggravated Indians (the gender and relationships of these relatives is linguistically ambiguous) submitted legal petitions to avoid tribute, "assuring the comfort and protection" of their daughters and sisters.[80] This language vividly describes the Indian family protecting its younger members from the burdens and worries of taxation. Although he identified the presence of *doncella* Indians on the tribute register, the mayor believed that these girls needed protection that *mulatas* might not legally deserve.

Like Navarres, the *fiscal* of the Real Audiencia would base his decision on his beliefs about *calidad*, gender, and blackness, in addition to established practices in the tribute regime. According to colonial ideals, all women were legal minors under the protection of watchful male relatives who had their best interests in mind, regardless of the *calidad* of the family members.[81] *Fiscal* Prudencio Antonio de Palacios stated that there was "no reason on which to base the exemption" since "even Indian girls, being of better *calidad* and *condición*, are not exempt from paying, except where there is no custom of it."[82] Being of better "*condición*" implied a wide variety of characteristics, including the differences between nobles and plebeians.[83] In central New Spain, it primarily referred to a free or enslaved legal status among Afromexicans, as evidenced in population counts in the Valley of Mexico from the mid-seventeenth century.[84] The term could be combined with caste labels ("a *mulato condición*"), but it was usually implied through phrases like "*mulato libre*."[85] The connection with slavery as well as personal disposition allowed administrators to use *condición* to recall African slavery and connect its legacy to Afromexican women.

The *fiscal* expressed his opinions regarding the negative qualities and nature of Afromexican women. He firmly believed that Afromexican and Indian women were unequal under the tribute regime. Palacios had experience with this question, having advised Philip V on the matter a year earlier. In the resulting *real cédula* of 1728, the king had decided that it would be best if "Indian *doncellas* were registered, without paying tribute, until they are married,"[86] and that the matter would be decided based on local practice. These hallmarks of femininity—a lack of reason and protection from labor and tax obligations—were inherent in Indian women. *Mulatas*, according to administrators, lacked these qualities, embodying only the most dishonest and negative aspects of womanhood.[87]

The case brought on behalf of Sebastiana and Juana reached the highest court in New Spain not because of the few pesos in dispute, but because the case pertained to a changing way of locating and categorizing Afromexican subjects. Local administrators did not necessarily want to engage in Afromexican tribute collection, especially when they deemed it incongruous with their experience as paternalistic leaders. These opinions registered in the legal proceedings along with those of mining elites and crown lawyers. Because of the lack of agreement between local officials and fiscal bureaucrats, as well as the importance of local custom, Afromexican women remained in a kind of tributary limbo until the 1780s. They were of inferior *calidad* and *condición*, concluded administrators in the Real Hacienda, but local customs continued to dictate Afromexican women's tributary status in the early eighteenth century.

Conclusions

Family and lineage were salient features of resistance to tribute payment and registration in the first half of the eighteenth century. Families placed emphasis on their honor and connections to Indians or Spaniards, which petitioners did not see as opposed to their familial blackness. Close family relationships that crossed boundaries of time, space, and caste were evident throughout discussions of tribute in these legal documents. Tribute registration and collection had immediate, quantifiable consequences for free people of African descent, combined with the genealogical and reputational effects that tributary status created. In central New Spain, some people sought opportunities to negotiate their incorporation into the tributary category while maintaining their family and community ties to each other and people of other castes. These petitioners clashed with Bourbon accountants and attorneys seeking new tributaries and firm definitions of tributary subjecthood and *calidad*. Additionally, petitioners had to in some way address the prevailing notion that free people of African descent did not belong, either in Indian towns or in Spanish lineages. The trope of the criminal *mulato* or the vagabond also fed into these official representations of Afromexicans as people without community who did not belong anywhere but in a place of forced labor.

Determined to revive the floundering Habsburg institution and enrich royal coffers, *oidores*, accountants, and advisers in Mexico City and Spain devoted considerable energy to royal tribute. The cooperation of local agents, interpersonal relationships among free people of African descent and across castes, and ideologies of family and gender played important roles in the early Bourbon agenda of reviewing and refashioning the standing tribute policy. Closer to New Spain's major cities of Mexico and Puebla, we find evidence of officials whose diligence and detail foreshadow the great data collection projects of the era of the Caroline Reforms. As Bourbon bureaucrats gained ground, they began to envision a system of recording and collecting that would be applicable across New Spain. Their exchanges with local officials and free people of color contributed to the process by which Bourbon reformers tracked tributary subjects and defined the obligations of blackness in the second half of the century.

Bureaucratic correspondence and opinions shed light on the nature and meanings of community and *calidad* for administrators, some of whom saw blackness as a condition diminishing the need for gendered as well as genealogical privileges. These opinions directly affected the meanings of *calidad* for Afromexican tributaries and arose in response to problems that local officials encountered as they attempted to implement the new standards. Sebastiana and Juana de la Encarnación, along with their lawyer, used their gender, lack of family ties, and poverty to attempt to avoid paying tribute. Unsatisfied with their arguments, officials and bureaucrats pondered the reputation and inherent qualities of blackness as it related to femininity, orphanhood, and *calidad*. When Philip V delineated his preference for registering Indian girls before marriage, he foreshadowed the late Bourbon practice of expanding tribute registers to include even those who would not pay (young children, widows, invalids, and such). At the same time, the king preserved the previous decrees of the seventeenth century exempting Indian women from payment.[88] When the sisters in this case were not afforded the same gendered privilege, *calidad* and the legacy of slavery marked the petitioners as tributary subjects more so than did their gender.

Free people of color responded to the tribute regime's administrative renaissance in the early Bourbon period by turning to older concepts that defined family in the Ibero-Atlantic. The enduring focus on the genealogical building blocks of tributary status allowed for the repeated use of the same tribute registers to establish a family history of paying, or lack thereof. In Acatlán and Piastla, in the previous chapter, the recycling of tributaries pointed to the logic of genealogical tributary status, and the stability of tributary community. In sharp contrast, members of the small *mulato* tributary populations of Lerma and Tenango del Valle struggled to avoid what they thought was the arbitrary imposition of taxes as a new regime underwent fiscal reform. Petitioner Antonio Lopes Bolaños associated himself with direct peninsular lineage, which brought imperial privileges unavailable to most residents of New Spain. Without denying their blackness, complainants defined themselves in terms of family and belonging, whether as honorable descendants or impoverished orphans.

These cases of families who claimed tribute privileges formed part of a wider discussion about taxation, reform, and privilege in New Spain that would, in subsequent decades, profoundly influence reform projects throughout the empire. The tribute regime was a forum for consideration of obligation and status, family and blood, and belonging or otherness that placed free people of color within a discourse of *calidad*. Had ordinary people not engaged with legal representatives, magistrates, priests, neighbors, friends and family, and others in support of their exemption cases, the arguments seen in this chapter might never have arisen. Certainly the terms of the debate would have differed, had only bureaucrats or local officials become interested in the meanings and permutations of tributary *calidad*. As these case studies make clear, the connections between the tribute register, family ties, and Afromexican *calidad* were contested in the heart of New Spain. Afromexicans' ideas and arguments informed *calidad* through local relationships with their officials and through the legal process. At the same time, these two channels also imposed *calidad* as a construct to limit the potential for self-definition and to control what the Bourbon regime viewed as a discrete community of taxpayers.

The connections free Afromexicans established with Indian and Spanish family members bolstered their claims to tribute exemption. Spanning decades, the genealogies that free people of color attempted to reconstruct rested on earlier colonial principles of reciprocity, military conquest, and service. While rare, these cases offer evidence of how families deployed documented lineages to achieve their goals. Like the descendants of elite Spaniards and Indians, free people of color sought the prestige associated with an illustrious Spanish ancestor or a cacique. Some petitioners tried to sustain this link as foundlings or illegitimate children, a strategy that allowed complainants to suggest a *calidad* of mestizo or Spanish without a sole focus on genealogy as a representation of family. For the petitioners from Actopan, the strategy seems to have proved ineffectual in the face of stricter definitions of *calidad* and tributary status as well as the divides within colonial administration regarding the privileges accorded to people of unknown parentage. For the Fernández de Cabrera family and the Lopes Bolaños brothers, this strategy that went beyond the all-encompassing notions of *calidad* and caste was risky. The materials presented as evidence were decades old. Officials claimed that all these men were known as *mulatos* or *pardos* or had family members who were so reputed. Yet, these families staked their reputations on their prized possession: lineage. This was not a lineage that negated their blackness, but one that affirmed their family's honor and place in the community.

4

Imperial Knowledge and the Expansion of Tribute

Registration of new tributaries of African descent in New Spain increased dramatically in the final decades of the eighteenth century as part of a general trend toward increased revenue extraction. While the methods that made possible this expansion arose from Atlantic currents in administrative reform and Enlightenment science, the growth of tributary numbers happened locally and was the product of interactions between Afromexicans, local officials, and royal agents. Although the Real Hacienda standardized and centralized certain aspects of tribute administration, many of the complex moving parts that made up tribute remained regionally distinctive and heterogeneous. We can understand this process of becoming a tributary in this period of fiscal and administrative reform using three kinds of documentary evidence: first, laws and instructions that went out from Mexico City; second, the observations and protests local officials made in response; and, finally, the nature of the data and payments officials successfully gathered. This chapter explains the process of creating tributaries through recording practices as well as the equally critical methods of extracting their cash and keeping accounts. The main characters in many of these documents are the *mulato* vagabond, the conniving commissioner, and the hardworking but overwhelmed local magistrate. Taking these with a grain of salt, I examine this process as a series of interpersonal interactions that ultimately had economic consequences for both tributaries and collectors. Commissioners and officials considered the possibility of false perceptions and fake documents that could allow tributaries to avoid registration or payment. I then discuss the expansion of collection through more rational modes of organizing data and the rapid increase in the registered tributary population. Chapter 5 then examines the social data that bureaucrats used to understand and track tributary families toward the goal of increasing the *cajas*. Chapter 6 treats the process by which individuals and families fought to remove themselves from the tribute registers as the registers swelled with families who became first-time tributaries.

The presentation of tributary data that came out of these reforms is important to consider as well as the actual amounts collected. One of the many objectives of Bourbon bureaucrats was to implement ways of knowing and seeing colonial tributaries that reflected trends in effective administration. Following the formation of the *padrones*, names and family structures were distilled into numbers of tributaries in a given area and that area's economic output. Even when they contained no personal names or residences, compilations of tributary data quantified nuclear families and delineated social groups as distinct from others. With new methods of data visualization and counting, colonial authorities constructed, tracked, and expanded the tributary population. The introduction of printed instruments aided not only in the tracking of tributary bodies but also in the construction of the tributary subject and its representation for an imperial audience. By creating a group of subjects who were economically and reproductively beneficial to projects like revenue expansion, Bourbon reformers represented free people of color as a productive part of the colonial society. At the same time, these authorities separated tributaries from nontributaries, a key function of the tributary regime by the late eighteenth century. Accountants in Mexico City communicated tributary data using charts (*mapas*) and summaries, following the example of a Castilian census from 1754 aimed at imposing a graduated tax under the direction of Zenón de Somodevilla, marquis of Ensenada.[1] Processing and representing imperial data, accountants could render the colony as a kind of "mathematical object."[2] In this Atlantic milieu, *calidad* demonstrated the nature and profitability of people and places as well as the streamlining of more objective data. These advances eventually led to an increase in royal tribute and tributaries of African descent, although communities frequently protested the imposition of new policies and population figures.

Economic data compiled between 1768 and 1788 suggest that standardized modes of collection and presentation of information streamlined the tribute regime. Large grids were the preferred method of visualizing the patterns of collection and distribution. Administrators in the tributes section of the Real Hacienda in Mexico City reviewed and compiled data each year in an effort to keep other bureaucrats apprised of the state of accounts. Free people of color paid tribute in more than 130 jurisdictions of New Spain, in numbers ranging from just one-half tributary individual in 1771 in Acapulco to the thousands registered in the mining zones of San Luis Potosí, León, and San Miguel el Grande.[3] Although some jurisdictional boundaries occasionally changed, there were around 150 jurisdictions counted on these vast states of accounts (*estados*).[4] Between 1768 and 1777, the amount of Afromexican tribute that reached regional treasuries in Guadalajara, Mexico City, and San Luis Potosí expanded—somewhat unpredictably at the local level—by 16.5 percent (table 4.1). The numbers of tributaries who were registered in these 150 jurisdictions between 1769 and 1788 increased 18.1 percent overall and 121.5 percent among *mulato* tributaries (table 4.2). These states of ac-

Table 4.1. Estimated tribute payments in pesos from *mulatos* in New Spain, 1768–77

Year	Estimated tribute from *mulatos*[a]	Estimated tribute from all tributaries	Estimated *mulato* tribute as % of total
1768	25,711	644,378	4.0
1769	25,393	644,471	3.9
1770	30,705	685,739	4.4
1771	41,397	725,143	5.7
1772	23,286	629,343	3.7
1773	29,112	708,548	4.1
1774	28,813	684,412	4.2
1775	26,394	704,473	3.7
1776	28,762	731,241	3.9
1777	29,574	752,253	3.9

Source: Archivo General de Indias, Audiencia de México leg. 2105.
[a]Official estimates have been rounded to the nearest peso.

Table 4.2. Total tributaries registered in the Kingdom of New Spain, 1769–88 (selected years)

Year	*Indios de pueblo*	*Mulatos*	*Indios laboríos*	Totals
1769	371,567.5	11,251.5	4,463.5	387,282.5
1770	367,084.0	10,522.5	4,412.5	382,019.0
1771	399,255.0	16,029.0	4,923.0	420,207.0
1772	404,414.0	14,823.0	3,290.0	422,527.0
1773	413,956.0	20,151.5	3,117.0	437,224.5
1774	404,928.0	17,997.5	3,388.0	426,313.5
1775	412,655.5	19,338.5	3,644.5	435,638.5
1776	432,368.5	24,366.0	6,414.5	463,149.0
1777	440,970.0	25,287.5	6,378.0	472,635.5
1778	424,053.5	13,837.5	3,829.0	441,720.0
1780	435,837.5	15,764.0	4,385.0	455,986.5
1782	443,602.0	17,154.0	4,591.0	465,347.0
1783	448,927.5	18,472.0	4,926.0	472,325.5
1784	449,580.0	19,501.5	5,101.0	474,182.5
1787	418,870.5	23,521.0	13,061.0	455,452.5
1788	419,582.5	24,926.0	12,874.5	457,383.0
% change	12.9	121.5	188.4	18.1

Source: Data from Archivo General de Indias, Audiencia de México legs. 2105 and 2106.

counts were intended to provide a description of the "amount of Royal Tributes of the Kingdom of New Spain intended for collection."[5] The documents referenced a host of taxes, their status as paid or unpaid, and the number of taxpayers charged in each jurisdiction. These documents, which rationalized and compiled local tribute data, complemented the tribute register in their design and purpose. Whereas the tribute register, a space oriented toward local families and social structures, spoke to the capital, these accounts would provide an overview of potential or current taxation in an imperial context.

Bourbon Reform and Renewal

Afromexican tribute was not a newfangled invention concocted in the laboratories of the Enlightenment. Rather, Bourbon rulers inherited a morass of laws and customs pertaining to an imperial tax administered across time and space with little continuity. Methodically and through repeated consultation across offices in the Real Hacienda, bureaucrats discussed the merits of petitions and potential projects under a kind of "collegial supervision" by committees like the Junta Superior de Real Hacienda.[6] These were not arbitrary decisions made hastily or without considerable debate and discussion. Reforms of this period emerged from conflict and a chorus of opinions rather than a single paradigm imposed from above.[7] Like other Bourbon reforms, the adjustments and new projects in the Real Hacienda reflected Atlantic ideas and negotiated outcomes dependent on a variety of interested groups. Major changes in the policies of the tribute regime originated with particular individuals as well as internal debates within the Real Hacienda. These late colonial influential figures included bureaucrats and accountants, among them Juan Ordóñez and Juan Domingo Lombardini, and reformers José de Gálvez and Juan Vicente de Güemes Pacheco de Padilla, who wielded power over tribute from their posts as *visitador general* (general inspector) and viceroy, respectively. The efforts on the part of Bourbon reformers to better manage and define Afromexican tribute resulted in valuable data on the scope and location of communities. This information would assist in the eventual collection of tribute and was crucial to a larger project of extending greater control over the lives of the king's colonial subjects.

The registration of Afromexican subjects and the collection of tribute expanded more rapidly in the final decades of the eighteenth century because of the successful implantation of reforms and new methods during the reigns of Charles III (1759–88) and Charles IV (1788–1808). The reigns of Philip V (1700–1746) and Ferdinand VI (1746–59) had provided templates for the development of methods of population registration that gave monarchs greater access to their subjects in Spain and its colonies.[8] Classic scholarship has recognized the far-reaching effects of fiscal and military expansion after 1763, paying particular attention to the crucial role of men like José de Gálvez, while other historians describe the reforms of Charles III's reign as a kind of "methodical incrementalism."[9] Although reforms to tribute were certainly not wholesale or abrupt, Bourbon bureaucrats during Charles III's reign did turn their attention to new and innovative ways of organizing data and effectively incorporating families further into the colonial regime. Quantitative data show the success of expanding Afromexican tribute, and repeated communication with local authorities demonstrates the impact of the reforms on the practices of alcaldes across New Spain. As entries on registers multiplied and amounts collected soared, tribute became an increasingly onerous institution for free people of color as Bourbon reformers sought to maximize revenue.

Reform projects sometimes ended in compromise, owing to the many local allegiances and specificities on the ground as well as differing opinions within the Real Hacienda itself. Indeed, many of the ambitious projects proposed during the reigns of Charles III and Charles IV revealed the "divergent ideological underpinnings of the reformers themselves" and their desire to avoid damaging confrontations with local elites.[10] This was true of tribute bureaucrats, though perhaps on a smaller, more procedural stage. Bureaucrats made a series of attempts to rationalize what had become a "tangled and fossilized system"[11] that continued and intensified in the Caroline period. For example, in 1753, *contador* Jose Rodríguez Gallardo argued before the Real Audiencia that the diversity of payment schedules and rates led to confusion among tributaries and officials. This was detrimental to tribute collection among Indians, who could not be accurately assessed and were paying at rates that were not regulated from the capital.[12] An experienced reformer, he took up this post in the capital after serving as a *visitador general* in Sonora and Sinaloa, where he had attempted to implement ambitious reforms, including harsh policies against Seri Indians.[13] Still, at the end of the century, Indians paid dozens of regionally variable rates based on long-standing customs and fears of local authorities that innovations would spark unrest. Reforms and proposed projects at midcentury were not always precursors to later practices of the Real Hacienda in New Spain or Spanish America.[14] Some solutions, especially those that involved introducing royal tribute where there was no custom of payment from free *mulatos*, met with skepticism. Other changes represented temporary measures to address immediate problems, rather than implement a logical, methodical series of reforms. Between 1777 and 1779, collection ceased in Mexico City's vast *parcialidades* of San Juan and Santiago owing to the high costs of collection.[15] The use of double-entry bookkeeping, introduced in the 1780s, met with opposition and conservative criticism.[16] While the reform process was gradual and encumbered by many conflicting methods, the push to centralize and rationalize the collection of data would eventually lead to a remarkable uptick in Afromexican tribute in certain jurisdictions and provinces of New Spain.

One of the central figures in New Spain's tribute reforms was *visitador general* and later minister of the Indies José de Gálvez. On completing his *visita* of 1764–72, Gálvez expressed concern that royal tributes did not represent the single greatest source of income for the Real Hacienda. Gálvez wrote that Indians, free *negros* and *mulatos*, and other *castas* "should pay [tribute] in recognition of their vassalage, and of the kind protection that the greatest and most pious monarch in the world provides them."[17] However justified the reforms seemed to the *visitador general*, the policies required force to carry out owing to their unpopularity with Indians and free people of color. In response to aggressive reforms, including the expulsion of the Jesuits, rebellions sprang up in 1766 and 1767 in the mines of Guanajuato and San Luis Potosí. Tribute played a role in further unrest in Valladolid, when rumors circulated that rates of payment might change and that *pardo* tributaries would no longer be refunded if overcharged.[18] Tributaries in Guanajuato, San Luis Potosí, and Valladolid paid elevated tributes as punishment for participation in uprisings in 1766 and 1767, revolts that had arisen, in part, over objections to tribute increases.[19] Ordinary people in New Spain resisted reform projects on occasion, though these localized uprisings were not nearly as destructive as the upheavals taking place in Peru and New Granada.[20] Although it hindered the implementation of reforms, this limited violence never posed a serious threat to the long-term administration of tribute.

Rebellions met with a combination of responses meant to quash the uprising and identify its true causes. Gálvez ordered harsh punishments, including gruesome public executions, for hundreds of those who had participated in the rebellions.[21] He also imposed a ban in Guanajuato on Indian men wearing "Spanish cloaks, causing them to be confused with mestizos, *mulatos*, and other castes" under pain of one hundred lashes. Indian women who failed to use their "own dress of *huipiles*" would be publicly stripped. The same directive went to *mulatos*, who were accused of using Indian clothing to alter their tributary status and "defraud the Real Hacienda." Officials agreed with the restrictions for *mulatos*, who had been able to achieve lower rates of tribute and avoid *alcabalas* by posing as Indians. But *fiscal* of the Real Hacienda Ramón Posada y Soto cautioned against preventing Indians from adopting Spanish styles. He saw the restrictions as detrimental to the long-term goal of encouraging Indians to wear Spanish clothing in the hope of bolstering colonial manufactures and "enriching the peninsula."[22] Free people of color would continue to be targeted as potential imposters, while Indians were a possible source of economic expansion through their participation in markets. Posada y Soto echoes the prediction of reformer José del Campillo y Cossío that Indian consumers thoroughly integrated into a rejuvenated economic system would provide new markets for Spanish products. According to Posada y Soto, Indians given access to Spanish manufactures would "leave behind their dress in favor of ours."[23] Here, the broader program of trade revitalization and reform intersected with a recent legacy of popular protests to tributary impositions. Even if some of the restrictions were lifted on rebellious Indians, one way or another, the Real Hacienda and metropolitan interests would profit from tributary subjects.

From his post as minister of the Indies (1776–87), Gálvez later oversaw a sweeping change to the administration of New Spain: the introduction of the intendancy. Reformers sought to impose new units of administration known as "intendancies" that would replace the colonial hodgepodge of provinces and kingdoms in the Americas. The system placed power in the hands of intendants from Spain, rather than creole appointees. The process of implementing the intendancy suffered multiple false starts and fierce opposition, but the new system prevailed. The Ordinance of Intendants, promulgated in Peru and New Spain in 1784 and 1786, respectively, reorganized colonial administration by limiting the powers of the viceroy, removing local officials, and creating new units of territorial division. Within the Real Hacienda, the Ordinance of Intendants (1786) restructured the responsibilities of individual branches, their organization, and their modes of accounting.[24] While these reforms promoted centralization and the incorporation of more subjects into the tax regime, they also created nodes of local authority under intendants in far-flung regions of the viceroyalty.[25] These intendants and subdelegates might mirror the former positions of the *alcaldes mayores*, but they were to receive increased resources to foster tribute collection and registration. In the capital, this ordinance would create a system of supervision to better regulate the administration of revenue through unified procedures and a clear chain of authority.[26] These administrative changes placed tribute at the center of multiple discussions of the problems with colonial rule and strategies for enriching the empire. The ordinance reevaluated militia privileges, reinforced bureaucratic separation between social groups, and introduced new methods and challenges to tribute and taxation.

For tributaries, one of the notable changes to administration was the attempt to do away with the figure of the *alcalde mayor* and replace him with an intendant, a salaried official who, in theory, would be less prone to embezzling tributary monies.[27] In 1774, Gálvez had recommended that every three years, the proposed intendants, commissioners, or subdelegates would review the "accounts of tributaries, keeping separate the Indians, *negros libres*, *mulatos*, and other castes."[28] However, attempts to replace *alcaldes mayores* with *alcaldes ordinarios* or subdelegates resulted in much the same setup as had previously existed. Subdelegates, also underpaid and overstretched, would not be able to personally oversee every aspect of tribute collection any more so than could the *alcaldes mayores* and appointed lieutenants to assist them.[29] In this aspect of tribute administration, the attempt to exercise greater control was unsuccessful. This ordinance also altered procedures for tributaries who wished to contest their status. Before 1786, cases were settled in local courts or at a tribunal devoted to tribute cases, overseen by the viceroy.[30] Under the Ordinance of Intendants, commissioners were unable to change the tribute registers once they were completed, reserving this power for the Contaduría General de Retasas in the capital. Therefore, though tributary identities depended on local reputations, the power to alter them officially rested with bureaucrats in the capital.

The Ordinance of Intendants made recommendations for tribute practices that were under scrutiny in previous decades. One of these was the elimination of the category of the half tributary for adult men. Officials in the Real Hacienda had already recommended more attention to Afromexican occupations and livelihoods, the legal status of spouses, and the category of the half tributary as it applied to *mulatas* in particular. In the 1760s, José Rodríguez Gallardo, the *contador general de reales tributos*, argued that this category had a deleterious effect on the royal treasuries. He argued for a reform to the practices of setting rates of tribute as well as registers of tributaries, with special attention to Afromexican men and women. First, the *contador* recommended the application of a law now hundreds of years old, which never seemed to function. This was the obligation of the *amos* who were to monitor Afromexican workers and were "charged with paying on their behalf."[31] Second, the practice of composing a single tributary unit out of various half tributaries seemed illogical to Rodríguez Gallardo. He cited the practice of charging two pesos in tribute for "the free *negra* or *mulata* who is married to an enslaved *mulato* or *negro* . . . from which it can be inferred that the two pesos are charged by head and not based on the unit of husband and wife." According to the *contador*, such a situation would render Afromexican women "more privileged, and by extension their husbands, than Indians" who paid double this rate.[32] His opinions resonated with Antonio Joaquín Rivadeneira y Barrientos, a prominent *fiscal* and later *oidor*. Breaking with earlier laws that defined an Afromexican tributary unit as a married couple, both men advocated for a higher rate of tribute based on individual contributions from men and women. Forcing tributaries to stay with *amos* and, in some cases, doubling rates of tribute would increase the intake of the Real Hacienda. But part of the problem in counting and tracking, observed another official in the Real Hacienda, lay with the "*justicias* and *agentes fiscales* who make [the lists] without any other information than age and marital status of tributaries without recording the *condición*, occupation, or trade of these people."[33] Without the broad distribution of detailed recording instruments, there could be no real conformity between local agents of tribute, such as *alcaldes mayores* and commissioners, and Mexico City bureaucrats and magistrates examining tributary practices on behalf of the Real Hacienda or the Real Audiencia.

Decades later, the Ordinance of Intendants proposed a new system of counting that eliminated the half tributary category among unmarried men and exogamous couples. This measure would supposedly stop discouraging tributaries from marrying, but imposition of a single tax rate met with opposition from the treasury.[34] In 1788, the Junta Superior de Real Hacienda ruled that enforcing a new standard of taxation went against locally determined privileges and rates. Disrupting this long-standing tradition would result in Indian protests.[35] These privileges arose from a legal tradition of negotiation and justice that accommodated local elites and, ideally, eased the tributary burden on ordinary people. The tradition of *tasación*—the process of evaluating the ability of a community to pay a certain rate of tribute—was the basis of forming new registers. Bureaucrats wary of political and economic strife opted for changes in certain districts, rather than a complete reformulation of the rate of tribute.

The question of the half tributary category was directly linked to the ambiguous status of women in the tribute regime. A clear policy did not exist for much of the eighteenth century. Occasionally collection from women was suspended while attorneys and accountants reviewed the various contradictory laws that had piled up.[36] Many tribute commissioners prioritized the family unit as a source of income and often omitted individuals, such as unmarried women, whose tributary status was uncertain. Juan de Villalba y Velázquez, a *corregidor* from Querétaro, wrote to the Real Audiencia in Mexico City in 1781 to complain that royal authorities wanted to register free women of color as tributaries, "against the established custom."[37] A 1758 royal decree had already granted tribute exemption to Indian women. Another order in 1763 stated that any free *mulatas* married to enslaved men would pay tribute.[38] Such a policy challenged the logic of the half tributary as a person married to a member of an exempt group, as enslaved people were not charged tribute. By 1786, following an investigation by the Real Audiencia, Charles III extended the privilege of exemption to Afromexican women.[39] This decision was possible in part because the potential loss of these tributes would not be very great, and the Audiencia sought to portray Afromexican women as impoverished and in need of protection from avaricious alcaldes.[40] Free people of color who were registered as tributaries "are all, in general, unhappily reduced to living by a meager wage, if they can get it, or to begging." Touching on the rhetoric of paternalism and protection, the Audiencia described unmarried Afromexican women as "poorer than Indian women, because they usually have plots or properties that once belonged to their husbands or fathers."[41] Poverty and protection were two established themes in discussions of tribute exemption that were not broadly applied to Afromexican women until nearly thirty years after the exemption for their Indian counterparts.

Although women would avoid collection based on their gender, other protected groups were forced to jealously defend their exemptions. Local and regional privileges came under scrutiny as bureaucrats sought new and underutilized sources of revenue. These regional variations were especially notable on the coasts, where large Afromexican populations had gained corporate militia exemptions, and in mining regions. Gálvez responded to a request by elites in Guanajuato that workers in the mines be exempted from tribute. Writing to the king, Gálvez warned that "if, in the royal mines, tribute is not charged of Indians and other castes who should pay it, the surrounding provinces, and even the more remote ones, will be deserted to the detriment of settlement and agriculture."[42] The Ordinance of Intendants would echo this sentiment, extending tribute to mine workers, cattle ranchers, and others who worked in Spanish settlements.[43] The retraction of tribute privileges among the *pardo* militia units was contested and did not dramatically change the exemptions of many companies through the 1780s. During the late eighteenth century, some authorities in Mexico City advocated curbing special privileges and exemptions and targeted the militias in particular.[44] The Real Hacienda reevaluated regional tribute privileges for Indian groups as well, with the exception of the Tlaxcalans, who were singled out in the Ordinance of Intendants as protected from tribute indefinitely.[45] The latter half of the century was a time of intense debate within the tribute regime regarding the merits of corporate exemptions. Yet, the preference for continuity in law and local custom prevented radical reforms to tribute for much of the period. It was not until the arrival of Viceroy Revillagigedo that the *pardo* militiamen lost many of their regional tribute privileges.

On his installment as viceroy in 1789, Revillagigedo began one of the most influential reform programs to tribute. He orchestrated downsizing of the *pardo* militias, thereby stripping them of any tribute privileges they had accrued.[46] Under his leadership, revenues continued to expand and ambitious new programs were put into effect. He was also a principal architect of the most complete census of the colonial period, which also employed forms and instructions to achieve accurate population counts. Although one of its detractors critiqued the labeling of some of the columns, and ordinary people feared the implementation of a census in order to extract more taxes, the census provided vital information for the colonial government.[47] In 1794, Revillagigedo wrote that at the beginning of his appointment, he had found tribute collection "in great decline" in Mexico City. In 1790, new regulations were put in place for a registration of free people of color in the capital that would result in collection from "without exception all those who because of their appearance, trade, or dress seem to be tributaries."[48] This proposal occasioned fierce debates, discussed in chapter 6, but the end result of these policies was to impose tribute on large swaths of the population of the capital. By 1793, the amount of tribute had doubled as a result of targeting migratory tributaries who lived and worked in and around the city.[49] Often remembered as a rational, enlightened, and pioneering statesman, Revillagigedo nonetheless had little regard for the concerns of ordinary people and the burdens of tributary status. As viceroy his concern was the success of New Spain as a colony of Spain and of its subjects as the most economically integrated and productive as possible. Although mindful of the need to preserve a sustainable relationship across the Atlantic, he believed that New Spain was "a colony which ought to depend on its origin, Spain, and to deal some profit in return from the benefits of protection."[50]

Under the direction of Revillagigedo, the "Ordinance for the Formation of Visitations, Censuses, and Rates of Tributaries of New Spain" (1793) aimed to further reform and standardize the process of collecting tribute from, and allowing exemptions for, Indians and free people of African descent.[51] In some ways similar to the recent population census, this didactic document contained new instruments for counting and prioritized categories that would preserve genealogical information, family ties, and *calidad*. The Council of the Indies had found it well within the bounds of the king's largesse to relieve unmarried women of African descent in New Spain from royal tribute.[52] Yet, the *calidad* and lineage a woman maintained in her community would continue to influence the designation of tributary status for her children. The ordinance of 1793 stipulated that no Indian or Afromexican woman "should pay, nor be placed in a half-tributary category; but nevertheless, they should be noted in the columns corresponding to the reserved class" of tributaries excused from payment but not of an exempt *calidad*.[53] Commissioners selected and created tributary subjects who met prevailing standards of patriarchal family construction. Some officials avoided unmarried women altogether, following local custom or their personal ambivalence about disrupting the paternalistic authority that allowed them to protect vulnerable community members. These ordinances envisioned tribute as a method of data collection, a symbol of integration of local populations into the Spanish Empire, and as a means of imperial finance.

Reorganizing information, bureaucrats reasoned, would yield greater Hacienda income; in the process, these statistical methods generated data that grouped free people of African descent into specific units spatially and socially. The men who created lists of tributary families had, for centuries, situated Afromexican individuals and how they supposedly lived and associated with others in their communities.[54] Bourbon administrators wanted to know who lived together in order to count tributary units and certify *calidad* at the local level. Registers mapped kinship and family relationships as part of an administrative "management of reality."[55] The proliferation of tribute registers, and especially their translation into printed grids, was part of a larger process in which states placed increasing value on numbers. In the sphere of Atlantic administration, in particular, the efficiency of data collection, the centrality of numeracy, and the need for visual representations such as charts were on the rise at the turn of the nineteenth century.[56] For peninsular and colonial administrators, seeing tribute through a grid, chart, or table fundamentally changed the portrait of tributary community.

For ordinary people, the register was the treasury's push for compliance with an onerous tax and an oppressive caste hierarchy, but, through a range of complaints and appeals, some families pushed back. Mistaken registration, a commonplace occurrence throughout New Spain, led to hundreds of court cases and petitions that fiscal authorities sought to prevent by standardizing tribute and centralizing its administration firmly in the capital. While this procedure fit the logic of Bourbon reform, it had markedly negative effects on tributaries who sought justice. Chronically underpaid and understaffed, the officials in the fiscal bureaucracy were under pressure to audit and review hundreds of account books as well as petitions.[57] The expectation that the treasury would seriously consider and sometimes grant temporary relief or permanent exemption demonstrated its interest in maintaining a public perception as a just and fair body.[58] For bureaucrats, a smooth, regularized process of collection and registration was preferable to the highly contested, halting series of interactions that were the reality of tribute collection and registration. The Ordinance of Intendants and the Ordinance for the Formation of Visitations from 1793 were targeted reforms that also regularized legal procedures and vocabularies for dealing with tribute complaints. Tributaries, and some local officials unhappy with demands emanating from Mexico City, saw the widening net of tributary status as an unwelcome sign of their obligations and precarious position vis-à-vis colonial government.

Procedures and Realities

An imaginary *mulato*, "Feliciano de tal," and his wife, "N. Española," were written into existence on a grid that Revillagigedo and his advisers developed to complement Article 134 of the Ordinance of Intendants. In this idealized process of tribute registration and collection, Feliciano would have received notice via a public proclamation in his hometown that he must see a tribute commissioner in person to be registered or face eight days in jail along with any other free people of African descent who "would hide themselves or maliciously delay the completion" of the register.[59] He was not to approach the commissioner with any extra gifts to try to influence the process of registration. The purpose of these measures was to prevent habitual fraud and flight on the part of tributaries as well as commissioners, who might be tempted into taking bribes in the form of money, food, or other gifts. The commissioner would work with other authorities in the town who knew Feliciano, such as a priest or an *hacendado*, and had access to his official records (birth certificates, marriage licenses, and the like).[60] With the full cooperation of the ideal vassal, diligent local officials, and unbiased royal officials, information would be compiled in an orderly fashion.

Once the accurate and current register was complete, the commissioner would leave it with a local magistrate or subdelegate, who would then orchestrate collection on the basis of this document three times a year in April, August, and

December. The alcalde or one of his representatives (*comisarios*) would come to the residence of each registered Afromexican tributary and collect a "moderate" amount of twenty-four reales from married adults and unmarried men, or one peso roughly every four months.[61] Feliciano might live in a tiny pueblo, in the head town at the center of local administration (*cabecera*), or with other tributaries on a hacienda. Wherever he and his family lived, they would all be present and accounted for when the collector came. Loyal to his king and ready to demonstrate his rootedness in his community, the fictional Feliciano would dutifully pay cash. Once tribute was paid, he might receive a written *carta de pago*, or receipt. Alternatively, he might make the payment for no other reason than to avoid jail time that awaited "any tributary who resists, hides, or attempts to evade payment."[62] If Feliciano possessed a written document explaining that his ancestors never paid tribute, and three witnesses were willing to verbally attest to the veracity of the claim, Feliciano could avoid registration and future payments.[63] While there were jurisdictions that adhered to these procedures in the late eighteenth and early nineteenth centuries, there were ample opportunities for this orderly process to unravel.

A tribute official beating an innocent child with a cane, a bankrupt alcalde fleeing his post to parts unknown, a wily neighbor penning a false list of tributaries for official use—the archive preserves examples of all these alternative outcomes to the process of collection and registration that reformers envisioned. Bourbon reformers, and above all José de Gálvez, attempted to diminish the power of corrupt local officials and the possibilities for wrongdoing by appointing evenhanded and decorous "Judges commissioned for the Registers of Tributaries."[64] The men commissioned to evaluate or create tributary registers were not a defined group. They could be anyone worthy of the "greatest confidence" of the intendant.[65] Unlike the *alcaldes mayores*, commissioners were assured a salary of three pesos per working day. This compensation assumed that he reviewed thirty-five whole tributaries per day, whose existence he verified either in person or through a worthy intermediary. Additional funds were available for lengthy travels.[66] Commissioners also had the assistance of local officials, language interpreters, priests, neighbors, and old registers to assist them in keeping accurate records. In 1789, commissioners and interpreters were paid in total 5,647 pesos for the creation of new registers.[67] Commissioners were expected to revise these registers every five years, taking careful notes of recent births, deaths, marriages, or absences of new or current tributaries. In any given community, tributaries might include free people of African descent, *vagos*, *indios laboríos*, and Indians in towns, although distinctions were often made only between the *indios de pueblo* and everyone else. As community outsiders appointed at higher levels of a renovated bureaucracy, these commissioners presumably could avoid the temptations of graft and the constraints of local politics in their unbiased construction of tributary instruments.

Unfortunately, some of these tribute commissioners did more than enough to inspire revulsion and fear in the communities they visited. In the first place, their lack of attachment to the community and disregard for local affairs often made them careless or ineffective. Second, the position seems to have attracted vindictive or violent people given over to public displays of punishment. One Andrés Gordoa, assigned to renew a register in Coatepec, caused a scandal when he took offense to a young Indian man who did not remove his sombrero in the presence of a commissioner. Gordoa promptly grabbed the youth by the hair and began beating him with a staff over his chest, "without regard for being in the cemetery when mass was beginning."[68] News spread of a commissioner in Huichapam who had attacked the son of an Indian official with a staff and threatened to beat others causing a public outcry that was only put down through the negotiations of the sheriff.[69] The images of the malevolent Spanish official in the town of hapless Indians was a widespread strategy in many petitions, but complainants narrated these events in such detail that some kind of abuse likely did occur.

Other visits by commissioners caused scandals through rumor, gossip, and damage to reputations, if not to physical bodies. In 1799, José Ortega Terradillos, a tribute commissioner, arrived unannounced in Xilotepec, some fifty miles north of Mexico City. Disregarding any official procedure, he received a series of "anonymous lists" of tributaries provided by a "wicked and bad-tempered" individual. Whoever penned the document named a local magistrate and his family as well as others who had historically enjoyed exemption for reasons of *calidad*. According to the complainant Alejandro Antonio Sánchez, the commissioner "proceeded with such flippancy and hastiness" that he seemingly made no effort to investigate this unverified and highly controversial document. He then went so far as to publicly call the names of the new tributaries, causing uproar and fueling gossip. Furthering the public uproar, the lists went "running through the town" to such an extent that "no one [could] ignore how many families have been unjustly damaged." Some of those accused were able to officially support their *calidad* through the procedures of Article 25 of the 1793 ordinance, which placed the responsibility of judging such complaints in the hands of the Junta Superior de Real Hacienda in Mexico City. Less fortunate residents were unable to take such measures because of their complete poverty and "continued unjustly registered." Outraged, the magistrate sent a complaint to Viceroy Miguel José de Azanza denouncing the new commissioner for his "pride and despotism." This "contemptible being" had impugned the reputations of many and was attempting to extort further funds from caciques.[70] The commissioner resorted to unsubstantiated rumors without examining the intricate hierarchies that tributary status and public reputation had built. The power to declare exemptions had been centralized for decades, and the Junta Superior continued to reserve for itself the final say in "understanding or declaring exempt" the *calidad* of any person, even if they had not been previously registered.[71] In this light, the commissioner appears not as a negotiator but as an agent of the Real Hacienda whose prerogative it was to expand the registers but not arbitrate who could be excluded from registration.

The shoddy work of commissioner José Ortega Terradillos came under scrutiny again in the course of an investigation in nearby Huichapam that considered the "lack of fixed residence that the *mulato* tributaries have." By Ortega Terradillos's documentation, the total amount that the subdelegate should have collected was 673 pesos for *mulato* tributaries, but he could only scrape together 548. If they could not collect from a highly mobile population, the responsibility of local officials was to determine and report a number of *vagos* in their jurisdictions and provide sworn testimony as to the situation.[72] To justify this discrepancy, a local judge brought witnesses to explain that "the class of *mulato* tributaries of this district [of Huichapam, Xilotepec] is in general made up of arrogant vagabonds with no formal residence that regularly work as servants to muleteers and as cowhands on haciendas and others doing nothing." Such a group of people, modeled exactly on previous tropes of the *mulato* vagabond discussed elsewhere in this book, provided an acceptable excuse for local officials who had not managed to charge an amount that reflected the current tribute registers. A past tribute collector and *vecino* of the town confirmed that collecting all the tributes corresponding to the register was simply impossible because he had never been able to find the people. These extremely crafty and irresponsible people, claimed another witness, "only end up in debt to their *amos* and then flee." As highly "dispersed" people without residence that was known to any collector, the *mulatos* of the area earned their living in mining, ranching, and transport, thus according themselves a freedom of mobility that frustrated tribute collectors and worried fiscal bureaucrats.

For the free Afromexicans who lived there, Huichapam offered them labor that would have been, at times, dangerous and difficult but also provided them with the means to move from place to place if they so chose. If the rate the Real Hacienda was attempting to collect—more than six hundred pesos a year—was anywhere near correct, then there were likely hundreds of free people of African descent nearby. This community appears to have been difficult to access for collectors and commissioners, suggesting that these free Afromexicans may have had greater control over the terms of their subjecthood or their *calidad*. Faced with a group of "dispersed" people who were difficult to reach, commissioner José Ortega Terradillos took considerable license with his task of creating tribute registers. According to witnesses, he made no effort to create "legitimate and truthful" lists, opting instead to copy names from previous lists without "seeking to inform himself if they exist." Even some of these had been on the previous register but had never paid previous collectors, either because they were absent or officials could not locate their residences. One of the witnesses in the account charged that "the commissioners, in the interest of not diminishing the numbers on their register, have put on it [names] from the previous list without stopping to determine whether many of the people were absent and their residences unknown." Another remarked that even when commissioners did "dispatch representatives to the markets of the royal mines to see if there they could find them [the *mulatos*], they return having achieved nothing." Clearly, Ortega Terradillos had no desire to personally go to the markets or employ someone else to seek out Afromexican shepherds and cowboys. Ultimately, the failure and finger-pointing arose from the uninspired methods of the commissioner, an outsider with little commitment to the veracity of the tribute register and plenty to gain from inflating the lists.[73]

The tribute registers were the guides collectors used to extract payment from families based on diverse rates determined based on geography and *calidad*. Although the Ordinance of Intendants and the Real Hacienda developed standard rates and explanations, distinct local customs and rates remained. Among Indians, there were more than fifty rates of payment from across New Spain in the eighteenth century, from just four reales to twenty-four reales, although sixteen and a half reales was common.[74] The Ordinance of Intendants established the rate of Indian tribute at sixteen reales and the tribute of free *negros* and *mulatos* at twenty-four reales.[75] In practice, these rates were not generalized at all. In Mexico City, the tax applied to married and unmarried couples at deflated rates: an Indian man married to a *parda* would pay 14.5 reales; a *pardo* married to an Indian woman would pay two pesos and 2.5 reales; and unmarried *pardos* would pay one peso and four reales.[76] A register of "Indians, *mulatos*, and other individuals of tributary caste," from the mining region of Zacualpan, charged married Indian couples eighteen reales and married *mulato* couples twenty, although a *mulato* half tributary paid twelve reales rather than ten. The system became more complex for exogamous couples, who were counted each at the same rate as a half tributary and then added together. The scribe noted that "the *mulato* married to an Indian pays twenty-one *reales*, twelve for himself and nine for his wife."[77] In contrast, an Indian man married to a *mulata* paid the same rate of twenty-one reales, contributing nine for himself and twelve for his wife.[78] Even when rates of tribute were irregular, collectors and commissioners often relied on the standard logic of the two halves of the tributary whole.

An inquiry into rates of payment in the town of Maquili in the jurisdiction of Motines, Valladolid, in 1801 provides an example of this reasoning. Enslaved Africans as well as Filipinos had worked in ranching and cacao production in this area, and by 1800 there were 165 Afromexican whole tributaries in Motines.[79]

Juan Ordóñez, head accountant in the Real Hacienda, explained that a married *mulato* couple in any part of Valladolid should be charged sixteen reales in royal tributes plus four more to be designated as *servicio real.* Half tributaries who were unmarried only owed eight reales for tribute, technically, but they were still required to contribute four more as their *servicio*. Ordóñez instructed officials in Motines to charge a *mulato* or *mulata* married to an Indian "as if he were unmarried," that is, twelve reales. The customary rates in the town of Maquili were 18.5 reales from every whole tributary, which included nine from cacao, 4.5 as the equivalent of the half *fanega* of corn, four for the *servicio real*, and another real to fund public legal insurance (*ministros*) and hospitals. Translating these rates to fit the logic of the *mulato* half tributary, Ordóñez wrote that a couple made up of an Indian and a *mulato* would have to pay twenty-one reales and three *granos* because the Indian spouse would be charged half the town's normal rate, but the *mulato* or *mulata* would pay a general rate of twelve reales to be charged throughout Valladolid. This revision made sense, Ordóñez explained, based in part on the visual demarcation of half tributaries on tributary registers.[80] The logics of the register and collection lined up and reinforced the legitimacy and rationality of tribute collection from intertwined populations and across *calidad*.

The men who collected tribute from free people of African descent were members of different castes and positions. Spanish governors and magistrates often led these efforts, employing others to help them locate tributary residences and collect small amounts of money door to door.[81] This system, though it made tribute collection more feasible, was poorly regulated according to bureaucrats in the capital who complained that some assistant collectors were "useless, and if they know how to read, they don't know how to write."[82] Indian officials might also collect Afromexican tribute in the absence of or in concert with a designated Spanish official. Afromexican men participated in the process as sources of oral information crucial for locating tributaries and as collectors themselves. In the second half of the seventeenth century, for example, free people of African descent were employed as collectors of tribute from Indians in Yucatán and Guatemala.[83] Corporate structures like guilds and militias also carried out tax collection, provided the group was not exempt.[84] *Amos* and employers were responsible for paying on behalf of their servants. The revenue was passed from the local level to regional treasuries. Monies deposited in the *cajas* were recorded in separate books from the registers of tributaries.[85] Like other aspects of public administration, tribute continued to use the medieval Iberian system of accounting of "*cargo y data*" (charge and discharge), which specified the amounts of money each official collected and remitted, the number of tributaries, and the jurisdiction.[86] These records were important for the functioning of the treasuries and allowed local officials to prove that they had followed the requirements of the current tribute register or provided an explanation for what had gone wrong.

The expected revenues required by the Real Hacienda were based on the tribute registers in advance of actual collection, which could lead to significant delays and investigations into the practices of local authorities. For their efforts in the difficult task of collection, Article 132 of the Ordinance of Intendants compensated the *alcalde ordinario* or subdelegate with 5 percent of the total collection and Indian officials with 1 percent.[87] Therefore, any compensation a local official could expect to receive depended on his success and the efficacy of his emissaries to Afromexican homes. Officials complained of the great costs of travel, especially in the large jurisdictions containing profitable mines, prompting the Real Hacienda to grant them 9 percent of their collection to cover expenses.[88] In 1788, alcalde Francisco Ballesteros received 862 pesos to compensate him for expenses incurred charging 612 Afromexican whole tributaries, as well as thousands of Indians, in Cuautla Amilpas.[89] Prior to the establishment of the intendancies, *alcaldes mayores* were often beleaguered by debts and obligations and had to offer guarantees of payments on many of the materials necessary for tribute collection, including paper.[90] As a longtime practice, the *alcaldes mayores* had one or more *fiadores* (guarantors) who were registered and known to the government along with the amounts they were each able to pay on the alcalde's behalf for the price of expected tributes.[91] The Real Hacienda had suffered great losses owing to its inability to depend on the incoming revenues from many indebted local magistrates.[92] The Ordinance of Intendants sought to remedy these chronic problems by implementing uniform rates of compensation and clear expectations for the work of commissioners and collectors.

The specter of ever-expanding registers haunted cash-strapped local authorities and vulnerable workers and registered within the Real Hacienda itself. Some bureaucrats became concerned with the detrimental effect that wholesale registration might have on unfortunate people who were not "of a tributary caste" but nevertheless would be "damaged in their reputation and interests" by overzealous registration efforts. Accountant for the Real Hacienda Juan Ordóñez observed that "for the Real Hacienda, it would be best to indiscriminately register as tributaries all who have the aspect and dress of a tributary while alleging *calidad*" and later force them to prove their lineage before the intendant.[93] However, this would have been an undue burden on many people registered as tributaries who were not in a position to make the journey or otherwise form a petition. While some commissioners clearly had no regard for people who were, to them, strangers and social inferiors, the consequences of tributary status were not lost on other agents of the Real Hacienda.

Each time an official charged Afromexican tribute or created its associated registers, he made choices about his constituents' *calidad* and that of their families. *Calidad* and tributary status were the product of multiple decisions made over a lifetime, by subjects, local officials, family and community members, clergy, the courts, and through other interpersonal relationships. Relationships between local agents and tributaries were often the primary determinants of tributary status, especially when written documentation regarding past registration, family history, or a detailed genealogy was scarce. Petitioners frequently complained that their interests did not align with those of the commissioner, who had sometimes allegedly insulted the reputations of taxpayers (*contribuyentes*) or local officials. The solutions to these problems, from the perspective of treasury bureaucrats, lay in streamlined methods and rational engineering that would continue to smooth the wrinkles out of the tributary regime and root the meanings of *calidad* in recognizable categories.

Grids, Columns, and the Restructuring of Registers

In their sweeping account of the history of the Real Hacienda, Fabián Fonseca and Carlos de Urrutia wrote that "the multitudinous masses of Mexico can be reduced to two classes, one exempt . . . and the other tributary." Tributaries included *negros*, *mulatos*, *lobos*, and other people of mixed ancestry, and the authors noted that it was "very important to distinguish the tributaries from those who were not or whose status was in doubt so that collection could be kept current."[94] Toward this end, local officials and bureaucrats in the Real Hacienda separated tributary subjects and visually represented them in tribute summaries to be archived in Seville (figure 4.1). In the name of speeding collection and amplifying revenue, Bourbon reformers managed to elevate the numbers of free people of color on tribute registers as well as squeeze an unprecedented amount of cash from some of these communities from the 1780s until the end of the colonial era. In turn, a primary divide across colonial society between tributary and nontributary functioned as a barrier to a potential breakdown of social categories that were increasingly difficult to establish with fixity at the turn of the nineteenth century.

Tribute registers and summaries were part of a wider process of imperial knowledge-making and visual representation of nature undertaken by bureaucrats, scientists, and travelers in the Ibero-Atlantic world.[95] Figures of collection and registration were rendered onto documents that mapped the physical location and distinguishing features of colonial populations, places, and goods to increase understanding across the Atlantic.[96] These tools shared commonalities with older methods of gathering information as well as newer imperial attempts at organizing data. Grids introduced at the end of the eighteenth century allowed commissioners to procure local knowledge and subsequently create visual representations toward the project of "filling out white space with local color."[97] Tribute commissioners, recording and representing *calidad*, mapped the status of families and their potential to generate revenue. Reformers beyond New Spain and its tribute regime applied similar methods to data collection, sometimes us-

Figure 4.1. *Cuadro de castas* (Painting of castes) (Anonymous, Museo Nacional del Virreinato, Tepotzotlán, Mexico, https://en.wikipedia.org/wiki/Casta#/media/File:Casta_painting_all.jpg)

ing the term *calidad* toward assessments of property. *Calidad* appears on the Catastro de Ensenada, the ambitious Castilian census from 1754, to describe the value and characteristics of properties and local products at the center of the empire. This usage, though distinct from the application of *calidad* in New Spain, illustrates the utility of this term for describing value and status. Questionnaires that outlined the productive potential and geography of colonial places, such as the *relaciones geográficas*, shared commonalities with tribute registers in their concern with accurate categorization and evaluation of local people and colonial geographies.[98] Ecclesiastics in Peru employed questionnaires to compile data on the far-flung peoples, customs, and productive capacity of local parishes.[99] Such questionnaires allowed local priests and informants to probe the "natural inclination" of subjects and discover "if there is any noticeable difference between Indians, Spanish, and other *castas*," and whether "they keep any commerce."[100] Using new printed instruments, tribute commissioners answered similar questions using quantitative approaches to potentially thorny and complicated questions. Empirical approaches to relaying information had been in development in the Spanish Atlantic since the sixteenth century.[101] More recent precedents for the bureaucratic interest in mapping and data representation came from the distant expeditions underwritten by the crown to better understand geography and its own territories. As it stretched the limits of colonial data management, the tribute regime became one of the many "intellectual laboratories" of administration in the Atlantic world.[102]

In practice, tribute registers were a diverse body of documents ranging from scrawled lists of names to highly regulated grids. The most detailed registers come from the late eighteenth and early nineteenth centuries, owing to late Bourbon attempts to break down families into their component parts, placing each individual into a discrete category. Registers are preserved from the first half of the eighteenth century that had more in common with Habsburg registers than with the rational methods of the end of the century. Even a bare minimum of detail would have required local knowledge to decode, a problem reformers sought to address as they invented new tools for tribute registration. The introduction of the commissioner from outside the community changed the methods of collection and representation of information. The commissioner and his agents might know little about the families in question, which could hinder their efforts but might also encourage them to record more information to best locate and distinguish tributaries in the future. Organizing this information so that it could be understood by a future commissioner, perhaps also an outsider, was one of the motivations behind the creation of new instruments. These efforts toward formalization and enforcement, unique to the late eighteenth century, were embodied in new tributary instruments issued from the capital.

Visual representations of tributary lists for Indians and free people of color were released to commissioners as early as the 1770s, and again in the years 1785, 1788, and 1796. In the 1770s and 1780s, the instruments focused on three categories that were essential to both payment and counting: the whole tributary, the half tributary, and those reserved from payment. Brief didactic exercises accompanied these grids (figure 4.2). Revillagigedo's 1793 ordinance contained a grid and examples that aimed to better educate commissioners and thereby standardize the process of registration among Indians and free people of color. The ordinance and its accompanying form were designed to avoid "obscurity or doubt because of defective methods of expressing names, *calidad*, caste, sex, and marital status of each individual, and their age."[103] Using the standard forms cut costs, saved time, and rationalized the system. Printing documents avoided crossing out categories and wasting paper, while ticking off categories on a grid streamlined the process of creating and copying registers. Using the same documents for Indian and Afromexican tribute joined them under a single rationale known to a wide array of administrators, both Spanish and Indian.

As an instrument of genealogical construction, spatial location, and *calidad* identification, the grids targeted all individuals who could be part of the tributary class and then disaggregated them accordingly. The separation between Indians and free Afromexicans split the population in two; yet, beyond this initial bifurcation, the instruments themselves did not prioritize the recording of other *calidad*-based data. Not only was there no column through which to specify *moreno*, *negro*, *mulato*, or otherwise, the only printed version of an Afromexican register that ever circulated was an Indian grid. The use of similar instruments unified the tribute regime, but this practice also signaled that subtleties of *calidad* among *negros* and *mulatos* were irrelevant within this institutional context. Bureaucrats viewed these communities as constituted by their tributary status, effectively defining a community that subsumed the distinctions of *calidad*.

As they designed the columns and instructions, Revillagigedo and his advisers were more concerned with recording *calidad* distinctions in the case of exogamous marriages between Afromexican tributaries and Indians, Spaniards, or mestizos. If an exempt individual married someone who was not, the exempt individual would also be registered. Marrying a tributary jeopardized an exempt individual's distance from royal tribute and associated documentation, as was true for a Spaniard named Vicente Zoria, alias "The Fat" ("*El Gordo*"), who married Ana María, a *mulata*, with whom he had a daughter.[104] The new grid reinterpreted unions such as this one with an eye toward creating future tributaries (see figure 4.2). The new instructions seemed to contradict directions from comptroller general Juan de la Riva in 1790 stating that any exempt man who married a tributary woman could expect to avoid registration along with their children.[105] In 1793, column 9 did not locate marriages between Afromexican men and exempt women; yet, examples instructed commissioners on how to deal with

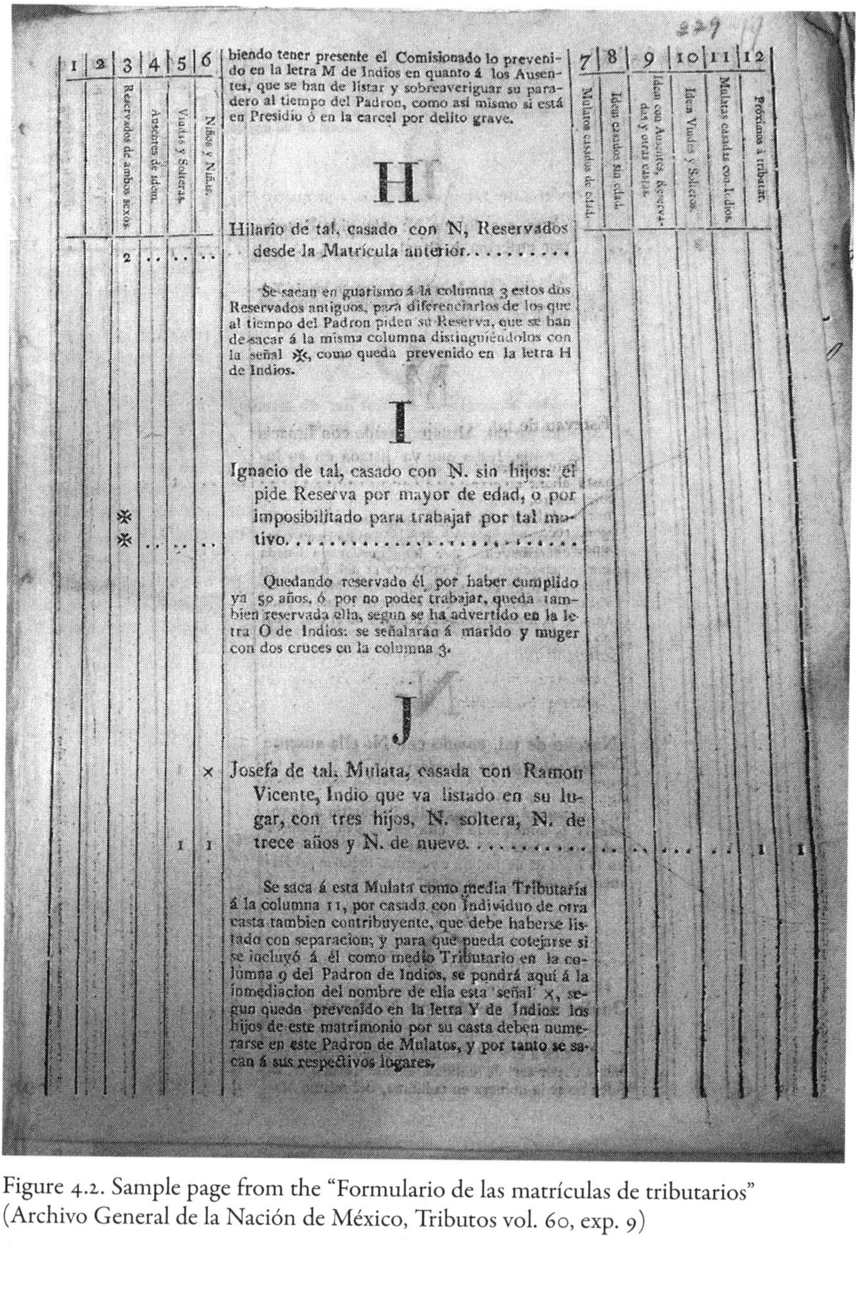

Figure 4.2. Sample page from the "Formulario de las matrículas de tributarios" (Archivo General de la Nación de México, Tributos vol. 60, exp. 9)

such marriages.[106] *Mulatos* gained the same half tributary status that their Indian counterparts received as the husbands of Spanish women or mestizas. But the sample register made it plain that "the children, following the *calidad* of the father, are listed here."[107] This 1793 register was explicit about the extent to which exogamous marriage between Afromexican men and Spanish women or mestizas could be beneficial. Regardless of the *calidad* of their mother, for tribute purposes, children of such unions were still future *mulato* tributaries. The practice anticipated a process of funneling entire families into a single tributary caste, eliminating the need for complex distinctions and technicalities.

Grids for both Indian and Afromexican tribute registers included the important distinction between "reserved" (*reservado/a*) or "exempt" (*exento/a*), both of which excused an individual from payment. Someone who was "reserved" experienced a kind of physical and temporal suspension that could revert at any time—part of the tributary class but not subject to payment. Such a reservation from royal tribute might be granted because of illness, injury, or advanced age. A temporary exemption might also be dispensed to a sick or unproductive individual; however, controversies persisted into the early nineteenth century regarding whether crop failures should qualify Indians for temporary relief.[108] Spanish and mestizo exempt individuals could not be obligated to pay tribute because they did not have a tributary *calidad*. These distinctions became confused when Afromexican women appeared in the sample supplied with the ordinance itself, despite the law's stipulation that all women receive automatic exemptions, regardless of "age, *calidad*, or marital status."[109] Their inclusion was geared toward preserving evidence of Afromexican tributary genealogies.

Distinctions of age and gender among free Afromexicans were the most important organizing principles of the grid. Registration was possible for everyone from a nursing infant to an elderly person. The columns disaggregated the population into those who had been temporarily relieved of tributary obligations but who remained tributaries (*reservados*); individuals who had once resided in the community but who had been absent for years (*ausentes*); widows and spinsters (*viudas y solteras*); boys and girls (*niños y niñas*); married couples of legal majority (*casados de edad*); married couples under eighteen years of age (*casados sin edad*); men who had married women who were absent, exempt, or Indians; widowers and bachelors (*viudos y solteros*); women whose husbands were absent or Indians; and male children who would soon reach the tributary age of eighteen (*próximos a tributar*). As Bourbon reformers rearticulated the economic importance of the labor of dependents in Enlightenment terms, bureaucrats translated these ideas into changing attitudes toward women and children of tributary castes. The *próximo* category was indicative of renewed interest in the economic potential of minors.[110]

Officials recorded a primary name, of a man or woman, followed by the names and ages of any dependents.[111] The language of the 1793 ordinance presumes the combination of a tributary and his wife, although the form itself taught commissioners to locate the names of widows.[112] The creators of the form were aware that Afromexican tributaries lived in a wide range of arrangements with myriad possibilities for social relationships. Up to a point, the grid allowed for this diversity and supported the incorporation of varied family types as tributaries. As long as these families contained at least one potential tributary, even if the arrangement did not fit nuclear norms, some commissioners were eager to locate as many free Afromexicans as possible.

Some officials continued Habsburg traditions of listing rather than categorizing individuals based on the grid. In places like Celaya, Mexico City, and Tlapa, the grid was subject to local interpretation. In practice, families were registered using the grid designed for Indians, leaving the columns for noble Indians and Indian officials blank (figure 4.3). Of the eighteen registers in this sample, nine used the printed grid for Indians, two used a letter grid issued before 1793, and the remaining seven used no grid at all (see table 4.1). This led to considerable variations on the placement of certain individuals, most notably men and women who married exogamously. The Celaya register followed the pattern of Indian registration: *mulatos* who married Indians would appear in column 9 and exogamous *mulatas* in column 11. In Ixcateopan, the handful of *mulatos* (n = 9) who married Indian women fell under column 11, which did designate "Indians with *mulatos*." The only marriage listed in column 9 on this register was that of a *mulato* Felipe de Jesús Cervantes, a cattle rancher who lived in Teloloapan with his Spanish wife, Manuela de Naxera, and their child, María.[113] A commissioner who recorded hundreds of exogamous couples likely developed a more consistent method than an official in Ixcateopan who encountered only a few such marriages.

The register was, in its ideal form, a clear map from one Afromexican tributary to others. By connecting free Afromexicans to people like them and to common spaces, the register recorded the regional characteristics of tributary populations. These registers reveal the family and social arrangements among Afromexican tributaries, offering details that related free Afromexicans to each other. The organization of the records speaks to the centrality of social and genealogical connection for the process of formation of the register, its inspiration, and its continued relevance. Administrators concerned themselves with who Afromexican subjects were, where they were, how they lived, and which people they knew. This last piece of information went beyond the economic purposes of taxation; administrators had elevated the ties between tributaries, genealogical and otherwise, as building blocks of a system of categorization.

In Mexico City, accountants kept copies of local tribute registers, amassing vast amounts of information about individuals and families. These data would

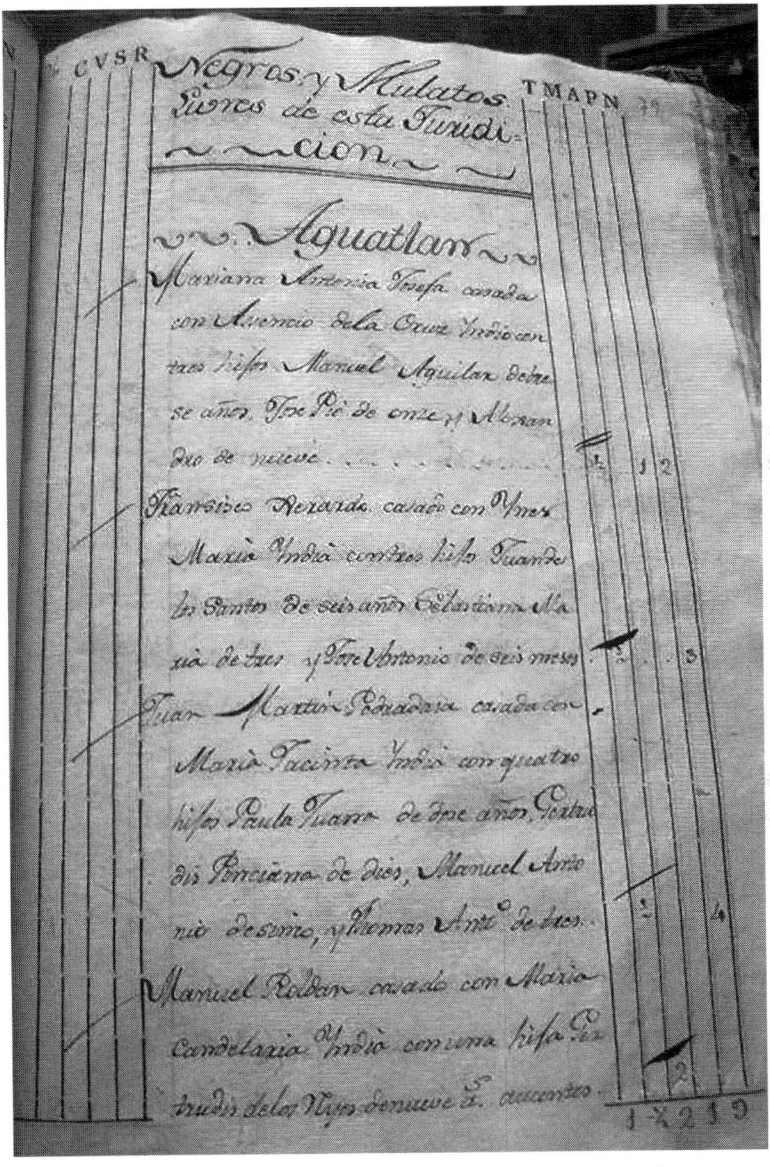

Figure 4.3. Selection from a 1786 register from Aguatlán using an alternate grid (Archivo General de la Nación de México, Tributos vol. 8, exp. 1)

eventually reach imperial authorities as a series of summaries of accounts produced consistently in the second half of the eighteenth century. These so-called states of accounts (*estados*), through their use of this term, embodied "the link between papers, charts, thoroughness and bureaucracy."[114] The idea of "*estadística*," or "that which is related to the state," came to encompass the more scientific, rational administration promoted within various arms of the bureaucracy of the Spanish Empire.[115] The summary and the *padrón* worked in tandem to convey information at different levels of government. The summaries represented further steps in the process of bringing information about tributary potential and production from local areas to the viceregal capital, and eventually to Spain. The combination of counting tributaries and collection in the same document further commodified the Afromexican tributary body. Whereas the tribute register focused on reproduction, family, and community, the summary is a reflection of massive amounts of data that translated into a commodification of tributary bodies. The summary combines demographic and economic data in ways that were easily understood and streamlined, producing an imperial vision of Afromexican tributaries and their importance for taxation.

The process of distilling, translating, and transferring information that began with the local tribute register continued in the Real Hacienda. A document from 1805 describes the local impact of tribute based on the number of individuals and their different social categories in various jurisdictions (figure 4.4).[116] Although this document has been used as a source of population data in other scholarly work, the visual structure and its meanings for representing Afromexican tributary data have not been studied.[117] The information was grouped visually into larger administrative units put into place under the Ordinance of Intendants. By standardizing the information, the accountants who created these documents each year attempted to approximate the annual value from what they saw as the varied and somewhat disorganized processes of each locale. This kind of mapping of local information allowed for easier evaluation and comparison of tributary output or potential.

This process brought together the total numbers of tributaries in various regions, evaluating their potential to increase the sizes of their tributary populations. For example, in the western coastal city of Acapulco, in 1804, a commissioner created or copied a list of Indians and free Afromexicans (see figure 4.4). When accountants in Mexico City reprocessed that list of thousands of names, they grouped people by caste and class, age, marital status, and legal status. These tributary classes represented another way in which tribute officials avoided caste as the sole basis for legal, social, and economic categories. Separated visually from other groups is the class of Indians in towns (*indios de pueblo*), who had specific legal and property rights, as well as obligations, within the colonial order. Next are listed the Indian wage laborers (*indios laboríos y vagos*), a group not defined

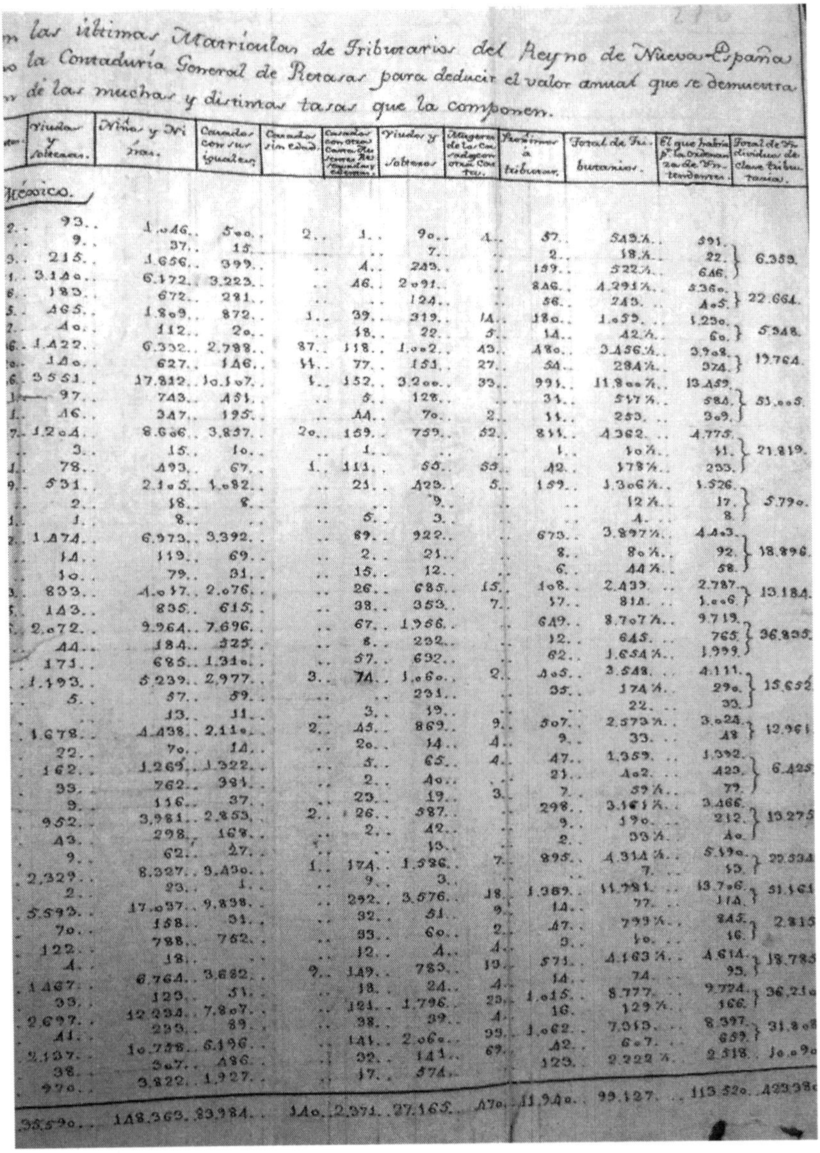

Figure 4.4. Selection from the "Estado general" from the Province of Mexico (Archivo General de la Nación de México, Tributos vol. 43, exp. 9)

by place of origin but by their work. Finally, the *negros y mulatos libres* are joined via a small bracket with the other wage laborers. Such illustrations exemplify the ways in which tribute subsumed categories based on caste, labor, and legal status to provide a standard method for counting people.

At the far end of the page are the total whole tributaries, counted as married couples. The viewer is then drawn to additional figures, also totals, based on manipulations of the data. After the total tributaries, bureaucrats would have seen a prediction of the total tributaries using a new method of counting implemented under the Ordinance of Intendants. This document takes on political undertones in its support of the counting methods introduced under the ordinance. Here we can see proof of improved counting methods, according to the treasury. In Acapulco, the total number of Indian tributaries increased by just 8 percent. But the new system of counting would increase Afromexican tributaries by nearly one-quarter. This general trend was true across New Spain: Afromexican numbers increased in the late eighteenth century (see table 4.2). Although some growth can be attributed to population expansion, the successes of Afromexican tribute were based largely on more aggressive registration and innovations in counting. Alternatively, some obstacles to registration can be attributed to disaster and disease, but others were clearly the work of free people of color who pushed back against the tax.

The translation of this information from local list to imperial map culminated in a different survey of all the funds collected and deductions made to royal tributes. The structure of this *estado* is placed on a grid to aid the reader and underscore the orderly nature of the state of accounts. These summaries of all the distinct charges were carefully constructed data sets, repackaged yet again to express an annual overview of tributary finance in New Spain. These grids and their production embody the centralization of knowledge and authority that scholars have long associated with late Bourbon rule. The documents are large, spanning more than thirty inches in height and around twenty inches in width. The visual priorities place economic value first, or what accountants saw as the end result of the demographic data gathered in the previous stages of documentation. The first column after name of the jurisdiction contains the "total value of the contribution of Indian, *mulato*, *laborío*, and *vago* tributaries."[118] At the far end is column 19, divided into four parts, which notes the number of "fixed Indians in towns," *laboríos* and *vagos*, free blacks and *mulatos*, and the total of these three groups. Additional columns deducted ecclesiastical taxes, exemptions, and other fees. In the final columns the viewer comes full circle, having seen both the value produced in each place and its populations of taxpayers. The large space of the map visualized the many jurisdictions that made up New Spain and further evoked the richness and breadth of the colony.

The Expansion of Tributary Populations and Payments

Tribute was part of an expansion of New Spain's Real Hacienda and a net gain in remittances for Spain's global empire. Income from the American colonies rose significantly in the final decades of the eighteenth century.[119] These growing remittances, of which Afromexican tribute formed a small part, provided much-needed funds as well as predictable income for Spain. As the result of targeted reforms, tribute collection increased by more than 30 percent between 1760 and 1780.[120] Local events and petitions, from groups of residents who claimed exemption or from *pardo* militias, were highly influential in determining the amounts of tribute collected. Some petitioners related their concerns to broader themes, especially defense, to justify their continued exemptions. In the 1780s, as Spain continued its war with Great Britain (1779–83), Viceroy Martín Mayorga felt compelled to grant exemptions to *pardo* militia units vital to the protection of the colony.[121] Yet as Bourbon bureaucrats searched for greater revenues, the need for more remittances eventually outweighed the traditional roles militias had played. In large part, the fluctuations in amounts collected from jurisdictions with Afromexican populations reflect the engagement of ordinary people and local authorities with legal mechanisms for temporary or permanent relief. Despite these unpredictable occurrences and decisions that were beyond the control of the Real Hacienda, a dynamic population of registered tributaries and greater revenue were achieved in multiple regions of the Kingdom of New Spain (map 4.1).

The challenges to collection came from the legal engagement of free Afromexican tributaries, and those erroneously registered as such, as well as the unwillingness of local authorities to impose the tax. Data from two jurisdictions illustrate the different situations Afromexican tributaries, commissioners, and collectors experienced between 1768 and 1788. First, we reexamine the area of Xilotepec and Huichapam,[122] discussed earlier. From 1769 to 1774, sixty-three Afromexican tributaries were expected to pay 179 pesos, or about 1 percent of the total tribute estimated from Xilotepec. There were between eight and ten thousand tributary Indians registered here, and their numbers increased by thousands in this period. In 1775, nearly two thousand more Indian tributaries were registered in addition to 110.5 *mulato* tributaries. Their estimated tributes rose to 317 pesos and four reales. These Afromexican tributaries were made up of twenty-eight married couples and 82.5 half tributaries in 1778. The tributary population expanded again in 1780 as Indian tributaries surpassed fourteen thousand and forty-five whole Afromexican tributaries joined 85.5 half tributaries on the register. By 1787, tribute had reached a standstill because of inaccurate registers full of names of deceased or absent individuals. The introduction of new pro-

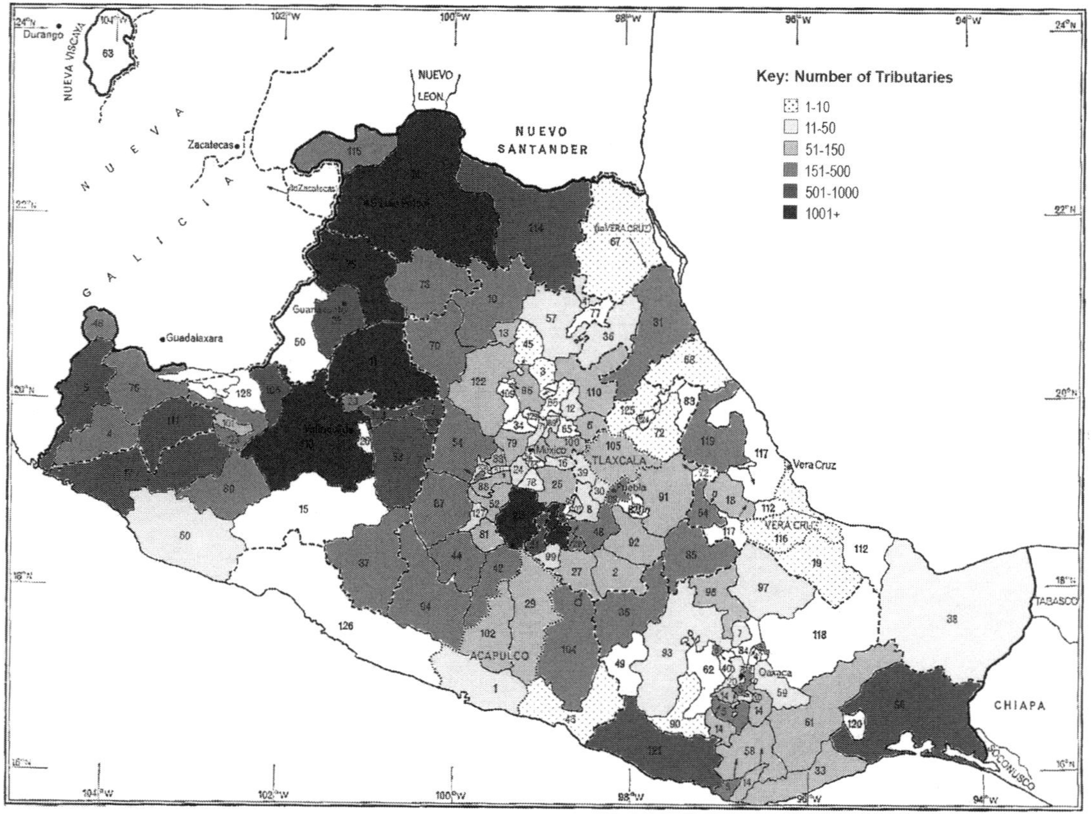

Map 4.1. Jurisdictions in the Kingdom of New Spain with more than four hundred Afromexican tributaries in 1787–88 (Adapted from Peter Gerhard, *A Guide to the Historical Geography of New Spain* [Cambridge: Cambridge University Press, 1972])

cedures with the figure of the commissioner and the Ordinance of Intendants had done more to change the tribute regime in Xilotepec than any other factor. Overall, the Afromexican tributary population doubled from 1768 to 1786, and, in this sense, the project of expanding registers was very successful. But the task of charging from *mulatos*, many of whom were unmarried workers on estates and in mines, eventually ground to a halt. The difficulties began in the wake of the administrative decision to designate the commissioner as author of the tribute register, a practice that greatly distressed local officials in Xilotepec at the end of the century.

Second, we return south to the jurisdiction of Acatlán and Piastla from chapter 2. The numbers of *mulato* tributaries and the amounts of expected and actual collection show the expansion of a small tributary population that had doubled by the 1780s. Between 1737 and 1743, Afromexican tributaries increased from 19.5 to twenty-seven whole tributaries and payments rose from forty-nine to 67.5 pesos (see table 2.4). In 1769 and 1770, free Afromexican tributaries had increased to forty-two, and the Real Hacienda expected 110 pesos from these subjects. From 1771 to 1775 the register showed fifty-four whole tributaries who were expected to pay 146 pesos. In the following two years, 68.5 tributaries were recorded and were expected to pay 178 pesos and four reales. At this point *mulatos* represented only 2.3 percent of the tributary population, but this was up from 1.7 percent in 1769, a 38.4 percent change. In 1777, their tribute was about 3 percent of the total payment from the jurisdiction. These incremental changes show a methodical effort to expand the Afromexican register at a rate that would exceed a normal population increase. Later data separate tributaries between whole tributaries made up of endogamous married couples and an aggregate of half tributaries, unmarried men and free Afromexicans married to members of exempt castes. In 1778, 68.5 whole tributaries were again recorded, but an additional fifty-four tributaries were also recorded made up of half tributary units. In 1780, the numbers were revised to fifty-four married tributaries and only 14.5 half tributaries. The population was reestablished from 1782 to 1784 at roughly the same number of tributary married adults and 19.5 half tributaries. In 1787 and 1788 there were a total of 81.5 Afromexican tributaries. These data show that, from 1768 to 1788, the Afromexican tributary population nearly doubled, though numbers rose and fell along the way. The amount of tribute Indians paid was about thirty times what these few dozen people were paying each *tercio*. Rather than ignore this tiny population, administrators focused on establishing a community of taxpayers from the early period of Bourbon reform through the dramatic growth of the 1780s. Here in Acatlán and Piastla this expansion was certainly significant (a nearly 40 percent increase), but it also reflected a longer trajectory of orderly registration and payment that stretched back to the earlier part of the century.

Both Afromexican and Indian tributary communities grew in this period.

Overall, the numbers are highly disparate: Indian tribute rose by around 13 percent, the low end of the estimate Charles Gibson gives for the period between 1797 and 1800.[123] In contrast, the number of Afromexican tributaries more than doubled between 1769 and 1788. The tribute from *indios laboríos* surged dramatically (see table 4.1). These rapid changes in tributary population, driven by local politics, environmental disasters, and mining concessions, affected the overall state of the tributary population. Among Indian tributaries in towns, the average change in all jurisdictions from 1769 to 1788 was 19.6 percent. Among free people of color, rapid changes in local tributary populations did not reflect huge population increases but rather were the result of dramatic changes in smaller communities. Removing outliers (gains of more than 500 percent), the average change between 1769 and 1788 was 144.6 percent.[124] Jurisdictions examined in this sample recorded losses and gains from year to year that could change the revenue from free people of color significantly in the short term.

These figures also point to rates of change in individual jurisdictions. Some of the most lucrative and populated jurisdictions periodically avoided registration. For example, in 1769 only six free people of color were registered in Valladolid, but 1,295.5 tributaries were registered in the same jurisdiction in 1788. Other profitable jurisdictions like Ixtlahuaca, Metepec, and Guazacoalco were in the middle of petitions by the *pardo* militias at the end of the 1760s. The militias made significant delays in the collection of Afromexican tribute in some jurisdictions where many Afromexicans lived. Another similar case is Xicayan, where no free people of color were recorded in 1769, but 725.5 were recorded in 1788.[125] Xicayan's militiamen believed they were exempt from tribute, a privilege Viceroy Antonio María Bucareli later upheld in 1773. He further specified that the exemption was not general and applied only to those enlisted in militia units.[126] Like the collection of information, the flow of tax revenues from individual jurisdictions varied based on region. Some were unstable, such as Celaya, San Luis Potosí, and Michoacán, all areas with large tax bases and large labor forces. Free people of color avoided tribute for two entire decades in twenty different jurisdictions, including the *parcialidades* of Mexico City and the mines at Zumpango. In the case of the capital, these problems were long-standing and had deprived the treasury of revenue for decades. Only 154.4 pesos were collected from Afromexican and Indian tributes in 1744, making Mexico City one of the least profitable areas subject to its *real caja* with regard to this tax.[127] Despite these failures in what might have been the most lucrative areas, overall collection was relatively stable between 1768 and 1784. By 1786, three consecutive years of temporary exemptions had resulted in significant debts from various regions that were, according to comptroller general Juan de la Riva, "unable or unwilling to pay the arrears on the pretext that a very high number of contributors had died in the epidemics."[128] In spite of these losses, the overall number of Afromexican tributaries continued to grow steadily from 1780 to 1788.

These accounts catalóged regional changes and showed the Afromexican tributary population, though often small, to be distributed across New Spain. Fewer than half of all jurisdictions contained more than one hundred Afromexican tributaries at any given time in the twenty-year period. The sixty-two jurisdictions that did contain larger populations were not limited to any particular part of the colony. Larger Afromexican tributary populations were especially prevalent in west central and northern New Spain. The wealthy mining areas at San Luis Potosí and Guanajuato, as well as the jurisdictions surrounding Guadalajara, seem to have experienced greater and more complete registration. Although numbers fluctuated over time, in 1787 and 1788 fifty jurisdictions had more than one hundred Afromexican tributaries, and more than twenty jurisdictions recorded four hundred tributaries or more in this category (see map 4.1). Regions that had smaller mining centers also had substantial numbers of Afromexican tributaries. The jurisdiction of Cuautla Amilpas had 612 Afromexican tributaries in 1787 and 814 by 1801.[129] Along the coasts, fewer free people of color were registered in 1788. Jurisdictions like Zacatula avoided registration in this twenty-year period, only to be incorporated by the tribute regime in later years.[130] These coastal and interior mining areas represented two extremes; the majority of jurisdictions contained small populations, most of which were growing. In 1788, the general tendency for a jurisdiction was to have a tributary population that was less than 10 percent Afromexican.[131]

Only eight jurisdictions contained an Afromexican tributary population that represented more than a quarter of the overall tributary group (table 4.3). These jurisdictions were Chietla in the Province of Puebla; Tancítaro, Xaso y Teremendo, Tlazazalca, and Xacona y Zamora in the Province of Valladolid; Autlan and Colima in the Province of Guadalajara; and San Luis Potosí in the Province of Potosí. Tributary numbers had changed considerably since summaries from various districts (*partidos*) were compiled in 1735. In that year, Chietla had only thirty-five Afromexican tributaries, Xacona had forty-eight, and Colima had fifty-one. In Autlan, 239 Afromexican tributaries registered, out of a total of 1,044, meaning registration was actually lower in 1769.[132] Fluctuating numbers speak to the changing nature of record keeping and implementation of tribute as well as the frequent problem of out-of-date registers. These jurisdictions contained urban areas, mines, ports, and ranches, demonstrating the wide variety of places tributaries lived and worked either permanently or in more mobile ways. Especially evident is the flux of tributaries in Valladolid, where markets were expanding and wage laborers in high demand. These data also show the importance and stability of other communities like that of Chietla, which bordered areas of

Table 4.3. Afromexican tributaries in eight jurisdictions, 1769–88 (selected years)

Year	Chietla	Tancítaro	Xaso y Teremendo[a]	Autlan	San Luis Potosí	Tlazazalca	Colima	Xacona y Zamora
1769	110.5	82.0	109.5	209.0	—	132.0	467.5	249.5
1770	108.5	156.0	109.5	—	—	132.0	—	249.5
1771	108.5	156.0	109.5	209.0	—	132.0	467.5	249.5
1772	108.5	156.0	109.5	259.0	—	132.0	467.5	490.5
1773	108.5	156.0	128.5	209.0	3,292.0	132.0	467.5	490.5
1774	108.5	156.0	128.5	657.5	3,292.0	146.0	471.5	490.5
1775	139.0	366.5	120.5	399.5	3,292.0	146.0	471.5	490.5
1776	139.0	366.5	120.5	399.5	3,292.0	146.0	471.5	490.5
1777	139.0	366.5	120.5	506.0	3,292.0	146.0	471.5	467.0
1778	139.5	366.5	167.0	506.0	—	146.0	471.0	467.0
1780	118.5	366.5	167.0	506.0	—	568.5	716.5	467.0
1782	118.5	402.5	167.0	506.0	—	568.5	716.5	467.0
1783	118.5	402.5	167.0	555.0	—	568.5	716.5	467.0
1784	118.5	402.5	167.0	555.0	—	568.5	716.5	1,468.0
1787	153.0	402.5	195.0	555.0	2,435.0	633.0	782.5	—
1788	153.0	402.5	195.0	555.0	2,435.0	633.0	782.5	—
% change	38.5	390.9	78.1	165.6	–26.0	379.5	67.4	488.4
% overall in 1788[b]	28.9	29.0	29.8	33.1	35.4	36.8	43.5	57.9

Source: See table 4.2.

[a]Xaso and Teremendo were towns within Valladolid after 1786.

[b]Afromexicans as a percentage of the tributary population in a single year. Data for Xacona y Zamora are calculated from the year 1784.

intense sugar production. In Chietla, about forty miles from Puebla City, free Afromexicans paid as many as five pesos per tributary couple in 1766.[133] In Autlan and Colima, both of which stood between Guadalajara and coastal ports like Manzanillo, populations seem to have fluctuated but grown like other jurisdictions with ties to Guadalajara. Finally, San Luis Potosí showed the same unpredictable stance toward Afromexican tribute that had bothered administrators at the beginning of the century. Potentially a lucrative area with thousands of Afromexican tributaries, this area periodically drew and lost workers and residents depending on economic cycles and local politics regarding taxation.

For the first ten years of these summaries, accountants included the estimated levels of collection (*tanteos*). Table 4.1 shows the estimated collection from *mulatos*, which increased modestly from 1768 to 1777. What authorities expected to gain from charging Afromexican tributaries was never the lion's share of local tribute payments. These payments were clearly never expected to surpass, or even approximate, those of Indian tributaries, yet accountants in Mexico City saw Afromexican tributaries as potential sources of untapped revenue. Expanding the tributary population of *mulatos*, though a smaller group than Indians, would disproportionately benefit the Real Hacienda because they paid a higher rate of royal tribute at the turn of the century. Between 1805 and 1810, the population of tributaries overall increased by 4.4 percent, but the number of *castas* who paid tribute rose by 9.5 percent.[134] The opportunity to draw more tributaries into the regime motivated Bourbon bureaucrats to target free Afromexicans, who often paid higher rates of royal tribute.

At its zenith, the tribute regime finally reached Afromexicans in the lucrative mining zones of the near north, or so accountants claimed. There, bureaucrats finally realized their goals of the early eighteenth century, having more than doubled the Afromexican tributary population in San Luis Potosí between 1794 and 1805 (table 4.4). This success was unparalleled by other regions, save Guadalajara. In Mexico and Valladolid, the increase in the Afromexican population (34 and 32 percent) more closely approximates that of the increase overall in all tributaries (39 percent). These rates show considerable expansion and demonstrate the increasing potential of the tribute regime to access and categorize tributary subjects. Yet, these documents must be considered cautiously, as they promoted sometimes unfathomable increases in taxable subjects. Whether all of the tributaries recorded on these new lists and counted using new methods could be subjected to collection would be an entirely different matter. What these figures do show is the commitment to shoring up tributary subjects and representing them as part of a productive colonial populace.

Even if all these subjects could not be taxed, some of them clearly were. Between 1795 and 1799, tribute from Indians and free Afromexicans made up about 22 percent of all direct taxes in New Spain.[135] Although still dependent on the

Table 4.4. Afromexican tributaries as percentage of total tributaries in 1794 and 1805

Province	Afromexican, 1794	Total tributaries, 1794	Afromexican, 1805	Total tributaries, 1805[a]	% increase in Afromexican	% increase in total tributaries
Veracruz	1,284.0	30,706.5	1,330.5	33,867.0	3.62	10.29
Arizpe	—	—	2,369.0	4,345.0	—	—
Puebla	2,405.5	94,350.5	2,400.5	113,174.0	−0.21	19.95
Oaxaca	2,460.0	81,679.0	2,905.5	95,952.0	18.11	17.47
Guanajuato	7,701.0	47,328.0	8,086.0	62,874.0	5.00	32.85
Mexico	8,159.5	197,088.5	10,923.0	257,230.0	33.87	30.51
Valladolid	9,457.0	36,203.5	12,455.0	46,804.0	31.70	29.28
Potosí	3,760.5	15,157.5	10,212.0	32,004.0	171.56	111.14
Zacatecas	—	—	12,768.0	23,459.0	—	—
Guadalajara	2,101.0	14,107.0	14,885.5	46,682.0	608.50	230.91
Totals	37,328.5	516,620.5	78,335.0	716,391.0	109.85	38.67

Sources: Data from Archivo General de Indias, Audiencia de México leg. 1583; Archivo General de la Nación de México, Tributos vol. 43, exp. 9.

[a]Calculated under the old system of counting.

power and behavior of local groups, such as the *pardo* militias and subjects who jointly filed petitions, the collection and registration of tributaries was a success. In this way, the tax resembled other economic burdens borne by the people of New Spain whose contributions acted as the backbone of imperial finance.

Conclusions

A series of experimental administrative reforms characteristic of expanding Bourbon bureaucracies across the Spanish Atlantic made possible a rapid expansion of the tributary population of both Indians and free Afromexicans. Bourbon reformers used a "visual epistemology" by which understanding depended on seeing as well as representing information.[136] The collection of data demanded new ways of organizing and understanding, embodied in the new printed instruments circulating in New Spain in the 1790s. Rather than the prevalent "lack of method and confusion" for creating tributary documents, Revillagigedo attempted to implant "a general and enduring method that in the future will assure the success of such an important matter."[137] Revillagigedo and his advisers showed, through their commitment to instruments, an intention to categorize, analyze, and separate different groups according to their tributary responsibilities. The accumulation of registers in the late eighteenth century, intended ultimately to expand coffers, also greatly increased bureaucrats' knowledge of Afromexican subjects.

Attempts to streamline the tributary population met with varying degrees of acceptance at the local level and had the potential to provoke a public scandal. Irresponsible and occasionally violent behavior on the part of royal officials commissioned for the process of gathering tributary knowledge seriously jeopardized the relationship between bureaucrats in Mexico City and the local authorities on which collection ultimately depended. Instructions in multiple colony-wide ordinances explained best practices for collection and registration. When ideal results could not be achieved, authorities might resort to blaming the age-old figure of the vagabond who disrupted the functionality of the tribute regime. The *mulato* vagabond trope was refashioned to contest the veracity of tributary registers controlled by outsiders and to relieve local authorities of the daunting task of charging tribute.

In the final decades of the eighteenth century, free people of African descent paid more tribute and registered as tributaries in greater numbers than ever before. The data suggest that these people were not, in fact, incorrigible vagabonds. By 1805, Bourbon officials had described the potential to demand large amounts of tribute from the Afromexican population. Still, bureaucrats continued to characterize Afromexican tribute as everything from an unmitigated disaster to a building block of colonial society. Given that many of them were accountants, it may be unsurprising that their strong beliefs on the issue of Afromexican tribute concerned the minutiae of collection and the delicate and orderly procedures of registration. Their internal discussions and disputes with local authorities led to a process of reform that was somewhat multivalent, although the justification for all reform was to bring more rational standards and greater income to the treasury. Free people of African descent themselves also influenced changes in policy through their petitions and opposition to Bourbon reforms.

5

Mapping Community on the Afromexican Tribute Register

Bourbon reformers used tribute documents to track the genealogical, spatial, social, and occupational characteristics of free people of color, constituting them as a distinct community in New Spain. At the turn of the nineteenth century, a *padrón* from the city of Celaya recorded the name of Petrona Palacios, a free woman of color better known as "The Pigeon" ("*La Pichona*"), sister of "*El Pichón*" the bullfighter.[1] These aliases related two family members in the absence of information concerning their whereabouts, parentage, or provenance. Tribute registers were repositories of local knowledge directed toward the goals of the Real Hacienda. Once they had gathered information available to community members, men commissioned to make these registers transmitted nicknames like "The Donkey" ("*El Burro*") or "Let's Eat" ("*Bamos comiendo*") to the capital in an effort to increase the colonial regime's power to define its subjects and expand its treasury.[2] Commissioners received or sought out aliases and other information as part of a process that ensured that tributaries would be recognizable to future officials collecting tribute and creating registers. The register became a bridge between Mexico City and thousands of far-flung settlements, allowing bureaucrats in the capital to analyze local knowledge in the form of quantitative data.

Connections between family members were the guiding principle for reformers as they maximized tributary registration.[3] *Padrones* cataloged interpersonal relationships and commissioner preferences or beliefs about Afromexican tributaries. Using data on spatial distribution, marriage patterns, and family structures, this chapter argues that the Afromexican tributary subject was constructed toward specific social and fiscal purposes. With that caveat in mind, the data commissioners left behind also offer valuable perspectives on the families and lives of free people of African descent. I use this inherent tension to discuss the purposes of the register and its constructed nature while using demographic data to draw conclusions about Afromexican communities. The chapter is organized around four central themes pertinent to Afromexican tributary subjecthood, the compilation of tribute registers, and the lives of many free people of color. First,

I show that Afromexican tributary patterns of residency shared basic characteristics and were related to community ties. Second, the data demonstrate the prevalence of exogamous marriage practices among certain tributary communities. Elsewhere, the registers belie commissioner biases in favor of endogamous marriages, which bounded community in the minds of officials. Next, the chapter analyzes the methods Bourbon bureaucrats and commissioners used to track free people of color and what the successes or failure of these methods tell us about the trope of the *mulato* vagabond. Even in New Spain, where tribute was fiscally successful, the mobility of tributaries could impede local collection. Finally, I consider the absence of *calidad* markers from the registers. Rather than *calidad*, other tributary qualities such as occupation, marital status, gender, and age formed the bedrock of these registers. Once an individual entered the space of the Afromexican tribute register, his or her specific caste and *calidad* were of secondary importance for bureaucrats and officials.

The following analyses draw on eighteen tribute lists compiled between 1774 and 1807 (table 5.1). They come from the intendancies of Arizpe (Sonora y Sinaloa), Guanajuato, Mexico, Puebla, Valladolid, and Veracruz. In total, the sample represents about 4 percent of the Afromexican tributary population of more than 380,000, as it was tallied in 1805 from provincial summaries.[4] All but two of the registers, those from Rosario and Aguatlán, were made after the Ordinance for Intendants in 1786. The two earlier registers show some distinctive features in their grids and language, such as increased attention to legitimacy, for Rosario, and color, for Aguatlán. In total, these eighteen registers collected information that would help the Real Hacienda locate about 14,870 people. These sample registers demonstrate the reach of the tribute regime and its limits across geography in the late Bourbon period. While it obscures some of the procedural and political changes discussed in the previous chapter, aggregating the data commissioners collected allows us to see glimpses of free Afromexican life across a wide geography. This methodology also allows us to quantify the regional differences in family structures as commissioners perceived them. Although these families are visible only through the distortions of fiscal documents, their names and attachments nonetheless remain an important source of historical information about ordinary Afromexicans in the late eighteenth and early nineteenth centuries.

Data from eighteen tribute registers analyzed in this study contained more than 7,500 records and belonged to fifteen territorial units (a full list can be found in table 5.1). Many of these registers were made in *cabeceras*, which were seats of administration, and smaller towns and estates subject to this regional authority. In the center of New Spain, in the Intendancy of Mexico, multiple registers came from the jurisdiction of San Cristóbal Ecatepec and the vast district of San Juan, one of the major sectors that made up Mexico City with more than

Table 5.1. Organization of eighteen tribute registers

Place	Intendancy	Year	Grid used	Afromexican records[a]	Separate Afromexican book
Rosario	Arizpe[b]	1774	Letter	350	No
Aguatlán	Puebla	1786	Letter	28	No
Guauchinango	Puebla	1789	None	528	Yes
Puebla	Puebla	1791	Indian	589	Yes
Tecpan	Mexico	1794	None	58	No
Celaya	Guanajuato	Unknown[c]	Indian	1,379	Yes
Ixmiquilpan	Mexico	Unknown[d]	Indian	58	No
Puebla	Puebla	1800	None	369	Yes
San Juan	Mexico	1800	Indian	623	Yes
Ixcateopan	Puebla	1801	Indian	636	Yes
Temascaltepec	Mexico	1801	Indian	121	No
Zacualpan	Mexico	1801	Indian	507	No
Huichapam	Mexico	1803	None	243	Yes
San Cristóbal Ecatepec	Mexico	1803	Indian	50	No
Zacualpan	Mexico	1804	None	57	No
Cozamaloapan	Veracruz	1806	None	775	Yes
Tlazazalca	Valladolid	1806	None	1047	No
San Juan	Mexico	1807	Indian	127	Yes

Sources: Archivo General de la Nación (AGN), Tributos vol. 8, exp. 1; AGN, Indiferente Virreinal c. 5555, exp. 31; AGN, Tributos vol. 51, exp. 6; AGN, Tributos vol. 40, exp. 11; AGN, Tierras vol. 1550, exp. 1; AGN, Padrones vol. 9, exp. 3; AGN, Padrones vol. 50, exp. 203; AGN, Padrones vol. 47, exp. 363; AGN, Padrones vol. 106, exp. 15; AGN, Indiferente Virreinal c. 1676, exp. 1; AGN, Indiferente Virreinal c. 6078, exp. 1; AGN, Padrones vol. 49, exp. 227; AGN, Indiferente Virreinal c. 4038, exp. 13; AGN, Padrones vol. 51, exp. 133; AGN, Indiferente Virreinal c. 315, exp. 5; Biblioteca Nacional de Antropología e Historia (BNAH), Puebla, rollos 43 and 44; and AGN, Provincias Internas vol. 247, exp. 16 (which is published in Benito Ramírez Meza, "Matrícula y retasa de tributarios del Real de Nuestra Señora del Rosario: Real del Rosario, abril de 1774," *Clío* 6, no. 22 [1998]: 161–97).

Note: The place-names written on the registers themselves, which may be variations on the most common versions, are preserved.

[a]The total number of records of Afromexican families does not reflect the total number of records on registers that included Indians in the same notebook.

[b]Also called Sonora y Sinaloa, an intendancy created before the general implementation of the system.

[c]Date unknown, probably after 1776.

[d]Date unknown.

10,000 residents. Here, many free men of African descent were recorded as members of guilds and registered at specific addresses. San Cristóbal Ecatepec, near Mexico City and now in the state of Mexico, had few *mulato* tributaries, most of whom lived in small towns. To the southeast, New Spain's second city, Puebla, was home to thousands of non-Indian families who lived within the city itself and practiced a dizzying variety of trades. Nearby, the sample includes Aguatlán, which after 1786 belonged to the jurisdiction of Izúcar. A jurisdiction where free people of color were the majority, Aguatlán had a few dozen Afromexican tributaries in the 1780s. A brief register from the head town of Temascaltepec listed any *negros* and *mulatos libres* who could be located in the head town and surrounding agricultural properties. Today part of the state of Mexico, the jurisdiction contained multiple royal mines as well as haciendas that produced sugar or raised cattle. In a contiguous jurisdiction, free men of African descent were listed as miners within Zacualpan, also located today in the state of Mexico. The community of Ixcateopan (or Iscateupa) was being administered from Zacualpan when a tribute register of free people of color was produced in 1801. Most free Afromexicans here worked on cattle ranches, as muleteers, or simply as "laborers" on the many haciendas that supplied the nearby mines.

To the north, the study draws on registers and lists from the head town of Huichapam (in the jurisdiction of Xilotepec), the jurisdiction of Celaya, and the jurisdiction of Ixmiquilpan. Today part of the state of Hidalgo, Huichapam was surrounded by small estates where free people of color raised cattle or sheep. Next to Xilotepec the small jurisdiction of Ixmiquilpan contained free people of color who had migrated there to work in the mines or were the descendants of enslaved Africans who had previously done the same labor. The thriving conurbation of Celaya in the same region was surrounded by dozens of estates and smaller towns where free people of African descent were a vital part of the labor force. Even farther north, the sample incorporates Tlazazalca, now in Michoacán, which joined Chilchota as a subdelegation in the Intendancy of Valladolid. A comparative register comes from Rosario, a northern silver mining center in what would become the intendancy of Sonora populated mostly by free people of mixed ancestry. The coastal regions of New Spain were home to many free people of color who participated in the militias as well as the tribute regime. On the west coast, the register from the head town Tecpan included a few smaller towns and haciendas within the large jurisdiction of Zacatula. Guauchinango and Cozamaloapa, both towns on the Gulf of Mexico in the Intendancy of Veracruz, had active coastal militias as well as fishing villages, ranches, and haciendas. Free people of African descent were involved in mining, agriculture, urban commerce, and long-distance trade and paid tribute in diverse communities and regions.

The interplay between qualitative and quantitative data on the registers bound together families as statistics within a household and individuals with fiscally

Table 5.2. Phrases describing family ties on Afromexican tribute registers, 1774–1807

Phrase	Son(s) of[a]	Daughter(s) of	Brother of	Sister of	Other family[b]	Total
Number of records	590	44	129	9	2	774
% of total	76.2	5.7	16.7	1.2	0.2	100

Sources: See table 5.1.

[a]Includes one record that contains both "brother of" and "son of" and five records that also contain daughters.

[b]Refers to instances of "grandson of" and "niece of."

relevant connections. Many commissioners and officials saw Afromexican communities, enslaved or free, as a web of interconnected families and individuals stretching across multiple households.[5] This attitude is exemplified in the constant use of language identifying unmarried people in tribute records: "son of," "sister of," and so on (table 5.2). "Widow of" and "brother-in-law of" or "stepson" might be used, and one long-absent couple in Zacualpan was described as "in the company of their father-in-law."[6] These people were not lone individuals but parts of a larger system of taxation based on their genealogies, social connections, and economic circumstance. Preserving lineages and family connections was to record *calidad* and fix it in time and bureaucratic space. The wider these tributary nets were cast within and across communities, the more towns and regions became characterized by the presence of Afromexican tributary subjects.

Bureaucrats in the capital used tributary status to break down the populace using only two categories that cut across boundaries of *calidad* and gender to improve administration. Eliminating the distinctions between the *calidad* of *morenos* and *mulatos* within tribute, authorities contained proliferating groups of *castas* who had different lineages of Indian, African, and European ancestry. Some of these distinctions remained meaningful for free people of color in other institutions,[7] but tribute nearly always relied on just one caste, that of the *mulato*. Out of the sample of more than fourteen thousand people, less than 1 percent (n = 14) contain an Afromexican who was not a *mulato*. Thousands more had no *calidad* specified at all beyond those listed in the title of the register itself. Within the tribute regime, the ideal of a single designation uniting all free people of color overwhelmed any investment individuals may have had in their *calidad* labels. The lack of attention to specificities of *calidad* on tribute registers points to the need for increased efficiency, streamlining, and digestion of information for an audience less familiar with or interested in an intricate local vocabulary.

The titles of registers themselves reflected the diversity of terms subsumed under Afromexican tribute. The terms "*mulato*," "*moreno*," and "*pardo*," used to describe people of mixed ancestry, frequently appeared in the titles of Bourbon tribute registers. This pattern was similar on the censuses, in which some subdelegates counted just *mulatos*, while others tallied *pardos*, *otras castas*, or *mulatos* and mestizos together. In the intendancy of Veracruz in 1805, for example, in Tamiahua there were 4,744 *mulatos*, while in Xalapa there were 2,009 *pardos*. In Yucatán in 1789, there were about 22,000 men and 22,000 women categorized as "*negros y mulatos*."[8] "*Negro libre*" ("free black") was less common on both census and tribute registers, reflecting demographic trends as well as a growing preference for the more euphemistic "*pardo*."[9] In the coastal region of Cozamaloapa in 1806, a commissioner created a town register of "*morenos, pardos,* and *chinos*"; *chino* was a word that had been applied to African and Asian captives who arrived in the port of Acapulco in the seventeenth century.[10] In jurisdictions where the militia presence was strong, like Guauchinango or Cozamaloapa, the titles of tribute registers reflected the terminology used in the names of militia units. In San Juan Tenochtitlán, a *parcialidad* of Mexico City, a register counted "the *pardos* who were found in the guilds of the capital." And an undated register from Celaya listed the "free *negros* and *mulatos*" of the city and its jurisdiction. While the titles of these registers varied, commissioners rarely categorized individual entries further between *chinos* and *mulatos*, or *negros* and *pardos*. Instead, the title signaled the collection of families and individuals brought together on a list that created a single tributary population out of a multitude of reputations and statuses.

Tributary Family Formation

Marital, genealogical, and adoptive relationships bound tributaries into social units that Bourbon reformers recognized as familial. These relationships were the cornerstone of tributary status and genealogies of privilege and obligation. The repeated use of family linkages such as "son of" and "mother of" were essential to tracking tributary dependents. While creating genealogies on some records would allow families to demonstrate residence or retain property, the tribute register created these genealogies to determine *calidad* as well as family ties. The data these registers provided, from a quantitative perspective, show the complexity of social groups. In everyday life, the idea of "family" in Bourbon New Spain was more fluid, determined by economic and social relationships that brought individuals together by birth, godparentage, marriage and sexual relationships, labor contracts, and adoption.[11] Tribute registers targeted productive workers and married couples, but they also made evident the ties free people of color formed through adoptive parentage and sharing dwellings. Indeed, commissioners and bureaucrats did not limit tributary units to a strict notion of "family," calling the

Table 5.3. Spatial distribution of heads of households on eighteen Afromexican tribute registers

Place type	Female primary name	Male primary name	Totals
Barrio	161	498	659
Cañada	0	7	7
Cabecera	112	842	954
City	37	990	1,027
Congregación	2	66	68
Cuadrilla	8	94	102
Curato	0	30	30
Estancia	7	129	136
Guild	1	368	369
Hacienda	69	1,514	1,583
Obraje	1	13	14
Paraje	6	118	124
Town	28	625	653
Puesto	0	25	25
Rancho	66	956	1,022
Royal Mint	0	15	15
Royal Mines	6	347	353
Region	1	12	13
Tobacco Factory	0	293	293
Unspecified	2	96	98
Totals	507	7,038	7,545

Sources: See table 5.1.

records on *padrones* "entries" (*partidas*) made up of component individuals related by place of residence, employer, kinship, or birthplace.

Entries on the tribute register began with a primary name and individuals related to the head of household. Commissioners in the sampled registers recorded 7,038 male primary names and 507 female primary names (table 5.3). Overall, the unit of the nuclear family with a male head of household was the norm, despite considerable variation attributable to commissioners' attitudes and choices. A total of 358 households in the sample were headed by widows, 126 by *solteras*, and another handful of records of women of unspecified status, girls not yet eighteen, and widows of other castes. From these groups combined, 135 women were recorded alone (four of these were servants identified with places of work, and therefore probably did not live alone), while another 368 households were headed by women and contained dependents. In mining regions, female primary names occasionally appeared. In Temascaltepec, a register of 121 families showed fifteen female primary names, thirteen widows, and two wives of men who had left from the jurisdiction but were still registered as potential tributaries. All but one of the widows living in and around the mines resided with their sons, many of them bachelors and miners. The sample from Mexico City shows slightly smaller numbers of households headed by a widow with children or additional dependents or residents (*agregados*), compared with the population census of 1790.[12] This arrangement existed in various types of households because of the many economic pressures they would have experienced. People with fewer economic resources on the edges of the city found their resources stretched thin in smaller households, where the number of individuals bringing in pay would have been reduced. These additional residents were likely tied by kinship to the widows, who as a group probably did not possess the resources to pay household workers.[13] Because women had been declared exempt from payment on numerous occasions, commissioners may have applied this exemption to registration, though instructions from the Real Hacienda and Viceroy Revillagigedo explicitly discouraged this practice.

The ambiguous status of free women of color in the tributary regime also affected the ways in which exogamous and endogamous marriage choices defined tributary subjects. Tributary status, tied to caste and *calidad*, was maintained or broken through marital and reproductive unions. The tribute registers from this study show high levels of Afromexican tributary endogamy, though exogamy did occur frequently in specific regions. Such discrepancies may point to a scarcity of marriage partners, opportunities for social mobility, emotional and social bonds that were unrelated to caste, commissioner bias, or some combination of these factors. One historian has posited that relationships between urban Indians and free people of African descent could indicate a kind of fascination across castes with an "other."[14] In general, tributaries in this sample maintained extended families of mostly Afromexican members. High rates of endogamy may also stem from a commissioner preference for identifying whole tributaries, which were more lucrative and recognizable as Afromexican. It is possible that levels of tributary endogamy exceeded those of free people of African descent throughout New Spain, though such an estimate would be preliminary at best. What is clear is that thousands of Afromexican tributary couples married endogamously and became tributaries.

The eighteen tribute registers in this sample show that free Afromexicans married with most frequency within their own caste, followed by unions with Indians, and finally with nontributary individuals (table 5.4). Across New Spain, free people of color showed varying degrees of preference for endogamous partners, depending on geography, gender, and trade. While most free people of color

Table 5.4. Castes of exogamous marriage partners of *mulato* tributaries on eighteen tribute registers

Caste	*Castizo/a*	*Español/a*	Exempt	*Indio/a*	Mestizo/a	Unspecified	Totals
Mulata	1	24	2	249[a]	12	1	289
Mulato	7	287	3	387[b]	144[c]	0	828
Totals	8	311	5	636	156	1	1,117

Sources: See table 5.1.

[a]Includes three Indians described as vagabonds.

[b]Includes one Indian from a *reducción* and one member of the Indian nobility.

[c]Includes three instances of a combination of "mestiza" and "*india*" to "*mestindia*."

showed an affinity for their own castes or for mestizo partners, local variations occurred (see table 5.4). Among the data examined, 39 percent of exogamous unions occurred between *mulatas* and Indians. Like most exogamous marriages in the sample, the majority occurred in the city of Celaya, a commercial hub in the Bajío, but Indian men did marry *mulatas* in Puebla, Huichapam, and Tlazazalca. In Tlazazalca, a jurisdiction of more than six thousand people, exogamous marriages were a factor of the availability of marriage partners as much as preference for exogamy or endogamy among *mulatos* or mestizos.[15] Tributary status would have had fewer effects on unions between Indians and free people of African descent, all subject to the tax, though at different rates. Such marriages, exogamous by caste, were still endogamous in terms of tributary status and joined individuals within the tributary class.

The group of Indians who married free people of African descent on these tribute registers encompassed different cultures, languages, modes of dress, legal statuses, family arrangements, and economic networks. Indians in New Spain maintained distinct cultural and linguistic identities, but the tribute regime recognized only some of this diversity toward fiscal ends. In and around Mexico City, the Indian category waxed and waned as individuals used or rejected this label to achieve different goals at the end of the colonial period.[16] Some Indian groups on frontiers were not subjected to tribute in exchange for their allegiance. In areas like the jurisdiction Tlazazalca, Indians received tributary distinctions based on their residence rather than their ethnicities. In the town of Chilchota, the commissioner distinguished between an Indian woman living in an Indian town (*india de pueblo*) and simply "Indian" (*india*) to demonstrate the legal privileges and responsibilities of Indians belonging to a corporate entity. In the neighboring head town of Tlazazalca, Juan Antonio Cabrera had married María Rosalía, an *india de reducción*.[17] This term associated María Rosalía with a contemporary dispute between missionaries, who believed in the importance of insulating Indians to promote their spiritual growth, and Bourbon reformers, who advocated for assimilating Indians into Spanish American society.[18] In Zacualpan, tribute commissioners also divided Indian women by descriptive markers rather than grouping them all as simply "*indias*." Here, women could be part of the group of "*indios vagos*," a somewhat negative term usually applied to temporary male workers unaffiliated with a town. This term could denote a lack of accountability to pay tribute, when migrant workers in mining regions were not associated with a hacienda or town.[19] Most commissioners left the more than six hundred records of marriages between Indians and free people of African descent without extra detail, perhaps noting what they saw as a relatively common occurrence that would eventually yield more tributaries and taxes to the Real Hacienda.

Urban areas simultaneously promoted more anonymity and more frequent contact with colonial institutions like the tribute regime. Puebla de los Ángeles, second only to the capital in its administrative apparatus and importance, possessed a dynamic economy and a historic Spanish population. It was also home to enslaved and free people of African descent, some of whom married outside their castes. These relationships seem to have severely altered the state of tributary registration in the city. Over the course of the final decade of the eighteenth century, the number of exogamous entries was cut in half.[20] By contrast endogamous Afromexican tributary couples remained relatively constant, even as the total number of entries fell. Two registers highlight the extent to which Spanish and other exempt people avoided registration alongside their Afromexican spouses. In 1794, twenty-nine *españolas* appeared married to Afromexican men, while that number decreased to eight in 1800. In the same year, Spanish men had disappeared entirely as marriage partners of tributaries. Forty-seven mestizas in 1794 dropped to only three in 1800.[21] These changes speak to the important local and interpersonal factors that shaped tribute registers. As in other cases, commissioners in 1800 may have interpreted the *calidad* of one marital partner based on that of the other. Second, it is possible that some exempt people wielded enough power at the point of registration that they could deny the commissioner access to their own information and protect their spouse and children. Even as some partners of Afromexicans escaped the tribute regime in Puebla, many other Spaniards and mestizos elsewhere joined their families of African descent on the registers.

Hundreds of nontributaries and Indians made their way onto Afromexican tribute registers every time these documents were drawn up. Afromexican male tributaries who married mestizas or Spanish women were numerous on certain registers in urban areas like Puebla, even at midcentury.[22] In the sample overall, 287 such marriages occurred between Afromexican men and exempt women (see table 5.4), and another twenty-four unions between women of color and Spanish men also appeared. On a 1774 register from Rosario, don Luis de Ochoa, *español*, appeared as the widower of a *mulata* named Theresa Noyola, with whom he raised three children. Now adults, Juan Andrés, twenty-four, Josef Rafael, eighteen, and their fourteen-year-old brother, Josef Antonio, appeared on the record with their father.[23] On their mother's death, these children remained tributaries, and, as long as they were tied to their father's reputation, he would appear on the tribute register. Urban couples from the middle classes were most common in cases of a marriage between a Spanish man and an Afromexican woman. Nine of these entries were registered in the barrios of Rosario, including other men who used the honorific "don." How don Pedro Rivera ended up registered in Rosario alongside his *mulata* wife Josefa Leuteria and their five children is not disclosed by the sparse details of the register. Their relationship had begun long before the creation of this register in 1774, when Francisco Agapito, their eldest, was already twenty-two years old. The youngest, Juana, was just three, demonstrating a long and publicly known relationship between a *mulata* woman and a man of some social standing. Such marriages are highly infrequent because most men of don Pedro Rivera's *calidad* were able to prevent their families from acquiring a tributary status.

The analyses of tribute registers in this chapter point to the influence of regional specificities on exogamy and the scope of the tributary institution. About one-fifth of all records from this sample contain intermarriages between Afromexicans and Indians, mestizos, or Spaniards. Nearly half of these marriages came from a single register, that of Celaya, where the majority of all marriages were exogamous (table 5.5). Other Afromexican populations formed fewer exogamous marital connections. In Rosario, just 9 percent of marriages were exogamous among all living Afromexican marriage partners. These remarkable differences in urban choices may be traced to a variety of local factors. Celaya was a multiethnic city, unlike Rosario, which, though a hub for trade and commerce, was mostly *mulato* and mestizo at the time.[24] Afromexican miners and their families lived and worked in and around Rosario, a center of non-Indian life in an area where many Indian groups had maintained their autonomy in the face of Spanish authority.[25] In addition, as of 1770, Afromexican tribute was not being charged in Rosario despite its fertile lands and productive mines. Eusebio Ventura Beleña, a *visitador* from the Real Hacienda, argued that the status Rosario had maintained as a frontier town should no longer exist.[26] The longtime experience with avoidance of tribute might have led to a relaxing of registration practices in Rosario, and there had been generalized problems creating registers owing to opposition from tributaries and their employers.[27]

Compared with cities and their surrounding barrios, rural areas had lower rates of exogamy on these tribute registers. The register of Tlazazalca, comparable in size to that of Celaya, contained one-quarter the number of exogamous marriages. Ixcateopan, a western agricultural jurisdiction that supplied the mines

Table 5.5. Distribution of exogamous and endogamous Afromexican marriages by tribute register

Place	Year	Afromexican records	Exog. marriages	Endog. marriages	Total marriages	Exog. as % of total marriages	Endog. as % of total marriages
Huichapam	1803	243	117	43	160	73	27
Puebla	1794	589	118	81	199	59	41
Celaya	Post-1776	1379	525	463	988	53	47
Ecatepec	1803	50	25	23	48	52	48
Ixmiquilpan	Unknown	58	28	27	55	51	49
Aguatlán	1786	28	9	11	20	45	55
Puebla	1800	369	44	79	123	36	64
Tlazazalca	1806	1,047	132	616	748	18	82
San Juan	1800	623	54	329	383	14	86
Zacualpan	1804	57	4	38	42	10	90
Rosario	1774	350	17	167	184	9	91
Guauchinango	1789	528	12	234	246	5	95
Zacualpan	1801	507	18	398	416	4	96
San Juan	1807	127	2	61	63	3	97
Temascaltepec	1801	121	2	87	89	2	98
Ixcateopan	1801	636	10	475	485	2	98
Tecpan	1794	58	0	37	37	0	100
Cozamaloapa	1806	775	0	558	558	0	100
Totals		7,545	1,117	3,727	4,844	23	77

Sources: See table 5.1.

at Taxco and Zacualpan, showed that just ten of more than four hundred marriages were exogamous. These were rural agricultural zones where farmers participated in local commerce supplied by the nearby mines, but they spent most of their time farming and working on ranches or haciendas. Their marriage patterns reflect large concentrations of Afromexican families in similar areas and a preference for endogamous, nuclear families among farmers. These patterns and bonds reflect those of Afromexican communities in other rural agricultural zones, where free people of African descent were numerous and exogamous partners scarce.[28] Central rural mining regions such as Zacualpan also had remarkably low rates of exogamy. Here, in 1801, only eighteen exogamous couples were recorded, just over 4 percent of total marriages. Half of these couples were made up of Spanish women and Afromexican men. Just one mestiza was present, suggesting that perhaps women with mixed Spanish and Indian ancestry lived instead as Spanish. This practice would have gone against the general trend of commissioners who recorded couples with similar *calidad* or who based the *calidad* of one spouse on that of the other. By far the most intermarriage occurred in the rural region of Huichapam, probably because the register was created toward a specific purpose (see table 5.5). The document describes people who were Afromexican tributaries, to prove that they had intermarried among other caste groups.[29] This outlier underscores the necessity of seeing these documents not as simple snapshots of a population but as the parts of a community that drew attention from commissioners.

Coastal tribute registers show the greatest discrepancy between population characteristics and tributary populations. These registers were closely related to military registers and prioritized male tributaries, sometimes exclusively. Some were drawn up as part of petitions from *pardo* militia units to achieve tribute exemptions.[30] Registers from Tecpan, to the west, and Cozamaloapa, in Veracruz, show that no Afromexican tributaries married outside their caste. While this is an interesting artifact of these tribute registers, it is impossible that these regions near major ports would experience no exogamy whatsoever (see table 5.5). What seems more plausible is that this is a counterpart to the military list, since it included none of the unmarried women or young children living in the Cozamaloapa jurisdiction. The commissioners who created these tribute registers envisioned them as male, Afromexican spaces.

Most of the primary names on these tribute registers belonged to men of legal majority who were married. Age was a defining characteristic of the tributary population, dividing children, adolescents, adults, and the elderly. When age was indicated on a record, it typically described the head of household and his dependents under eighteen. The *doncellas*, adolescent girls and young women, were an exception, since this measure of youth was based as much on honor as on age.[31] Those asking for relief from tribute often listed age, especially when this was a characteristic that drove the exemption. Some commissioners were interested in the organization of household by age, going as far as to list that certain children were twins. Seven families contained twins: five sets of identical twin girls, one set of boys, and one fraternal pair. In Ixcateopan, a salt merchant called Toribio Hurtado and his wife had infant twins Micaela and Gerónima. Linking these sets of siblings as twins was intended to further prevent future attempts to achieve tribute relief based on age. If Micaela denied tributary status in the future, a commissioner could consult the status of Gerónima, her twin and therefore tributary counterpart.

Commissioners had been directly advised in the Ordinance for Intendants to record servants and dependents of wealthy and elite residents if they belonged to the tributary class. Just seven records pertained to young girls who were registered independently of any family, most of them servants. Nearly all these girls were living in urban areas at the time of their registration. María Antonia Borge, Barbara Torres, and María Gertrudis all served in elite residences or workshops in Puebla in 1794.[32] By 1800, the girls' names had disappeared from the tributary record.[33] Other *doncellas* appeared in coastal regions as well as the Bajío, though such entries were rare. A few young girls who were not servants were listed with the names of their deceased fathers. This practice was the equivalent of connecting young *soltero* men to a family member and a reputation, even if the ancestor listed was absent or had passed away. The presence of girls on multiple registers confirms the prevalence of young Afromexican domestics in elite households, in workshops, and outside cities. The infrequent recording of these individuals further underscores the difficulties commissioners experienced when dealing with reluctant elites or people who "hid" tributaries from registration to the detriment of the Real Hacienda.

Tribute registers reveal households headed by unmarried adult women in rural and urban settings (table 5.6). Most such houses, whether boarding houses or brothels, were run by sisters. Only one woman out of thousands recorded was labeled "divorced" in the coastal town of Santiago Tamiahua in Veracruz. In 1786, the commissioner for Guauchinango found Estefania Chávez, the sister of Juan Miguel Chávez, a fisherman and unmarried tributary. Both were children of María Antonia Chávez and Juan Miguel Chávez, now deceased. She lived as a divorced woman, though her earlier marriage is unspecified, with her only son, Felipe, age four.[34] Divorced individuals were unable to remarry while their spouse still lived,[35] so it is possible that Felipe had a living father. The fact that few women were divorced was in keeping with the norm at the time, when divorce was difficult to obtain, costly, and socially frowned on. Unmarried women were of particular interest to commissioners when they lived in groups. In Rosario, María Confianza Villela, a forty-year-old *soltera*, and her sister Antonia, thirty, with whom she lived, were described as orphans and daughters of Josefa.[36]

Table 5.6. Gender distribution of households headed by Afromexican tributaries in rural and urban areas

Head of household	Female, rural	Male, rural	Female, urban	Male, urban
Total number of households	192	4,018	311	3,024
% of all urban or rural records	5	95	9	91
% of total records	3	53	4	40

Sources: See table 5.1.

How exactly the sisters maintained their property is unclear from the record. The same silence surrounds septuagenarian Ylariona Artieda and her fifty-year-old sister Manuela Josefa Artieda. These two women managed their own affairs at the same time that they raised twelve-year-old orphan Mariano, who, according to the record was of "unknown parentage." This vague category of illegitimacy placed Mariano on a continuum between bastard and legitimate child, one that he might navigate as an adult to remove this marker through legal means.[37]

Across the sample, brothers and sisters lived together without parents or spouses, as pairs of adults or as caretakers for younger siblings. Siblings frequently lived under the same roof in cities like Celaya and the capital. Caretaker roles were more common among men who had never been married, who undertook responsibilities of guardianship for younger siblings in at least fourteen instances on the register. In Tamiahua, Manuel López, the son of Mateo, lived with his two sisters, both *doncellas*. Manuel requested that he be relieved of tribute duties (*reserva*) owing to a long-term illness that would have affected his livelihood as a fisherman and decreased his ability to pay tribute.[38] These living arrangements would have allowed free people of African descent to support and raise younger members of the family, forming bonds that went beyond rigid definitions of "parent" and "child."

The presence of children on the register demonstrates the dual purpose of the document as a tracking device for potential tributaries and as a tool for categorizing the Afromexican population from an early age (table 5.7). For the tribute registers in this sample, nearly one-third (32.8 percent) of all individuals recorded were children. They were more frequent on some tribute registers than others. In the royal mines of Zacualpan, for example, only 8 percent (n = 28) of Afromexican families recorded had children, with an average of about two each.[39] The register indicates nearly two hundred married couples with no dependents whatsoever, an overrepresentation that was unlikely given the rate of population change among free people of color across New Spain.[40] Other tribute commissioners and *visitadores* inflated the numbers in the category of adolescents reach-

Table 5.7. Children in households listed under female primary names on eighteen tribute registers

Marital status	No. of records	Adult sons[a]	Adult daughters	Avg. associated individuals	Total individuals
Mulata widow	363	105	29	2.82	1,024
Mulata soltera	125	9	1	2.31	289
Divorced *mulata*	1	0	0	2.00	2
Unspecified	5	0	0	2.25	10
Unmarried *mulata* girl	6	0	0	1.00	6
Indian widow	4	0	0	3.50	14
Mestiza widow	2	0	0	2.00	4
Spanish widow	1	0	1	2.00	2
Total	507	114	31	2.66	1,351

Sources: See table 5.1.
[a]Does not include unmarried sons with unknown whereabouts.

ing the tributary age of eighteen as well as the number of children to give the appearance of diligence and a growing, productive and compliant population.[41]

Young people with no known biological relationship to their families presented a special circumstance for tribute commissioners. Details regarding the adoptive and birth families, the age of the orphan, whether both parents were deceased, and where the orphan had come from were typical pieces of information a commissioner might include. This information was modeled on the instructions of the grids discussed in chapter 4. One set of directions fabricated a fictitious "Pedro de tal, Mulato, an orphan fifteen years of age, and under the care of F. de tal." This representative example instructed commissioners to insert Pedro as an adolescent nearing the tributary age (*próximo a tributar*) and to keep track of his whereabouts using the name of an adult person responsible for him.[42] While under the care of this unnamed individual, Pedro might have been a servant or apprentice, or simply an adopted son. Across the total sample, sixty-two records showed households containing minors who were not the biological children of the heads of household. Within this group were minors labeled orphans, stepchildren, nephews and nieces, grandchildren, in-laws, and godchildren. Thirty-eight households contained adopted orphans, twenty-seven contained children with some defined relationship to the heads of household, and three both orphans and adopted family members. The sexes of the children are relatively even, with twenty-nine male orphans and twenty-one female. An additional twenty-nine adopted family members were boys, while only thirteen were girls were taken in by kin. Adoptions were most prevalent on the tribute registers of Rosario (n = 12), Celaya (n = 11), Guauchinango (n = 14), and Ixcateopan (n = 13); however, adoptions never accounted for more than 3 percent of records on any one register. The diversity of examples confirms that adoption was not a wholly urban or rural phenomenon and served multiple and overlapping purposes for adults and children.

Cross-caste adoptions were rare on the tribute register, though they certainly occurred throughout New Spain.[43] Families formed from adoption dot the registers, and sometimes commissioners attempted to understand the nature of these bonds. On a hacienda in Celaya, a *mulato* and mestiza couple lived without biological children while caring for four children of an "*indio* now deceased."[44] These children, three sons ages eight to twelve and one *soltera*, were listed "in their place," meaning on the Indian register. What relationship a *mulato*-mestiza couple had with a deceased Indian remains open to speculation, but the couple had added four additional children to their household, a fact significant for the commissioner. These mixed households, complicated by the presence of children born to other individuals in the community, demanded close scrutiny on the part of officials who wished to categorize and stabilize what appear to be somewhat fluid relationships of responsibility and child rearing.

Why families adopted orphans or minors from other households is never explicit on the register, but the variations in these relationships demonstrate the many interconnected families and community ties linking free people of color. Godparentage, adopting the brothers and sisters of a spouse, or caring for a spouse's children from another marriage were all expectations tied to Catholic relationships that had economic outcomes as well.[45] Some couples who conceived outside wedlock might welcome their own children as "orphans" to preserve their reputations.[46] For those who chose to adopt orphaned children with no clear relationship to the adults, the presence of more members of the house provided more labor and created more responsibilities. In a royal mine in Zacualpan, a *mulato* called Felipe Fatoya and his wife Anastacia Ortiz cared for a thirteen-year-old son, Juan, and an orphan named María Franquilina, a *soltera*.[47] Her age when she was adopted would not appear in the record, but her status as a *soltera* implies that she was old enough to earn a wage or contract a marriage. Adopting orphans could also have been a method of caring for unrecognized offspring, though presumably many of these orphans had deceased parents. Finally, some couples who adopted children are described as "without children" (*sin hijos*), meaning they did not have biological children. José Andrés García and his wife, Juana María of Temascaltepec, may just have adopted orphan Joaquín out of a desire to raise children.[48]

"Guardianship" referred in these records to a circumstance that involved some level of caretaking as well as responsibility for the purposes of taxation. These relationships could have connotations of family as well as labor status. Using the phrase "like a son" ("*como hijo*"), adults justified these informal adoptive relationships that involved labor obligations on the part of the minor.[49] This group of "guardians" and their households included people who lived in someone else's house or were placed under the care of an adult, sometimes a Spaniard. The term "charge of" (*a cargo de*) occurred twenty-one times in the sample and sometimes in reference to adoptions. In other cases, men or women who might be artisans, elites with servants, or owners of boarding houses took responsibility for locating Afromexican tributaries. Another term, "*arrimado*," could be used to describe adoption of illegitimate children but might also connote servitude or apprenticeship. In a town in the jurisdiction of Celaya, a young boy called Juan Antonio Sánchez, already labeled "*soltero*" even at age eleven, was associated with a Spaniard named José Francisco Mireles.[50] Juan Antonio was part of a handful of individuals who could be found "close to" (*arrimado*) or "added to" (*agregado*) households, terms that could refer to living arrangements or simply to registration. These methods showed how enmeshed the process of locating and describing populations was for commissioners and point to what one historian has described as a "language of affection or affinity as bureaucratically ritualized formulas."[51] Echoing back the early colonial ideal that free people of color live with designated masters, the terms of closeness linked free people of color to guardians who could shoulder their tributary payments and may also have formed close personal connections to tributaries. At the same time, this practice dragged Spanish names and residences onto Afromexican tribute registers, a place that could prove a dangerous space for reputational and caste-based confusion.

Places and Spaces

The tribute register functioned as a kind of bureaucratic space as well as a physical space that characterized Afromexican communities. Individuals and families could move across geographies and on and off tribute registers and often made both transitions simultaneously. The fact that tributaries, including women and children, were tied to specific locations further reinforces the status of the Afromexican tributary as fixed, either to place or to networks of family and labor. The idea that free people of African descent were mobile and had no place of permanent residence permeated both popular discourse in the late eighteenth century and the logic of tribute. The tribute registers themselves eroded these stereotypes or worked to "correct" behavior. To root people to a particular spot, tribute commissioners noted place of residence or work, especially among urban guilds. Outside of cities, commissioners often described free people of color based on their residences on or relationship to a hacienda. Some descendants of enslaved Africans held prominent positions administering haciendas in the southwest, while the property owners lived in Mexico City.[52] Ordinary laborers were still somewhat mobile and might take on different occupations in the hacienda and its regional or local market over time. Commissioner attempts to connect people to economic production and fixed location had the effect of contradicting the very stereotypes attached to them. What emerges from tribute registers is a construction, through data production, of families who maintained residences and created multiple connections in their communities.

Physical and bureaucratic spaces show patterns of mobility and stability, and these spaces overlapped. In Mexico City, registration blurred the lines between the residential limits of tribute and the legal spaces of the Spanish and Indian republics. Part of the Indian legal structure of the capital, San Juan de Tenochtitlán was one of two *parcialidades*, administrative units that included the Indian barrios surrounding the center of Mexico City. In 1811, these *parcialidades* had 12,797 residents, some of whom were Afromexican.[53] Although the domain of Indian government supposedly contained its barrios, the authority of the *parcialidad* within the tribute regime extended to Indians living and working all over the capital, and to free people of color as well.[54] In this complex case, the tributary status shared by Indians and Afromexicans, and the necessity of registration, mattered more to Bourbon bureaucrats than did decrees that people of African descent be forcibly separated from Indian spaces.

Registers mapped tributary status onto the physical space of the family's residence or workplace. This aspect of registration was the first step in locating tributaries in the present, which would lay the foundations for the long-term process of establishing future tributary lineages. Some kind of location is given on 825 of the sample records, or 11 percent of the total, and 749 of them came from Puebla and Mexico City. These place-names might describe independent houses, landmarks, streets, elite homes, places of employment, or the last town where a person was seen. A total of 386 records described casas, many of which were probably workshops, though some were numbered residences situated on streets. These details might not mean exact places of residency, but they associated Afromexican tributaries with certain kinds of activities and associates: twenty-six records in Mexico City used a tavern (*pulquería*) as a reference point. Such features of tributary status, which were determined as much by caste as by class, informed the term "tributary class," which was popular at the end of the eighteenth century. Outside Mexico City, this level of detail rarely reached the registers. While some references to general place of residence do appear, the information given could amount to little more than "in the town" or the occasional note, "dead."[55] The use of grids and printed instruments improved the recording of the names and locations of dwellings, but such specificity was simply impossible in some rural communities where houses did not have numbers and commissioners were not tasked with creating maps of small towns and haciendas.

Afromexican families lived and worked in cities and surrounding Indian barrios; in towns that were administrative centers (*cabeceras*) and subject towns; in rural settlements and hamlets (*congregaciones, parajes, puestos*); on rural agricultural and cattle estates (*estancias, ranchos, haciendas*); as laborers in workshops (*obrajes*); and in mines (*reales de minas*). Rural families might live near mining haciendas in *cuadrillas*, areas designated for workers' family dwellings.[56] Families also lived in improvised situations, in unrecognized hamlets, as "*arrimados*," often near agricultural and cattle estates where they worked (see table 5.3). Slightly less than half (n = 3,335) of all records in this sample came from urban areas where Afromexican male tributaries followed typical trades like shoemaking and textile production and women served as domestics. The remaining records showed people laboring on rural properties or living in towns (n = 4,210). In Celaya alone, one hundred haciendas appeared on the tribute register, indicating the importance of hacienda labor for the local economy and the abundance of free black labor in the area. The more than eight hundred families that lived on these haciendas in Celaya cemented the close connections between city, mine, and hacienda. These tributary trends match what other historians have observed about the large number of male, Afromexican wage laborers in trades, farming, and unskilled work.[57] The registers show sites of labor like haciendas, *obrajes*, mines, and guilds, where commissioners could locate groups of Afromexican men and women. As contemporaries observed, hundreds of women labored in mines breaking up and carrying ore as it was extracted.[58] Other men and women provided food, shelter, and transportation to travelers to and from the mines. Free people of color filled the transportation gap between hacienda and city, as in the case of Celaya where *mulatos* held more than 30 percent of such jobs.[59] Recording free people of color at a place of work created a feasible site of future collection as well as a designated responsible party, such as the property owner, who would have to pay on behalf of any tributaries who evaded collection.

The spatial distribution of female primary names across different types of geography confirms scholarship that has located unmarried female heads of household in colonial cities (see table 5.6).[60] In such environments, women had greater access to what one scholar has termed "everyday credit," by which women managed money through pawning and other housekeeping strategies specific to urban life.[61] The presence of unmarried women is especially notable within the 44 percent of the Afromexican tributary population who lived in cities and their barrios. Nearly two-thirds of all such households could be found in urban areas. Indian barrios were the most common place to find households headed by widows and those run by unmarried women called *solteras*. The presence of women on urban tribute registers reflected the increased opportunities for female employment in cities, but women tributaries in rural areas had their own livelihoods as property owners and farmers.[62] The 192 records that list a woman's name first in the rural zones attest to the fact that commissioners were also concerned with tracking and taxing these families (see table 5.6). A female-headed household was potentially home to a family of farmers who would have the capacity to pay tribute.

Residence predicted occupation and, as a result, tributary status. Certain blocks of Mexico City were more likely to have tributaries subject to the *parcialidad* of San Juan, like Chiconautla Street, where six tributary families lived in 1800 and two in 1807. Of these records, four contained workers in the tobacco industry. Workers earned better wages if more than one person worked in a factory from the same family, a practice that could account for this pattern.[63] Another eight families lived in the first district (*cuartel*) on the Calle de la Amargura, just behind the old royal tobacco manufactory and the tavern called Las Papas. These workers were easily accessible to both commissioners and employers owing to their proximity to royal factories. In Puebla, more than 150 tributary records represented heads of household who were recorded in the same workshop or house as another tributary family. Textile workshops, like the Obraje de Manzano in Puebla, created another ideal environment for registering large numbers of tributaries at the same place of business. Finally, Afromexican artisans were exposed to tributary registration. For as many as 750 tributary households in this sample, guild membership offered little in the way of protection.

Many free people of color in late colonial New Spain lived in the households of persons with greater means. Some records in the sample name a *don* or *doña*, as well as clergy, in whose residences free people of color lived and served as domestics. The inclusion of these free servants addressed a plea by the Ordinance of Intendants that all tributaries should pay, "even if they are the domestic servants of the viceroys, magistrates, prelates, and any other powerful or exempt persons, because they should deduct from the salary they pay their servants who belong to the indicated tributary classes."[64] A total of fifty-one records connect Afromexicans to people who were probably their employers, such as don Pioquinto and his servant, Antonio Gutiérrez, who resided with his Indian wife Petra de la Cruz in Ixmiquilpan. The couple had raised Eugenio, an unmarried adult, as well as Cayetano, seven, María, fifteen, and Gertrudis, twelve. Having spent many years as tributaries already, the couple asked to be excused from payment owing to their old age. Whether all those people lived in don Pioquinto's own home is unclear, but he was attached to all of them and to some extent responsible for their financial obligations. Through these connections between employers and tributaries, powerful and wealthy individuals appeared on the register alongside their servants.

Registers from rural areas lacked this level of specificity but provided occupational and familial data to link free people of color. Immigrants in the rural region of Igualapa tended to "cluster" in certain areas, particularly agricultural *estancias*, along with friends and family.[65] Two sisters, María de las Nieves Avila and María Sinforosa, lived on a *hacienda* outside Celaya.[66] These two women each had multiple children, and they were connected through a practice that situated individuals and families within larger networks of extended family and community. These links also anchored people to a particular rural place, physically or on the register itself. This record keeping was nonexclusive to free people of color, as it served a purpose for the documentation of rural Indian workers as well. Linking individuals to haciendas or *estancias* and to other tributaries stabilized what some officials believed to be a mobile population while asserting the importance of family.

In the present sample of more than 7,500 tributary records, few individuals or families show a history of spatial mobility. People who changed residence routinely may never have been registered in the first place, thereby skewing the data toward people with fixed residences. A minority of records, many of them rural, detailed the movements of tributaries. In Celaya, Indians married across barrios and non-Indians sought partners in nearby towns.[67] In similar cases, tracking tributaries through physical space was a task that commissioners approached using multiple methods. Sometimes, the inclusion of a neighborhood where a spouse was born or a certain nickname, such as "The Tabascan," would alert a future reader to a family's spatial history. Other registers attest to the movements of larger groups of laborers, such as the preponderance of people "from La Florida," a nearby hacienda, who now lived near the mines at El Cardonal.[68] Whether great or small, any distance traveled caused a disturbance in the place-based methods of identifying and rooting tributaries, drawing the notice of commissioners to migrations of all kinds. The more common devices commissioners used related to social and familial relationships, rather than a history of moving from place to place. This genealogical information would have greater meaning than a house or a means to a livelihood, and many of the connections forged on these registers would endure beyond death.

Methods of Tracking Tributaries

The families that commissioners portrayed on tribute registers appeared deeply interconnected by bonds of blood, love, and place. Instead of the roaming vagabond removed from normal social pursuits, registers described hundreds of familial, marital, and other social ties that embedded Afromexican tributaries into communities. This vision, in turn, made Afromexican tributaries easier to locate and rendered their genealogies clear and accepted. The most prominent method of tracking tributaries on registers was the use of phrases that related them to other tributaries, often in the absence of a surname. The phrase "son of" ("*hijo de*") appears nearly six hundred times across the registers (see table 5.2). Officials commonly attached it to the name of a *soltero*, a bachelor, though they occasionally used the phrase to describe a member of a married couple. This practice was already used in early modern censuses in Europe as a method of establishing connections among taxable individuals.[69] Records containing "son of" include the names and sometimes the *calidad* of one or both parents. When both parents' names were present, the tributary gained the legitimacy that came with having known parents in the community, but also the burden of tributary lineage. The use of both parental names, however, was a local phenomenon specific to the city of Puebla. On the 1800 register, parental information was only provided for *solteros*, and within this group about 88 percent of the time. Of the 205 *solteros* on the register, 179 were listed with both parental names, making up nearly 99 percent of those recorded with parental information.[70] On this register, parental *calidad* is always absent and was assumed through the tributary status of the child. Simply their inclusion on the register itself was enough to mark the entire family as Afromexican.

Connections between records that provided only one parental name were usually between fathers and sons. Tributary status was, by technical definition, passed through the father's *calidad*, although on the ground these distinctions were not often important to commissioners. Of a more practical nature, the father's name could direct the reader to another record on the same register, often recorded near the record in question. "Son of the preceding" ("*hijo del anterior*"), a convenient method for organizing individuals related by blood if not household, appeared about fifty times. In the Real de Tecacipan, now in the state of Mexico, Jose Antonio Chimalpopoca lived with Juana Trinidad Rivas and their two sons, both bachelors. Five records previously, another of their sons appeared in another record as the son of the same Chimalpopoca.[71] The commissioner of the same register underscored the importance of father-son relationships by specifying not only when fathers were deceased, but also by using language such as "who still lives."[72] In 1806, Jorge Clemente Robledo, who resided on a ranch in Tlazazalca, was listed simply as a bachelor and "son of María."[73] An association with a mother's name only could have been due to commissioner neglect, but was likely the result of a female-headed household.[74]

A reference to a father's name could also give clues about occupation, reputation, or physical residence. In Cozamaloapa, a man called Guillermo, a bachelor, was noted as the son of the soldier Lermo Balentín, most likely a member of the *pardo* militia.[75] In Actopan, don Francisco Cortés Monroy was recorded as a bachelor "son of don Julián." His father was recorded five records later as the same don Julián Cortés y Monroy, married to doña María Francisca Peña.[76] Both Guillermo Balentín and Francisco Cortés Monroy would have enjoyed prestige because of their relationships to their fathers, who were people of some station in their communities either because of wealth or occupation. An elevated social standing might have protected family members from collection, if not from registration.

Occurring much less frequently, the phrases "daughter of" ("*hija de*") and "his/her/their daughter" ("*su hija*") served the same purpose of linking tributaries' families. Antonio Victoriano Romero had married an Indian woman named María Concepción with whom he was raising three young children on a hacienda in Celaya. In addition, he had an unmarried adult son who appeared alone. After him, listed as "his brother," is José Lucas Romero, the widower of an Indian woman, with whom he had an infant daughter. Antonio Victoriano also had an adult daughter who was recorded separately from her parents as a single woman with no children in her house. She did have at least one child during her life, listed two records later, a bachelor named José Dolores Romero who was tied to his mother's name with the distinction that she was a *soltera*, an unmarried woman.[77] These degrees of bureaucratic attention reflected the unusual circumstances of exogamy, extramarital children, and multigenerational tributary lineages contained in the records of one family.

The memory of deceased parents followed unmarried men and women, who might not have any other relationships recorded on the register. Nearly one-quarter of all records marked with "son of" named deceased fathers, making genealogy an especially important marker for those without any current familial connections to other tributaries. Outside the city of Celaya, María Venancia Secundina Paredes, a young girl and child of a deceased *mulato* named Joaquín Paredes, was recorded alone.[78] Such an action on the part of the commissioner would reduce María Venancia's chances of changing her *calidad* or caste later in life, perhaps at marriage. Commissioners included a deceased parent if the living parent's *calidad* might call into question the child's *calidad* or tributary status. Another eight-year-old girl, also the daughter of a deceased *mulato*, had been placed in the care of ("*a cargo de*") her Indian mother, who had been placed on an Indian register as well.[79] This situation merited the inclusion of more detail so that the girl's *calidad* could remain classified as Afromexican, preventing her, at least at this particular documentary moment, from joining her mother as an Indian. In multiple familial situations, the *calidad* of a deceased parent could not shield children from tributary status. In the jurisdiction of Huichapam, a young bachelor was listed as the son of Vicente Sáenz, a deceased *castizo*.[80] Vicente was known as a *castizo* at this time, and therefore nontributary, but his children followed their mother's *calidad*. These cases demonstrate the ability of the register to stabilize *calidad* by spreading Afromexican tributary status to children of a variety of genealogies.

Stabilizing *calidad* was a method that commissioners used among siblings, though it was more common among married couples. In an Aguatlán-based family with no surname given, one Cayetano Alberto was married to Marcelina

Antonia, mestiza, with whom he had a two-month-old son. The following record named Jose Ramón as Cayetano's brother. A third record following this one described another man as the "brother of the preceding" and a bachelor.[81] The thread of brothers solidified the Afromexican status of Cayetano Alberto, in spite of his exogamous marriage, which might draw into question the status of his children. Commissioners relied on accurate connections on registers to establish which children would be obligated to pay tribute, a task often complicated by the tendency of free Afromexicans to marry exogamously. If children were siblings born to the same parents, the *calidad* of the firstborn could be used as an indicator of the status of the others.

Stressed on the didactic form that accompanied the ordinance of 1793, the status of orphans on the tribute register raised questions about the standardization of Afromexican community from the perspective of the Real Hacienda.[82] The number of records containing orphans on the sample registers totaled 128, and, of these, forty-one recorded instances of adoption. The large number of orphans with no adoptive or biological family present greatly outnumbered the mere seven who gave an account of one or more biological parents. One of two individuals in the total sample described as "orphans of" deceased *mulato* men, Simón López, a bachelor, was the son of Manuel López and lived in Temascaltepec.[83] The record of this information would have prevented Manuel López from seeking tribute privileges awarded to orphaned children of unknown parentage. In Aguatlán, a commissioner recorded twelve-year-old *moreno* Matías as the "orphan of the deceased Miguel Antonio."[84] The commissioner included Matías's *calidad* to leave no doubt about his tributary status. Commissioners were aware of the special, though still controversial, status of orphans and its attendant royal, ecclesiastical, and social concessions. Orphans or not, these two young men would be next in line to tribute. In the absence of obvious genealogical and social connections such as living parents, spouses, or children, the register fashioned kinship networks that would stabilize potentially slippery tributaries.

When parents adopted children, some commissioners sought the names of the birth parents or other guardians. Such information might prove useful because adoption could also represent a form of movement, one that necessitated a register to keep minors in place. Moving through physical space or between legal statuses were changes tracked on registers for Afromexican and Indian tributaries, especially young people. Celaya registers preserved key examples of the movements of children, whose original guardians are recorded, perhaps to provide a trail to the children's place of origin. In one small town, a *mulata* married an Indian with whom she had no biological children, but the couple was effectively caring for two children, ages fifteen and twelve, described as the "stepchildren of Pablo."[85] Pablo may have been a *mulato*, because these children are listed with their adoptive mother on the Afromexican register, as opposed to the more common practice of listing children with their Indian fathers. Tracking such children on the tribute register would have been particularly important, as tributary and nontributary households adopted *casta* children.[86]

Foreshadowing debates about the status of foundlings in the tribute regime that would not be resolved until the nineteenth century, one register in the sample used legitimacy and parental recognition to categorize tributaries. In Rosario, most residents were *mulatos*, making legitimacy status a useful division for commissioners classifying tributaries.[87] However, the status of foundlings, known as *expósitos*, would become the subject of debate in the late eighteenth century. Foundlings were tributaries in some parts of Spanish America such as New Granada, where illegitimate children automatically assumed tributary status.[88] In Rosario in 1774, twelve of the total 350 records of *mulato* families contain one or more individuals described as the child of "unknown parents." Unknown parentage on this register was linked to dependent or vulnerable social positions, such as those of servants, single women, and orphans. Three orphaned *mulatos* of unknown parentage in their twenties were all unmarried servants in the house of don Vizente Gagiola.[89] In the absence of a father, these tributaries were known through their connections to their employer, who would be responsible for their tribute payments. The use of legitimacy terminology underlines the linkages of residency, genealogy, labor, and parentage with tribute.

These registers mark moments in time and interpersonal relationships that came to the attention of commissioners and local officials. If the same tributaries were registered at different moments in time, their social characteristics, including *calidad*, could change on the register. These constructions of tributary subjecthood were time sensitive and underscored the episodic nature of tribute. For all their efforts, bureaucrats might gain just a fleeting glimpse of local populations from time to time. However, when different commissioners drew up new registers, they were not simply copying the same lists, as in the case of Puebla de los Ángeles, New Spain's second city. A close look at the situation in Puebla in the last decade of the eighteenth century offers a more nuanced view of the tribute register and its efficacy. Tribute registers did gather large amounts of information for Mexico City bureaucrats interested in tracking and seeing Afromexican families. However, they were not always seeing the same families from one cycle to the next.

Puebla de los Ángeles, founded as a Spanish settlement, had been exempt from tribute in the sixteenth century.[90] Two hundred years later, New Spain's manufacturing center enjoyed no such exemptions because of its sizeable tributary workforce. Puebla's jurisdiction, where 71,366 people lived in and around the city in 1777, was home to some 2,899 *mulatos* and thirty-one *negros*.[91] Between its Indian and Afromexican residents, the city of Puebla alone brought in more than eleven thousand pesos in tribute per year at the end of the eighteenth century.[92]

In the larger Intendancy of Puebla, tribute contributions to the Real Hacienda more than doubled in the last decades of the eighteenth century.[93] This region was lucrative, as it brought in a total of about a million pesos in average total income annually between 1790 and 1799.[94] In the late eighteenth century, Atlantic conflicts primed intercolonial markets for goods from Puebla, but unpredictable economic cycles plagued the manufacturing and agricultural sectors.[95] At the start of the nineteenth century, Puebla was perhaps as industrialized as eastern Pennsylvania and some areas of New England.[96] Africans and their descendants played an integral role in the story of industrialization of the city.[97] Since the seventeenth century, Puebla had been characterized by its textile *obraje* labor, which propelled the region to economic prosperity. Puebla's proximity to the capital and its importance for international trade afforded a comparatively diverse occupational structure. Free Afromexicans in Puebla held a variety of professions at the end of the eighteenth century, but the tribute burden would have weighed heavily on the majority, who made low and modest wages as artisans.[98] The construction of tribute registers reflected bureaucrats' concerns with promoting manufacturing, and tribute registers of the late eighteenth century focused on male members of particular professions. For these reasons, the Afromexican tribute registers in this city demonstrate colonial economic trends and local professional structures.

Two tribute registers allow us to observe the tributary patterns of Afromexican individuals from the city of Puebla in 1794 and 1800. Although the 1791 register was copied onto a grid form in 1794, which is the version preserved in the archive, it was nearly completely distinct from the 1800 register. In total, Puebla's Afromexican registration numbers for the jurisdiction dwindled from 589 in 1791 to 369 records in 1800. Beyond the drop in raw numbers, different commissioners were rarely capable of counting the same people in both years. The position transferred from José González del Castillo, who served as commissioner in 1791, to Francisco Monroy, who served in 1800. A subdelegate of a nearby district, he had already held a similar post in 1794 for the register of Guayacocotla.[99] In spite of his experience, he was unable to locate hundreds of families inscribed on the grid of 1791.

Between the two registers, only about thirty records contain repeated primary names, and out of that small group only fifteen can be definitively matched across the years. When couples were located in both years, one striking phenomenon was that of caste-shifting among wives of tributary men. The following two extended families exemplify this trend of instability. In 1791, José Mendoza, a weaver on the Calle de Sayas, was married to a mestiza called Ana Antonia Ponce.[100] At this time, this match would have been typical of exogamy patterns among *mulatas* and *mulatos* alike in the area.[101] Their two eldest sons were nearing tributary age ("*próximos a tributar*"), but four other young children were all under the age of eight. A little more than half of all *mulato* men living in Puebla Intendancy were married.[102] But within the heavily *soltero* tributary group, José Mendoza was a memorable resident. His marital status and fixed residence may have drawn a new commissioner to him when the next registration occurred. In 1800, José Mendoza had reached forty years of age and the household had changed.[103] Three of their children—two girls, Margarita, now thirteen, and María Josefa, who would be turning nine, as well as Francisco, eight—were absent and in an undisclosed place. A new baby had been born, Marcelino and Joaquín had grown up, and Ana Antonia had changed her *calidad* to that of a *castiza*. This subtle shift in terminology did not directly affect the family's tributary payments in the short term. What it might do was alter the caste or even tributary status of the new baby, José Ygnacio, or future children. Although the children of a *mulato* man and a *castiza* woman would still be tributaries in the strictest sense, Ana Antonia and José Mendoza's future children would have a better chance of contesting their status the more Spanish blood they could accrue in their favor.

The brothers José and José Joaquín Heredia, both tanners, were listed in succession on the two registers. In 1791, José had asked for temporary tax relief because he was above the age of 60.[104] In the same entry is his son Manuel who practiced the most common Afromexican tributary trade as a shoemaker.[105] José Joaquín, described as the brother of José Heredia, lived at the Casadería de Blanco. These links among family members provided caste stability in Puebla. Although individual caste labels are not provided, the brothers were very likely to have the same caste.[106] But the spouses of the two men were not listed with their families of origin and so had greater caste mobility. By 1800, José Joaquín's wife, María Francisca Escobar, had established herself as a mestiza sufficiently to be entered as such into the register. With her husband, now simply Joaquín, aged thirty, she had three young children, María Antonia, Joaquín, and José Simón. Significantly reducing the financial burden on the family, the couple paid a half tributary rate owing to her status as a mestiza. In 1800, in contrast, José Heredia was connected to fewer potential tributaries than before. He remained the widower of one Hilaria Cayetano Veramonte, and now his son Manuel had disappeared from the 1800 register. Perhaps he sought work elsewhere and started a family of his own, or, like many, escaped registration.

Fleeing registration and hiding individuals appear to have been common practices in Puebla at the turn of the nineteenth century. The number of registered Afromexican tributary families for the jurisdiction dropped by more than one-third between 1791 and 1800. Married men in the sample were relatively few, appearing in around a third of all records (n = 122) from Puebla in 1800. Most of the Afromexican tributaries in New Spain's second city were skilled or semiskilled craftsmen who would have remained in the city with a workshop or master artisan. This was not an inherently mobile group, but commissioners did not manage to locate this population and record its characteristics over a ten-year period. Grids and columns could stabilize *calidad*, to a certain degree, yet these new instruments could not prevent individuals from hiding from or lying to commissioners. The distinctive population recorded on each tribute register suggests that the Afromexican population was much larger than either grid reveals. Officials in Puebla, like those in Mexico City, relied heavily on occupational characteristics to locate male tributaries. Yet, the unit of the family, as Bourbon reformers had argued, provided the most stable site of repeated registration. Outside Puebla and Mexico City, the uneven incorporation of women and children into the tributary group strengthened the tribute regime and allowed it to augment the numbers of tributaries significantly.

The Absence of Individual *Calidad*

Commissioners frequently failed to trace individuals and families, but one piece of information seems to have been removed almost entirely: explicit references to an individual's Afromexican *calidad*. Beyond the tribute register, including in petitions and tribute disputes, markers of *calidad* or *casta* were modifiers in the two classes of tributaries and nontributaries. Within the tribute register, *calidad* rarely appears as a marker of individual status. Commissioners titled their lists of tributaries using distinct terminologies of *calidad*, even if they were absent from the body of the register itself. The use of imperial instruments to apply categories across a local group shows the ways in which place and social identification were interrelated for the tribute regime. The disconnect between the variety of caste markers listed on the titles of tribute registers but not in the body of the documents shows the streamlining of these documents to funnel all free people of African descent into a single tributary class divided by place and family connections rather than by caste terminology. The Afromexican tributary population spanned individuals of a variety of castes and *calidades* ranging from *mulatos* and *pardos* to *morenos* and *negros*. Most references to *calidad* appeared only in the titles of the registers rather than alongside individual names. The creation of a blanket label for hundreds of families means that any caste designations must be treated with analytical caution. The presence or absence of caste markers would have been heavily dependent on commissioner preferences. However, the appearance of caste markers on these registers does reveal the care with which certain individuals were labeled, namely, those who were not *mulatos*. In the eighteenth century, the homogeneous absence of *calidad* on the register pointed to a goal of this institution—to label as many people as possible *mulatos*, and to label *mulatos* tributary.

The handful of Afromexican individuals who were not *mulatos* likely received this specification from a commissioner because they married outside their caste or *calidad*. Only fourteen records (0.2 percent of the total sample) contain free

Table 5.8. *Moreno, negro*, and *pardo* tributaries and spouses on eighteen tribute registers

Caste	Unknown (absent spouse)	*Español/a*	*India*	*Mulata*	None	Reserved (excused from payment)	Total
Moreno	0	0	0	0	1	1	2
Negro	0	1[a]	1	1	2	0	5
Negra	1	1	0	0	0	0	2
Pardo	0	1	0	0	2	0	3
Parda	0	2[b]	0	0	0	0	2
Total	1	5	1	1	5	1	14

Sources: See table 5.1.
[a]Includes one Spanish widow.
[b]Includes one man who "claimed to be Spanish."

people of African descent who were not labeled *mulato* or left without any designation of status. This small number of records named seven *negros*, five *pardos*, and two *morenos*, all free. The use of "*moreno*" was confined to Aguatlán in Izúcar, where the local industry of sugar production had led to the forced migration of enslaved Africans to the area. Distinctions between *negro, moreno, pardo*, and *mulato* existed in places like Izúcar where enslaved Afromexicans remained into the late eighteenth century. Other terms were scattered throughout tribute registers. None of these individuals married endogamously, and five were *solteros*. The most common intermarriages between these free people of African descent and other castes were with people who were recorded as (or claimed to be) of Spanish ancestry. As shown in table 5.8, such individuals did not have generalizable marriage patterns but were more likely to be male. The Guauchinango register showed *español* Eugenio de Castro as the husband of Rosalía, a *negra*, along with their two sons and two daughters.[107] *Pardo*, a common term in the titles of tribute registers for Afromexican tribute, appears three times in San Juan Tenochtitlán in relation to exogamous couples. Caste terminologies were used in specific instances to track distinctive marriages or, very rarely, to indicate the potential for such marriages among *solteros*. Unmarried men received a handful of caste markers, perhaps in anticipation that they might enter into exogamous marriages. These individuals were not the norm and received special attention from the commissioner in their community because they did not have a *mulato calidad*.

A total of 365 records of free people of African descent in the sample specified *calidad*, though this number is skewed by the preference of the Rosario commissioner who recorded families specifically as *mulato* in 338 cases.[108] As the oldest register examined in this study, the Rosario data may reflect a practice that late colonial reformers discouraged in favor of streamlining and abandoning individual labels. After Rosario, *calidad* terminology was most common in Celaya, San Juan Tenochtitlán, and Zacualpan. The use of caste terminology depended on the commissioner, who might never write the term "*mulato*" except in the title of his register. When caste is specified, however, the patterns suggest a predominance of other free people of color over *negros*, who by definition had no Spanish or Indian ancestors. Even the five enslaved people in the sample were not listed as "*negros*." Instead, they were simply a "slave" or, in two cases, a "*mulata esclava*." In Huichapam, Juan de Dios, the slave (*esclavo*) of don Manuel Villagran, was recorded with an Indian wife, with whom he had two young sons.[109] These recording methods did not conform to the instructions of the 1790s, which required not only that the enslaved person be named but that his or her master also be recorded.

The presence or absence of terminologies of *calidad* on these registers demonstrates the attention commissioners paid to this social marker. This practice did not reflect arbitrary idiosyncrasies after the 1780s, but rather a general practice. From the perspective of the Real Hacienda, the men who made tribute registers need not concern themselves with the specificities of Afromexican *calidad*. The difference between a *moreno* and a *mulato* amounted to little in the schemes of fiscal bureaucrats. The introduction of printed grids was precisely to do away with the intricacies of caste and *calidad*, abandoning them in favor of more rational modes of social division based on a bifurcated society. Ordinary people expressed a wide range of sentiments on the subject as evidenced in their petitions for tribute exemption. Some petitioners, as discussed in chapter 6, cared about the details of genealogy within tribute. Others, however, simply wished to define themselves against the idea of a "tributary quality," a *calidad tributaria*. These conflicting interpretations among ordinary people and commissioners shaped the Bourbon project to incorporate *calidad* into a simpler structure divided between tributary and nontributary. Into the 1790s, debates wore on in the Real Hacienda about how tributaries could reasonably be identified with some sort of reliability.

Conclusions

Through tribute, officials brought Indians and Afromexicans together in a single bureaucratic space, cordoning them off from Spanish men and their children with Indian women. Bourbon officials in Mexico City imagined registers as uniform exercises, but the documents show this was wishful thinking. In fact, very few registers conform to all the detailed instructions emanating from Mexico City in the late eighteenth century. As representations of free people of color through the eyes of local officials, registers provide an approximation of Afromexican tributary demography as well as insight into the success of bureaucratic goals at the local level. The presence of non-*mulatos* demonstrated the ways in which the register reflected Bourbon concerns with relationships as well as the possibilities for interaction among groups of people at local levels. Other adults, children of Indians and *mulatos*, as well as some guardians of *mulato* children, also found themselves associated with Afromexican tribute.

The register was a space in which relationships with free people of color determined social and genealogical webs. If mestizos or Spaniards became associated with free people of color, exempt names and families would be inscribed into this space as well. Previous chapters have argued that some Afromexican tributaries lived, sometimes as Indians or as the children of Spaniards, in communities that crossed boundaries of *calidad*. The efforts of the bureaucracy to divide Indians and Afromexican tributaries resulted in data that demonstrated the fantasy of physical and bureaucratic separation between free people of African descent and Indians. Connections with free people of African descent, within bureaucratic or physical space, could—accidentally or by malicious means—mark individuals of any *calidad* as a source of revenue for the crown.

To register and know all the Afromexican tributaries in New Spain was a lofty goal. In the process of partially meeting it, Bourbon attempts to expand tribute may have encouraged free people of African descent to attempt to change their *calidad* to avoid high tribute costs. Other evidence from rapid declines in tributaries, such as in Puebla, suggests that urban residents managed to escape registration. Taking this into account, the Real Hacienda still claimed to have registered more than a quarter million free people of African descent by the turn of the nineteenth century. A selection of these registers yields details from the lives of more than fourteen thousand people. Exogamy was a particular focus of the register, and the registers in the sample managed to aggregate more than a thousand such marriages. The tribute regime described individuals as the "products" of a place,[110] the outcome of reproductive unions, and the continuing expression of social ties. Many of these connections were genealogical constructions naming parents and their progeny, but siblings created a vertical and horizontal linkage that implied shared lineage as well as a direct relationship at the level of the current generation. Families were tracked in a fairly uniform fashion through phrases relating them by blood or marriage.

The register was the primary indicator of tributary status from the perspective of the Real Hacienda. Many complaints and exemption cases would focus on the register itself as more odious than the actual collection of payment. The payment of tribute was one part of the story, but appearing on the Afromexican register at all would impact local reputation in a way that many found intolerable. Although registers recorded relatively little information, they were powerful tools of bureaucratic organization, and residents of New Spain recognized this reality.

Creating numeric data from qualitative sources had the effect of distilling caste labels, family lineages, and other interpersonal relationships into delimited tributary categories. These categories were meaningful in an Atlantic context because they allowed for comparisons across empire and without any firsthand knowledge of the individual or regional situations.[111] By sending commissioners to make these tax registers, Bourbon authorities attempted to control the representation of information and increase their knowledge of colonial subjects. The first step in this process, the local tribute register, gave bureaucrats in Mexico City access to certain characteristics of Afromexican tributaries. While some data upheld Bourbon discourses about family, such as the importance of appropriate female labor, they undermined other stereotypes. Popularly disparaged as uprooted drifters, Afromexicans who were registered as tributaries instead formed close bonds in rural communities where they lived among other family members who paid tribute. Another aspect that many of these tributary portraits of free people of African descent shared was a connection between economic production and sexual reproduction. Many of the categories that interested colonial authorities as they gathered data on local families and communities show tribute as a site of production and reproduction of blackness. At the level of the jurisdictional summary, these minutiae of interpersonal connections were erased, as names turned to tallies and tallies to totals.

6

Genealogy and Disputed Tributary Status

In 1787, a group of Indians from the town of Almoloya, part of Apan in the Intendancy of Mexico, aired their grievances against several prominent local leaders. The petitioners claimed that their predominantly Indian community was plagued by a group of people who were masquerading as Tlaxcalans and Indian nobles, or caciques, and enjoying privileges to which only those with noble lineage were entitled. One of these was exemption from the economically onerous and socially stigmatized royal tribute, which had symbolized the relationship between the Spanish monarch and Indians and people of color since the sixteenth century.[1] The concern with the mixture of Indian and African blood resonated in Apan and in other areas where Tlaxcalan, Nahua, or other Indian groups enjoyed place- and genealogy-specific tribute privileges.[2] Throughout the colonial period, descendants of Tlaxcalans could claim tribute and other tax exemptions, land rights, and a legal status distinct from those of free people of African descent and other Indians.[3] But, the Apan complainants reasoned, the exemption should be conferred only on select descendants, those who had pursued marital unions that preserved a lineage "without degeneration from the class of Indians or *mestizos de españoles*."[4] A Tlaxcalan genealogy established not only colonial privileges but also a more generalized "cultural and military superiority over other 'Indians.'"[5] How, reasoned the Almoloya petitioners, could people from a publicly reputed line of Afromexican ancestors claim and prove a Tlaxcalan genealogy?

The Almoloya petition reflected anger that these "notorious *mulatos*" had gained exemptions awarded to Tlaxcalans who had served in Spanish conquests more than two and a half centuries before. To prove their suspicions that these people were tributaries, those lodging the complaint turned to lineage. The Almoloyans called out more than a dozen people who lived as caciques, in spite of the fact that those same individuals were "mixed with blacks and *mulatos* and should be registered and pay tribute with those of that class." Despite their attempts to fashion themselves as caciques, the accused families had not been able to erase from communal memory the occupations, castes, and places of origin of their various ancestors, all of which were weighed by the community and its authorities in determining reputation, or *calidad*. Thus, members of the Sánchez family were "grandchildren of a *negro* shoemaker called Martín," and the Granillos were "descendants of Juan Granillo, married to a known *mulata* servant." The list of putative Afromexicans was exhaustive.[6]

The "pure Indians" of Almoloya, as they called themselves in their initial petition and subsequent documents, relied on genealogy to stake their claims. They upheld proof of ancestry as a prerequisite for exercising privileges, a legal argument favored by Indian elites at the time.[7] The use of the word "*degeneración*" to describe the targets of the petition drew on an older rhetoric of purity as well as concepts of heredity that would gain greater attention in the nineteenth century.[8] The term also recalls scientific characterizations of New World flora and fauna as degraded, weak, and savage. The so-called pure Indians asserted that, in fact, only people of mixed ancestry and unclean nature deserved such a designation, not the original inhabitants of the region.[9] The repeated references to the "mixed nature" and "inferior *calidad*" of the people targeted in the petition was intended to undermine their authority as caciques, a status that was typically predicated on publicly regarded and written genealogies.[10] The opposition of the petitioners rested on the genealogical concept of *limpieza de sangre*, or blood purity, which had risen to prominence as a form of communal memory following mass conversions of Jews in medieval Iberia.[11] In New Spain, *limpieza de sangre* would evolve to equate genealogical impurity with the presence of African ancestry as well.[12] Pitting the idea of an inferior, mixed, and *mulato calidad* against Indian purity, the petitioners used the language of genealogy to upend local hierarchies.

The power of genealogy was clear to ordinary people who engaged in tribute disputes from the 1780s to the 1800s, as the Almoloya case demonstrates. Here as elsewhere in New Spain, genealogy took a prominent place in disputes involving local privileges, rivalries, and migration, and its importance corresponds to the emphasis given to genealogical determinations by Bourbon rulers. In Almoloya's surrounding jurisdiction, the number of *mulato* tributaries nearly doubled between 1781 and 1788, while Indian tributaries in the same period dropped by 10 percent.[13] On a register made at the end of the year 1800, no caciques were listed at all, though 407 Indians and twenty-one *mulatos* were registered as reserved from payment.[14] The basis of the Almoloya petition was that the accused caciques, failing to prove beyond doubt their genealogy, should be considered (or had always been considered, in the eyes of their accusers) *lobos*, *mulatos*, and *negros*, reputations that were only confirmed by the immigrant status of some families.[15] Thus the Almoloya plaintiffs' reliance on a Tlaxcalan genealogy proved to be untenable.[16] The caciques were not alone: across New Spain, Bourbon authorities had begun to strip privileged groups of their claims to Tlaxcalan ancestry. A weak genealogy, coupled with a Bourbon desire to streamline tributary groups and dispense with privileged status, forced many accused families to forfeit their privileges.

The disgruntled accusers succeeded in ousting alleged immigrants, *mulatos*, and *lobos* from their positions as caciques and thus stripped them of their rights to use communal property and authority over local affairs. In spite of the ruling, conflict continued into the next decade. Accusations surfaced that these non-Indians had refused to pay for their use of Indian lands and had reacted violently to the change in their status. In 1790, Viceroy Revillagigedo sent the former cacique Juan José Espinoza to jail along with his wife, their son, and son-in-law for throwing stones at the tribute collector. The same fate awaited Domingo Martínez, who had attempted to strike the alcalde. Other men and women resisted the imposition of Afromexican status by refusing to leave lands they had planted as part of the Indian community. The targeted families made a public display of their anger and refusal to comply. Women in particular were accused of disturbing the peace and spreading gossip in order to further inflame emotions in the town. In the midst of the scandal, some of the accused maintained that they were not Afromexican. One official snidely wondered if their continued insistence represented a kind of "sleepless hope of new regeneration from which the *mulato* can never escape."[17] In the eyes of colonial authorities, these families had been relegated to the tributary class, one that united castes and qualities under the shared and shameful burden of tribute.

For families like those accused in Almoloya, being or becoming an Afromexican tributary represented a social and financial burden that would mark future generations as both taxpayers and people of African descent. This chapter shows how petitioners attempted to circumvent the application of Afromexican tributary status on themselves and their families after the implantation of the intendant system. At the core of the discussion is genealogy, the principle underlying tributary status in the minds of bureaucrats and ordinary people. Petitioners who challenged Afromexican tributary status, most of them adult men, took a variety of strategies to establish genealogy, drawing on oral and written testimony from witnesses regarding their reputation and ancestry and social constructs concerning gendered honor, *calidad*, marriage and reproduction, and local histories. As they "consciously engaged in forms of *casta*-like genealogical mathematics," patriarchs excised certain lines of descent in order to shield family members from tributary status.[18] Thus the resolutions of these petitions defined families as well as tributary status and what constituted it.

Among bureaucrats also, contemporary debates about tributary status incorporated and reinterpreted concepts of heredity, physiognomy, genealogy, and *calidad*. Over time, however, governing bodies in New Spain and the Council of the Indies decided that genealogy, and not other elements of a person's identity, would be the defining feature of tributary status. Genealogy was thus central to the framework of self-definition and bureaucratic categorization within the tribute regime, and interpretations of *calidad*, gender, and family—and thus tributary status—were subject to it into the nineteenth century.

The petitions for exempt tributary status encapsulate the fundamental constructs of lineage and privilege evident in colonial Spanish America. Tribute exemption arguments reveal the "archival and genealogical practices" that characterized multiple kinds of petitions in the Spanish Atlantic.[19] Ordinary people, as well as bureaucrats, voiced diverse ideas about lineage, preserved in legal petitions like the proof of *limpieza de sangre*, requests for an official change to one's caste under the *gracias al sacar*, and the tribute exemptions discussed here. In seeking an exempt tributary status that relied on notions of purity, lineage, and colonial privileges, petitioners were addressing the themes that underpinned Spanish colonial governance and regulated the interactions between the crown and Afromexican subjects. The tribute regime, which spanned more than two hundred years, provided a means for Spanish rulers to profit from and incorporate free people of color as members of colonial societies.

Seeking Tribute Exemption in the Late Eighteenth Century

When tributaries sought exemption, they and their legal representatives constructed genealogical, legal, or social resources that could avoid or reverse tributary status. An exempt genealogy connected a family to ancestors—usually men—who had possessed a nontributary *calidad*, nobility, or privileges granted by colonial authorities. These practices had been in place since Habsburg rule and persisted into the late colonial period. Afromexican men across New Spain successfully petitioned for privileges usually reserved for Spaniards and mestizos, such as bearing arms or, for members of militia companies, tribute exemption. Successful petitions established the possibility for free people of color to employ the tropes of masculine honor and service.[20] Within the tribute regime, many of the discussions about the meanings of *calidad* and tributary status arose out of individual, familial, or corporate petitions describing or disputing family or community histories of tributary registration.

In petitions seeking exemption, tributary status was explicitly linked to words indicating caste, *calidad*, and class. Frequent substitutions in written records among the terms "tributary quality," "tributary caste," and the "tributary class" suggest that these designations were mutually dependent, even circular. The same people who comprised the tributary class would also have tributary qualities and belong to a tributary caste. Extending this line of thought, Bourbon reformers sought to implement a clearly delineated structure that would subsume caste, class, and *calidad* under the categories of tributary and nontributary, thereby denying the weight of any single element. Tributary status could not be defined by any one element; focus on any one of these destabilized the others. No matter the weight of caste, class, and *calidad* in one's self-definition, those qualities were still, nonetheless, subject to bureaucratic categorization.

The transition to *calidad* as the defining element in considering tribute disputes and petitions occurred in the eighteenth century. Petitioners and their legal representatives often associated *calidad* with both caste and class, reflecting a growing focus on socioeconomic status as a social marker. By the eighteenth century, tributary vocabulary had thoroughly incorporated *calidad*, a marker of reputation that described color, caste, occupation, and ancestry, among other characteristics. As colonial authorities and ordinary people began to use the term to describe appearance, reputation, and occupation in the same phrase, this approach to classification came to combine elements of class and caste.[21] *Calidad* condensed caste and socioeconomic status, making it the ideal social marker for determining who would be determined a tributary.

Petitioners who contested their tributary status were acutely aware of the meanings of genealogy and *calidad* in the tribute regime and its community politics. Since Spaniards, mestizos, and elite Indians did not pay tribute, tributary status was a de facto indication of an Indian commoner or African *calidad* in a family's lineage or marital ties. Thus, the negative social weight of a rumored or confirmed tributary status rendered registration and payment not only financially onerous but also a public disgrace. Even when a person's registration among tributaries with a *mulato* or *negro calidad* proved to be a mistake, it could fuel gossip and damage reputations. In addition, some petitioners used *calidad* to insult their neighbors by implying their tributary status, whereas others employed converse genealogical tactics to protect their own families. As the potential economic effects of tributary status lurked in the background, arguments about lineage and *calidad* dominated petitions requesting exemption from Afromexican tribute in the late eighteenth century.

The process of disputing tributary status became more structured and centralized in the late eighteenth century, providing historians with a wealth of information about tribute disputes in Mexico City after 1786. Although petitioners' legal representatives certainly influenced the ways in which people expressed themselves in writing, the labels and arguments people chose to present in legal documents help us understand how they thought about themselves within the colonial regime.[22] To illustrate these kinds of choices, in this chapter I examine two individual petitions and two petitions on behalf of large groups of men from frontier towns, all four from eighteenth-century records. I have drawn evidence for the analyses of these cases from petitions and other legal documents that discussed tribute exemption from the last forty years of the eighteenth century. Eighteen cases were requests from militiamen and their representatives for tribute exemption based on service to the crown.[23] The focus of this chapter is on the language and logic of the cases rather than on demonstrating their degree of success in securing exemption for petitioners. Whether or not petitioners were successful, their interpretations of tribute allow us to better understand the connections between *calidad*, blackness, tributary status, and family.

Petitions followed a set of procedures that changed multiple times in the eighteenth century and drew on centuries of Iberian and Ibero-American precedent. In Castile, individuals could gain royal tax exemptions through "*pleitos de hidalguía*," petitions that rested on genealogy and nobility.[24] The term "pleito," uncommon in tribute exemptions in New Spain, appeared when tributaries accused local officials or bureaucrats of poor administration or of using tribute for personal vendettas. Petitions in New Spain, in contrast, occasionally complained of an overzealous official, but most maintained the kind of deference inherent in their genre. Cases for tribute exemption often took the form of a petition to the viceroy. These initial documents would then be supplemented with additional evidence. Intendants and local magistrates testified in administrative matters pertaining to the collection and registration of families and individuals. Copies of these proceedings then went to the Real Hacienda in Mexico City. Accountants, as well as the tribute administrator, made frequent appearances in these disputes. Finally, the *fiscal* of the Real Hacienda was also consulted, as his recommendations were central to the functioning of the tribunal that dealt with royal accounts.[25]

The reorganization of colonial administration following the Ordinance of Intendants in 1786 limited the powers of the viceroy and created new units of territorial division. Revillagigedo's Ordinance for the Formation of Visitations, Censuses, and Rates of Tributaries of New Spain (1793) revised collections procedures and streamlined review of exemptions for Indians and free Afromexicans. One of the key changes for tribute petitioners was the definition of the tribute commissioner as any person who had gained the "confidence" of the intendant.[26] Although local reputation often determined tributary status, only bureaucrats in the capital had the official capacity to correct the data; the commissioners were unable to change the tribute registers once they were completed. The authority to approve, redact, and archive lists rested with the accountants of the Real Hacienda.

Tributaries complained when officials did not accurately create the "exact registers of all inhabitants" described in the Ordinance of Intendants. Most petitioners sought to remove themselves from any tribute register, not just from the list of free people of African descent. But some individuals and families did seek to adjust their status, even if it did not mean exemption from payment. In 1806, the Office of Tribute Accounts in the Real Hacienda transferred don Joseph María de Ayala and his family from the register of *mulatos* to that of Indians in the jurisdiction of Puruándiro, located halfway between Mexico City and Guadalajara. As "second-class mestizos" by their Indian father and Spanish mother, the Ayalas were tributaries despite their Spanish lineage.[27] Located in the jurisdiction of Valladolid, which was home to thousands of Afromexican tributaries at the time, these tributaries may have been registered in Puruándiro alongside many other free people of African descent. As mestizos registered as Indian tributaries, the Ayala family could expect to root themselves in their community while establishing a mestizo status. The family prepared documents for the distant offices of the Real Hacienda in the hope of modifying, rather than opposing, their tributary status.

Tributary status was made manifest in public performances testifying to the tributary's *calidad*, including the very act of registration and the delivery of payment to the tribute regime. Thus, petitioners for exemption were often able to call on a lack of tributary history, bringing in witnesses to attest to the fact that, for generations, no one in the family had ever been seen paying tribute in the community. Tributary status was based on written and reputational genealogies and public behaviors like those just mentioned. Tributary status might be read from a prepared list by a collector. In this way, tributary status mirrored *calidad* as a social marker, with its basis on appearance as well as family actions and behaviors, past and present. A lineage of nonpayment could bolster a petition to resolve tributary status in favor of a petitioner, so long as friends and neighbors were willing to attest to a long tradition of nonpayment in previous generations. A lineage of payment would bolster the opposite effect.

The process of proving one's *calidad* relied on written documentation of lineage as well as public reputation. Presented on behalf of individuals or groups, petitions for exemption gathered together documents that established genealogies, usually a combination of marriage and baptismal records and previous tribute registers. In tribute cases, community opinion could be estimated through witness testimony, which yielded the tributary genealogy of an individual or family as perceived by others. A *calidad* based on witness testimony was inherently unstable, as it depended on the personal opinions and *calidad* of the witness. Proofs of genealogy were not guaranteed over time, and labels of caste, *calidad*, *limpieza de sangre*, and tributary status were not always permanent. During a case, some individuals or families might be granted tribute relief provisionally, until higher authorities had time to review the case thoroughly; thus, "*con calidad de por ahora*."[28] Indeed, any tribute exemption could be temporary, and repeated legal proceedings were necessary to achieve the long-term desires of the petitioner.

Tributary Status in Flux

This kind of instability in administration directly affected petitioners' perceptions of justice and honor. In 1786, a *vecino* of Cuernavaca calling himself don Nicolás Gerardo Zedano asserted that he and his wife, doña María Josefa Ortiz, were "known and reputed" to have Spanish ancestry in their community "without there ever having been anyone to doubt their *calidad*" or tributary status.[29] The phrase "without a doubt" appears repeatedly in their petition, yet the basis of the case was the confusion surrounding the tributary status of the couple, who had been registered as *mulato* tributaries in 1785 and 1786. To clarify the situation, don Nicolás presented a battery of witnesses from Cuernavaca and beyond. These included numerous creoles, a peninsular Spaniard, and the Indian governor as well as the parish priest and the *alcalde mayor*, all of whom named the petitioner as a Spaniard. None of the witnesses so much as mentioned that the Zedano family had been registered among the *mulato* tributaries, perhaps opting to set that fact aside so as to advance the petition. In witness testimony, the Zedanos appeared to be a well-connected family with ties to prominent community members and a solid reputation as nontributaries.

The procedure for obtaining tribute exemptions required communication between bureaucrats in the capital and local officials, a tenuous connection that could alter and deteriorate over time. Following this initial petition, don Nicolás Zedano and María Josefa obtained a temporary exemption from the Real Hacienda, only to be registered again by a different agent of the same entity in 1789. This action forced the *alcalde mayor*, who had testified in Zedano's favor in the first instance, to charge him royal tribute. Aware of the alcalde's predicament, Zedano observed that the alcalde was forced to ignore "the certification which I showed him because once I was registered and counted in the *tasación*, the amount of my tribute would have to come from his own pocket." Don Nicolás floridly described the episode as "not only not conforming to justice, but diametrically opposed to it." The petitioner asked that his name and that of his wife be "erased" from the list in question, and that a note be placed "in the margin which will convey the reason for erasing us and so that we may not be registered again."[30] Only in 1792 did the Real Hacienda reaffirm the exemption, demonstrating the uncertain situation in which even successful petitioners often found themselves and their families.

Another resident of the Valley of Mexico learned that the evidence he had presented in the effort to remove himself from an Afromexican tribute register was not admissible. Vicente Pérez Abreu, a *vecino* of Coyoacán, brought his complaint in 1799 to protest his registration, in spite of his parents' being "free of any bad race [*raza*]." The use of the term "*raza*" rather than "*casta*" showed the petitioner's perception of the permanence of an Afromexican status and its irreparable damage to blood purity (Jewish ancestry was similarly known as a "bad race").[31] The complainant claimed to have "no idea" why the commissioner had registered him "among the tributaries, having no proof that I or my ancestors had been subject to the contribution . . . being of Spanish *calidad*."[32] Pérez Abreu returned to his town of origin, nearby Xochimilco, submitted ecclesiastical documents, and presented witness testimony on the part of Spaniards from the community in favor of his case. However, the fiscal for the Real Hacienda believed the information lacked proper certifications. At this point, the burden fell on Pérez Abreu to resubmit his case with the proper additions and corrections, a costly and time-consuming process. His case hung in the balance, his tributary genealogy firmly recorded unless and until it could be erased by orders from Mexico City. Pérez Abreu conveyed his shock and dismay at being registered as a *mulato* by a commissioner who did not seem to know his reputation and lacked justification to demand payment of the tax.

The figure of the commissioner as ignorant and greedy outsider was one that petitioners frequently evoked in disputes of Afromexican tributary status. Confrontations between the official and potential tributaries could encompass entire communities. Frontier regions in particular produced petitions decrying the commissioner's disregard for the genealogies of families or towns. In the Huasteca, large groups of petitioners constructed genealogies that focused on place as well as *calidad*. These petitioners were aware of their importance for colonial defense and trade in the region, which was agriculturally productive yet politically volatile.[33]

The following two examples are drawn from the Valley of Metztitlán, a fertile, majority-Indian area of the Huasteca that provided agricultural products for the mines at Pachuca.[34] Towns within Metztitlán were also tied to regional trade routes on which goods moved within the Huasteca and on to interior cities.[35] The valley was also the center of a profitable tribute-producing region, with more than fourteen thousand pesos charged in 1788.[36] Potential tributaries in this and other parts of the Huasteca used the region's commercial position to their advantage. Registered residents rejected their status as tributaries, citing nontributary genealogies resulting from the combination of ancestral privilege and *calidad*.

The concept of privilege based on a variety of "qualities" surfaced in tribute cases, as the meanings and permutations of the word "*calidad*" allowed petitioners to use it rather generously. Some requests for exemption involved men claiming to be the descendants of conquistadors. These arguments could prove compelling in Mexico City, and some were decided favorably. Petitions from the district of Metztitlán (today in the state of Hidalgo) provide two successful examples of arguments based on ancestral honor, both arising at the turn of the nineteenth century. In 1796, residents of San Agustín Metzquititlán offered proof of tribute exemption, citing how "our ancestors personally assisted in the conquest with their arms and horses," language that placed the petitioners on the same footing as conquistadors and their descendants.[37] Legal representatives often used phrases in a similar vein, as did the Augustinian Fray Juan Zapata y Sandoval, who argued in 1609 that privileges be dispensed to men of Spanish descent who had supported colonial rule "at their own expense" and "with their strength and industry."[38] Thirty-seven cases, comprising more than ninety men, claimed exemptions based on *calidad* and ancestral ties to the conquistadors of the Sierra Gorda and New Santander. Spaniards, *castizos*, and mestizos, these men sought recognition of their genealogies of service and *calidad*, which they hoped would lead to exemption.

Many complaints were presented in these cases; most stemmed from the perceived ignorance of the commissioner, a community outsider, who had mistakenly categorized many families as *mulatos* or Indians. This commissioner, the community protested, had no respect for the place-specific privileges that villagers perceived as grounds for their designated compensation: the participation of their ancestors in expensive and dangerous frontier conquests and settlement. The complaints presented in these cases reveal the discrepancies and doubts that led to an overhaul of the 1796 Afromexican register, even though only twenty-seven of the original petitioners were in fact confirmed as exempt.[39]

Efforts to dismantle the inflated tributary list began with a group of formulaic petitions from male heads of household. Luis Antonio de Torres, a literate descendant of a Spanish man and a *castiza*, filed such a petition on behalf of himself and his two sons, José and Vicente; it sought to remove them from the *mulato* register. With the testimony of witnesses, Luis Antonio tried to establish his own status as a Spanish man, buttressed by a family history that did not include paying tribute, and the *calidad* of his wife Felipa. Luis Antonio's witnesses were themselves men involved in the larger dispute over the accuracy of the new register. The first witness described Luis Antonio as the child of a Spanish man and a *castiza* and Felipa as a Spanish woman, making José and Vicente Spanish as well. A second witness called Luis Antonio's parents a Spanish man and a mestiza, and, thus, Luis Antonio a mestizo. A final witness described Luis as a mestizo by virtue of being the child of a *castiza* and a Spanish man; his children were also mestizos according to this witness.[40] Only the first of these witnesses addressed the progressions that supposedly allowed individuals to become Spanish by blood and thus exit the tribute register.

The witnesses did not agree on the precise caste of Luis Antonio, yet the technicalities of caste were not the real issue to these men. Rather, they understood tribute as a dividing line between privilege and obligation. As long as Luis Antonio and his family could preserve a mestizo, *castizo*, or Spanish *calidad*, they could avoid paying tribute. Although Luis Antonio believed his reputation was at risk, he and his sons were eventually listed as nontributaries who had never been registered.

Attacks or threats by hostile Indians created a necessity of allegiance between subjects and government. In the district just mentioned, a petition involving hundreds of people from the town of Molango (in present-day Hidalgo) sought to stabilize their "privileged *calidad*," based on their service, caste, and *limpieza de sangre*. Following a 1797 case before the Real Audiencia, the residents gained a temporary exemption from tribute because of their "special merit" for having maintained colonial control in the face of the "frontier with the Mecos."[41] The people in Molango had been called on at a time when uprisings were occurring in the Sierra Gorda region.[42] They argued that this reciprocal relationship should make them eligible for the conferral of tributary privileges. However, in 1798 disgruntled petitioners reported that a "malicious" commissioner had targeted "all the families of the town of Molango, intending to obscure in the most ignominious way the origin and birthplace of the families that have given certified proofs of their *limpieza de sangre*."[43] On the basis of their military allegiance and geographical importance, the residents submitted genealogical proofs of *calidad* for their legal representative to compile and present.

The investigation conducted by the Real Hacienda in Mexico City and local officials in Molango resulted in the creation of multiple lists of people based on distinctions of tributary status and further organized by family unit. Among these were married couples and unmarried men particularly concerned about their potential status as *mulato* tributaries. The lists that arose from the investigation would reflect not only the tributary status of individuals but familial bonds as well: men would be recorded with their wives or, in the case of unmarried men, their brothers. The threat to reputation was so great that 122 people who had never been registered as *mulato* tributaries provided proof that they were not *mulatos*, lest they be accused later on. An additional eighty people who were registered in 1791 as *mulatos* could not provide evidence of another *calidad*. A third group of twenty-nine people were registered as *mulatos* in 1791 but were granted an exempt *calidad* after investigation and petitioning. These people attempted to gain privileges due inhabitants "as children of Spanish men married to Spanish women, Indians, mestizas, or *castizas*."[44] A nontributary *calidad* was the priority of all of the petitioners, though at least two men defined themselves as Indian tributaries who had been registered as *mulatos*. With the consultation of branches of the Real Hacienda, Viceroy Félix Berenguer de Marquina approved the petition in 1801. This victory for the residents of Molango undermined the authority of the commissioner, an outsider who had infringed on their protected privileges based on genealogy.

Other tribute commissioners provoked frustration, confusion, and outrage among residents who claimed exemptions based on *calidad*. With the implementation of the Ordinance of Intendants, genealogy became the preferred method of proving nontributary *calidad*, but at the same time it provided commissioners with a flexible criterion they could use to inflate tribute registers. Commissioners were representative of an overarching Bourbon project to enhance revenue collection and dissolve colonial privileges that had structured relationships between authorities and subjects for centuries. Because their earnings were based on the amount of tributes collected, commissioners had little incentive to honor communal memory of privilege or local interpretations of *calidad*. At times, an entire community accused a commissioner of disregarding long-standing privileges and failing to evaluate *calidad* accurately, and the ensuing investigations often found numerous cases of mistaken identity. The methods for evaluating tributary status included review of ecclesiastical records and witness testimony, but the most influential was a previous tribute register. When a former nontributary was added to the register, witnesses protested that no other commissioner had recorded such an individual or family, thereby casting doubt on the new commissioner's reasons for doing so. In the cases of Metzquititlán and Molango, investigations revealed worries that commissioners would attempt to register individuals who had never been part of the Afromexican tributary group. These community outsiders did not value the reputations of the families and lineages that would become tributary in the event of registration.

Marriage, Adoption, and Inheritance of Tributary Status

Attitudes about marriage and reproduction in relation to *calidad* were at the foundation of Bourbon tribute policy. The Royal Pragmatic promulgated in New Spain in 1778 criticized "unequal" marriages between people of different *calidades*, with reference to free people of color.[45] Parents and guardians could petition authorities to declare a potential marriage invalid due to concerns about differences in *calidad*.[46] Yet, one historian has argued that the primary purpose of this legislation was to affirm the importance of obedience to father and crown and thus "fortify the paternalist, hierarchical bonds on which the empire was thought to rest."[47] Male petitioners concerned with tributary status sought not so much to contest the marriage itself as invalid on grounds of *calidad*, but rather to separate themselves from individual marital choices that threatened familial reputation. In such petitions, male family members acted as interpreters of the tribute regime, declaring the actions of younger female members unrepresentative of the family's *calidad* in order to privilege their own position. This disapproval of marriage choices reflected a Bourbon criticism of freedom of choice, and therefore patriarchal authority, in marriage; the opposition was to a marriage that would unite people deemed ill-suited for each other on the basis of their tributary status and *calidad*. By the time a tribute dispute occurred, the marriages in question had often already given rise to tributary offspring.

Late colonial reforms and genealogical debates had a strong influence on how families attempted to mitigate the effects of Afromexican tributary lineage. If either parent were a tributary, the children would inherit that status. Revillagigedo's 1793 ordinance stated that *mulato* and Indian men would pay only half the rate of tribute if they married exempt women, but that their children would remain on the register of tributaries.[48] Thus, such children retained their father's *calidad*, due to the presence of African blood in their lineage. The lack of distinction between maternal and paternal bloodlines in determining tributary status points to the determination to expand the tribute regime. The genealogical intricacies of maternal versus paternal lineage could not release children from the Afromexican tributary category.

The meanings of lineage and marriage dominated a 1797 case presented by a man from Zacatlán de las Manzanas, a Huasteca town near the regional trading hub of Tulancingo. When José Agustín González Muñiz returned after a long absence to his home town, tribute collectors demanded he pay royal tribute. Fearing that his name would be recorded among the *mulato* tributaries, he anticipated the "prejudice" that would affect his children and grandchildren, who still enjoyed the "good reputation, religious education, and good customs" of a Spanish family.[49] If he were assigned an Afromexican *calidad* in the tribute regime, the family would no longer retain its strong associations with good behavior.[50] Furthermore, the future of his descendants would become uncertain, all because of a single act of tributary registration. With these consequences in mind, González Muñiz petitioned for his removal from the list of *mulato* tributaries, using an argument based on genealogy.

González Muñiz and his legal representative chose to describe his status and establish his *calidad* by genealogical means. The centerpiece of the life history that they constructed and supported with witness testimony was González Muñiz's adoption. The petitioner used the term "*huérfano*," which allowed him to construe his childhood as one without parents but not without lineage, thus avoiding having to present himself as an *expósito*—a person without known parents and thus without a lineage. For González Muñiz and other petitioners unable to formulate convincing nontributary genealogies, presenting oneself as a foundling with a lineage, but one that could not be confirmed, was an attractive alternative. In 1794, Charles IV had extended new privileges to people of unknown parentage (the *expósitos*) like González Muñiz, who had been deposited in adoptive homes.[51] Although he might have been eligible to claim *expósito* status, González Muñiz determined that presenting himself as a *huérfano* instead would establish a stronger separation from his adoptive parents. He stated that he had been raised in the home of his godmother, doña Antonia Coronela, where he was originally placed as a baby. While he was still a young child, his godmother had died, leaving him under the care of the Morgados. His adoptive mother, Juana Morgado, was a *mulata* from a family of what one mestizo community member disparaged as "*negritos*."[52] Because the Morgados were publicly known to be *mulatos*, the petitioner speculated that his residence in their house "must have been the motive" for his inclusion among members of that "same *calidad*."[53] González Muñiz related this aspect of his childhood as an episode in his life, which he carefully detached from his own identity by pointing to the community memory of his biological father to distance himself from the Morgados (he described his relationship with the Morgados as tenuous). As an *expósito* under the new law, he might have been able to leave his *calidad* in doubt and thus open to determination; instead, he followed a strategy that distanced him clearly from his adoptive past.

Thus, a genealogical narrative of ties with people of Spanish ancestry served as the petition's argument. To make his case, González Muñiz first claimed to be a *castizo* mistakenly registered in the tributary "class of *mulatos*." He requested that he be "excluded from this caste" in the documents of the Real Hacienda and on the "General Count and Tributary Register of this jurisdiction of Zacatlán." Promising that witnesses "would give account of [his] lineage and *calidad*," he offered a description of his "*sanguinidad*," thereby evoking the importance of blood in the transference of tributary status. In this petition, he argued that "*casta*" and "*clase*" might define the bureaucratic distinction that made one a *mulato* tributary, but that the terms "*sanguinidad*," "*linaje*," and "*calidad*" were the building blocks of genealogy and, therefore, the basis for exemption. His genealogical relationship to his Spanish father, whom he never knew, outweighed his adoption into a *mulato* family.

Witness testimony eventually revealed the name and *calidad* of González Muñiz's biological father, a master gunsmith of Spanish lineage. This discovery was key to his case: when an orphan's parents were known to the community, the *calidad* of the child was no longer doubtful. This kind of "blend of public and private information" was already common in other petitions to confirm legitimacy and lineage.[54] Relying on the unwritten public reputation González Muñiz enjoyed as the illegitimate child of a Spaniard, witnesses in the case repeatedly asserted that ancestry was critical in determining tributary status. The caste of González Muñiz's adoptive parents should have little direct impact on his *calidad*, they said, and they clearly had no doubt that the petitioner's *calidad* should be determined from that of his biological parents. In the context of these arguments, Spanish genealogy and *calidad* shared an immutable feature that even deep familial bonds with *mulatos* could not negate.

Since González Muñiz's use of the circumstances of his adoption had proven successful in presenting his petition, he decided to use the same ideas about inherent qualities and blood lineage to construct the genealogies of his daughters (figure 6.1). The connection between fathers and daughters was not unique to this case or the region, and other men used information about their wives and daughters to protect the family.[55] For the daughters of Agustín González Muñiz, however, their involvement in his arguments did not necessarily work to their advantage. Tribute registers from previous years did not show Agustín González Muñiz or his wife as tributaries, but their daughters were registered as *mulatas*, creating confusion about reputation and tributary status within the family. The elder daughter, Bernabela Antonia, had contracted a first marriage to a tributary Indian with whom she had four children. In the eyes of her father, this alliance lacked what one historian has called "strategic conjugality."[56] Later Bernabela remarried, choosing a mestizo, as did her younger sister María Josefa. The local Indian governor testified that he did not understand why the two sisters had been registered as tributaries, unless it was because of their father's adoptive upbringing in a *mulato* household.[57] González Muñiz's petition had benefited from public recognition of his lineage, but his daughters' cases took a different trajectory. In January 1799, the commissioner who had created the contested register appeared in Mexico City to explain how he had made his decisions regarding who to record in Zacatlán. He claimed he had never registered González Muñiz but that he did register Bernabela Antonia as a *mulata*. To the commissioner, Bernabela's past registration as a tributary justified placing her name on the new register. Although Bernabela explained to him that "she was Spanish because her father was," the commissioner said he had asked neighbors and local officials but "could not determine the truth." Only a few community members claimed to know Bernabela's *calidad*. As for her sister, the commissioner saw her as a tributary by virtue of being "sister of Bernabela by father and mother."[58] In the commissioner's mind, the uncertainties surrounding Bernabela's *calidad* automatically spread to her sister owing to their similar genealogies.

Determining who had the authority to decide tributary status was a fundamental issue as the investigation into the family developed. González Muñiz asked the commissioner to erase his family from the tribute register "because his daughters and grandchildren were as Spanish as he and his ancestors."[59] When the commissioner informed him that the list could be revised only by the Real Hacienda, González Muñiz pointed to the confirmation of his own nontributary status by the Real Audiencia. "I the father of these [daughters] already proved my *calidad* in the ways provided by the Royal Ordinances," his petition stated, underscoring his role as protector and guardian.[60] Positioning himself as an expert on tribute during the proceedings, he declared that he himself would evaluate which of his grandchildren would inherit the familial tribute exemption. By his genealogical calculations, María Josefa's children should not be registered because the combination of her *castiza* genealogy and her husband's mestizo genealogy gave

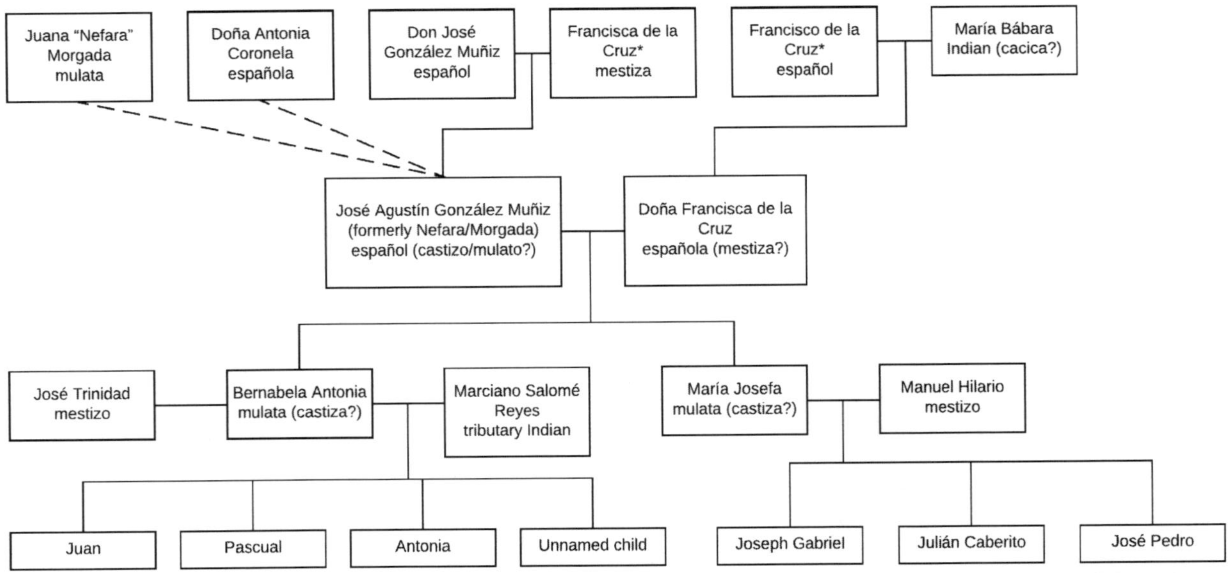

Figure 6.1. Family tree of José Agustín González Muñiz (asterisk = no relation; dashed line = adoptive relationship) (Norah Gharala)

the children enough Spanish blood to justify exemption. If both sisters were *castizas*, then Bernabela's children from her marriage to an Indian would become tributaries because they were not mestizos by technical definition. This careful attention to the designations of blood indicated González Muñiz's understanding of the repercussions of Bernabela's choice of marriage partners. Her past actions had resulted in the permanent obligation of her children to pay royal tribute. Agustín González Muñiz himself saw that obligation as the consequence of his daughter's disadvantageous marriage to an Indian, a union that would mark an entire branch of the family as tributaries.

While most of the case focused on genealogy and its proofs, exclusive of physical appearance, a brief statement at the end of the document shows how appearance and lineage were related in evaluations of tributary status. For Bernabela and María Josefa, the eligibility for exemption rested on the reputations of their father Agustín and their deceased mother Francisca de la Cruz, daughter of a Spaniard and a *cacica*. Although her genealogy was known in the community, a new parish priest stated that Francisca was already dead at the time of his installment and that he therefore "did not see her aspect, which she manifested related to her *calidad*."[61] This is the only explicit reference to phenotype in the case, and this interpretation of *calidad* did not come from the petitioner himself. Even in the absence of Francisca, the priest drew not only on genealogical characteristics but also on notions of physiognomy that long predated concepts of *calidad*.[62] His interest in seeing Francisca in order to "know" her *calidad* underscores the complex nature of *calidad* and its unstable dependence on everyday interpretations and individual opinions. But for the González Muñiz family, the case could not hinge on Francisca alone; they understood tributary status as a familial matter, deeply rooted in genealogy, rather than a condition that could be isolated to one individual.

Individual members' *calidad* and marital choices could have wide effects on the tributary status of the family. Once an exogamous marriage took place, it could be nearly impossible for a family to set itself apart from the choice made by a single member. The 1799 case of Cristóbal Martínez and his family, from Tenango in Chalco (southeast of Mexico City), illuminates the effects of marriage on a nontributary reputation. Warning the *oidores* in the capital that a rogue magistrate was on the loose, Cristóbal Martínez complained that his family had been unfairly targeted in the tribute commissioner's attempt to expand the local Afromexican register. The petition portrayed the temporal legal connection of marriage as quite different from the deeper bonds of blood between parent and progeny. Martínez stressed that he and his brother were of Spanish descent, and that his brother had married his wife's sister, also reputed to be Spanish. The mutual familial and marital connections between wives and husbands ensured that, as Martínez stated, "all the children that he and I procreated are legitimate Spaniards." However, Martínez's niece Mónica had married a *lobo*, and the commissioner wanted to register the entire family as *mulatos*. He argued that Mónica's husband, whatever caste he may have possessed before he died, did not "share at all in our blood." Furthermore, Mónica did not "have any succession" of children who would now be part of the family, effectively truncating this line of descent.[63] By this logic, this association was purely legal and thus could not affect a nontributary's genealogy. In spite of the petitioner's assertion that he did not have the funds to solicit the necessary ecclesiastical documentation to prove his *calidad*, the case was referred to the subdelegate for further review pending receipt of more documentary proofs.

Petitioners in the cases discussed above demeaned and discounted the place of marriages in their families and upheld genealogy as the determining factor in tributary status. For instance, Agustín González Muñiz urged legal authorities to look at his status as an illegitimate child of a Spaniard, rather than to consider him the adopted child of *mulatos*. As a natural son, González Muñiz could not claim all the prestige associated with his father, but he could avoid the genealogical implications of tributary status and the onus of passing it on to his children. In the Martínez case, the publicly perceived association with a tributary *calidad* jeopardized the status of the entire family. Mónica's marriage to a man of questionable tributary status diminished her standing in the eyes of tribute officials. If children had resulted from the union, the addition of Afromexican ancestors to the Martínez family would have fundamentally changed its "blood."

Physiognomy and Genealogy

The genealogical and legal identities created by marriage and reproduction far outweighed physiognomy in determinations of tributary status among petitioners. Nevertheless, many bureaucrats believed physiognomic characteristics were inextricably linked to tributary status, though this viewpoint tended to mix and match notions of heredity and genealogy as well as physiognomy. The tradition of judging the caste or noble lineage of an individual by sight was not new and often depended on dress, material possessions, and behavior.[64] When lineage was unknown or unclear, these behavioral and visual factors became especially important for determining classifications, resulting as the century came to a close in confusion regarding the distinctions between *mulatos* and Indians by sight.[65] Coinciding with a growing consensus in European scientific and medical communities that human biological heredity could be used as a "causal, explanatory notion," certain officials in Mexico City began to apply concepts of heredity to the transmission of tributary markers, such as dark skin.[66] But these newer ideas coexisted with an older fixation on physical "signs" that indicated a deeper nature. Therefore, the focus was not on skin color or phenotype alone but on a "symbolic quality of physical appearance."[67] The use of expressions like "*color de pardo*" may point to racial phenotype for determining status at the end of the colonial period,[68] but this focus could have also been rooted in physiognomic thinking.

As they sought more efficient methods of registering and charging a vast tributary populace, bureaucrats floated numerous proposals that would enable collectors and commissioners to cut genealogical corners. The problem of identifying tributaries in the capital was, by the end of the century, a somewhat exhausted yet unresolved topic in the Real Hacienda. In 1790, tribute administrator Juan Domingo Lombardini pushed commissioners to register "without exception all those who because of their appearance (*aspecto*), trade (*oficio*), or dress (*trage*) seem to be tributaries." The capital contained massive numbers of mobile tributaries, and Lombardini believed the best way to tackle the issue would be to use the tools of seeing. He further justified his position by reiterating the ideals of the Ordinance of Intendants and subsequent discussions that only the Real Hacienda, and not commissioners on the ground, had the power to grant exemptions to any individual. The job of the commissioner or collector was to locate anyone he believed might be subject to payment and allow the parties involved to take it up with magistrates later. Bernardo Bonavía y Zapata, at the time Intendant of Mexico, invented another method for easily identifying tributaries without regard to lineage or physiognomy. He explained his experiment thus: "My idea is to identify as a tributary anyone who is poorly dressed and as exempt anyone who is well dressed, even when that person may be of a privileged class according to the law and the other is a tributary." Bonavía y Zapata reasoned that charging people for the price of clothing would balance out any losses in the tributary category, echoing the proposals of Campillo y Cossío's *Nuevo sistema de gobierno económico para América*. Both men were inspired by new scientific administrative methods and ways of seeing that they believed could be applied to a muddled and complex tributary population. At the same time, both reformers melded much older methods of understanding human difference in New Spain, culturally and physiognomically, into their plans.[69]

Debates about the tributary status of foundlings or illegitimate children showed the role of color where it was admixed with caste, *calidad*, and class. Royal paternalism, combined with Enlightenment thought, inspired Charles IV to include foundlings as legitimate. A royal decree of 1794, mentioned earlier, granted unprecedented and ambiguous privileges to the *expósitos*, including the ability to claim nontributary status and to be treated as if they had honorable Spanish lineage. The king did not offer additional instructions about implementing this new policy and likely believed that most individuals who would concern themselves with questions of honor were the descendants of Spaniards.[70] But the decree was not to resolve the status of the *expósitos* so easily. The radical reforms in favor of people of unknown parentage upset local hierarchies and worried elites and bureaucrats in New Spain and beyond.[71] In response to the decree, Juan Ordóñez, *contador de retasas* in Mexico City, argued that all free people of color, regardless of *expósito* status, would continue to pay tribute "because they are plebeians" with certain obligations to the crown. He believed class to be the overriding factor in determining tributary status. Simply because someone had no genealogy did not mean that he or she could avoid the obligations associated with being a vassal. Ordóñez observed that "to know [the *calidad*] of all the foundlings in which there is a frequent mixture of Spaniards, Indians, and *mulatos*, seems impossible," and he favored a strategy that privileged color and class in the absence of genealogical proofs. He recommended that the monarch not grant exemptions to "*expósitos* who are black in color, who do not leave any doubt about their *calidad* . . . and those who in their color, hair, and features are known as *mulatos* or another of the castes that result from a mixture of blacks."[72] Ordóñez was calling on a language of physiognomy that had appeared in Spanish America before caste terminologies became widespread; its popularity within the tribute regime spanned more than two centuries.

However, not all bureaucrats approved of physiognomy as a method of categorization; there were those who opposed what they saw as outdated thinking. Another official in the Real Hacienda identified only as "Beltrán" (perhaps Joseph María of the same surname) countered Ordóñez directly, stating that Ordóñez advocated a method of tributary identification based on a backward school of thought. Beltrán insisted that it had been proven that "the extrinsic features of the body do not coincide with the qualities (*qualidades*) of the soul." Beltrán was outraged at the notion that "the color of the face, the lack of a beard, the toughness, straightness, or curliness of the hair demonstrate that the *expósito* is a child of Indians or blacks or *mulatos* or comes from other castes." He was well aware of the paradoxes of physiognomy and *calidad* in the face of tributary status and the law. To this end, he challenged his opponents, "And shall it be lawful that *calidad* be doubtful and the imposition of tribute certain?"[73] Contemporary writers and thinkers shared the distaste for outdated physiognomic thinking, including Afroperuvian surgeon and writer José Pastor de Larrinaga, who argued similarly that, "the difference in the colour of one's skin does not affect the qualities of one's soul, and those of dark and olive-coloured skin alike enjoy the blessing of being wise if they have the necessary attributes to be so."[74] Furthermore, the method proposed by Ordóñez was not nearly as simple as he made it out to be, since it would "not be easy . . . because the signs of color, hair, and physiognomy" left many people's status in doubt.[75] This issue was not confined to the tribute regime, and signs or aspect had already begun to gradually permeate considerations for posts in the ecclesiastical bureaucracy as well.[76] The conflicting views of officials, bureaucrats, and intellectuals about the meanings of color, physical features, and lineage show that labels of tributary status and *calidad* intended to categorize society along clear-cut lines had resulted in further confounding identification of who was who in the caste hierarchy.

Woven into the tribute discussions was a case that contested the tributary status of an *expósito* in Mexico City begun in 1797. The case involved a hodgepodge of appeals to gendered honor, service, and class, interwoven with pieces of recent debates surrounding *expósito* status. Don José Francisco Prieto, a literate master blacksmith, requested an exemption as a subject "numbered in the class of good men." His petition did not confirm or deny allegations that he was Afromexican. In fact, he admitted that it was "impossible to prove [his] *calidad*" because he was adopted. He based his argument on his notion of a tributary class, which the petitioner associated with the "inferior rank of plebeians," and from which he clearly intended to distinguish himself.[77] People of this class lacked the skill he exercised as a master in his trade, he claimed; his attainments and economic position distanced him from the working poor. He bolstered these arguments by claiming that he was an *expósito* raised by a militiaman of African ancestry, himself exempt from tribute—unable to demonstrate his own blood lineage, he constructed a parental connection to an exempt man. By downplaying blood ties and focusing on the nontributary status of the adoptive parent, the petitioner and his representatives hoped that blood lineage would be rendered irrelevant.

Those opposed to the exemption were unmoved by Prieto's appeal to honor and upbringing and instead focused on his shaky bloodline. The case found its way to Juan Domingo Lombardini, who showed a distinct lack of sympathy for exemption claims. Even if the petitioner did not know his biological parents, Lombardini asserted that, in spite of Prieto's being a foundling, "it is undeniably clear from his presentation, color, and exterior characteristics that [his parents] are *pardos* or other *castas*."[78] His use of "undeniably" asserted that this way of seeing provided the objectivity that bureaucrats in the Real Hacienda craved. Lombardini was convinced that exterior characteristics were clear markers of tributary status, an inherited condition that could be tracked through its physical manifestations. The petitioner's physical presentation confirmed his blood lineage, overriding any of the privileges supposedly accorded to *expósitos* based on the impossibility of knowing their *calidad*.

Fortunately for Prieto, the judges of the Junta Superior de Real Hacienda ruled in 1801 that all *expósitos* were exempt from tributary responsibilities. The resolution stated that "the basis of color is very fallible for determining the castes of *expósitos*." Ever focused on the fiscal implications of decisions related to *calidad*, proponents of this resolution pointed out that any losses in Afromexican tributes would be recouped elsewhere by way of *alcabalas* or other taxes.[79] The recognition that *expósitos* could be "decent plebeians" did not disrupt the overall tributary structure or the growth of the Real Hacienda. *Expósitos* were not without *calidad* or exempt from the obligations of vassalage but simply of a caste and genealogy indeterminable under the law. The Real Hacienda's resolution reaffirmed the extent to which subjects could improve their social status but still remain in the same tributary category.[80] The fractured opinions of the bureaucracy in cases similar to Prieto's demonstrate the coexistence, however contradictory, of multiple theories of *calidad* based on blood or sight or both. The range and diversity of these theories gave petitioners many ways to construct genealogies or marshal other evidence to distance themselves from tributary status, without referencing physical characteristics.

For some bureaucrats, the master blacksmith José Francisco Prieto was clearly defined more by his color than his prestige. Although he placed his class and *calidad* foremost, he initially encountered a judicial audience more interested in his appearance than his reputation. Doubtless, certain tribute officials were willing to allow physical characteristics to take priority over an individual's local reputation and community understandings of lineage and *calidad*. But at the highest levels of government, color and appearance did not satisfy bureaucrats searching for a fixed, rational method of identifying tributaries. Seeking to close the loopholes free people of color exploited in the tribute regime, Bourbon high courts refused to acknowledge color—a characteristic with the potential to become as subjective as caste itself—as the basic tributary marker.

Accountants and bureaucrats probed the implications of the 1794 royal decree by mixing new ideas about heredity with entrenched desiderata of genealogy, purity, and caste. The question eventually reached the Council of the Indies, which approved the Real Hacienda's 1801 resolution in 1802, with the caveat that it "not circulate in the Indies as a general ruling."[81] Thus, the council upheld the continued importance of the "diverse practices" entailed in counting and registering tributaries of different castes. In New Spain, most authorities continued to favor genealogical proofs, already prevalent in tribute and other institutions, as the preferred method of identifying tributaries.

Conclusion

Colonial notions of tributary caste, tributary class, and tributary qualities existed in arguable concert, with little consensus as to their precise meanings. The flexibility of these terms persisted, despite multiple efforts on the part of creative bureaucrats to nail down the specific meanings of tributary status. Their shared significance and intelligibility derived from genealogical underpinnings and created a self-sustaining bureaucratic organization for drawing families into the tributary category. All three markers could be manipulated to achieve genealogical goals, whether in the claim of a determined petitioner or the response of a scrutinizing official. For bureaucrats, identifying tributaries by genealogical means appeared to be the least subjective way to do so, and genealogy held its place as the preferred method of tracing ancestry and privilege. People seeking to avoid their own registration as Afromexican tributaries also looked to genealogy as a method of defining their privileges within the colonial regime.

At this most basic level, petitioners and judges agreed that genealogy was the cornerstone of tributary status. Membership in the class of tributaries depended on the status of one's ancestors. Whether this genealogical method could be supplemented with interpretations of color and certain physical features remained a point of contention, but all the while genealogy retained its primary position as an indispensable personal and legal marker in New Spain. It is important to clarify that the family histories recounted in disputes of Afromexican tributary status did not necessarily seek to create a pure and prestigious ancestry but simply to distance some or all family members from a financial obligation. In these ways, these stories of genealogical creation or establishment differ from processes such as the proof of *limpieza de sangre*. Petitioners employed genealogy as a tool to negotiate the obligations of their subjecthood, whether or not that determination resulted in genealogical purity. The absolute essential for many of these petitioners was to rid the family of the stain of tribute. In pursuit of this goal, ordinary people articulated their positions within their own families, towns, and a larger colonial hierarchy of *calidad*.

The late eighteenth century was a time of changing attitudes and rhetoric regarding the absolute and relative value of genealogy, *calidad*, and color in determining social categorization. Against this trend toward innovation and diffusion, tribute petitioners claimed and preserved Afromexican tributary status as a genealogical, rather than a physical, characteristic. Of the hundreds of individuals involved in tribute disputes examined for this study, no petitioner argued that color alone should be the central or deciding factor in proving a specific lineage or an exempting *calidad*. Petitioners whose cases reached the higher levels of bureaucracy in the capital relied on genealogy as the strongest basis for their appeals.[82] Those who avoided tribute payment did so using the same vocabulary of genealogy and privilege that subjected others less lucky to pay the tax. In an era of political change in New Spain, the desire to maintain established genealogical means of determining tributary status united most petitioners with the bureaucrats who judged them. Both sides were wary of depending on phenotypic vocabularies for authority in defining *calidad*.

Genealogy prevailed because it satisfied Bourbon bureaucrats and at the same time provided a culturally sanctioned vocabulary of self-authentication familiar to ordinary people. Tribute complaints evoke deeply ingrained popular ideas about the interdependence of marriage and family, reproduction and gender, and *calidad* and lineage. To contest their tributary status, families relied on genealogy to help them document marital and reproductive relationships that would reflect favorably on the family's tributary lineage and, therefore, on the *calidad* of the petitioner as well. In the context of tribute, people presented themselves as participants in and inheritors of an ongoing family history, which seemed, to them, more compelling than any attempt to define oneself according to an assortment of physical characteristics.

By the late eighteenth century, the imposition of tributary status as a genealogical marker had simplified the meaning of African ancestry for the purposes of the Bourbon colonial regime. The lens of tribute, then, distilled multiple categories into one recognizable term, suited for export across the Atlantic. For various reasons, considerations of caste and *calidad* had become unattractive to bureaucrats searching for quick, efficient determinations of tributary status. One of the underlying problems was the inability of bureaucrats to deconstruct tributary status to each other's satisfaction: some believed tributary status could be determined by color, while others favored a genealogical approach. They debated, and ultimately upheld, the early modern belief that the body was a changeable expression of difference.[83] Genealogy, having long served as a tool to negotiate subjective interpretations of physical features, came to trump physical aspect. Concurring, the Real Hacienda of New Spain would eventually find color and physical appearance insufficient for determining tributary status.

Conclusion

Manuel Abad y Queipo, the future bishop of Michoacán, in 1799 penned impassioned words to King Charles IV regarding free people of African ancestry and the injustice of charging the tribute tax: "They are tributaries, and because the counts are made with such precision, tribute becomes for them an indelible mark of slavery that they cannot erase with time, nor with the mixing of races in successive generations." He supported the abolition of tribute for Indians and free people of African descent on the grounds that it degraded entire communities, condemning in particular legislation that had separated Indians from the rest of colonial society.[1] Furthermore, he argued that "there are many who, because of their color, physiognomy and conduct would be elevated to the class of Spaniards, if it were not for this impediment by which they are dragged down into this class." Because of this impediment, *mulato* tributaries were "dishonored by law, poor, and dependent."[2] Conceived as a tax on formerly enslaved subjects, the tribute tax on blackness hindered the economic mobility of free people of color and marked their genealogies indefinitely.

Bishop Abad y Queipo's objections to the power of the tributary status illustrate how damaging it often was for those whom it forever relegated to a "dishonored" position in colonial society. However, as *Taxing Blackness* demonstrates, at no point did the Real Hacienda or its local emissaries have the satisfaction of successfully imposing tributary status on all whom the bureaucrats tried to designate as *negros, mulatos*, or *pardos*. Fiscal bureaucrats continually debated how tributary subjects could be better identified, categorized, and controlled. As they developed different methods to expand the Afromexican tributary population, that population reacted through petitions and occasional lawsuits. Free people of color may have felt an obligation to obey the crown, but their response to tribute indicates that they expected the Real Hacienda to administer just government. Debating these obligations and expectations, ordinary people and bureaucrats engaged in a process of defining tributary status through negotiation. Those free people of color who gained exemption took pride in their avoidance of the tax, strengthened their reputations, and attempted to pass these privileges on to their descendants.

The immediate effects of tribute exemption could change the fate of an entire lineage, but these decisions also sparked debates about the general status of distinct groups within the colonial hierarchy. Don José Francisco Prieto, the master blacksmith who considered himself "counted in the class of good men," became part of an Atlantic quandary as a result of his rejection of tributary status that he felt lowered him to the "inferior rank of plebeians."[3] Because of petitions and inquiries from colonial subjects, magistrates addressed the use of *calidad* and appearance in determining tributary status and sometimes found them lacking. Thus, when free people of color sought support for their causes and petitioned for tribute relief, they forced the issue of *calidad* to the forefront of the bureaucracy. They advocated their own interpretations of justice and the obligations of their vassalage, thus mobilizing a kind of politics based on their status as tributaries.[4] The reverberations of their efforts went beyond the scope of their individual, familial, and corporate petitions. Free people of African descent, and anyone else concerned about allegations of tributary status, engaged actively in the development of what *calidad* was. What began as individual or familial petitions could extend to entire communities and eventually affect the privileges or possibilities for a wider network of *castas*.[5] Magistrates and bureaucrats would have the final say in demarcating the relative importance of *calidad* and genealogy in determining tributary status, but free people of color used their own knowledge of their family histories and reputations to press their cases and assert their worth.

The Fall of Tribute and Persistence of *Calidad*

The Napoleonic Wars and the crisis of legitimacy they engendered in the Spanish Empire after 1808 eventually led to Mexican independence and the abandonment of the tribute regime. Despite the political turmoil, the fall of royal tribute was far from immediate in the early nineteenth century. More than two hundred thousand pesos of Afromexican tribute were collected in 1805 and 1810, in addition to more than a million pesos of Indian tribute in each of those years.[6] To shore up Indian support for Spanish rule, the Regency Council in Spain ended Indian tributes in New Spain in 1810.[7] In October of that year, insurgent José María de Ansorena published a *bando* reporting the position of leader Father Miguel Hidalgo y Costilla on the abolition of slavery and slave trading and the tribute tax on free people of African descent. The succinct message stated that tribute would be "totally abolished forever for all kinds of castes whatever they may be."[8] Initially hesitant to upend colonial social hierarchies, Hidalgo associated the collapse of royal tribute with the fall of the colonial regime rather than an overhaul of *calidad*.[9] Revolutionary leader Father José María Morelos later signed another *bando* abolishing royal tribute as well as slavery. To achieve more extensive changes, Morelos declared that Mexico's "inhabitants will not be qualified as Indians, *mulatos* nor other castes, but rather as Americans (*americanos*)."[10] This language made clearer the illegitimacy of tribute, caste, and *calidad* in the eyes of the proposed new government of independent Mexico. In 1816, Félix María Calleja, first count of Calderón and viceroy of New Spain, attempted to reintroduce tribute as a "contribution" rather than a "tribute" to rid the tax of its negative associations with blackness or Indianness. However, imperial bureaucrats knew that it would be impossible to reinstate the tax and never published Viceroy Calleja's *bando*.[11] The regional differences that had characterized tribute for so long ensured that it was still practiced in pockets of New Spain throughout the war. Only in 1822 would there be a complete and definitive halt to tribute collection following the rupture between Mexico and Spain.

Royal tribute collection eventually ended with the fall of the colonial regime, but the terms of tributary categories and *calidad* lingered in ecclesiastical documents into the nineteenth century.[12] Mexicans continued the colonial practice of using separate registers of births or baptisms for Spaniards, Indians, and *castas* and produced caste-based genealogies and proofs of lineage.[13] The very recent past, so dominated by genealogical logics, did not fade immediately from institutional records or popular imagination. Morelos's passionate and far-reaching reforms to colonial society failed to dislodge the pernicious effects of caste and the memory of tributary status. The end of the tributary category likely allowed some colonial *indios* and *pardos* to become mestizos for the purposes of the liberal state.[14] Overall, however, the official end of royal tribute and the bans on the legal use of caste terms did not eradicate the thinking that had permeated most aspects of colonial society. Free people of African descent might now be, in name, Mexicans and *americanos* free from arbitrary taxation, but their economic and political situations left much to be desired. In the first decades of independence, free people of African descent put pressure on political leaders, and a few did achieve regional political representation in places like Xalapa in Veracruz.[15] Like other free blacks in the Atlantic world, many former tributaries struggled to realize economically as well as socially the gains that freedom symbolized.[16]

The political meanings of tributary status rang hollow as the bloody wars for independence raged and a hard-won peace ended colonialism. The fiscal importance of tributes from Indians and free people of African descent had fluctuated in the eighteenth century, but tribute always retained elements of its original purpose of organizing vassals who recognized their king. Bureaucrats and reformers insisted that tribute registration and collection could (and should) be more expansive and effective for the good of the colonial social order as well as the treasury. Not only did tribute provide a steady stream of revenue in the late eighteenth century, its imposition also symbolized the relationships of obligation between vassal and monarch. According to some officials, these symbols of loyalty and obedience solidified categories of *clase*,[17] which would have seemed especially useful in the stratified urban setting that bureaucrats in the capital experienced daily. Bureaucrats continued to see tribute as an essential mode of classification, manifested in the reorganization of Mexico City's tributary structure in the 1790s.[18] The rupture of the colonial regime put an immediate end to the use of tribute itself as an underpinning of the colonial hierarchy, but its removal did not totally eradicate the more insidious social effects of the tax.

Calidad and tribute became entwined and entrenched through a century of events, ideas, and actors in the tribute regime, from meticulous accountants to stone-throwing tax dodgers. Collecting tribute from and registering tributaries among free people of African descent provided the Spanish crown with scant revenue vis-à-vis other sources, but it promised a wealth of information about a cross section of colonial subjects. The administration of royal tribute produced historical sources that represented and described the Afromexican tributary subject. These were not simply representations of demographic and economic trends; commissioners collected and displayed these data to illustrate Afromexican community for imperial administrators. Therefore, tribute records were constructions of community that reflected demographic patterns through a lens of bureaucratic selection. Through these documents, bureaucrats saw often idealized, lucrative, stable, and well-ordered Afromexican populations ready to be taxed. The establishment of an Afromexican tributary subject was a bureaucratic success in the eighteenth century, one that proceeded from rational administration and long-running debates within the Real Hacienda.

The persistence of caste and *calidad* following independence was linked to the success of the previous tax regime, which implanted categories broadly, if not completely coherently. In the last three decades of the eighteenth century, the proliferation of summaries and printed instruments that represented tributaries resulted from an emphasis on accuracy, numeracy, and order. This administrative effort required the participation of royal officials, local elites, clergy, and ordinary people to extract information. The lofty tribute ordinance Viceroy Revillagigedo dispatched in 1793 depicted a studious and dedicated commissioner as he prepared his "detailed and timely comparison" of ecclesiastical documents with the current *padrón* of the jurisdiction to which he was assigned. The ordinance described how the commissioner would "note the differences he may find" and "form a calculation" using more rational instruments of administration in the form of printed grids. This was to be a "most perfect and comprehensive" endeavor.[19] The tribute register was, ideally, supported by ecclesiastical documents, previous registers, and the careful oversight of commissioners and accountants. The use of these standardized methods and the acts of copying and recalculating data served to ingrain *calidad* as an administrative concept. Its use permeated government and fiscal administration, leaving behind a strong legacy of colonial record keeping and a widely used vocabulary of difference.

The abolition of slavery and the emergence of independent nations in Latin America took different forms depending on the legacies of blackness and slavery across the region. With a very small population of enslaved people at the time of independence, full abolition in Mexico occurred soon after the establishment of the new nation, in 1829. Rather than adopting racial discourses that justified the continuing subjugation of Africans and their descendants in the absence of slavery, as would occur in Brazil, Mexican leaders abolished distinctions of caste.[20] Fashioning itself as a nation characterized by *mestizaje*, principally between Indians and Europeans, the Mexican state tended to ignore blackness as part of a national paradigm.[21] These categories echo through official discourses of race in present-day Mexico.[22] Mexican *mestizaje* became a discourse that denied the presence of black people in nineteenth- and twentieth-century Mexico and "erased them from the face of the nation."[23] Yet, even in the context of mestizo nationalism, ideas of purity have seen a recent resurgence as many people acknowledge that genetics, rather than race, determines human biological difference and so-called biogeographical ancestries. Somewhat ironically, a well-worn Iberian framework seems to have reemerged in this context. Peter Wade recently concluded that "purity might appear an anachronistic concept, but insofar as it stands in for 'racial difference,' one can still detect its magnetic field in constant tension with 'mixture.'"[24] The colonial administrative interest in official categories and combinations did not completely dissolve with the rise of the nation-state. Abandoned concepts like *calidad* and caste, once the obsession of scientific-minded bureaucrats, may yet take on renewed relevance through their commonalities with DNA testing and genetic science.

Calidad and Proximity to Blackness

Archival evidence presented in *Taxing Blackness* deepens and enriches historical understanding of *calidad* as a key marker of social organization among free people of color in Bourbon New Spain. *Calidad* not only connected free people of African descent to one another, it also served the purpose of associating blackness with people who formed close connections with Afromexicans. Because *calidad* was not completely genealogical, the status of a family name could change by becoming attached to a free person of color. The tribute register was key in giving *calidad* this influence over entire family reputations. Being close to a free person of color could result in a kind of "*calidad*-by-association," a change in one's status because of proximity to blackness genealogically, residentially, or in a bureaucratic space like the tribute register. Specific caste terminologies became less important on tribute registers than connections to blackness embodied in the *padrones de negros y mulatos*, as entire families took on tributary reputations merely through the presence of their names in these documents.

This kind of *calidad*-by-association coexisted and clashed with genealogical logics in the tribute regime. Tribute was inseparable from genealogy from its inception, when noble lineage was a hallmark of social organization for Indians under early Spanish rule. By the eighteenth century, many colonial subjects as well as authorities held that public reputation was fundamental to a person's status and that of his or her family. *Calidad* could pass among friends, neighbors, employers, and spouses; it was also transmissible through family lines. Established artisans as well as illiterate plebeians used family history, written proofs, and popular opinion to construct genealogies. Ordinary people, local officials, and Bourbon bureaucrats all concerned themselves with questions of genealogy and its effects on caste and *calidad*. It was widely understood that tributary status was a condition that would be created or broken through bonds of marriage and reproduction. Marriages that crossed boundaries of caste and *calidad* were especially troubling when Spanish women wed Afromexican or Indian men, as attested by the complaints of parents opposed to the decisions of young, non-tributary women who chose tributary husbands.[25] These marital and reproductive connections were the basis of tributary status and transferred it to other members of the family. The danger that Afromexican *calidad* and tributary status posed to a family manifested through the social and legal ties of the marriage at the current generation as well as through expected genealogical relationships in the future.

Genealogy and physiognomy, *calidad* and tributary status all factored into blackness at the end of the colonial period. Colonial authorities and ordinary people held their own opinions about which markers were key to determining blackness, but the end result of the late Bourbon renovations to tribute was the expansion of the tax. That the Council of the Indies seemed to embrace genealogy over appearance in arguments about unknown *calidad* at the turn of the nineteenth century did not change the outcome of tributary status for hundreds of thousands of colonial subjects in New Spain. The process of debate and discussion within the tribute branch of the treasury meant that bureaucrats voiced their own ideas and weighed in on issues of concern to the viceroy and their colleagues. Hereditary, physiognomic, and racial thinking had clearly made inroads among accountants by the late decades of the eighteenth century. They were challenged by others who saw these modes of thinking as flawed and preposterous and, instead, preferred cautious and less expansive modes of finding tributaries. Although unsatisfactory at the highest levels of administration and never completely codified, modes of categorizing based on appearance and *calidad* seemed justified to outspoken officials in the Real Hacienda. Associations with free people of color, or the presence of some physical feature that could be construed as a marker of blackness, reduced the burden of proof on commissioners and collectors. Accountants in Mexico City believed they had sound economic reasoning for this policy throughout the eighteenth century, which allowed them to seek the enrichment of royal coffers by what they understood to be the most efficacious means at their disposal.

The intensified efforts by authorities in the Real Hacienda to identify and categorize people had already taken significantly new forms in the late eighteenth century when the regime introduced standardized printed registers on which any individual connected to free people of color could be identified as a potential source of tribute revenue for the crown. As repositories of local information about tributary families, *padrones* of *mulatos* and *negros* functioned as maps of tributary social and genealogical relationships. Throughout the colonial period, tribute registers had served as a bureaucratic barrier between people of African descent and *indios de pueblo* and justified the recognition of free people of color as a distinct community for the purposes of taxation. Colonial officials used tribute registers as tracking devices for communities, a space in which blackness had specific economic meanings. The register was also a space in which relationships with free people of color determined social and genealogical webs for Indian, Spanish, and mestizo men and women. Connections with free people of African descent could mark individuals of any *calidad* as likely tributaries.

While the register indicates potential reputational risks associated with blackness, it also provides data that call into question official discourses that associated free people of color with vagrancy. Using the information gathered in the last decades of colonialism in what would become Mexico, this book has shown that families who paid tribute did not conform to contemporary assumptions about their mobility. Many people lived in communities in which they had familial ties to other residents, regardless of caste. Tribute officials took pains to record information pertaining to family as an organizing principle on the register. They created or observed families as units of employed fathers who cared for their families; mothers who labored and raised children; adult boarders, children, or siblings; and adolescents, children, and infants. In their eagerness to produce more revenue, officials chipped away at the negative stereotypes of the *mulato* vagabond operating in the Real Hacienda and in popular culture.

This book interrogates the persistence of the vagabond trope in the late eighteenth century, when many free people of color did live in settled communities that were well known to bureaucrats. The stability of these communities weakened widespread stereotypes within the regime itself and in popular imagination. Yet, some bureaucrats and local officials clung to these narratives, despite convincing evidence to the contrary that they had themselves amassed. Labeling free people of African descent as vagabonds facilitated the tribute regime at the lower levels of administration, where local officials often struggled to conform to the expectations of the Real Hacienda. The vagabond *mulatos* who could never be found, whether real or exaggerated, provided an important explanation for the dysfunction of tribute. At the higher levels of the regime, bureaucrats could rehash centuries-old logics about *amos* and fixed residences to justify their control over the labor and movement of free people of color along an increasingly blurred gradient of *calidad* and color. We can imagine that some free people of color paid tribute partially in response to persistent and detrimental mentalities that condemned them to be permanent outsiders, vagabonds, or invaders. Although certainly an unwelcome economic burden, free people of African descent would have understood the symbolism of tribute. Through their payments and registration, they asserted their belonging and loyalty, their familial ties, their close connections with the places they called home.

The Fate of Blackness

Tributary status in New Spain separated Spaniards and mestizos from free people of color and Indians. Afromexican tribute was rooted in the connections between blackness, slavery, caste, and *calidad*. If the frequent marital unions among people of different castes determined, as one historian has argued, that "the equation of black with slave lost its meaning,"[26] then tribute had existed in part to amplify the echoes of slavery through its imposition as a kind of manumission tax. That tribute was demanded of *mulatos* but not mestizos made blackness particularly damaging to reputation and social standing regardless of whether a *mulato* had less Spanish ancestry than a comparable mestizo. Based on the logic of caste progressions and blood purity, African ancestry, unlike Indian ancestry, was nearly impossible to change.[27] Among proponents of categorizing people using the hippocratic-galenic tradition, humors "derived from African bodies . . . were conceived of as physically tenacious" beyond the current generation.[28] Elite Spaniards believed that African blood also had permanent characteristics that overrode others,[29] a view reflected in the practice of using maternal and paternal lineages of blackness to determine tributary status. While the symbolic meanings of African blood, fluids, and impurity were generally clear, the actual process of identifying the descendants of Africans posed practical challenges for collectors, commissioners, and bureaucrats.

Bourbon officials expended considerable effort to stabilize the meanings of labels like "*mulato*" or "*pardo*" and policies assigning blackness to those whom the regime slated for taxation. But the proliferating signifiers of blackness that bureaucrats felt obliged to ponder stymied efforts to relegate Afromexicans to a single recognizable social category. Color, *casta*, and *calidad* became so entangled and sometimes contradictory that bureaucrats found their usefulness often limited at best. One of the underlying problems was the inability of bureaucrats to decipher tributary status to one another's satisfaction: some believed tributary status could be determined by assessing an individual's color, while others searched a petitioner's genealogy for signs of blackness in the family line. As shown in the previous chapter, the Council of the Indies in the first years of the nineteenth century would eventually find color and physical appearance insufficient for determining tributary status.

The delegate to the Cortes de Cádiz (1810–14) from Tlaxcala, José Miguel Guridi y Alcocer, alluded to the fact that the problem of tributary categories remained unsolved a decade later. The Cortes, the national assembly that passed the Constitution of 1812, became a new arena for the debates about the qualities of *castas* that could make them citizens or exclude them on the basis that they were descended from Africans and thus not fully deserving of inclusion as Americans. Guridi y Alcocer argued that it was impossible in the first place to definitively distinguish *castas* from others in New Spain, and he employed the example of tribute collection to make this point. "Not a quarter of what should be collected from *castas* is ever collected, because they have always managed to confuse themselves either with Indians or with Spaniards, calling themselves such, depending on their darker or lighter color," he observed.[30] The delegate from Guadalajara, José Simeón de Uría, spoke passionately in favor of granting full citizenship to *pardos* on the basis that many free people of African descent in New Spain were of mixed ancestry and not wholly African.[31] Article 22 of the eventual constitution only narrowly extended citizenship to free men of African descent, requiring them to have provided outstanding service to the *patria*.[32] Although delegates from what would become Mexico looked favorably on granting citizenship to free people of color, the larger problem of *casta* citizenship depended on Spanish and other colonial delegates who were unwilling to consider the prospect of a *casta* citizenry capable of upsetting the balance of power concentrated in the hands of Spaniards and their creole descendants.

Using petitions and the occasional lawsuit, free people of color pushed back against the vicious prejudices of some elite creoles and the simplifying impulses of Real Hacienda bureaucrats intent on reducing the complexities of caste and *calidad*. For free Afromexicans, being a respected and settled member of a community was complicated by the simultaneous requirement of paying tribute and its stigma. The socially shameful aspects of tributary status were tightly bound to ideas about impurity and blackness. Some families who rejected tributary status did so by denying African ancestry. But the use of genealogical proofs toward specific ends was also a strategy for families who wished to solidify their tax privileges or social standing as nontributaries without asserting that they were not *mulatos*. In cases discussed in chapter 3, privileges were not necessarily, for petitioners, in conflict with identifications with blackness. Although genealogical preoccupations may be more readily identifiable among elite creoles or caciques, questions of genealogy mattered to Afromexican families in search of a better status.

In the eighteenth century, families of *pardos*, *morenos*, and *mulatos* found the means to avoid or confront restrictions on their advancement without rejecting the legitimacy of colonialism. The most direct of these was the whitening petition, the *gracias al sacar*, though it was quite rare. People who sought to remove their *pardo* or *mulato* status legally had often attained prestige through unofficial means.[33] Similarly, free people of color in New Spain probably sought legal relief from tribute as a last resort, having already attempted to avoid the tax by building sterling reputations and publicly known genealogies. Former tributaries who asserted their privileges and questioned the meanings of *calidad* managed, in their own lives and those of people around them, to increase their prestige. In contrast to the *gracias al sacar*, tribute exemption cases did not always reject the presence of blackness in the family. Some of these petitioners had access to basic literacy, practiced skilled trades, and amassed good standing and honor in the eyes of their peers. Free people of color who, despite barriers, attained education and circulated their ideas in newspapers and literary publications further complicated social hierarchies at the turn of the nineteenth century. The goals and talents of these individuals spurred "colonial rhetoric regarding the dual nature of their detrimental influence yet vital contributions to society."[34] Even when they attained a certain level of prestige, free people of color remained the object of suspicion. If targeted by zealous commissioners or vindictive neighbors, families could easily lose their prized tribute exemptions.

Free people of color found distinct opportunities for negotiating tributary status based on geographic variations. Blackness was not confined to a single geography in New Spain, and neither was royal tributary status. Documents related to the tribute regime confirm Bourbon interest in regulating the cities as well as understanding the rural and provincial side of Afromexican life. Free people of African descent lived and worked on large estates and built strong ties to haciendas and ranches in the hinterlands of New Spain.[35] Towns that faced incursions from hostile Indian groups sought group exemptions based on service, just as entire coastal communities claimed militia privileges.[36] Service could become part of a genealogy in the case of a town that had once been part of a frontier zone but, thanks to the loyal service of the town's past residents, now was home to the descendants of *pobladores*. In interior regions close to the capital, associations with a tribute register, and therefore with blackness, offered few benefits vis-à-vis state structures. Coastal regions and frontier zones, on the other hand, provided an association with privileges embodied in militia units or a history of military service. When free people of color protested tribute collection, they could reference their historic and present defense of Spanish territories and the connections between blackness and militia service. Families who lacked such a connection, however, were more likely to deny a genealogy of blackness as a strategy to tribute exemption.

Free people of African descent entered Atlantic debates about *castas* and tribute whose terms they intimately understood, and whose outcomes they could influence somewhat but not control. These petitioners did not convince the most rabid proponents of physiognomy, heredity, and racial notions of difference in the capital. Bureaucrats bent on improving the income of the Real Hacienda rarely took an interest in the plight of ordinary people of color. The ability to push legal outcomes in a favorable direction sometimes necessitated strength in numbers, a corporate status. Historians have argued that the militias of *pardos* and *mulatos* successfully upheld their own prestige, masculinity, and a kind of blackness that was tinged with loyalty and pride.[37] These assertions certainly affected entire regions of New Spain and thus went beyond the men of the militias themselves. The long-term results of the petitions and lawsuits of ordinary people who had no such connections are more difficult to gauge. The local impact of their petitions was significant and could, if continually reestablished, stretch for generations into the future. However, these petitioners did not settle the debate about the meanings of *calidad*, heredity, and race that was raging in the Real Hacienda itself. Clearly, ordinary people in New Spain and authorities on both sides of the Atlantic held differing opinions on the importance of sight versus genealogy in determining *calidad*.

The questions surrounding tributary status within the colonial bureaucracy and among colonial subjects did not result in a wholesale revision of policy based on the input of free people of African descent. As free *mulatos* and *pardos* repeatedly petitioned for greater privileges for their families, towns, or descendants, bureaucrats in Mexico City were focused on new and more efficient ways of categorizing tributaries. The daily concerns of the Real Hacienda addressed the problem of identifying tributaries, rather than awarding exemptions. The strongest supporters of *calidad* as a direct indicator of tributary status, especially those who relied on physical signs, dismissed petitioners' more nuanced formulations of blackness and their genealogies. For administrators and accountants who understood tribute to be a fraught endeavor that barely functioned, the simpler methods that did not require a sophisticated understanding of genealogy seemed preferable. Ordinary people contested these notions and forced imperial bureaucrats to seriously consider the possible detriments of *calidad*-by-sight and *calidad*-by-association on upstanding people caught up in widening tributary nets. But their periodic complaints that reached Mexico City, and eventually Spain, never threatened the gradual expansion of tribute that spread through the cities and countryside at the end of the eighteenth and into the nineteenth century. Thousands of new tributaries and families were recorded, and lineages created, as a result of improved methods of registration and expansive categories that swept up millions of colonial subjects in New Spain. In terms of its logics and laws, free people of color did eventually influence the tribute regime and its Atlantic understandings of blackness and *calidad*. However, these decisions in the first years of the nineteenth century would not undo the tremendous expansion of the previous decades.

The terms of tributary status and *calidad*, and therefore the legacy of blackness in New Spain, belonged to ordinary people as well as fiscal bureaucrats. While the latter group always held disproportionate power, the Real Hacienda was never able to fully enforce categories of tributary status and *calidad* among New Spain's hundreds of thousands of free people of African descent. *Calidad* and tribute were multifaceted, encompassing economic obligations and the legacy of slavery as well as dutiful vassalage and loyal engagement with the crown. They embodied the complex nature of blackness itself, which brought with it social and economic repression that weighed heavily on thousands of free people of African descent. The tribute regime also preserves instances of petitioners who argued that their *mulato* qualities were incidental, and still others who claimed their blackness was passed to them by an honorable ancestor. The meanings of *calidad* were at once institutional and personal, physiognomic and genealogical, Atlantic and local. Despite its conflicting interpretations and possibilities, *calidad* remained a meaningful concept through which thousands of free people of color established their relationship to the Spanish Empire.

Notes

Introduction

1. At this time, the silver peso was equal to one dollar. See Carlos Marichal, *Bankruptcy of Empire: Mexican Silver and the Wars between Spain, Britain, and France, 1760–1810* (Cambridge: Cambridge University Press, 2007), 17.

2. Archivo General de la Nación de México (hereafter AGN), Tributos vol. 44, exp. 9, f. 219.

3. Vicente L. Rafael, *Contracting Colonialism: Translation and Christian Conversion in Tagalog Society under Early Spanish Rule* (Durham, NC: Duke University Press, 1993), 143.

4. Libro 7, Título 5, Ley 1, in *Recopilación de leyes de los reynos de las Indias*, vol. 2 (Madrid: Julián de Paredes, 1681; Madrid: Ediciones Cultura Hispánica, 1973), 320. The use of "adquirir," which lexicographer Sebastián de Covarrubias defined in 1611 as "allegar y juntar hazienda," suggests payment or acquiring by economic means. See *Tesoro de la lengua castellana o española* (Madrid: L. Sánchez, 1611).

5. Libro 7, Título 5, Ley 1, *Recopilación*, 2:320.

6. The Codex Mendoza, though compiled around 1541–42, describes the tributes of goods and labor exacted from Aztec provinces before the arrival of the Spanish. See Frances Berdan and Patricia Rieff Anawalt, *The Essential Codex Mendoza* (Berkeley: University of California Press, 1992). Tribute structured social and economic relationships in the provinces of the Kingdom of Kongo, where governors and local chiefs exchanged luxury and tribute goods. See Anne Hilton, *The Kingdom of Kongo* (Oxford: Clarendon Press, 1985), 43–44.

7. María Elena Martínez, *Genealogical Fictions: Limpieza de Sangre, Religion, and Gender in Colonial Mexico* (Stanford, CA: Stanford University Press, 2008), 3.

8. I borrow this phrase from María Elena Martínez's influential study of investigations of blood purity, generally limited to elite Spaniards and Indians, which were based on "genealogical understandings of difference that despite their invented nature were no less effective at shaping social practices, categories of identity, and self-perceptions." See Martínez, *Genealogical Fictions*, 61.

9. Richard Konetzke, *Colección de documentos para la historia de la formación social de Hispanoamérica*, vol. 3, pt. 2 (Madrid: Consejo Superior de Investigaciones Científicas, 1953–62), 789–90.

10. Another ten thousand Afromexicans were enslaved. See Herbert S. Klein and Ben Vinson III, *African Slavery in Latin America and the Caribbean*, 2nd ed. (Oxford: Oxford University Press, 2007), 197.

11. Libro 7, Título 5, Ley 1, in *Recopilación*, 2:320.

12. The independence of Portugal from Spain in 1640 dramatically reduced the number of slaves being sold in New Spain and helped facilitate the transition to wage labor. Slavery persisted in certain industries and regions well into the eighteenth century, even as free people of color became more numerous overall. See Colin A. Palmer's classic study, *Slaves of the White God: Blacks in Mexico, 1570–1650* (Cambridge, MA: Harvard University Press, 1976). For African slavery in the middle period, see Frank T. Proctor, *Damned Notions of Liberty: Slavery, Culture, and Power in Colonial Mexico, 1640–1769* (Albuquerque: University of New Mexico Press, 2010).

13. Ismael Sánchez-Bella, *La organización financiera de las Indias: Siglo XVI* (Seville: Escuela de Estudios Hispano-Americanos, 1968), 72.

14. Marichal, *Bankruptcy of Empire*, 54.

15. Silvio Zavala, *Ordenanzas del trabajo, siglos XVI y XVII* (Mexico City: Editorial Elede, 1947), 264–65.

16. María Elisa Velázquez Gutiérrez, "Juntos y revueltos: Oficios, espacios y comunidades domésticas de origen africano en la capital novohispana según el censo de 1753," in *Pautas de convivencia étnica en la América Latina colonial (Indios, negros, mulatos, pardos y esclavos)*, ed. Juan Manuel de la Serna (Mexico City: Universidad Nacional Autónoma de México, 2005), 345–46.

17. David A. Sartorius, *Ever Faithful: Race, Loyalty, and the Ends of Empire in Spanish Cuba* (Durham, NC: Duke University Press, 2013), 10. Enslaved people in Cuba also used "hegemonic ideologies," such as a close connection to the king, to seek "entitlements and prerogatives." See María Elena Díaz, *The Virgin, the King, and the Royal Slaves of El Cobre: Negotiating Freedom in Colonial Cuba, 1670–1780* (Stanford, CA: Stanford University Press, 2000), 316.

18. Archivo General de Indias (hereafter AGI), Audiencia de México leg. 1043, cuaderno 16, f. 1569. Free Africans and people of African descent in Minas Gerais took a similar strategy of situating themselves at the center of their community, using the language of vassalage, to petition the king regarding abuses by white residents. See Mariana L. R. Dantas, "Humble Slaves and Loyal Vassals: Free Africans and Their Descendants in Eighteenth-Century Minas Gerais, Brazil," in *Imperial Subjects: Race and Identity in Colonial Spanish America*, ed. Andrew B. Fisher and Matthew D. O'Hara (Durham, NC: Duke University Press, 2009), 115–17.

19. Ann M. Wightman, *Indigenous Migration and Social Change: The Forasteros of Cuzco, 1570–1720* (Durham, NC: Duke University Press, 1990), 4.

20. AGI, Audiencia de México leg. 1043, cuaderno 16, f. 1569v.

21. Tamar Herzog, *Defining Nations: Immigrants and Citizens in Early Modern Spain and Spanish America* (New Haven, CT: Yale University Press, 2003), 62.

22. Ann Twinam, *Purchasing Whiteness: Pardos, Mulatos, and the Quest for Social Mobility in the Spanish Indies* (Stanford, CA: Stanford University Press, 2015), 81–122. For two rich new studies on ordinary litigants, in particular enslaved Africans and their descendants, see Michelle A. McKinley, *Fractional Freedoms: Slavery, Intimacy, and Legal Mobilization in Colonial Lima, 1600–1700* (New York: Cambridge University Press, 2016); and Bianca Premo, *The Enlightenment on Trial: Ordinary Litigants and Colonialism in the Spanish Empire* (New York: Oxford University Press, 2017).

23. Palmer, *Slaves of the White God*, 184.

24. Andrew B. Fisher and Matthew D. O'Hara, "Introduction: Racial Identities and Their Interpreters," in *Imperial Subjects: Race and Identity in Colonial Latin America*, ed. Andrew B. Fisher and Matthew O'Hara (Durham, NC: Duke University Press, 2009), 2. I translate "*indios*" directly to "Indians," instead of "indigenous peoples" or "natives," to reflect the ways in which the *indio* construct reinforced Spanish justifications for charging tribute. See Brian Owensby, *Empire of Law and Indian Justice in Colonial Mexico* (Stanford, CA: Stanford University Press, 2008), 24.

25. Charles Gibson, *The Aztecs under Spanish Rule: A History of the Indians of the Valley of Mexico* (Stanford, CA: Stanford University Press, 1976), 194–219.

26. See Nancy M. Farriss, *Maya Society under Colonial Rule: The Collective Enterprise of Survival* (Princeton, NJ: Princeton University Press, 1984), 39–47; Robert S. Chamberlain, *The Pre-Conquest Tribute and Service System of the Maya as Preparation for the Spanish Repartimiento-Encomienda in Yucatán* (Coral Gables, FL: University of Miami Press, 1951); and Ross Hassig, *Trade, Tribute, and Transportation: The Sixteenth-Century Political Economy of the Valley of Mexico* (Norman: University of Oklahoma Press, 1985).

27. For demography and movements of people, see Sherburne Friend Cook and Woodrow Wilson Borah, *Essays in Population History*, vol. 1, *Mexico and the Caribbean* (Berkeley: University of California Press, 1971); Wightman, *Indigenous Migration and Social Change*; and Nicolás Sánchez-Albornoz, *Indios y tributos en el Alto Perú* (Lima: Instituto de Estudios Peruanos, 1978). For prices, see Woodrow Wilson Borah, *Price Trends of Royal Tribute Commodities in Nueva Galicia, 1557–1598* (Berkeley: University of California Press, 1992). For natural disasters, see the work of América Molina del Villar, especially "Tributos y calamidades en el centro de la Nueva España, 1727–1762: Los límites del impuesto justo," *Historia Mexicana* 54, no. 1 (2004): 15–57.

28. See José Miranda, *El tributo indígena en la Nueva España durante el siglo XVI*, 2nd ed. (Mexico City: Colegio de México, 2005). Fabián Fonseca and Carlos de Urrutia also provide a lengthy discussion in their chapter "Tributos y servicio real" of the issuing and consequences of decrees related to the Real Hacienda in Mexico with attention to the tributes paid by Indians and free people of African descent. See *Historia general de Real Hacienda*, vol. 1 (Mexico City: V. G. Torres, 1845–53).

29. Studies that provide sustained treatment of gendered production in Indian communities include Susan Kellogg, *Weaving the Past: A History of Latin America's Indigenous Women from the Prehispanic Period to the Present* (New York: Oxford University Press, 2005), 63–71; and Bianca Premo, "From the Pockets of Women: The Gendering of the Mita, Migration, and Tribute in Colonial Chucuito, Peru," *The Americas* 57, no. 1 (2000): 63–93. For the case of free people of African descent, see also Cynthia Milton and Ben Vinson III, "Counting Heads: Race and Non-native Tribute Policy in Colonial Spanish America," *Journal of Colonialism and Colonial History* 3, no. 3 (2002).

30. See Aaron Pollack, "Hacia una historia social del tributo de indios y castas en Hispanoamérica: Notas en torno a su creación, desarrollo y abolición," *Historia Mexicana* 66, no. 1 (2016): 65–160; and Rafael Castañeda García, "Hacia una sociología fiscal: El tributo de la población de color libre de la Nueva España, 1770–1810," *Fronteras de la Historia* 19, no. 1 (2014): 152–73.

31. See Leon G. Campbell, "Black Power in Colonial Peru: The 1779 Tax Rebellion of Lambayeque," *Phylon* 33, no. 2 (1972): 140–52; Ben Vinson III and Matthew Restall, "Black Soldiers, Native Soldiers: Meanings of Military Service in the Spanish American Colonies," in *Beyond Black and Red: African-Native Relations in Colonial Latin America*,

ed. Matthew Restall (Albuquerque: University of New Mexico Press, 2005), 15–52; Paul Lokken, "Useful Enemies: Seventeenth-Century Piracy and the Rise of Pardo Militias in Spanish Central America," *Journal of Colonialism and Colonial History* 5, no. 2 (2004); and Ben Vinson III, "The Loathed Tax," in *Bearing Arms for His Majesty: The Free-Colored Militia in Colonial Mexico* (Stanford, CA: Stanford University Press, 2001), 132–72.

32. See Andrew Fisher, "Negotiating Two Worlds: The Free-Black Experience in Guerrero's Tierra Caliente," in *Black Mexico: Race and Society from Colonial to Modern Times*, ed. Ben Vinson III and Matthew Restall (Albuquerque: University of New Mexico Press, 2009), 51–71. For microhistories that use tribute data, see José Miguel Romero de Solís, *Padrón de negros en Colima de la Nueva España (siglo XVI)* (Colima: Archivo Histórico del Municipio de Colima, 2007); and *Negros y mulatos en Colima de la Nueva España (siglo XVI)* (Colima: Archivo Histórico del Municipio de Colima, 2007). Outside of Mexico, see Silvia G. Álvarez and Cecilia Mejía de Rubira, *Parentesco, política y prestigio social en los pueblos de indios del partido de Santa Elena: Padrón de 1803* (Guayaquil: Archivo Histórico del Guayas, 2011).

33. See Herman L. Bennett, *Africans in Colonial Mexico: Absolutism, Christianity, and Afro-Creole Consciousness, 1570–1640* (Bloomington: Indiana University Press, 2003); Nicole von Germeten, *Black Blood Brothers: Confraternities and Social Mobility for Afro-Mexicans* (Gainesville: University Press of Florida, 2006); and Ben Vinson III, *Bearing Arms for His Majesty: The Free-Colored Militia in Colonial Mexico* (Stanford, CA: Stanford University Press, 2001).

34. Three distinct yet equally relevant examples of this scholarship are Herman Bennett, *Colonial Blackness: A History of Afro-Mexico* (Bloomington: Indiana University Press, 2009); Matthew Restall, *The Black Middle: Africans, Mayas, and Spaniards in Colonial Yucatán* (Stanford, CA: Stanford University Press, 2009); and Ann Twinam, *Purchasing Whiteness: Pardos, Mulatos, and the Quest for Social Mobility in the Spanish Indies* (Stanford, CA: Stanford University Press, 2015).

35. David Sartorius shows how enslaved and free black "social subordinates could figure as loyal subjects," thereby gaining greater access to justice or challenging the excesses of the powerful. See *Ever Faithful*, 92. Bianca Premo has recently argued that enslaved people, through their engagement with the law in Spanish America, "were instrumental in plotting out the liberation teleology that so dominates Western thought." See *The Enlightenment on Trial: Ordinary Litigants and Colonialism in the Spanish Empire* (New York: Oxford University Press, 2017), 192. In Peru, enslaved people's actions pushed ahead the halting process of individual manumissions. See Christine Hünefeldt, *Paying the Price of Freedom: Family and Labor among Lima's Slaves, 1800–1854* (Berkeley: University of California Press, 1994), 200.

36. Robert McCaa, "Calidad, Clase, and Marriage in Colonial Mexico: The Case of Parral, 1788–90," *Hispanic American Historical Review* 64, no. 3 (1984): 477–78. For the use of this term in Brazil, see Mariana L. R. Dantas, *Black Townsmen: Urban Slavery and Freedom in the Eighteenth-Century Americas* (New York: Palgrave Macmillan, 2008), 174.

37. Joan Bristol has addressed the influence of ritual practice and religiosity on Afromexican *calidad* before the eighteenth century. See *Christians, Blasphemers, and Witches: Afro-Mexican Ritual Practice in the Seventeenth Century* (Albuquerque: University of New Mexico Press, 2007), 26–27.

38. Vinson, *Bearing Arms*, 4; and María Elena Martínez, "The Language, Genealogy, and Classification of 'Race' in Colonial Mexico," in *Race and Classification: The Case of*

Mexican America, ed. Ilona Katzew and Susan Deans-Smith (Stanford, CA: Stanford University Press, 2009), 42.

39. Martínez, *Genealogical Fictions*, 247.

40. Magali Carrera, *Imagining Identity in New Spain: Race, Lineage, and the Colonial Body in Portraiture and Casta Paintings* (Austin: University of Texas Press, 2003), 5. Studies of the caste system published during the mid-twentieth century proposed that caste differences were based on physical traits that came to constitute a complex taxonomy that starkly divided colonial society. See Gonzalo Aguirre Beltrán, *La población negra de México, 1519–1810: Estudio etno-histórico*, 2nd ed. (Mexico City: Fondo de Cultura Económica, 1972), 163–79. Magnus Mörner also stressed the importance of a "pigmentocracy" while acknowledging the possibility of "passing" among *castas*. See *Race Mixture in the History of Latin America* (Boston: Little, Brown, 1967), 68–70.

41. See Bristol, *Christians, Blasphemers*, 26; and Robert H. Jackson, *Race, Caste, and Status: Indians in Colonial Spanish America* (Albuquerque: University of New Mexico Press, 1999), 6.

42. Ann Twinam, *Public Lives, Private Secrets: Gender, Honor, Sexuality, and Illegitimacy in Colonial Spanish America* (Stanford, CA: Stanford University Press, 1999), 65.

43. Max S. Hering Torres, "Purity of Blood: Problems of Interpretation," in *Race and Blood in the Iberian World*, ed. María Elena Martínez, David Nirenberg, and Max-Sebastián Hering Torres (Zurich: LIT Verlag, 2012), 27.

44. Verena Martinez-Alier, *Marriage, Class, and Colour in Nineteenth-Century Cuba: A Study of Racial Attitudes and Sexual Values in a Slave Society* (Cambridge: Cambridge University Press, 1974), 26.

45. Aguirre Beltrán, *La población negra de México*, 153–78. For artistic production and the *castas*, see Magali Carrera, *Imagining Identity in New Spain: Race, Lineage, and the Colonial Body in Portraiture and Casta Paintings* (Austin: University of Texas Press, 2003); and Ilona Katzew, *Casta Painting: Images of Race in Eighteenth-Century Mexico* (New Haven, CT: Yale University Press, 2004). For recent work on the precursors to caste, see Robert C. Schwaller, *Géneros de Gente in Early Colonial Mexico: Defining Racial Difference* (Norman: University of Oklahoma Press, 2016); and Joanne Rappaport, "'Asi Lo Paresçe Por Su Aspeto': Physiognomy and the Construction of Difference in Colonial Bogotá," *Hispanic American Historical Review* 91, no. 4 (2011): 601–31. Rappaport has further cautioned scholars against indiscriminately applying principles of caste to early colonial contexts. See *The Disappearing Mestizo: Configuring Difference in the Colonial Kingdom of New Granada* (Durham, NC: Duke University Press, 2014), 224–25.

46. Rebecca Earle, *The Body of the Conquistador: Food, Race, and the Colonial Experience in Spanish America, 1492–1700* (Cambridge: Cambridge University Press, 2012), 6.

47. Sarah C. Chambers, *From Subjects to Citizens: Honor, Gender, and Politics in Arequipa, Peru, 1780–1854* (University Park: Pennsylvania State University Press, 1999), 90.

48. David Tavárez, "Legally Indian: Inquisitorial Readings of Indigenous Identity in New Spain," in *Imperial Subjects: Race and Identity in Colonial Spanish America*, ed. Andrew B. Fisher and Matthew D. O'Hara (Durham, NC: Duke University Press, 2009), 82.

49. A recent exploration of this practice is Cristian Berco, "Perception and the Mulatto Body in Inquisitorial Spain: A Neurohistory," *Past and Present* 231, no. 1 (2016): 33–60.

50. See Ben Vinson III, "From Dawn 'til Dusk: Black Labor in Late Colonial Mexico," in *Black Mexico: Race and Society from Colonial to Modern Times*, ed. Ben Vinson III and Matthew Restall (Albuquerque: University of New Mexico Press, 2009), 96–135.

Patricia Seed has argued that occupation influenced the application of caste and *calidad* labels on the census of 1753 in Mexico City. See "Social Dimensions of Race: Mexico City, 1753," *Hispanic American Historical Review* 62, no. 4 (1982): 569–606. In Cartagena in the 1770s, blacks were generally relegated to difficult manual labor, while *mulatos* and whites were able to procure more skilled positions. See Aline Helg, *Liberty and Equality in Caribbean Colombia, 1770–1835* (Chapel Hill: University of North Carolina Press, 2004), 97.

51. David Cahill, "Colour by Numbers: Racial and Ethnic Categories in the Viceroyalty of Peru, 1532–1824." *Journal of Latin American Studies* 26, no. 2 (1994): 325–46.

52. See Frederick Cooper, *Colonialism in Question: Theory, Knowledge, History* (Berkeley: University of California Press, 2005), 59–90.

53. Ruth Hill, *Hierarchy, Commerce, and Fraud in Bourbon Spanish America: A Postal Inspector's Exposé* (Nashville: Vanderbilt University Press, 2005), 229–30.

54. Restall, *Black Middle*, 92.

55. See Kathryn Burns, "Unfixing Race," in *Histories of Race and Racism: The Andes and Mesoamerica from Colonial Times to the Present*, ed. Laura Gotkowitz (Durham, NC: Duke University Press, 2014), 57–71; Diego A. von Vacano, *The Color of Citizenship: Race, Modernity, and Latin American/Hispanic Political Thought* (New York: Oxford University Press, 2012); M. Hering Torres, "Colores de piel: Una revisión histórica de larga duración," in *Debates sobre ciudadanía y políticas raciales en las Américas Negras*, ed. C. Mosquera (Bogotá: Universidad Nacional de Colombia, 2010), 113–60; Peter Wade, *Race and Ethnicity in Latin America*, 2nd ed. (London: Pluto Press, 2010); and James H. Sweet, "The Iberian Roots of American Racist Thought," *William and Mary Quarterly* 54, no. 1 (1997): 143–66.

56. Norma Angélica Castillo Palma, *Cholula, sociedad mestiza en ciudad india: Un análisis de las consecuencias demográficas, económicas y sociales del mestizaje en una ciudad novohispana (1649–1796)* (Mexico City: Plaza y Valdés Editores, 2001), 145.

57. See Rebecca Earle, "The Pleasures of Taxonomy: Casta Paintings, Classification, and Colonialism," *William and Mary Quarterly* 73, no. 3 (2016): 433. On the same topic, see R. Douglas Cope, *The Limits of Racial Domination: Plebeian Society in Colonial Mexico City, 1660–1720* (Madison: University of Wisconsin Press, 1994), 56–57.

58. Bennett, *Africans in Colonial Mexico*, 27.

59. Patrick James Carroll, *Blacks in Colonial Veracruz: Race, Ethnicity, and Regional Development*, 2nd ed. (Austin: University of Texas Press, 2001), 114.

60. Laura Lewis, *Hall of Mirrors: Power, Witchcraft, and Caste in Colonial Mexico* (Durham, NC: Duke University Press, 2003), 32–33.

61. R. Douglas Cope, *The Limits of Racial Domination: Plebeian Society in Colonial Mexico City, 1660–1720* (Madison: University of Wisconsin Press, 1994), 78.

62. See Graham T. Nessler's discussion of liberty suits in which individuals established themselves as people "considered" free in *An Islandwide Struggle for Freedom: Revolution, Emancipation, and Reenslavement in Hispaniola, 1789–1809* (Chapel Hill: University of North Carolina Press, 2016), 168–84. See also Rebecca J. Scott's recent discussion of how taking on the behaviors of a free person could become a pathway to legally becoming free in "Social Facts, Legal Fictions, and the Attribution of Slave Status: The Puzzle of Prescription," *Law and History Review* 35, no. 1 (2017): 9–30. On public knowledge and witness testimony, see Donald Ramos, "Gossip, Scandal, and Popular Culture in Golden Age Brazil," *Journal of Social History* 33, no. 4 (2000): 887–912.

63. Martínez, *Genealogical Fictions*, 199.

64. Two masterful studies on these topics are Martínez, *Genealogical Fictions*; and Peter B. Villella, *Indigenous Elites and Creole Identity in Colonial Mexico, 1500–1800* (New York: Cambridge University Press, 2016).

65. Twinam, *Purchasing Whiteness*, 124–27.

66. Twinam, *Purchasing Whiteness*, 115.

67. Rebecca J. Scott and Jean M. Hébrard, *Freedom Papers: An Atlantic Odyssey in the Age of Emancipation* (Cambridge, MA: Harvard University Press, 2012), 172.

68. Bianca Premo, "Familiar: Thinking beyond Lineage and across Race in Spanish Atlantic Family History," *William and Mary Quarterly* 70, no. 2 (2013): 30.

69. The historiography on marriage and family among people of African descent in colonial Latin America is substantial. For works that consider black kinship in New Spain beyond nuclear family ties, see Carroll, *Blacks in Colonial Veracruz*; Herman L. Bennett, *Africans in Colonial Mexico: Absolutism, Christianity, and Afro-Creole Consciousness, 1570–1640* (Bloomington: Indiana University Press, 2003); Von Germeten, *Black Blood Brothers*; Bennett, *Colonial Blackness*; and, more recently, María Elisa Velázquez and Carolina González Undurraga, eds., *Mujeres africanas y afrodescendientes: Experiencias de esclavitud y libertad en América Latina y África, Siglos XVI al XIX* (Mexico City: Secretaría de Cultura, Instituto Nacional de Antropología e Historia, 2016).

70. Nicole von Germeten's *Black Blood Brothers* explores blackness and religiosity as markers of community through confraternity membership. On the potential for community among people of African descent in Yucatán, see Matthew Restall, *The Black Middle: Africans, Mayas, and Spaniards in Colonial Yucatán* (Stanford, CA: Stanford University Press, 2009), 200–246. For a broad treatment of family life, Christian belief, and the private sphere among Afromexicans, see Bennett, *Colonial Blackness*. On marriage choices and the impact of the end of the slave trade, see Proctor, *Damned Notions of Liberty*, 37–67.

71. Vinson, *Bearing Arms*, 138–39.

72. These structures were pervasive beyond New Spain. Free people struggled to overcome numerous social barriers, even as they lived and worked in close proximity to people considered "white." See Jay Kinsbruner, *Not of Pure Blood: The Free People of Color and Racial Prejudice in Nineteenth-Century Puerto Rico* (Durham, NC: Duke University Press, 1996), 141. On policies in the education sector, see Rafael L. López Valdés and Ricardo E. Alegría, *Pardos y morenos esclavos y libres en Cuba y sus instituciones en el Caribe hispano* (San Juan, PR: Centro de Estudios Avanzados de Puerto Rico y el Caribe, 2007), 83. Some of these same means to social control were aimed at enslaved people who had access to autonomy. See Kathleen J. Higgins, *"Licentious Liberty" in a Brazilian Gold-Mining Region: Slavery, Gender, and Social Control in Eighteenth-Century Sabará, Minas Gerais* (University Park: Pennsylvania State University Press, 1999).

73. Palmer, *Slaves of the White God*, 28.

74. For the quote, see Philip D. Morgan, "British Encounters with Africans and African-Americans, circa 1600–1780," in *Strangers within the Realm: Cultural Margins of the First British Empire*, ed. Bernard Bailyn and Philip D. Morgan (Chapel Hill: University of North Carolina Press, 1991), 161–62. For the politics of death and disease in slave societies, see Vincent Brown, *The Reaper's Garden: Death and Power in the World of Atlantic Slavery* (Cambridge, MA: Harvard University Press, 2008).

75. Dantas, *Black Townsmen*, 125.

76. Sherwin K. Bryant, *Rivers of Gold, Lives of Bondage: Governing through Slavery in Colonial Quito* (Chapel Hill: University of North Carolina Press, 2014), 10.

77. For a recent example, see Carolina González Undurraga, *Esclavos y esclavas demandando justicia: Chile, 1740–1823; Documentación judicial por carta de libertad y papel de venta* (Santiago de Chile: Editorial Universitaria, 2014), 27.

78. Christopher J. Bryant has used "freedom tax" to refer to the many taxes required of free blacks in slave states in the United States. See "Without Representation, No Taxation: Free Blacks, Taxes, and Tax Exemptions between the Revolutionary and Civil Wars," *Michigan Journal of Race and Law* 21, no. 1 (2015): 99–103 and 107–10.

79. Léo Elisabeth, "The French Antilles," in *Neither Slave nor Free: The Freedmen of African Descent in the Slave Societies of the New World*, ed. David William Cohen and Jack P. Greene (Baltimore: Johns Hopkins University Press, 1972), 144.

80. See Rafael Castañeda García, "Hacia una sociología fiscal: El tributo de la población de color libre de la Nueva España, 1770–1810," *Fronteras de la Historia* 19, no. 1 (2014): 158–61.

81. Fonseca and Urrutia, *Historia general de Real Hacienda*, 1:434–35.

82. On rural free Afromexican populations, see Fisher, "Negotiating Two Worlds"; Carroll, *Blacks in Colonial Veracruz*, 112–29; and Ben Vinson III, "The Racial Profile of a Rural Mexican Province in the 'Costa Chica': Igualapa in 1791," *The Americas* 57, no. 2 (2000): 269–82. For the early establishment of rural black communities in the Spanish Caribbean, see David Wheat, *Atlantic Africa and the Spanish Caribbean, 1570–1640* (Chapel Hill: University of North Carolina Press, 2016), 181–215.

83. See Bennett, *Colonial Blackness*, 114–18; Frederick Bowser, *The African Slave in Colonial Peru, 1524–1650* (Stanford, CA: Stanford University Press, 1974), 157–58; Sidney Chalhoub, "Illegal Enslavement and the Precariousness of Freedom in Nineteenth-Century Brazil," in *Assumed Identities: The Meanings of Race in the Atlantic World*, ed. John D. Garrigus and Christopher Morris (College Station: Texas A&M University Press, 2010), 88–115; Lewis, *Hall of Mirrors*, 78–80; María Elena Martínez, "Space, Order, and Group Identities in a Spanish Colonial Town: Puebla de los Angeles," in *The Collective and the Public in Latin America: Cultural Identities and Political Order*, ed. Luis Roniger and Tamar Herzog (Brighton: Sussex Academic Press, 2014), 13–36; Palmer, *Slaves of the White God*, 131; Schwaller, *Géneros de Gente*, 79–82; and Von Germeten, *Black Blood Brothers*, 76.

84. Martínez, "Space, Order, and Group Identities in a Spanish Colonial Town," 13–14.

85. This term denoted a lack of fixity, certainty, or direction. See Real Academia Española, *Diccionario de Autoridades*, vol. 4 (Madrid: F. del Hierro, 1739).

86. Patrick J. Carroll, "Black-Native Relations and the Historical Record in Colonial Mexico," in *Beyond Black and Red: African-Native Relations in Colonial Latin America*, ed. Matthew Restall (Albuquerque: University of New Mexico Press, 2005), 249; Ursula Camba Ludlow, *Imaginarios ambiguos, realidades contradictorias: Conductas y representaciones de los negros y mulatos novohispanos, siglos XVI y XVII* (Mexico City: El Colegio de México, 2008), 151.

87. See Gabriel B. Paquette, *Enlightenment, Governance, and Reform in Spain and Its Empire, 1759–1808* (Basingstoke: Palgrave Macmillan, 2008); and Matthew O'Hara, *A Flock Divided: Race, Religion, and Politics in México, 1749–1857* (Durham, NC: Duke University Press, 2010), 91–22.

88. On Mexico as a "fiscal submetropolis" with a great fiscal surplus, see Marichal, *Bankruptcy of Empire*, 16–47. See also Carlos Marichal and Matilde Souto Mantecón, "Silver and Situados: New Spain and the Financing of the Spanish Empire in the Carib-

bean in the Eighteenth Century," *Hispanic American Historical Review* 74 no. 4 (1994): 588–89; Regina Grafe and Alejandra Irigoin, "The Spanish Empire and Its Legacy: Fiscal Re-distribution and Political Conflict in Colonial and Post-Colonial Spanish America," *Journal of Global History* 1, no. 2 (2006): 252; and Herbert S. Klein and Jacques A. Barbier, "Recent Trends in the Study of Spanish American Colonial Public Finance," *Latin American Research Review* 23, no. 1 (1988): 52.

89. Richard L. Kagan, *Lawsuits and Litigants in Castile, 1500–1700* (Chapel Hill: University of North Carolina Press, 1981), 4.

90. Quoted in Mörner, *Race Mixture in the History of Latin America*, 69.

91. Alan J. Kuethe and Kenneth J. Andrien, *The Spanish Atlantic World in the Eighteenth Century: War and the Bourbon Reforms, 1713–1796* (Cambridge: Cambridge University Press, 2014), 303.

92. For the intendancy system as a "revolution in government," see D. A. Brading, *Miners and Merchants in Bourbon Mexico, 1763–1810* (Cambridge: Cambridge University Press, 1971), 33–92. See also Lillian Estelle Fisher, *The Intendant System in Spanish America* (New York: Gordian Press, 1969).

93. José del Campillo y Cossío, *Nuevo sistema de gobierno económico para la América* (Madrid: Imprenta de Benito Cano, 1789), 292.

94. In 1765 and 1766, accountants claimed that no tribute had been charged in the capital district of San Juan Tenochtitlán owing to disease. Subsequently, officials had difficulty finding a qualified administrator willing to oversee collection efforts. See AGI, Audiencia de México leg. 2104, *plano* for 1769.

95. In 1773, the *alcalde mayor* of San Miguel el Grande claimed that it was "impossible to collect" tribute in full, which would have totaled 13,445 pesos and 6 *tomines* (where eight *tomines* are equal to one peso) from Indians in towns along with 5,650 pesos from *mulatos*. See "*Relaciones juradas*" included with the description of accounts of 1773 in AGI, Audiencia de México leg. 2104.

96. John Leddy Phelan, "Authority and Flexibility in the Spanish Imperial Bureaucracy," *Administrative Science Quarterly* 5, no. 1 (1960): 59.

97. AGN, Indiferente Virreinal c. 6316, exp. 13, f. 5.

98. Vinson, *Bearing Arms*, 138.

99. Ann Laura Stoler, *Carnal Knowledge and Imperial Power: Race and the Intimate in Colonial Rule* (Berkeley: University of California Press, 2010), 8.

CHAPTER 1

1. Peter Gerhard, *A Guide to the Historical Geography of New Spain* (Cambridge: Cambridge University Press, 1972), 272.

2. AGN, Indiferente Virreinal c. 1151, exp. 15, f. 1.

3. For Tenango del Valle, see Deborah E. Kanter, *Hijos del Pueblo: Gender, Family, and Community in Rural Mexico, 1730–1850* (Austin: University of Texas Press, 2008), 35. Laws aimed at separating free people of African descent from Indian populations were issued repeatedly throughout the colonial period. A law from 1785 instructed ecclesiastics to force "*mulatos, negros*, and other *razas*" to leave Indian towns. See Richard Konetzke, *Colección de documentos para la historia de la formación social de Hispanoamérica*, vol. 3, pt. 2 (Madrid: Consejo Superior de Investigaciones Científicas, 1953–62), 589–90. *Mulatas* who lived and did business in Indian barrios and towns might adopt a different caste status, a strategy taken by market women in New Spain and beyond as they navigated

commercial spaces and colonial rules. For examples of these shifts in caste among market sellers, see the work of Jane E. Mangan, *Trading Roles: Gender, Ethnicity, and the Urban Economy in Colonial Potosí* (Durham, NC: Duke University Press, 2005), especially 82–92; and "A Market of Identities: Women, Trade, and Ethnic Labels in Colonial Potosí," in *Imperial Subjects: Race and Identity in Colonial Latin America*, ed. Andrew B. Fisher and Matthew O'Hara (Durham, NC: Duke University Press, 2009), 61–80.

4. AGN, Indiferente Virreinal c. 1151, exp. 15, ff. 1–iv.

5. Miguel Artola, *La Hacienda del Antiguo Régimen* (Madrid: Alianza, 1982), 32.

6. In addition to royal tributes (the *tributo real* and the *servicio real*), Indians paid a host of other taxes described in Nancy Farriss, *Maya Society under Colonial Rule: The Collective Enterprise of Survival* (Princeton, NJ: Princeton University Press, 1984), 40–41; and Charles Gibson, *The Aztecs under Spanish Rule: A History of the Indians of the Valley of Mexico* (Stanford, CA: Stanford University Press, 1976), 205.

7. Robert S. Chamberlain, *The Pre-Conquest Tribute and Service System of the Maya as Preparation for the Spanish Repartimiento-Encomienda in Yucatán* (Coral Gables, FL: University of Miami Press, 1951), 30–31.

8. Although the English quickly realized that the vast tributary potential in goods and labor found in Spanish America would not be repeated, the Virginia Company did attempt to impose a tribute in goods and labor in 1609. It would prove a failure owing to Indian resistance to the system. See J. H. Elliott, *Empires of the Atlantic World: Britain and Spain in America, 1492–1830* (New Haven, CT: Yale University Press, 2006), 42.

9. Herbert S. Klein, *Royal Income and Expenditures in Colonial Mexico, Peru, and Bolivia, 1680–1809* (Albuquerque: University of New Mexico Press, 1998), 20.

10. Ismael Sánchez Bella, Alberto de la Hera, and Carlos J. Díaz Rementería, *Historia del Derecho Indiano* (Madrid: Editorial MAPFRE, 1992), 229–30.

11. C. H. Haring, "The Early Spanish Colonial Exchequer," *American Historical Review* 23, no. 4 (1918): 782.

12. Herbert S. Klein and Ben Vinson III, *African Slavery in Latin America and the Caribbean*, 2nd ed. (Oxford: Oxford University Press, 2007), 197.

13. Sherburne Friend Cook and Woodrow Wilson Borah, *Essays in Population History*, vol. 1, *Mexico and the Caribbean* (Berkeley: University of California Press, 1971), 340.

14. See Yovana Celaya Nández's interpretations of the *informe* to Viceroy Antonio Bucareli in "José de Gálvez: Pensamiento, evaluaciones y proyectos en la Hacienda novohispana, 1765–1786," in *Pensar la Hacienda pública: Personajes, proyectos y contextos en torno al pensamiento fiscal en Nueva España y México (Siglos XVIII–XX)*, ed. Ernest Sánchez Santiró (Mexico City: Instituto Mora, 2014), 63.

15. John Leddy Phelan, *The People and the King: The Comunero Revolution in Colombia, 1781* (Madison: University of Wisconsin Press, 1978), xviii.

16. Free blacks paid tribute to the Seminole Nation, in addition to the Spanish Empire, to secure safety from British enslavement. See Jane Landers, *Black Society in Spanish Florida* (Urbana: University of Illinois Press, 1999), 68. For the case of the Comanche, see Pekka Hämäläinen, *The Comanche Empire* (New Haven, CT: Yale University Press, 2008), 181–82. The costs of maintaining a tribute regime and other signs of imperial governance on frontiers allowed Bourbon officials to "see practical advantages to abandoning long-held claims." See David Weber, *Bárbaros: Spaniards and Their Savages in the Age of Enlightenment* (New Haven, CT: Yale University Press, 2005), 205.

17. Carlos Marichal, *Bankruptcy of Empire: Mexican Silver and the Wars between Spain, Britain, and France, 1760–1810* (Cambridge: Cambridge University Press, 2007), 58.

18. The precise figure given by Ernest Sánchez Santiró is 112,462 people. See Sánchez Santiró, *Padrón del Arzobispado de México 1777* (Mexico City: Archivo General de la Nación, 2003), 55.

19. Alexander von Humboldt, *Ensayo político sobre Nueva España*, trans. Vicente González Arnao, vol. 3, book 4 (Paris: Libreria de Lecointe, 1836), 302. Mexico had outpaced the Andean zone in terms of its mining exports to Europe by the 1660s. See Herbert S. Klein, *The American Finances of the Spanish Empire: Royal Income and Expenditures in Colonial Mexico, Peru, and Bolivia, 1680–1809* (Albuquerque: University of New Mexico Press, 1998), 14. John J. TePaske gives the figure at 45 percent for 1492–1810. See *A New World of Gold and Silver*, ed. Kendall W. Brown (Leiden: Brill, 2010), 17.

20. See Gibson, *Aztecs under Spanish Rule*, 208; and Marichal, *Bankruptcy of Empire*, 62–63.

21. Marichal, *Bankruptcy of Empire*, 61.

22. AGN, Tributos vol. 43, exp. 9. This summary includes the provinces of Arizpe, Guadalajara, Guanajuato, Mérida, Mexico, Oaxaca, Potosí, Puebla, Valladolid, Veracruz, and Zacatecas.

23. Miguel Ángel Ladero Quesada, *Fiscalidad y poder real en Castilla (1252–1369)*, 2nd ed. (Madrid: Real Academia de la Historia, 2011), 25–26.

24. C. H. Haring, *The Spanish Empire in America* (New York: Harcourt, Brace and World, 1963), 263.

25. Miguel Artola, *La Hacienda del Antiguo Régimen* (Madrid: Alianza, 1982), 63–64. Occasionally, eighteenth-century administrators, ordinary people, and commissioners used the term "*servicio*" in reference to royal tribute for free people of African descent or Indians.

26. A. C. de C. M. Saunders observes that a few free blacks in Lisbon and beyond had access to small properties or had skills that allowed them to live comfortably. See *A Social History of Black Slaves and Freedmen in Portugal, 1441–1555* (Cambridge: Cambridge University Press, 1982), 144.

27. Free people who continued to work in a master's or mistress's home often struggled to collect a salary in fifteenth-century Valencia. See Debra Blumenthal, *Enemies and Familiars: Slavery and Mastery in Fifteenth-Century Valencia* (Ithaca, NY: Cornell University Press, 2009), 245–51. Manumitted women occasionally received a dowry to secure their future marriage. See William D. Phillips, *Slavery in Medieval and Early Modern Iberia* (Philadelphia: University of Pennsylvania Press, 2014), 142.

28. Andrés Lira González, "Aspecto fiscal de la Nueva España en la segunda mitad del siglo XVIII," *Historia mexicana* 17, no. 3 (1968): 374.

29. Konetzke, *Colección de documentos*, vol. 3, pt. 2, 789.

30. See "*fidalgo*" in Sebastián de Covarrubias Orozco, *Tesoro de la lengua castellana o española* (Madrid: L. Sánchez, 1611).

31. Juan Beneyto Pérez, *Historia social de España y de Hispanoamérica* (Madrid: Aguilar, 1961), 216.

32. Alvin Rabushka, *Taxation in Colonial America* (Princeton, NJ: Princeton University Press, 2008), 22.

33. Ismael Sánchez Bella, Alberto de la Hera, and Carlos J. Díaz Rementería, *Historia del Derecho Indiano* (Madrid: Editorial MAPFRE, 1992), 313–15.

34. The term *principal* became increasingly interchangeable with *cacique* to signal importance in the community. James Lockhart argues that "Spaniards were mainly concerned with rulers and lords as figures of authority, not with nobles and nobility as such."

Yet, caciques could pass on an exempt status to their firstborn children, thus retaining a genealogical element to this title within the tribute regime. See James Lockhart, *The Nahuas after the Conquest: A Social and Cultural History of the Indians of Central Mexico, Sixteenth through Eighteenth Centuries* (Stanford, CA: Stanford University Press, 1991), 133.

35. See Colin M. MacLachlan, *Spain's Empire in the New World: The Role of Ideas in Institutional and Social Change* (Berkeley: University of California Press, 1991), 9–10; and J. H Elliott, *Imperial Spain 1469–1716*, 2nd ed. (London: Penguin Books, 2002), 164–212.

36. Karen B. Graubart, *With Our Labor and Sweat: Indigenous Women and the Formation of Colonial Society in Peru, 1550–1700* (Stanford, CA: Stanford University Press, 2007), 45.

37. José Miranda, *El tributo indígena en la Nueva España durante el siglo XVI*, 2nd ed. (Mexico City: Colegio de México, 2005), 21.

38. Miranda, *Tributo indígena en la Nueva España*, 51–52.

39. Gibson, *Aztecs under Spanish Rule*, 206.

40. Miranda, *Tributo indígena en la Nueva España*, 235–42.

41. Miranda, *Tributo indígena en la Nueva España*, 110.

42. Ronald Escobedo Mansilla, *El tributo indígena en el Perú: Siglos XVI y XVII* (Pamplona: Ediciones Universidad de Navarra, 1979), 27.

43. Gibson, *Aztecs under Spanish Rule*, 199–202.

44. Jon Cowans, *Early Modern Spain: A Documentary History* (Philadelphia: University of Pennsylvania Press, 2003), 28–31. Reprinted in English translation from Francisco de Zabálburu and José Sancho Rayón, eds., *Nueva colección de documentos inéditos para la historia de España y sus indias*, vol. 6 (Madrid: Imprenta de Manuel G. Hernández, 1896).

45. Woodrow Wilson Borah, *Price Trends of Royal Tribute Commodities in Nueva Galicia, 1557–1598* (Berkeley: University of California Press, 1992), 6.

46. Ross Hassig, *Trade, Tribute, and Transportation: The Sixteenth-Century Political Economy of the Valley of Mexico* (Norman: University of Oklahoma Press, 1985), 227–28.

47. Fabián Fonseca and Carlos de Urrutia, *Historia general de Real Hacienda,* vol. 1 (Mexico City: V. G. Torres, 1845–53), 425.

48. Real Academia Española, *Diccionario de la lengua castellana* (Madrid: D. Joaquín Ibarra, 1780), 675.

49. Real Academia Española, *Diccionario de la lengua castellana*, 611.

50. Although these two terms had different definitions, they were often used interchangeably and both derive from the same Latin roots *syllabus* and *catalogus*. "Tribute register" will serve as a translation for both "*padrón*" and "*matrícula*."

51. Cook and Borah, *Essays in Population History*, 19–22.

52. See Article 137 published in Marina Mantilla Trolle, Rafael Diego-Fernández Sotelo, and Agustín Moreno, *Real Ordenanza para el establecimiento e instrucción de intendentes de ejército y provincial en el reino de la Nueva España: Edición anotada de la Audiencia de la Nueva Galicia* (Guadalajara: Universidad de Guadalajara, 2008), 296.

53. See "Capitación" in José Canga Argüelles, *Diccionario de hacienda*, vol. 2 (London: Imprenta Española de M. Calero, 1826), 39.

54. See Escobedo Mansilla, *El tributo indígena en el Perú*, 24–25. In the Andes, their activities included agricultural work, textile production, and herding. See also Bianca Premo, "From the Pockets of Women: The Gendering of the Mita, Migration, and Tribute in Colonial Chucuito, Peru," *The Americas* 57, no. 1 (200): 63–93.

55. Libro 7, Título 5, Ley 2, in *Recopilación de leyes de los reynos de las Indias*, vol. 2 (Madrid: Julián de Paredes, 1681; Madrid: Ediciones Cultura Hispánica, 1973), 320.

56. Libro 7, Título 5, Ley 2, *Recopilación*, 2:320.

57. Robert C. Schwaller, "'Mulata, Hija de Negro y India': Afro-Indigenous Mulatos in Early Colonial Mexico," *Journal of Social History* 44, no. 3 (2011): 889.

58. Libro 7, Título 5, Ley 1, *Recopilación*, 2:320.

59. Robert C. Schwaller, *Géneros de Gente in Early Colonial Mexico: Defining Racial Difference* (Norman: University of Oklahoma Press, 2016), 76–77.

60. Rafael Castañeda García, "Hacia una sociología fiscal: El tributo de la población de color libre de la Nueva España," *Fronteras de la Historia* 19, no. 1 (2014): 156.

61. Libro 7, Título 5, Ley 1, *Recopilación*, 2:320.

62. Cynthia Milton and Ben Vinson III, "Counting Heads: Race and Non-native Tribute Policy in Colonial Spanish America," *Journal of Colonialism and Colonial History* 3, no. 3 (2002): 15.

63. This practice did exist in the Andes for landless male Indians and those whose land use was otherwise restricted. See Herbert S. Klein, *Haciendas and Ayllus: Rural Society in the Bolivian Andes in the Eighteenth and Nineteenth Centuries* (Stanford, CA: Stanford University Press, 1993), 88–89.

64. Frederick P. Bower, "Colonial Spanish America," in *Neither Slave nor Free: The Freedmen of African Descent in the Slave Societies of the New World*, ed. David W. Cohen and Jack P. Greene (Baltimore: Johns Hopkins University Press, 1972), 42.

65. Christopher Lutz, *Santiago de Guatemala, 1541–1773: City, Caste, and the Colonial Experience* (Norman: University of Oklahoma Press, 1994), 254.

66. Paul Lokken, "La recaudación del tributo de laborío y la formación burocrática de identidades sociales en la provincia de Guatemala, 1608–1644," *Boletín de la Asociación para el Fomento de los Estudios Históricos en Centroamérica* 51 (2011): 17–18.

67. AGI, Audiencia de Panamá leg. 237, cuaderno 11, ff. 47–47v.

68. See Archivo General de la Nación de Colombia, Colonia, Tributos t. 8, fs. 657–84, "Nicolás de Munar, arrendador de tributos de indios, mulatos, negros y zambos de Santa fé hace una petición para poder apremiarlos por la tributación" (1756) and Katherine Bonil Gómez, *Gobierno y calidad en el orden colonial: Las categorías del mestizaje en la provincia de Mariquita en la segunda mitad del siglo XVIII; Primera edición* (Bogotá: Universidad de los Andes, 2011).

69. See Ronald Escobedo Mansilla, "El tributo de los zambaigos, negros y mulatos en el virreinato peruano," *Revista de Indias* 41, no. 163 (1981): 43–54.

70. Juan de Solórzano y Pereira, *Política Indiana*, book 2 (Madrid: Diego Díaz de la Carrera, 1648), 248.

71. Herbert S. Klein and John J. TePaske, "Arica" and "Potosí," in *Las cartas cuentas de la Real Hacienda de la América española, siglo XVI a principios del siglo XIX* (CD-ROM) (Mexico City: Colegio de México, 2004).

72. Konetzke, *Colección de documentos*, vol. 3, pt. 1, 86.

73. Klein and TePaske, "Santiago de Chile," in *Cartas cuentas*.

74. See Alex Borucki, *From Shipmates to Soldiers: Emerging Black Identities in the Río de la Plata* (Albuquerque: University of New Mexico Press, 2015), 71; and Ignacio Telesca, "Sociedad y afrodescendientes en el proceso de independencia del Paraguay," in *"Negros de la patria": Los afrodescendientes en las luchas por la independencia en el antiguo Virreinato del Río de la Plata*, ed. Silvia Mallo and Ignacio Telesca (Buenos Aires: Editorial SB, 2010), 164.

75. Luis Ramos Gómez and Carmen Ruigómez Gómez, "Una propuesta a la corona para extender la mita y el tributo a negros, mestizos y mulatos (Ecuador, 1735–1748)," *Revista Complutense de Historia de América* 25 (1999): 109.

76. María Eugenia Chaves, "Slave Women's Strategies for Freedom and the Late Spanish Colonial State," in *Hidden Histories of Gender and the State in Latin America*, ed. Elizabeth Dore and Maxine Molyneux (Durham, NC: Duke University Press, 2000), 111.

77. See Borucki, *From Shipmates to Soldiers*, 105; and Carlos J. Díaz Rementería, "En torno a un aspecto de la política reformista de Carlos III: Las matrículas de tributarios en los virreinatos de Perú y Río de la Plata," *Revista de Indias*, 37 (1979): 58–59.

78. Konetzke, *Colección de documentos*, vol. 2, pt. 2, 628–31.

79. Carlos J. Díaz Rementería, "El régimen jurídico del ramo de tributos en Nueva España y las reformas peruanas de Carlos III," *Historia Mexicana* 28, no. 3 (1979): 405.

80. Leon G. Campbell, "Black Power in Colonial Peru: The 1779 Tax Rebellion of Lambayeque," *Phylon* 33, no. 2 (1972): 145.

81. Klein and Vinson, *African Slavery*, 274 (table 2).

82. Klein and Vinson, *African Slavery*, 197.

83. Klein and Vinson, *African Slavery*, 196–97.

84. Frank Proctor, "Afro-Mexican Slave Labor in the Obrajes de Paños of New Spain, Seventeenth and Eighteenth Centuries," *The Americas* 60, no. 1 (2003): 35.

85. Using data from TePaske and Klein, Vinson calculates annual rates of increase or decrease fluctuating as much as 76 percent. See *Bearing Arms*, 140.

86. América Molina del Villar, "Tributos y calamidades en el centro de la Nueva España, 1727–1762: Los límites del impuesto justo," *Historia Mexicana* 54, no. 1 (2004): 28–29.

87. John Tutino, *Making a New World: Founding Capitalism in the Bajío and Spanish North America* (Durham, NC: Duke University Press, 2011), 175–79 and 529 (appendix C).

88. Peter Gerhard, *The North Frontier of New Spain* (Princeton, NJ: Princeton University Press, 1982), 272.

89. Miranda, *Tributo indígena en la Nueva España*, 198–99.

90. Libro 7, Título 5, Ley 1 in *Recopilación*, 2:320.

91. Eberhard Isenmann, "Medieval and Renaissance Theories of State Finance," in *Economic Systems and State Finance*, ed. Richard Bonney (Oxford: Oxford University Press, 1995), 31.

92. Men who held this opinion included Solórzano, Juan Ortiz de Matienzo, José de Acosta, and Juan Zapata y Sandoval. See Miranda, *Tributo indígena en la Nueva España*, 161–62; and Escobedo Mansilla, *El tributo indígena en el Perú*, 137.

93. Mario Góngora, *Studies in the Colonial History of Spanish America* (Cambridge: Cambridge University Press, 1975), 73.

94. Silvio Arturo Zavala, *Las instituciones jurídicas en la conquista de América*, 2nd ed. (Mexico City: Editorial Porrúa, 1971), 64–70.

95. Nancy E. van Deusen, *Global Indios: The Indigenous Struggle for Justice in Sixteenth-Century Spain* (Durham, NC: Duke University Press, 2015), 2.

96. Silvio Arturo Zavala, *Los esclavos indios en Nueva España*, 2nd ed. (Mexico City: Colegio Nacional, 1981), 24–25.

97. Lesley Byrd Simpson, *Studies in the Administration of the Indians in New Spain*, vol. 3 (Berkeley: University of California Press), 4–5.

98. Zavala, *Esclavos indios*, 155.

99. Zavala, *Esclavos indios*, 152–53.

100. An estimated 151,618 blacks lived in New Spain in 1646. Of these, 35,089 were born in Africa. See Gonzalo Aguirre Beltrán, *La población negra de México, 1519–1810: Estudio etno-histórico*, 2nd ed. (Mexico City: Fondo de Cultura Económica, 1972), 219.

101. Aguirre Beltrán, *La población negra de México*, 270 and 282. These uncommon or "forgotten castes" are the subject of a recently published work by Ben Vinson III on racial dynamics and identities at the extremes of the caste spectrum. See *Before Mestizaje: The Frontiers of Race and Caste in Colonial Mexico* (Cambridge: Cambridge University Press, 2017).

102. Vinson, *Bearing Arms*, 134.

103. Libro 7, Título 5, Ley 3, *Recopilación*, 2:320.

104. Libro 6, Título 5, Ley 23 in *Recopilación*, 2:244.

105. Silvio Zavala identifies this label as that of a free wage laborer. See Silvio Arturo Zavala and María Castelo, *Fuentes para la historia del trabajo en la Nueva España* (Mexico City: Fondo de Cultura Económica), 271, cited in Manuela Cristina García Bernal, *La Sociedad de Yucatán, 1700–1750* (Seville: Escuela de Estudios Hispano-Americanos, 1972), 28. By the eighteenth century, *laboríos* in Guatemala could be "(1) Indian tributaries who claimed *laborío* status based on military service and (2) the offspring of Indian women and either naboría, free mulatto, or free black fathers." See Christopher Lutz, *Santiago de Guatemala, 1541–1773: City, Caste, and the Colonial Experience* (Norman: University of Oklahoma Press, 1994), 270n31.

106. AGN, Indiferente Virreinal c. 6578, exp. 17, f. 1718. In Guatemala after 1680, Lutz claims that *laborío* tribute was only collected from free people of African descent. See Lutz, *Santiago de Guatemala*, 270.

107. Rachel Sarah O'Toole, *Bound Lives: Africans, Indians, and the Making of Race in Colonial Peru* (Pittsburgh: University of Pittsburgh Press, 2012), 30–31.

108. Fonseca and Urrutia, *Historia general de Real Hacienda*, 1:447–48.

109. AGN, General de Parte vol. 79, exp. 277, f. 241.

110. Accounts of Indian towns requesting relief from tribute due to famine, drought, and disease can be found in Virginia García Acosta, Juan Manuel Pérez Zevallos, and América Molina del Villar, *Desastres agrícolas en México: Catálogo histórico, tomo 1: Epocas prehispánica y colonial (958–1822)* (Mexico City: CIESAS, 2003). Although less common, it was not impossible for Afromexican families to get these temporary exemptions on the grounds of poverty. Free *mulato* Balthazar Senteno of Celaya made such a petition in 1714. See AGN, Indiferente Virreinal c. 6627, exp. 37.

111. AGN, Tributos vol. 28, exp. 1, f. 32v.

112. See Kevin Terraciano, *The Mixtecs of Colonial Oaxaca: Ñudzahui History, Sixteenth through Eighteenth Centuries* (Stanford, CA: Stanford University Press, 2001), 234; and Gibson, *Aztecs under Spanish Rule*, 219.

113. See Jane G. Landers's discussion of former maroons and free black towns in "Cimarrón and Citizen: African Ethnicity, Corporate Identity, and the Evolution of Free Black Towns in the Spanish Circum-Caribbean," in *Slaves, Subjects, and Subversives: Blacks in Colonial Latin America*, ed. Jane G. Landers and Barry M. Robinson (Albuquerque: University of New Mexico Press, 2006), 121–32. Here, Landers makes an intriguing point disputing the widely accepted position that a free black republic, or a "República de Negros," did not exist. See "Cimarrón and Citizen," 130. Although some officials advocated for the creation of *pueblos de negros*, other historians argue that this idea was never put into general practice. See Vinson, *Bearing Arms*, 156. A failed experiment along these lines occurred in Paraguay in 1741 at San Agustín de la Emboscada, where 572 free *pardos* were relocated to the town by 1761. See Telesca, "Sociedad y afrodescendientes," 164.

114. Miranda, *Tributo indígena en la Nueva España*, 198.

115. O'Toole, *Bound Lives*, 86–87.

116. The *padrones* created for *mulatos* in Mizque provide a curious example of the ways in which free people of African descent might assert their status and negotiate the impact of tribute on their finances and labor. See Lolita Gutiérrez Brockington, *Blacks, Indians, and Spaniards in the Eastern Andes: Reclaiming the Forgotten in Colonial Mizque, 1550–1782* (Lincoln: University of Nebraska Press, 2006), 283–84.

117. A reproduction of this treaty can be found in Jean-Pierre Tardieu, *Resistencia de los negros en el Virreinato de México, siglos XVI–XVII* (Madrid: Iberoamericana, 2017), 174.

118. Tardieu, *Resistencia de los negros*, 187–88.

119. See Ben Vinson III, "From Dawn 'til Dusk: Black Labor in Late Colonial Mexico," in *Black Mexico: Race and Society from Colonial to Modern Times*, ed. Ben Vinson III and Matthew Restall (Albuquerque: University of New Mexico Press, 2009), 117; and Susan Deans-Smith, *Bureaucrats, Planters, and Workers: The Making of the Tobacco Monopoly in Bourbon Mexico* (Austin: University of Texas Press, 1992), 192–95.

120. Silvio Zavala, *El servicio personal de los indios en la Nueva España*, vol. 7 (Mexico City: Colegio de México, 1984), 266.

121. The sample is taken from eighteen regions and is described further in chapters 4 and 5 herein. Of the 7,545 records in the sample, 1,953 specified a form of livelihood such as guild membership, farming, or trade. About one-fifth of all those employed were farmers.

122. AGN, General de Parte vol. 79, exp. 277, f. 240v.

123. Karen B. Graubart, "The Creolization of the New World: Local Forms of Identification in Urban Colonial Peru, 1560–1640," *Hispanic American Historical Review* 89, no. 3 (2009): 474.

124. Milton and Vinson, "Counting Heads," 6.

125. See Vinson and Restall, "Black Soldiers, Native Soldiers," 15–52; Lokken, "Useful Enemies"; and Vinson, *Bearing Arms*, 132–72.

126. Regina Grafe and Alejandra Irigoin, "A Stakeholder Empire: The Political Economy of Spanish Imperial Rule in America," *Economic History Review* 65, no. 2 (2012): 613.

127. Tribute registers in New Spain and Peru contain what María Elena Martínez contends are the most common caste names (Indian, Spanish, black, mestizo, *mulato*, *castizo*, *morisco*, *zambaigo*) as well as *lobo*, *coyote*, *pardo*, *moreno*, and *chino* for the eighteenth century. See María Elena Martínez, *Genealogical Fictions: Limpieza de Sangre, Religion, and Gender in Colonial Mexico* (Stanford, CA: Stanford University Press, 2008), 166.

128. Schwaller, *Géneros de Gente*, 228.

129. Martínez, *Genealogical Fictions*, 162.

130. David Nirenberg, "Mass Conversion and Genealogical Mentalities: Jews and Christians in Fifteenth-Century Spain," *Past and Present* 174, no. 1 (2002): 3–41.

131. Martínez, *Genealogical Fictions*, 221.

132. Martínez, *Genealogical Fictions*, 205.

133. AGN, Indios vol. 2, exp. 182, f. 47.

134. See Cheryl English Martin, *Rural Society in Colonial Morelos* (Albuquerque: University of New Mexico Press, 1985), 13–14; and Ernest Sánchez Santiró, *Azúcar y poder: Estructura socioeconómica de las alcaldías mayores de Cuernavaca y Cuautla Amilpas, 1730–1821* (Mexico City: Editorial Praxis, 2001), 38.

135. Herman Bennett, *Colonial Blackness: A History of Afro-Mexico* (Bloomington: Indiana University Press, 2009), 115.

136. Robert C. Schwaller, "'For Honor and Defence': Race and the Right to Bear Arms in Early Colonial Mexico," *Colonial Latin American Review* 21, no. 2 (2012): 239–66.

137. AGN, Hospital de Jesús vol. 50, exp. 4.

138. Aguirre Beltrán, *La población negra de México*, 171.

139. The quotation is reproduced in Aguirre Beltrán, *La población negra de México*, 269–70.

140. Ben Vinson III, "Facetas del concepto de castas: Observaciones sobre la interpretación y el significado de "*casta*" en la Nueva España," in *Vicisitudes Negro Africanas en Iberoamerica: Experiencias de Investigación*, ed. Juan Manuel de la Serna (Mexico City: Universidad Autónoma de México, 2012), 360–61. See also Carolina González Undurraga, "De la casta a la raza: El concepto de raza; Un singular colectivo de la modernidad, México, 1750–1850," *Historia Mexicana* 60, no. 3 (2011): 1501–2.

141. See Aaron P. Althouse, "Contested Mestizos, Alleged Mulattos: Racial Identity and Caste Hierarchy in Eighteenth Century Pátzcuaro, Mexico," *The Americas* 62, no. 2 (2005): 152. Jean-Paul Zúñiga has located an example of the confusion surrounding the term "*morisco*" in Guadalajara and Madrid as a religious or a caste category. See "Visible Signs of Belonging: The Spanish Empire and the Rise of Racial Logics in the Early Modern Period," in *Polycentric Monarchies: How Did Early Modern Spain and Portugal Achieve and Maintain a Global Hegemony?*, ed. Pedro Cardim, Tamar Herzog, José Javier Ruiz Ibáñez, and Gaetano Sabatini (Brighton: Sussex Academic Press, 2012), 125.

142. O'Toole, *Bound Lives*, 165.

143. Ruth Hill, *Hierarchy, Commerce, and Fraud in Bourbon Spanish America: A Postal Inspector's Exposé* (Nashville: Vanderbilt University Press, 2005), 210.

144. For an example, see Rachel Sarah O'Toole, "To Be Free and Lucumí: Ana de la Calle and Making African Diaspora Identities in Colonial Peru," in *Africans to Spanish America: Expanding the Diaspora*, ed. Sherwin K. Bryant, Ben Vinson III, and Rachel Sarah O'Toole (Urbana: University of Illinois Press, 2012), 73–92.

145. AGN, Indiferente Virreinal c. 630, exp. 7, ff. i–iv.

146. Laura A. Lewis, *Hall of Mirrors: Power, Witchcraft, and Caste in Colonial Mexico* (Durham, NC: Duke University Press, 2003), 4.

147. Miranda, *Tributo indígena en la Nueva España*, 319.

148. See "Leyes y ordenanzas nuevamente hechas por S. M. para la gobernación de las indias, y buen tratamiento y conservación de los indios," in Joaquín García Icazbalceta, *Colección de documentos para la historia de México: Versión actualizada* (Alicante: Biblioteca Virtual Miguel de Cervantes, 1999). Available online at http://www.cervantesvirtual.com/nd/ark:/59851/bmc4b2z9.

149. AGN, Tributos vol. 33, exp. 13, f. 108.

150. See Joan Bristol, "Patriarchs, Petitions, and Prayers: Intersections of Gender and *Calidad* in Colonial Mexico," in *Women, Religion, and the Atlantic World, 1600–1800*, ed. Daniella Kostroun and Lisa Vollendorf (Toronto: University of Toronto Press, 2009), 180–204; and Juan de Solórzano Pereira, *Política Indiana* (Madrid: Diego Díaz de la Carrera, 1648), 2: chap. 30.

151. Real Academia Española, *Diccionario de Autoridades*, vol. 2 (Madrid: F. del Hierro, 1729).

152. Magali Carrera, *Imagining Identity in New Spain: Race, Lineage, and the Colonial Body in Portraiture and Casta Paintings* (Austin: University of Texas Press, 2003), 5.

153. Nancy E. van Deusen, *Global Indios: The Indigenous Struggle for Justice in Sixteenth-Century Spain* (Durham, NC: Duke University Press, 2015), 173.

154. María Elena Martínez, "The Language, Genealogy, and Classification of 'Race' in Colonial Mexico," in *Race and Classification: The Case of Mexican America*, ed. Ilona

Katzew and Susan Deans-Smith (Stanford, CA: Stanford University Press, 2009), 37. Magali Carrera observes the same pattern in multiple laws in the second half of the eighteenth century. See *Imagining Identity in New Spain*, 48.

155. AGN, Tributos vol. 50, exp. 9, f. 186.

156. Marcelo da Rocha Wanderley, "Mulatos libres, redes personales y cogniciones en la Nueva España (siglos XVII–XVIII)," in *Esclavitud, mestizaje y abolicionismo en los mundos hispánicos*, ed. Aurelia Martín Casares (Granada: Universidad de Granada, 2015), 139.

157. Joan Bristol, *Christians, Blasphemers, and Witches: Afro-Mexican Ritual Practice in the Seventeenth Century* (Albuquerque: University of New Mexico Press, 2007), 26. Bristol has argued that the relationship between gender and *calidad* was not constant and could be "disentangled, manipulated, and linked in tactical ways by people at different levels of the colonial power structure." See "Patriarchs, Petitions, and Prayers," 198–99.

158. Sonya Lipsett-Rivera, *Gender and the Negotiation of Daily Life in Mexico, 1750–1856* (Lincoln: University of Nebraska Press, 2012), 4.

159. Matthew O'Hara, *A Flock Divided: Race, Religion, and Politics in México, 1749–1857* (Durham, NC: Duke University Press, 2010), 54.

160. An in-depth discussion of this case can be found in Tania Itzel Martínez Aldana, "Amor y matrimonio: Familia, mestizaje y movilidad social: En un estudio de caso del Querétaro de finales del siglo XVIII," *Dos Puntas* 12 (2015): 143–52.

161. AGN, General de Parte vol. 78, exp. 96, f. 144v. Similarly, *limpieza de sangre, condición, casta*, and *calidad* could be found in Inquisitional documents by the late eighteenth century, where caste and *calidad* might be freely substituted. See Martínez, *Genealogical Fictions*, 247.

162. Vinson, "Facetas del concepto de castas," 360.

Chapter 2

1. AGI, Audiencia de México leg. 1043, cuaderno 6, f. 660. In Zacatecas, tributes and draft labor were absent until the turn of the nineteenth century. See Dana Velasco Murillo, *Urban Indians in a Silver City: Zacatecas, Mexico, 1546–1810* (Stanford, CA: Stanford University Press, 2016), 4 and 186–87. In Guanajuato, only ninety-five Afromexican tributaries were recorded in a compiled set of tributary lists from 1735. The total tributaries recorded amounted to more than three thousand. See Sherburne Friend Cook and Woodrow Wilson Borah, *Essays in Population History*, vol. 1, *Mexico and the Caribbean* (Berkeley: University of California Press, 1971), 229.

2. Silvio Zavala, *Ordenanzas del trabajo, siglos XVI y XVII* (Mexico City: Editorial Elede, 1947), 84.

3. R. Douglas Cope, *The Limits of Racial Domination: Plebeian Society in Colonial Mexico City, 1660–1720* (Madison: University of Wisconsin Press, 1994), 126.

4. Virginia García Acosta, Juan Manuel Pérez Zevallos, and América Molina del Villar, *Desastres agrícolas en México: Catálogo histórico*, vol. 1, *Epocas prehispánica y colonial (958–1822)* (Mexico City: Centro de Investigaciones y Estudios Superiores en Antropología Social, 2003), 1685–88.

5. AGI, Audiencia de México leg. 1043, cuaderno 7, f. 786v.

6. Scarlett O'Phelan Godoy, *Rebellions in Revolts in Eighteenth Century Peru and Upper Peru* (Cologne: Bohlau Verlag, 1985), 75.

7. See William B. Taylor, *Drinking, Homicide, and Rebellion in Colonial Mexican Villages* (Stanford, CA: Stanford University Press, 1979), 113–52.

8. Alejandro Montoya, *San Luis Potosí Novohispano: Origen y evolución sociodemográfica de un real de minas* (San Luis Potosí: Universidad Autónoma de San Luis Potosí, 2009), 134–36.

9. AGI, Audiencia de México leg. 1043, cuaderno 7, f. 790v.

10. See AGI, Audiencia de México leg. 1043, cuaderno 7, ff. 72 and 74, for examples.

11. Fabián Fonseca and Carlos de Urrutia, *Historia general de Real Hacienda*, vol. 1 (Mexico City: V. G. Torres, 1845–53), 439.

12. Nicole von Germeten has argued this point using a longer version of this quotation, which she points to as an important foundation of "the long-enduring myth of the violent African vagabond." See *Black Blood Brothers: Confraternities and Social Mobility for Afro-Mexicans* (Gainesville: University Press of Florida, 2006), 76.

13. Miners and local governments in seventeenth-century San Luis Potosí organized *cuadrillas* of enslaved and free laborers across *calidades*. See Woodrow Borah, "Un gobierno provincial de frontera en San Luis Potosí (1612–1620)," *Historia Mexicana* 13, no. 4 (1964): 537–38; and Felipe Durán Sandoval, "Las condiciones para la utilización del trabajo de negros y afrodescendientes en la minería en San Luis Potosí durante la primera mitad del siglo XVII," in *Interculturalidad y relaciones interétnicas en afroindoamérica*, ed. J. Jesús Serna Moreno and Israel Pineda Ángeles (Mexico City: Universidad Nacional Autónoma de México, 2015), 186–87.

14. Silvio Zavala, *El servicio personal de los indios en la Nueva España*, vol. 7 (Mexico City: Colegio de México, 1984), 24–25.

15. Charles Gibson, *The Aztecs under Spanish Rule: A History of the Indians of the Valley of Mexico* (Stanford, CA: Stanford University Press, 1976), 206.

16. See Fonseca and Urrutia, *Historia general*, 432; and Zavala, *Servicio personal*, 7:56.

17. Felipe Durán Sandoval, "Pueblos de indios y acceso a la tierra en San Luis Potosí, 1591–1767," *Revista Historia y Justicia* 5 (2015): 27.

18. AGI, Contaduría leg. 809. This excuse is given for Cirándano y Guimeo and other locations in 1701. Much of the document is rendered illegible by water damage.

19. José María Mariluz Urquijo, *El agente de la administración pública en Indias* (Buenos Aires: Instituto Internacional de Historia del Derecho Indiano, 1998), 331–32.

20. AGN, Indiferente Virreinal c. 6520, exp. 15, f. 14.

21. AGI, Contaduría leg. 809. In Puebla, the 134 *mulatos* who were charged paid a total of 336 pesos. They were part of a much larger group of 30,772.5 tributaries who paid 7,436 pesos. In Cholula, five *mulato* tributaries paid 15 pesos, while a total of 3,443.5 tributaries paid 5,681 pesos for the entire jurisdiction. The document is badly water damaged.

22. Fonseca and Urrutia, *Historia general de Real Hacienda*, 1:434.

23. AGI, Audiencia de México leg. 1043, cuaderno 16, f. 1572v.

24. In 1579, the Real Audiencia of Mexico rejected a petition filed by a hatter regarding tributes he refused to pay on behalf of a group of Afromexican tributaries who had left his "house and service." See AGN, Tierras vol. 2810, exp. 1, f. 2.

25. Kendall Brown, *A History of Mining in Latin America* (Albuquerque: University of New Mexico Press, 2012), 16.

26. Laurent Corbeil, "Identities in Motion: The Formation of a Plural Indio Society in Early San Luis Potosí, New Spain, 1591–1630" (PhD diss., McGill University, 2014), 69–70.

27. Montoya, *San Luis Potosí Novohispano*, 138.

28. Frank T. Proctor, *Damned Notions of Liberty: Slavery, Culture, and Power in Colonial Mexico, 1640–1769* (Albuquerque: University of New Mexico Press, 2010), 23–24.

29. Peter Gerhard, *A Guide to the Historical Geography of New Spain* (Cambridge: Cambridge University Press, 1972), 236.

30. AGI, Audiencia de México leg. 1043, cuaderno 1, ff. 35v–37v.

31. John Tutino, *Making a New World: Founding Capitalism in the Bajío and Spanish North America* (Durham, NC: Duke University Press, 2011), 160.

32. Amalia Gómez Gómez, *Las visitas de la real hacienda novohispana en el reinado de Felipe V: 1710–1733* (Seville: Editorial CSIC, 1979), 81–85.

33. AGI, Audiencia de México leg. 1043, cuaderno 1, ff. 68–68v.

34. AGI, Audiencia de México leg. 1043, cuaderno 1, f. 70.

35. AGI, Audiencia de México leg. 1043, cuaderno 1, f. 70.

36. Von Germeten, *Black Blood Brothers*, 76.

37. See Joan Bristol, "From Curing to Witchcraft: Afro-Mexicans and the Mediation of Authority," *Journal of Colonialism and Colonial History* 7, no. 1 (2006): 14; and Andrew B. Fisher, "Creating and Contesting Community: Indians and Afromestizos in the Late-Colonial Tierra Caliente of Guerrero, Mexico," *Journal of Colonialism and Colonial History* 7, no. 1 (2006): 4.

38. AGI, Audiencia de México leg. 1043, cuaderno 1, ff. 67–67v.

39. Montoya, *San Luis Potosí Novohispano*, 137.

40. AGI, Audiencia de México leg. 1043, cuaderno 1, f. 13v.

41. Frank T. Proctor, "La familia y la comunidad esclava en San Luis Potosí y Guanajuato: 1640–1750," in *Rutas de la esclavitud en África y América Latina*, ed. Rina Cáceres Gómez (San José: Editorial de la Universidad de Costa Rica, 2001), 223–50.

42. Montoya, *San Luis Potosí Novohispano*, 215.

43. AGI, Audiencia de México leg. 1043, cuaderno 1.

44. Robert McCaa, "Calidad, Clase, and Marriage in Colonial Mexico: The Case of Parral, 1788–90," *Hispanic American Historical Review* 64, no. 3 (1984): 493.

45. AGN, Tributos vol. 33, exp. 13, f. 108.

46. AGN, Tributos vol. 33, exp. 13, f. 108.

47. AGI, Audiencia de México leg. 1043, cuaderno 1, f. 261.

48. AGI, Audiencia de México leg. 1043, cuaderno 1, f. 261v.

49. Montoya, *San Luis Potosí Novohispano*, 139.

50. Gómez Gómez, *Las visitas*, 84.

51. AGI, Audiencia de México leg. 1043, cuaderno 3, f. 481.

52. The total number of individuals of tributary status recorded in 1711 was 2,778. Among the Indian tributaries of legal majority were 1,206 married people and 208 unmarried Indian men under fifty. The free tributaries of African descent included 296 married people and 67 unmarried men under fifty. Another 164 people were temporarily exempted from payment as *reservados*, and 837 were children. See AGI, Audiencia de México leg. 1043, cuaderno 15.

53. AGI, Audiencia de México leg. 1043, cuaderno 3, f. 597.

54. AGI, Audiencia de México leg. 1043, cuaderno 7, f. 837.

55. Cristina Masferrer León, *Muleke, negritas y mulatillos: Niñez, familia y redes sociales de los esclavos de origen africano en la ciudad de México, siglo XVII* (Mexico City: Instituto Nacional de Antropología e Historia), 141. Children worked as farriers on haciendas on these *padrones* and included an unnamed "*coyotillo*" in addition to the *mulatillos*.

56. AGI, Audiencia de México leg. 1043, cuaderno 16, ff. 1566 and 1568.

57. AGI, Audiencia de México leg. 1043, cuaderno 16, f. 1537.

58. Real Academia Española, *Diccionario de Autoridades* (Madrid: F. del Hierro, 1739).

59. AGI, Audiencia de México leg. 1043, cuaderno 16, f. 1569.

60. Cheryl English Martin, *Governance and Society in Colonial Mexico: Chihuahua in the Eighteenth Century* (Stanford, CA: Stanford University Press, 1996), 44–45.

61. AGI, Audiencia de México leg. 1043, cuaderno 16, f. 1569v.

62. AGI, Audiencia de México leg. 1043, cuaderno 2, f. 240v.

63. AGI, Audiencia de México leg. 1043, cuaderno 16, f. 1572.

64. One person is registered nearby in 1712 but not on the hacienda.

65. AGI, Audiencia de México leg. 1043, cuaderno 16, f. 1498v.

66. AGI, Audiencia de México leg. 1043, cuaderno 7, f. 771v.

67. See Francisco de Solano, ed., *Relaciones geográficas del Arzobispado de México, 1743* (Madrid: Consejo Superior de Investigaciones Científicas, 1988); and José Antonio de Villaseñor y Sánchez, *Theatro Americano: Descripción general de los reynos y provincias de la Nueva España y sus jurisdicciones*, ed. María del Carmen Velázquez (Mexico City: Editorial Trillas, 1992).

68. Villaseñor y Sánchez, *Theatro americano*, 263–64.

69. Ernesto Sánchez Santiró, "Plata y privilegios: El Real de minas de Huautla, 1709–1821," *Estudios de Historia Novohispana* 26, no. 26 (2002): 101. In the 1770s and 1780s, Huautla drew laborers from Chila de la Sal in Acatlán and Piastla.

70. Ursula Ewald, *La industria salinera de México, 1560–1994* (Mexico City: Fondo de Cultura Económica, 1997), 75.

71. AGI, Contaduría leg. 809. In Acatlán and Piastla, 547.5 Indian tributaries paid 1,098 pesos.

72. Cook and Borah, *Essays in Population History*, 228.

73. Gerhard, *A Guide*, 43. The 1743 register tallied 2,160 families.

74. Gerhard, *A Guide*, 109.

75. For the case, see AGN, Indiferente Virreinal c. 5657, exp. 49. For the surrounding area, see Miguel Ángel Cuenya, *Puebla de los Ángeles en tiempos de una peste colonial: Una mirada en torno al matlazahuatl de 1737* (Puebla: Benemérita Universidad Autónoma de Puebla, 1999); and América Molina del Villar, "Las prácticas sanitarias y médicas en la Ciudad de México, 1736–1739," *Estudios del hombre* 20 (2005): 39–58.

76. Among the seventeen couples who were entered identically across three different years, only three appeared in 1741. The summary from this year did not attribute the change in population to any specific effect of epidemics or tribute policy, and the lack of payments from 1741 could also be due to delinquency.

77. AGN, Tributos vol. 46, exp. 28, f. 273.

78. Following the steady rate used in the following years, 19.5 tributaries would have paid forty-eight pesos and six *tomines* in total. An extra two *tomines* might have been collected in back payments or can be attributed to clerical error.

79. AGN, Tributos vol. 46, exp. 28, f. 162v.

80. Von Germeten, *Black Blood Brothers*, 129 and 163.

81. See McCaa, "Calidad, Clase, and Marriage," 477–501; and Jake Frederick, "Without Impediment: Crossing Racial Boundaries in Colonial Mexico," *The Americas* 67, no. 4 (2011): 495–515.

82. María Elisa Velázquez Gutiérrez, *Mujeres de origen africano en la capital novohispana, siglos XVII y XVIII* (Mexico City: Instituto Nacional de Antropología e Historia, 2006), 230.

83. Cope, *Limits of Racial Domination*, 82.

84. AGN, Real Hacienda Casa de Moneda vol. 119, exp. 8.

85. María Cristina Torales Pacheco, *Ilustrados en la Nueva España: Los socios de la Real Sociedad Bascongada de Amigos del País* (Mexico City: Universidad Iberoamericana, 2001), 288.

86. Yovana Celaya Nández, *Alcabalas y Situados: Puebla en el sistema fiscal imperial, 1638–1742* (Mexico City: El Colegio de México, 2010).

87. José Miranda, *El tributo indígena en la Nueva España durante el siglo XVI*, 2nd ed. (Mexico City: Colegio de México, 2005), 198–99.

88. Ernest Sánchez Santiró, *Corte de caja: La Real Hacienda de Nueva España y el primer reformismo fiscal de los Borbones (1720–1755)* (Mexico City: Instituto Mora, 2014), 252–53.

89. Cynthia Milton and Ben Vinson III, "Counting Heads: Race and Non-native Tribute Policy in Colonial Spanish America," *Journal of Colonialism and Colonial History* 3, no. 3 (2002): 2.

90. Ben Vinson III, *Bearing Arms for His Majesty: The Free-Colored Militia in Colonial Mexico* (Stanford, CA: Stanford University Press, 2001), 132–72.

Chapter 3

1. AGN, General de Parte vol. 19, exp. 50, f. 56.

2. See "*calidad*" in Sebastián de Covarrubias Orozco, *Tesoro de la lengua castellana o española* (Madrid: L. Sánchez, 1611).

3. Ann Twinam concludes that free women of African descent had greater opportunities to seek connections to white males through marital or otherwise sexual relationships that would benefit their children. *Pardo* men, left with fewer opportunities, could seek "relationships with peers whose fathers were white or with plebeian white women." See *Purchasing Whiteness: Pardos, Mulatos, and the Quest for Social Mobility in the Spanish Indies* (Stanford, CA: Stanford University Press, 2015), 412. For a Brazilian case of *pardo* descendants of white fathers, see Mariana L. R. Dantas, *Black Townsmen: Urban Slavery and Freedom in the Eighteenth-Century Americas* (New York: Palgrave Macmillan, 2008), 151–52.

4. Nicole von Germeten, *Black Blood Brothers: Confraternities and Social Mobility for Afro-Mexicans* (Gainesville: University Press of Florida, 2006), 11.

5. See Danielle Terrazas, "Capitalizing Subjects: Free African-Descended Women of Means in Xalapa, Veracruz during the Long Seventeenth Century" (PhD diss., Duke University, 2013), 211–72.

6. Joan Cameron Bristol has explored the possibilities for Afromexican honor and status extensively throughout her work on seventeenth-century New Spain. See "From Curing to Witchcraft: Afro-Mexicans and the Mediation of Authority," *Journal of Colonialism and Colonial History* 7, no. 1 (2006): 1–37, and her discussion of Juana Esperanza de San Alberto in *Christians, Blasphemers, and Witches: Afro-Mexican Ritual Practice in the Seventeenth Century* (Albuquerque: University of New Mexico Press, 2007), 47–61.

7. María Elisa Velázquez Gutiérrez, *Mujeres de origen africano en la capital novohispana, siglos XVII y XVIII* (Mexico City: Universidad Nacional Autónoma de México, 2006), 233.

8. Robert C. Schwaller, "'For Honor and Defence': Race and the Right to Bear Arms in Early Colonial Mexico," *Colonial Latin American Review* 21, no. 2 (2012): 260.

9. Aaron Pollack, "Hacia una historia social del tributo de indios y castas en His-

panoamérica: Notas en torno a su creación, desarrollo y abolición," *Historia Mexicana* 66, no. 1 (2016): 95–96.

10. Ben Vinson III, *Bearing Arms for His Majesty: The Free-Colored Militia in Colonial Mexico* (Stanford, CA: Stanford University Press, 2001), 222.

11. Russell Lohse, *Africans into Creoles: Slavery, Ethnicity, and Identity in Colonial Costa Rica* (Albuquerque: University of New Mexico Press, 2014), 166–67.

12. Rachel Sarah O'Toole, *Bound Lives: Africans, Indians, and the Making of Race in Colonial Peru* (Pittsburgh: University of Pittsburgh Press, 2012), 29–33.

13. See the allegations of a robbery supposedly committed against an indigenous muleteer by an enslaved *mulato* in 1666 in the Chicama valley discussed in Rachel Sarah O'Toole, "Mobilizing Muleteer Indigeneity in the Markets of Colonial Peru," in *To Be Indio in Colonial Spanish America*, ed. Mónica Díaz (Albuquerque: University of New Mexico Press, 2006), 106–7.

14. Tatiana Seijas, "Indios Chinos in Eighteenth-Century Mexico," in *To Be Indio in Colonial Spanish America*, ed. Mónica Díaz (Albuquerque: University of New Mexico Press, 2006), 125–27.

15. AGN, Indios vol. 50, exp. 213. When Indian suits also involved free people of color, the latter entered a juridical space reserved for matters of Indian justice. See Woodrow Wilson Borah, *Justice by Insurance: The General Indian Court of Colonial Mexico and the Legal Aides of the Half-Real* (Berkeley: University of California Press, 1983), 227–55.

16. AGN, Indios vol. 50, exp. 213, f. 373v.

17. He refers to the residence of "*algunos indios del pueblo de Coyoacán y algunos* mulatos *que inquietan, como cabecillas de los naturales*," in the barrio of Aguatepec. AGN, Indios vol. 50, exp. 213, f. 373v.

18. AGN, Indios vol. 50, exp. 213, f. 374.

19. Patrick Carroll identifies a *mulato* called Miguel de Chabarria who lived in Tepecoacuilco, near Taxco. He had resided in the Indian village for years but eventually offended local residents in 1759 when he began to take on Spanish customs. See "Black Aliens and Black Natives in New Spain's Indigenous Communities," in *Black Mexico: Race and Society from Colonial to Modern Times*, ed. Ben Vinson III and Matthew Restall (Albuquerque: University of New Mexico Press, 2009), 79–80.

20. Palacios served in Havana from 1713 to 1716 as Teniente General y Auditor de Guerra and later as an investigator of corruption among royal officials. In New Spain, he was *fiscal* in civil matters for the Real Audiencia in Mexico, and finally a *consejero* in the Council of the Indies. See Amalia Gómez Gómez, *Las visitas de la real hacienda novohispana en el reinado de Felipe V: 1710–1733* (Seville: Editorial CSIC, 1979), 110–12.

21. AGN, Indios vol. 50, exp. 213, f. 375.

22. AGN, Indios vol. 50, exp. 213, f. 375v.

23. Susan Kellogg, "From Parallel Equivalent to Separate but Unequal: Tenocha Mexica Women, 1500–1700," in *Indian Women of Early Mexico*, ed. Susan Schroeder, Stephanie Gail Wood, and Robert Stephen Haskett (Norman: University of Oklahoma Press, 1997), 139.

24. AGN, Indios vol. 50, exp. 213, f. 375v.

25. Tamar Herzog, *Defining Nations: Immigrants and Citizens in Early Modern Spain and Spanish America* (New Haven, CT: Yale University Press, 2003), 4.

26. Carroll, "Black Aliens and Black Natives," 81.

27. Richard Boyer, "Negotiating *Calidad*: The Everyday Struggle for Status in Mexico," *Historical Archaeology* 31, no. 1 (1997): 66–67.

28. See also Matthew Restall's distinction between urban relationships between Spaniards and Afro-Yucatecans ("attached subordination") versus the more autonomous integration of free people of color into Maya pueblos in *The Black Middle: Africans, Mayas, and Spaniards in Colonial Yucatán* (Stanford, CA: Stanford University Press, 2009), 221–22.

29. See María Teresa Jarquín Ortega, *Formación y desarrollo de un pueblo novohispano: Metepec en el Valle de Toluca* (Metepec: Colegio Mexiquense, 1990), 225–82.

30. Luis Enrique Miranda Nava, *La esclavitud en el Valle de Toluca, 1558–1630* (Toluca de Lerdo: Gobierno del Estado de México, 2010), 48–49.

31. AGI, Escribanía c. 187A, f. 2.

32. Peter Gerhard gives the number of non-Indians as 1,375 in towns and on haciendas and *obrajes*, including enslaved blacks. See *A Guide to the Historical Geography of New Spain* (Cambridge: Cambridge University Press, 1972), 248.

33. AGI, Escribanía c. 187A, ff. 105–105v.

34. AGI, Escribanía c. 187A, f. 2v.

35. AGI, Escribanía c. 187A, f. 133.

36. AGI, Escribanía c. 187A, ff. 136–136v.

37. AGI, Escribanía c. 187A, ff. 139–139v.

38. Decades later, petitioners who sought whiteness through the *gracias al sacar* also requested exceptions to rules that degraded free people of color and their families. These arguments subtly attacked the logic that blackness was a totalizing, negative quality worthy of discrimination against an entire lineage of people. See Twinam, *Purchasing Whiteness*, 413.

39. AGI, Escribanía c. 187A, f. 139.

40. Alejandro Cañeque, *The King's Living Image: The Culture and Politics of Viceregal Power in Colonial Mexico* (New York: Routledge, 2004), 164.

41. AGI, Escribanía c. 187A, "Filiación de real nobleza de Juan Fernandes Cabrera," f. 3.

42. AGI, Escribanía c. 187A, f. 44.

43. AGI, Escribanía c. 187A, f. 140.

44. Francisco de Solano, ed., "Jurisdicción de Santa Clara de Lerma" in *Relaciones geográficas del Arzobispado de México, 1743*, vol. 1, ed. Francisco de Solano (Madrid: Consejo Superior de Investigaciones Científicas, 1988), 130–44. Some witnesses used "*calidades*" and others "*naciones*" to describe people who were neither Indian nor Spanish. The city of Lerma was home to about forty Spanish families, eighty Indian families, and 120 families of another *calidad*.

45. AGN, Indiferente Virreinal c. 5434, exp. 37, f. 8. This document is water damaged.

46. Sherburne Friend Cook and Woodrow Wilson Borah, *Essays in Population History*, vol. 1, *Mexico and the Caribbean* (Berkeley: University of California Press, 1971), 227.

47. Another 643 families of Indians and fifty-seven Spanish families also lived in Lerma and its surroundings. See Gerhard, *A Guide*, 169.

48. AGN, Indiferente Virreinal c. 5434, exp. 37, ff. 3–4.

49. AGN, Reales Cédulas Duplicadas vol. D20, exp. 25.

50. For this case, see Paul Lokken, "Angolans in Amatitlán: Sugar, African Migrants, and *Gente Ladina* in Colonial Guatemala," in *Blacks and Blackness in Central America: Between Race and Place*, ed. Lowell Gudmundson and Justin Wolfe (Durham, NC: Duke University Press, 2010), 45.

51. AGN, Indiferente Virreinal c. 5434, exp. 37, ff. 8v–11.

52. Laura A. Lewis, *Hall of Mirrors: Power, Witchcraft, and Caste in Colonial Mexico* (Durham, NC: Duke University Press, 2003), 76–77. Lewis observes that "no mulatto invoked black or Indian paternity or maternity in support of a petition, because Indian-

ness and blackness did not improve one's sanctioned status," as far as privileges associated with lineage were concerned. Similarly, the cases I have located do not focus on blackness as an explicitly positive feature of lineage, but neither do they deny its presence.

53. Maira Cristina Córdova Aguilar, "Procesos de convivencia de negros, mulatos y pardos en la sociedad de Oaxaca: Siglos xvii y xviii" (PhD diss., Universidad Nacional Autónoma de México, 2017), 266–73.

54. The totals collected from the head town of Metepec and its subject towns were seventy pesos from twenty-eight *mulato* tributaries, as well as 17,454 pesos from 7,962.5 Indian tributaries. See AGI, Contaduría leg. 809.

55. AGN, Indiferente Virreinal c. 5434, exp. 37, ff. 26–27v.

56. AGN, Indiferente Virreinal c. 5434, exp. 37, f. 56v.

57. By 1769, Lerma had just 4.5 *mulato* tributaries and 586.5 Indian tributaries. Metepec, still a head town, counted its tributaries at 14.5 *mulatos* and 5,828.5 Indians. See "Importe del ramo de Reales Tributos y Servicio Real de indios, de pueblos de mulatos y laboríos del año de 1769" in AGI, Audiencia de México leg. 2105. In 1801, only ten *mulato* tributaries were counted in Lerma. See AGN, Tributos vol. 62, exp. 1.

58. AGN, Indiferente Virreinal c. 5434, exp. 37, ff. 47–57.

59. AGN, Tributos vol. 50, exp. 5, ff. 84–86v.

60. AGN, Tributos vol. 50, exp. 5, f. 84. The issue of *expósitos* and their tributary status would be addressed, though not resolved, at the end of the century. The sixteenth-century status of *expósitos* is mentioned in Ondina E. González, "Down and Out in Havana: Foundlings in Eighteenth-Century Cuba," in *Minor Omissions: Children in Latin American History and Society*, ed. Tobias Hecht (Madison: University of Wisconsin Press, 2002), 111n18.

61. For this strategy in Quito, see Cynthia Milton, *The Many Meanings of Poverty: Colonialism, Social Compacts, and Assistance in Eighteenth-Century Ecuador* (Stanford, CA: Stanford University Press, 2007), 145.

62. Phelipe refers to himself in the petition as "I, said Phelipe" and the rest of the copetitioners as "we." For the list on which his name appears, see AGN, Tributos vol. 50, exp. 5, f. 93.

63. Cynthia Milton, *The Many Meanings of Poverty: Colonialism, Social Compacts, and Assistance in Eighteenth-Century Ecuador* (Stanford, CA: Stanford University Press, 2007), 66.

64. Bianca Premo, *Children of the Father King: Youth, Authority, and Legal Minority in Colonial Lima* (Chapel Hill: University of North Carolina Press, 2005), 180.

65. In Peru in the 1720s, authorities began to impose broader constraints on poor people across caste and color. Rachel Sarah O'Toole has argued that "as crown and viceregal authorities issued fewer stark comparisons of Indians and blacks, they articulated more concerns with control of all people of color." See *Bound Lives*, 32.

66. AGN, Criminal vol. 136, exp. 74, f. 445.

67. Deborah E. Kanter, *Hijos del Pueblo: Gender, Family, and Community in Rural Mexico, 1730–1850* (Austin: University of Texas Press, 2008), 82. In a specifically female context, this punishment indicated the internment of women in a private house or institution of *recogimiento*. See also Asunción Lavrin, "In Search of the Colonial Woman in Mexico: The Seventeenth and Eighteenth Centuries," in *Latin American Women: Historical Perspectives*, ed. Asunción Lavrin (Westport, CT: Greenwood Publishing, 1978), 35–37.

68. Cheryl English Martin, *Governance and Society in Colonial Mexico: Chihuahua in the Eighteenth Century* (Stanford, CA: Stanford University Press, 1996), 174.

69. Kanter, *Hijos del Pueblo*, 5.

70. AGN, Tributos vol. 33, exp. 13, f. 104.

71. Herman L. Bennett, *Colonial Blackness: A History of Afro-Mexico* (Bloomington: Indiana University Press, 2009), 184. Nicole von Germeten has also observed this possibility for some free women of African descent in eighteenth-century New Granada. See *Violent Delights, Violent Ends: Sex, Race, and Honor in Colonial Cartagena de Indias* (Albuquerque: University of New Mexico Press, 2013), 191.

72. AGN, Tributos vol. 33, exp. 13, f. 105.

73. AGN, Matrimonios vol. 67, exp. 19, f. 82.

74. AGN, Tributos vol. 33, exp. 13, f. 112.

75. AGN, Tributos vol. 33, exp. 13, f. 112v.

76. AGN, Tributos vol. 33, exp. 13, f. 113.

77. AGN, Tributos vol. 33, exp. 13, f. 113. The girls also accused the Navarres of "asking them for *pesos*," a sum that would have totaled eighty reales rather than the expected ten.

78. "*Patria potestad*" refers to the body of laws and customs that governed the patriarch's authority over his dependents, including his wife, children, servants, and any other legal minors.

79. AGN, Tributos vol. 33, exp. 13, f. 114, contains the phrase "enjoying this freedom, many of the age of twenty-five to thirty years did not marry." This phrase borrows from Libro 6, Título 5, Ley 7 in *Recopilación de leyes de los reynos de las Indias*, vol. 2 (Madrid: Julián de Paredes, 1681; Madrid: Ediciones Cultura Hispánica, 1973), 241.

80. AGN, Tributos vol. 33, exp. 13, f. 114.

81. Pilar Gonzalbo Aizpuru, *Las mujeres en la Nueva España: Educación y vida cotidiana* (Mexico City: El Colegio de México, 1987), 289.

82. AGN, Tributos vol. 33, exp. 13, f. 114v.

83. Real Academia Española, *Diccionario de Autoridades*, vol. 2 (Madrid: F. del Hierro, 1729). A secondary definition of "*condición*" was "*la naturaleza, calidad y distintivo del nacimiento de los hombres.*"

84. AGN, Indiferente Virreinal c. 3537, exp. 27.

85. Nicole von Germeten has located a reference to a lawyer, don Cristóbal Polo de Águila, who was described as being of a "*condición mulato*" in 1765. See Alonso de Sandoval, *Treatise on Slavery: Selections from De Instauranda Aethiopum Salute*, trans. Nicole von Germeten (Indianapolis: Hackett Publishing, 2008), xii.

86. Richard Konetzke, *Colección de documentos para la historia de la formación social de Hispanoamérica*, vol. 3, pt. 2 (Madrid: Consejo Superior de Investigaciones Científicas, 1953–62), 197.

87. For a more detailed discussion of the rise of these negative European and American perceptions of African womanhood and sexuality, see Jennifer Morgan, *Laboring Women: Reproduction and Gender in New World Slavery* (Philadelphia: University of Pennsylvania Press, 2004), 12–49.

88. Libro 6, Titulo 5, Ley 19, *Recopilación*, 2:244.

Chapter 4

1. John Lynch, *Bourbon Spain, 1700–1808* (Oxford: Basil Blackwell, 1989), 168.

2. Antonio Lafuente and Nuria Valverde, "Making Scientific Objects and Setting Standards: Values, Technology, Government, and the Enlightenment," *EMPIRIA: Revista de Metodología de Ciencias Sociales* 18 (2009): 140.

3. See "Estados, cortes y tanteos de tributos" from 1771 in AGI, Audiencia de México leg. 2104.

4. The names of these jurisdictions were, as of 1785: Acapulco, Acayuca, Acatlán, Actopan, Aguas del Venado, Aguatlan, Amula, Apan, Atitalaquia, Atlatlahuca, Atlixco, Autlán, Cadereyta, Celaya, Cempoala, Chalco, Chiautla, Chichicapa, Chietla, Chilapa, Chilchota, Chimapan, Chinantla, Cholula, Chimapan, Cimatlán, Coatepec, Coautitlán, Coautla Amilpas, Colima, Cosamaluapam, Cuernavaca, Cuicatlán, Cuitceo, Cuyoacan, Escateopan, Goanaxoato, Guadalcazar, Guatlatlauca, Guatulco, Guexolotitlan, Guimeo, Huanxuapa, Huauchinango, Huayacoctla, Heuxotcingo, Huexutla, Yguala, Ygualapa, Yxcuintepéc, Yxmiquilpan, Yxtepexi, Yxtlahuaca, Yzatlán, Yzucar, Lerma, Macuilsuchil, Malinalco, Maravatío, Mechoacán, Mestitlán, Metepéc, Mexicalcingo, Miahuatlan, Mizantla, Misquiahuala, Mitla, Justlahuaca, Motines, Nexapa, Nochistlán, Oaxaca, Orizava, Otumba, Pachuca, Panuco, Papalotipác, Papantla, Parcialidades de Mexico, Puebla, Quatro Villas, Queretaro, Salvatierra, San Antonio Guatusco, San Cristoball Ecatepéc, San Juan de los Llanos, San Juan Teotihuacan, San Luis de la Paz, San Luis Potosí, San Miguel el Grande, Santiago Tecali, Tacuba, Tancitaro, Tasco, Tehuacán, Tehuantepéc, Temascaltepéc, Tenango, Teococuilco, Teotalco, Teozacoalco, Tepeaca, Tepexi de la Seda, Teposcolula, Tetela del Rio, Tetela y Xonotla, Tetepango, Teusitlan, Teutila, Teutitlán, Texcuco, Tinouindin, Tixtla, Tlalpuxahua, Tlapan, Tlaxcala, Tlayacapa, Tlazazalca, Tochimilco, Toluca, Tonalá, Tula, Tulantcingo, Tuxpa, Tuxtla, Veracruz, Villa de Leon, Villa de Valles, Villa-alta, Xacona, Xalapa, Xalatcingo, Xaso, Xicayan, Xilotepec, Xiquilpan, Xuchimilco, Yagualica, Yanguitlan, Zacatlan, Zacatula, Zayula, Zacualpan, Zochicoatlan, Zultepéc, and Zumpango.

5. This was a standard formula reproduced on a variety of grids from the period. For examples, see AGI, Audiencia de México legs. 2105 and 2106.

6. Linda Arnold, *Bureaucracy and Bureaucrats in Mexico City, 1742–1835* (Tucson: University of Arizona Press, 1988), 9.

7. Alan J. Kuethe and Kenneth J. Andrien, *The Spanish Atlantic World in the Eighteenth Century: War and the Bourbon Reforms, 1713–1796* (Cambridge: Cambridge University Press, 2014), 303.

8. The *matrícula de mar* in 1726 registered coastal communities with the goal of expanding the Spanish Navy. See Christopher Storrs, "Felipe V: Caesura or Continuity?" in *Early Bourbon Spanish America*, ed. Francisco A. Eissa-Barroso and Ainara Vázquez Varela (Leiden: Brill, 2013), 12–13. See also Concepción Camarero Bullón, "Averiguarlo todo de todos: El catastro de Ensenada," *Estudios Geográficos* 63, no. 248/49 (2002): 493–531.

9. For the former position, see D. A. Brading, *Miners and Merchants in Bourbon Mexico, 1763–1810* (Cambridge: Cambridge University Press, 1971); and Herbert I. Priestley, *José de Gálvez: Visitor-General of New Spain (1765–1771)* (Berkeley: University of California Press, 1916). For an example of the latter, see Stanley J. Stein and Barbara H. Stein, *Apogee of Empire: Spain and New Spain in the Age of Charles III, 1759–1789* (Baltimore: Johns Hopkins University Press, 2003), 27. See also Linda K. Salvucci, "Costumbres viejas, 'hombres nuevos': José de Gálvez y la burocracia fiscal novohispana (1754–1800)," *Historia Mexicana* 33, no. 2 (1983): 224–64.

10. Gabriel B. Paquette, *Enlightenment, Governance, and Reform in Spain and Its Empire, 1759–1808* (Basingstoke: Palgrave Macmillan, 2008), 153.

11. Daniela Marino, "El afán de recaudar y la dificultad de reformar: El tributo indígena en la Nueva España tardocolonial," in *De colonia a nación: Impuestos y política en*

México, 1750–1860, ed. Carlos Marichal and Daniela Marino (Mexico City: El Colegio de México, 2001), 62.

12. Fabián Fonseca and Carlos de Urrutia, *Historia general de Real Hacienda*, vol. 1 (Mexico City: V. G. Torres, 1845–53), 429–30.

13. Thomas E. Sheridan has proposed Rodríguez Gallardo as a forerunner to Gálvez. See *Empire of Sand: The Seri Indians and the Struggle for Spanish Sonora, 1645–1803* (Tucson: University of Arizona Press, 1999).

14. Ernest Sánchez Santiró, *Corte de caja: La Real Hacienda de Nueva España y el primer reformismo fiscal de los Borbones (1720–1755)* (Mexico City: Instituto Mora, 2014), 342–43. See, for example, a failed midcentury plan to implement royal tribute from free people of African descent in Ecuador. Luis Ramos Gómez and Carmen Ruigómez Gómez, "Una propuesta a la corona para extender la mita y el tributo a negros, mestizos y mulatos (Ecuador, 1735–1748)," *Revista Complutense de Historia de América* 25 (1999): 99–110.

15. Fonseca and Urrutia, *Historia general de Real Hacienda*, 1:443.

16. Pedro Martínez Santos, "Reforma de la contabilidad colonial en el siglo XVIII," *Anuario de Estudios Americanos* 17 (1960): 531–34.

17. Marino, "Afán de recaudar y la dificultad de reformar," 67.

18. Felipe Castro Gutiérrez, *Nueva ley y nuevo rey: Reformas borbónicas y rebelión popular en Nueva España* (Zamora: El Colegio de Michoacán, 1996), 163–64.

19. Marta Terán, "El movimiento de los indios, las castas y la plebe de Valladolid de Michoacán en el inicio de la guerra por la independencia, 1809–1810," in *Las guerras de independencia en la América española*, ed. Marta Terán and José Antonio Serrano Ortega (Zamora: El Colegio de Michoacán, 2010), 286.

20. See Scarlett O'Phelan Godoy, *Rebellions and Revolts in Eighteenth Century Peru and Upper Peru* (Cologne: Bohlau Verlag, 1985); and John Leddy Phelan, *The People and the King: The Comunero Revolution in Colombia, 1781* (Madison: University of Wisconsin Press, 1978). For a more recent treatment, see Charles F. Walker, *The Tupac Amaru Rebellion* (Cambridge, MA: Belknap Press of Harvard University Press, 2014).

21. D. A. Brading, *Miners and Merchants in Bourbon Mexico, 1763–1810* (Cambridge: Cambridge University Press, 1971), 27. See also Priestley, *José de Gálvez*, especially chap. 6, 210–33.

22. AGN, Tributos vol. 44, exp. 9, ff. 219–21.

23. José del Campillo y Cossío, *Nuevo sistema de gobierno económico para la América* (Madrid: Imprenta de Benito Cano, 1789), 125.

24. Luis Jáuregui, *La Real Hacienda de Nueva España: Su administración en la época de los intendentes, 1786–1821* (Mexico City: Universidad Autónoma de México, 1999), 98–99.

25. Jordana Dym, *From Sovereign Villages to National States: City, State, and Federation in Central America, 1759–1839* (Albuquerque: University of New Mexico Press, 2006), 60.

26. Horst Pietschmann, *Las reformas borbónicas y el sistema de intendencias en Nueva España: Un estudio político administrativo*, trans. Rolf Roland Meyer Misteli (Mexico City: Fondo de Cultura Económica, 1996), 202.

27. Brading, *Miners and Merchants*, 50.

28. Rafael Diego-Fernández Sotelo, *El proyecto de José de Gálvez de 1774 en las ordenanzas de intendentes de Río de la Plata y Nueva España* (Zamora: El Colegio de Michoacán, 2016), 311.

29. Brading, *Miners and Merchants*, 74–76.

30. José Ignacio Rubio Mañé, *El Virreinato: Orígenes y jurisdicciones y dinámica social de los virreyes*, vol. 1, 2nd. ed. (Mexico City: Instituto de Investigaciones Históricas, Universidad Autónoma de México, 1983), 78.

31. AGN, Indiferente Virreinal c. 5670, exp. 56, f. 4.

32. AGN, Indiferente Virreinal c. 5670, exp. 56, f. 5.

33. AGN, Indiferente Virreinal c. 5670, exp. 56, f. 12.

34. Rafael García Pérez, "El régimen tributario en las intendencias novohispanas: La Ordenanza para la formación de los autos de visitas, padrones y matrículas de Revillagigedo II," *Anuario Mexicano de Historia del Derecho* 11–12 (2000): 282–83.

35. García Pérez, "Régimen tributario," 283.

36. AGI, Audiencia de México leg. 2103. For instance, a suspension occurred between 1731 and 1747.

37. Richard Konetzke, *Colección de documentos para la historia de la formación social de Hispanoamérica*, vol. 3, pt. 2 (Madrid: Consejo Superior de Investigaciones Científicas, 1953–62), 604.

38. Fonseca and Urrutia, *Historia general de Real Hacienda*, 1:439.

39. Fonseca and Urrutia, *Historia general de Real Hacienda*, 1:434–35.

40. These arguments are discussed in detail in Rafael Castañeda García, "Hacia una sociología fiscal: El tributo de la población de color libre de la Nueva España, 1770–1810," *Fronteras de la Historia* 19, no. 1 (2014): 159–60.

41. Castañeda García reproduces the text of part of these arguments from AGN, Tributos vol. 20, exp. 1, in "Hacia una sociología fiscal."

42. Silvio Zavala, *El servicio personal de los indios en la Nueva España*, vol. 7 (Mexico City: Colegio de México, 1984), 263.

43. Lillian Estelle Fisher, *The Intendant System in Spanish America* (New York: Gordian Press, 1969), 194.

44. Ben Vinson III, *Bearing Arms for His Majesty: The Free-Colored Militia in Colonial Mexico* (Stanford, CA: Stanford University Press, 2001), 164.

45. Fisher, *Intendant System in Spanish America*, 193. See also José M. Portillo Valdés, *Fuero indio: Tlaxcala y la identidad territorial entre la monarquía imperial y la república nacional, 1787–1824* (Mexico City: El Colegio de México, 2015), 55–106.

46. Vinson, *Bearing Arms*, 40. For the effects of fiscal and military reforms on the tribute exemptions of *pardo* militia units, see Vinson, *Bearing Arms*, 161–72.

47. Aurea Commons, "La población de Nueva España en 1790," *Tempus: Revista de Historia de Facultad de Filosofía y Letras* 3 (1995): 7–111.

48. AGN, Indiferente Virreinal c. 6610, exp. 20, f. 6.

49. Ernesto de la Torre Villar, *Instrucciones y Memorias de los Virreyes Novohispanos*, vol. 2 (Mexico City: Editorial Porrua, 1991), 1196.

50. Quoted in Brading, *Miners and Merchants*, 29.

51. AGN, Tributos vol. 60, exp. 9.

52. Konetzke, *Colección de documentos*, vol. 3, pt. 2, 604–5.

53. AGN, Tributos vol. 60, exp. 9, f. 237.

54. Philip II issued a decree in 1577 calling for a tribute register "with their names and people with whom they live." See Libro 7, Título 5, Ley 3 in *Recopilación de leyes de los reynos de las Indias*, vol. 2 (Madrid: Julián de Paredes, 1681; Madrid: Ediciones Cultura Hispánica, 1973), 320.

55. I borrow this phrase from Catarina Madeira Santos, "Administrative Knowledge

in a Colonial Context: Angola in the Eighteenth Century," *British Journal for the History of Science* 43, no. 4 (2010): 543.

56. Maeve E. Adams, "Numbers and Narratives: Epistemologies of Aggregation in British Statistics and Social Realism, c. 1790–1880," in *Statistics and the Public Sphere: Numbers and the People in Modern Britain, c. 1800–2000*, ed. Tom Crook and Glen O'Hara (New York: Routledge, 2011), 103.

57. Arnold, *Bureaucracy and Bureaucrats*, 84–85.

58. Ernest Sánchez Santiró, "El orden jurídico de la fiscalidad en la Real Hacienda de Nueva España: Un análisis a partir de la calidad, el estado y la clase de los contribuyentes," *Espacio, Tiempo y Forma* 4, no. 27 (2014): 100–101.

59. AGN, Tributos vol. 60, exp. 9, f. 231.

60. Vinson, *Bearing Arms*, 135.

61. Fisher, *Intendant System in Spanish America*, 194.

62. These words come from a 1790 instruction for Mexico City, but imprisonment was a common punishment. AGN, Indiferente Virreinal c. 6610, exp. 20, f. 78.

63. Accountant Juan Ordóñez of the Real Hacienda wrote in 1799 that these could be declarations made by official or out-of-court witnesses. See AGN, Tributos vol. 27, exp. 6, f. 157.

64. AGN, Tributos vol. 60, exp. 9, f. 230.

65. AGN, Tributos vol. 60, exp. 9, f. 230.

66. AGN, Tributos vol. 60, exp. 9, f. 239.

67. AGN, Indiferente Virreinal c. 4804, exp. 43, f. 69v.

68. AGN, Tributos vol. 27, exp. 7, f. 193.

69. AGN, General de Parte vol. 76, exp. 211, f. 154.

70. AGN, General de Parte vol. 76, exp. 211, ff. 154–154v.

71. AGN, Tributos vol. 60, exp. 9, ff. 235–36.

72. Fonseca and Urrutia, *Historia general de Real Hacienda*, 1:509–10.

73. AGN, Indiferente Virreinal c. 998, exp. 7, ff. 1–6v.

74. Ernest Sánchez Santiró, *La imperiosa necesidad: Crisis y colapso del erario de Nueva España (1808–1821)* (Mexico City: Instituto de Investigaciones Dr. José María Luis Mora, 2016), 261.

75. Fisher, *Intendant System in Spanish America*, 194.

76. Fonseca and Urrutia, *Historia general de Real Hacienda*, 1:447.

77. AGN, Indiferente Virreinal c. 315, exp. 5, f. 1.

78. AGN, Indiferente Virreinal c. 315, exp. 5, f. 1.

79. Peter Gerhard, *A Guide to the Historical Geography of New Spain* (Cambridge: Cambridge University Press, 1972), 194.

80. AGN, Indiferente Virreinal c. 4607, exp. 47.

81. Depending on the area, these Spanish officials could be alcaldes, *ordinarios*, *gobernadores*, *corregidores*, or *alcaldes mayores*. In the absence of an *alcalde ordinario*, any of the other officials listed could act as a judge of first instance in a tribute dispute. See José Ignacio Rubio Mañé, *El Virreinato: Orígenes y jurisdicciones y dinámica social de los virreyes*, vol. 1, 2nd. ed. (Mexico City: Instituto de Investigaciones Históricas, Universidad Autónoma de México, 1983), 77.

82. AGN, Indiferente Virreinal c. 6610, exp. 20, f. 43.

83. See Matthew Restall, *The Black Middle: Africans, Mayas, and Spaniards in Colonial Yucatán* (Stanford, CA: Stanford University Press, 2009), 129; and Konetzke, *Colección de documentos*, vol. 2, pt. 2, 746.

84. John K. Chance, *Race and Class in Colonial Oaxaca* (Stanford, CA: Stanford University Press, 1978), 178.

85. Luis Jáuregui, *La Real Hacienda de Nueva España: Su administración en la época de los intendentes, 1786–1821* (Mexico City: Universidad Autónoma de México, 1999), 140–44.

86. Esteban Hernández Esteve, "Reflexiones sobre la naturaleza y los orígenes de la contabilidad por partida doble," *Pecvnia* 1 (2005): 93–124.

87. Fisher, *Intendant System in Spanish America*, 189–90.

88. Fonseca and Urrutia, *Historia general de Real Hacienda*, 1:435–36.

89. AGN, Indiferente Virreinal c. 4804, exp. 43.

90. Brian Hamnett, *Politics and Trade in Southern Mexico, 1750–1821* (Cambridge: Cambridge University Press, 1971), 6.

91. AGN, Indiferente Virreinal c. 3138, exp. 26.

92. José Antonio de Villaseñor y Sánchez, *Theatro americano: Descripción general de los Reinos y Provincias de la Nueva España y sus jurisdicciones*, ed. María del Carmen Velázquez (Mexico City: Editorial Trillas, 1992), 94–95.

93. AGN, Tributos vol. 27, exp. 6, f. 157.

94. Fonseca and Urrutia, *Historia general de Real Hacienda*, 1:444.

95. See Daniela Bleichmar, *Visible Empire: Botanical Expeditions and Visual Culture in the Hispanic Enlightenment* (Chicago: University of Chicago Press, 2012); and Jorge Cañizares-Esguerra, *Nature, Empire, and Nation: Explorations of the History of Science in the Iberian World* (Stanford, CA: Stanford University Press, 2006).

96. See Neil Safier, *Measuring the New World: Enlightenment Science and South America* (Chicago: University of Chicago Press, 2008). On cataloging ethnographic objects, see Paula de Vos, "The Rare, the Singular, and the Extraordinary: Natural History and the Collection of Curiosities in the Spanish Empire," in *Science in the Spanish and Portuguese Empires, 1500–1800*, ed. Daniela Bleichmar (Stanford, CA: Stanford University Press, 2009), 271–89.

97. Bleichmar, *Visible Empire*, 184.

98. See René Acuña, *Relaciones geográficas del siglo XVI*, vol. 8 (Mexico City: Universidad Nacional Autónoma de México, Instituto de Investigaciones Antropológicas, 1982); and Francisco de Solano, ed., *Relaciones geográficas del Arzobispado de México, 1743*, vol. 1 (Madrid: Consejo Superior de Investigaciones Científicas, 1988).

99. Emily Berquist Soule, *The Bishop's Utopia: Envisioning Improvement in Colonial Peru* (Philadelphia: University of Pennsylvania Press, 2014), 52–54.

100. Berquist Soule, *Bishop's Utopia*, 55.

101. See Antonio Barrera-Osorio, "Empiricism in the Spanish Atlantic World," in *Science and Empire in the Atlantic World*, ed. James Delbourgo and Nicholas Dew (New York: Routledge, 2008), 177–202.

102. Madeira Santos, "Administrative Knowledge," 539.

103. AGN, Tributos vol. 60, exp. 9, f. 241v.

104. AGN Indiferente Virreinal c. 5555, exp. 31, f. 41.

105. AGN Indiferente Virreinal c. 6610, exp. 20, f. 152.

106. AGN, Tributos vol. 60, exp. 9, f. 248v.

107. AGN, Tributos vol. 60, exp. 9, f. 247v.

108. Lorgio Cobá Noh, *El "indio ciudadano": La tributación y la contribución personal directa en Yucatán, 1786–1825* (Mérida: Universidad Autónoma de Yucatán, 2009), 67.

109. AGN, Tributos vol. 60, exp. 9, f. 237.

110. Bianca Premo, *Children of the Father King: Youth, Authority, and Legal Minority in Colonial Lima* (Chapel Hill: University of North Carolina Press, 2005), 137–38.

111. AGN, Tributos vol. 60, exp. 9, f. 233v.

112. AGN, Tributos vol. 60, exp. 9, f. 249.

113. AGN, Padrones vol. 9, exp. 3, f. 33.

114. Antonio Lafuente and Nuria Valverde, "Making Scientific Objects and Setting Standards: Values, Technology, Government, and the Enlightenment," *EMPIRIA: Revista de Metodología de Ciencias Sociales* 18 (2009): 116–17.

115. Esteban Terreros y Pando, *Diccionario Castellano con las voces de ciencias y artes y sus correspondientes en las tres lenguas Francesca, Latina é Italiana*, vol. 2 (Madrid: Ibarra, Hijos, 1787), 108.

116. AGN, Tributos vol. 43, exp. 9.

117. Sherburne Friend Cook and Woodrow Wilson Borah, *Essays in Population History*, vol. 1, *Mexico and the Caribbean* (Berkeley: University of California Press, 1971), 283–84.

118. See examples from "Estados, cortes y tanteos de tributos" between 1769 and 1785 in AGI, Audiencia de México leg. 2104.

119. See Carlos Marichal, "Beneficios y costes fiscales del colonialismo: Las remesas americanas a España, 1760–1814," *Revista de Historia Económica* 15, no. 3 (1997): 475–505.

120. Vinson, *Bearing Arms*, 162, using figures from Fonseca and Urrutia, *Historia general de Real Hacienda*, vol. 1.

121. Vinson, *Bearing Arms*, 170–71.

122. The accounts branch of the Real Hacienda counted 150 jurisdictions for the purpose of tribute collection at this time. These units depended on shifting boundaries at the district level. In addition to those numbered jurisdictions of figure 4.4, other jurisdictions were listed in general states of accounts from 1785. These jurisdictions were smaller pieces of territorial units that included Acayuca (part of Guazacualo), Aguatlán (part of Izucar), Atitalaquia (part of Tetepango Hueypustla), Atlatlahuca (part of Chalco), Chichicapa (part of Cimatlan), Chilchota (part of Tlazazalca), Chinantla (part of Teutila), Cuicatlán (part of Teutitlan del Camino), Guadalcazar (part of San Luis Potosí), Macuilsuchil (part of Mitla y Tlacolula), Mizantla (part of Vera Cruz Vieja), Papalotipác (part of Teutitlan del Camino), Salvatierra (part of Celaya), Tonalá (part of Guaxuapa), Xalatcingo (part of Xalapa de la Feria), Xaso (part of Valladolid), and Yagualica (part of Sochicoatlan).

123. Charles Gibson, *The Aztecs under Spanish Rule: A History of the Indians of the Valley of Mexico* (Stanford, CA: Stanford University Press, 1976), 208.

124. These data are calculated from "Cuentas del ramo de tributos" in AGI, Audiencia de México legs. 2105 and 2106.

125. AGI, Audiencia de México legs. 2105 and 2106.

126. Vinson, *Bearing Arms*, 166–69.

127. Ernest Sánchez Santiró, *Corte de caja: La Real Hacienda de Nueva España y el primer reformismo fiscal de los Borbones (1720–1755)* (Mexico City: Instituto Mora, 2014), 256.

128. Description of "Cuentas del ramo de tributos" from the year 1787 in AGI, Audiencia de México leg. 2106.

129. Gerhard, *A Guide*, 93; and AGI, Audiencia de México leg. 2106.

130. Gerhard, *A Guide*, 396.

131. In 1788, only one jurisdiction in New Spain registered more than half of its tribu-

taries as *negros* or *mulatos*. Another four jurisdictions contained a tributary population that was 30–50 percent Afromexican. Seven had populations in which Afromexicans made up 20–30 percent of the total tributary population. (See table 4.3 for additional information on areas where free people of color made up large percentages of the tributary population.) Another twenty-one jurisdictions showed between 10 and 20 percent of tributaries registered as Afromexicans. The common trend for fifty-four jurisdictions was to have between 1 and 10 percent *negro* or *mulato* tributaries. Slightly smaller was the group of jurisdictions where less than 1 percent of all tributaries were Afromexicans (n = 52). Fourteen jurisdictions had no data for the year 1788. See AGI, Audiencia de México leg. 2016.

132. Cook and Borah, *Essays in Population History*, vol. 1, *Mexico and the Caribbean*, 228–29.

133. Carlos Paredes Martínez and Blanca Lara Tenorio, "La población *negra* en los valles centrales de Puebla: Orígenes y desarrollo hasta 1681," in *Presencia Africana en México*, ed. Luz María Martínez Montiel (Mexico City: Consejo Nacional para la Cultura y las Artes, 1994), 58.

134. Sánchez Santiró, *La imperiosa necesidad*, 262–63.

135. Sánchez Santiró, *La imperiosa necesidad*, 248.

136. Daniela Bleichmar develops this concept in *Visible Empire*.

137. AGN, Tributos vol. 60, exp. 9, f. 240v.

Chapter 5

1. AGN, Indiferente Virreinal c. 5555, exp. 31.

2. For José "El Burro" Gómez, see AGN, Padrones vol. 51, exp. 133. For Josef Antonio "Bamos comiendo" Rodríguez of Rosario, see Benito Ramírez Meza, "Matrícula y retasa de tributarios del Real de Nuestra Señora del Rosario: Real del Rosario, abril de 1774," *Clío* 6, no. 22 (1998): 193.

3. The tribute regime mirrored the focus on family units in Spanish imperial policy enacted under minister of the Indies José de Gálvez. Allyson M. Poska, "Babies on Board: Women, Children, and Imperial Policy in the Spanish Empire," *Gender and History* 22, no. 2 (2010): 270.

4. This total is 381,941. See AGN, Tributos vol. 43, exp. 9. Another 3.2 million Indian tributary individuals were recorded in the same summary.

5. For an example from an inventory of slaves described based on their social ties to each other, see Brígida von Mentz, "Esclavitud en centros mineros y azucareros novohispanos: Algunas propuestas para el estudio de la multietnicidad en el centro de México," in *Poblaciones y culturas de origen africano en México*, ed. María Elisa Velázquez Gutiérrez and Ethel Correa Duró (Mexico City: Instituto Nacional de Antropología e Historia, 2005), 259–80.

6. AGN, Indiferente Virreinal c. 315, exp. 5.

7. See Ben Vinson III, *Bearing Arms for His Majesty: The Free-Colored Militia in Colonial Mexico* (Stanford, CA: Stanford University Press, 2001), 206–7; and Nicole von Germeten, *Black Blood Brothers: Confraternities and Social Mobility for Afro-Mexicans* (Gainesville: University Press of Florida, 2006), 140 and 192.

8. Aurea Commons, "La población de Nueva España en 1790," *Tempus: Revista de Historia de Facultad de Filosofía y Letras* 3 (1995): 52–55.

9. Adriana Naveda Chávez-Hita, "Denominaciones raciales en archivos locales,"

in *Pardos, Mulatos y Libertos: Sexto Encuentro de Afromexicanistas*, ed. Adriana Naveda Chávez-Hita (Xalapa: Universidad Veracruzana, 2001), 195–206.

10. Tatiana Seijas, *Asian Slaves in Colonial Mexico: From Chinos to Indians* (Cambridge: Cambridge University Press, 2014), 5.

11. See Silvia Arrom, *The Women of Mexico City, 1790–1857* (Stanford, CA: Stanford University Press, 1985); Pilar Gonzalbo, *Familia y educación en Iberoamérica* (Mexico City: Centro de Estudios Históricos, Colegio de México, 1999); and Richard E. Boyer, *Lives of the Bigamists: Marriage, Family, and Community in Colonial Mexico* (Albuquerque: University of New Mexico Press, 2001).

12. Marta Vera Bolaños, "La composición de la familia en la ciudad de México en 1790: Una reconstrucción demográfica," in *La población de la ciudad de México en 1790: Estructura social, alimentación y vivienda*, ed. Manuel Miño Grijalva and Sonia Pérez Toledo (Mexico City: Universidad Autónoma Metropolitana, Unidad Iztapalapa, 2004), 124.

13. Ben Vinson III, "From Dawn 'til Dusk: Black Labor in Late Colonial Mexico," in *Black Mexico: Race and Society from Colonial to Modern Times*, ed. Ben Vinson III and Matthew Restall (Albuquerque: University of New Mexico Press, 2009), 131.

14. See Norma Angélica Castillo Palma, "Cohabitación y conflictividad entre afromestizos y nahuas en el México Colonial," in *Pautas de convivencia étnica en la América Latina colonial: (Indios, negros, mulatos, pardos, y esclavos)*, ed. Juan Manuel de la Serna Herrera (Mexico City: Universidad Nacional Autónoma de México, 2005), 163–86.

15. Leon Yacher, "Marriage Migration and Racial Mixing in Colonial Tlazazalca, 1750–1800," Syracuse University Department of Geography, Discussion Paper Series, no. 32 (1977), 8. For the population figure, see Commons, "Población de Nueva España en 1790," 62.

16. Matthew O'Hara, *A Flock Divided: Race, Religion, and Politics in México, 1749–1857* (Durham, NC: Duke University Press, 2010), 198–203.

17. AGN, Indiferente Virreinal c. 4038, exp. 13, f. 5v.

18. David Weber, *Bárbaros: Spaniards and Their Savages in the Age of Enlightenment* (New Haven, CT: Yale University Press, 2005), 104.

19. D. A. Brading, *Miners and Merchants in Bourbon Mexico, 1763–1810* (Cambridge: Cambridge University Press, 1971), 258.

20. See Biblioteca Nacional de Antropología e Historia (hereafter BNAH), Puebla, rollos 43 and 44. The drop in tributary numbers is discussed in greater detail in the last part of this chapter.

21. BNAH, Puebla, rollo 43.

22. See Norma Angélica Castillo's analysis of an Afromexican tributary register in 1751 in "La pérdida de la población de origen africano en la región de Puebla," in *Poblaciones y culturas de origen africano en México*, ed. María Elisa Velázquez and Ethel Correa (Mexico City: Instituto Nacional de Antropología e Historia, 2005), 325.

23. Benito Ramírez Meza, "Matrícula y retasa de tributarios del Real de Nuestra Señora del Rosario. Real del Rosario, abril de 1774," *Clío* 6, no. 22 (1998): 175.

24. Peter Gerhard, *The North Frontier of New Spain* (Princeton, NJ: Princeton University Press, 1982), 272.

25. Ignacio del Río, *La aplicación regional de las reformas borbónicas en Nueva España: Sonora y Sinaloa, 1768–1787* (Mexico City: Universidad Nacional Autónoma de México, 1995), 130.

26. Silvio Zavala, *El servicio personal de los indios en la Nueva España*, vol. 7 (Mexico City: Colegio de México, 1984), 575–76.

27. Zavala, *Servicio personal*, 604.

28. Ben Vinson III, "The Racial Profile of a Rural Mexican Province in the 'Costa Chica': Igualapa in 1791," *The Americas* 57, no. 2 (2000): 278–79.

29. AGN, Tierras vol. 1550, exp. 1.

30. AGN, Tributos vol. 51, exp. 6.

31. Herman L. Bennett, *Colonial Blackness: A History of Afro-Mexico* (Bloomington: Indiana University Press, 2009), 194.

32. BNAH, Puebla, rollo 43.

33. BNAH, Puebla, rollo 44.

34. AGN, Tributos vol. 40, exp. 11, f. 209.

35. Arrom, *Women of Mexico City*, 208.

36. Ramírez Meza, "Matrícula y retasa," 189.

37. Ann Twinam, *Public Lives, Private Secrets: Gender, Honor, Sexuality, and Illegitimacy in Colonial Spanish America* (Stanford, CA: Stanford University Press, 1999), 26.

38. AGN, Tributos vol. 40, exp. 11, f. 215v.

39. AGN, Padrones vol. 51, exp. 133.

40. Between 1742 and 1793, the Afromexican population increased by as much as 30 percent. See Vinson, *Bearing Arms*, 1.

41. Daniela Marino, "Visitas, padrones y tributo: Una lectura política de la demografía indígena y la fiscalidad borbónica en Charcas," *Anuario IEHS: Instituto de Estudios histórico sociales* 12 (1997): 311.

42. AGN, Tributos vol. 3, exp. 3, f. 152.

43. The secondary literature on sexuality and marriage occasionally references these cross-caste adoptions. See Boyer, *Lives of the Bigamists*, 95. Boyer has described a *loba* farmer named María who was raised by an Indian called Antonio.

44. AGN, Indiferente Virreinal c. 5555, exp. 31, f. 133v.

45. R. Douglas Cope, *The Limits of Racial Domination: Plebeian Society in Colonial Mexico City, 1660–1720* (Madison: University of Wisconsin Press, 1994), 92–93.

46. Ann Twinam, "Honor, Sexuality, and Illegitimacy in Colonial Spanish America," in *Sexuality and Marriage in Colonial Latin America*, ed. Asunción Lavrin (Lincoln: University of Nebraska Press, 1989), 131.

47. AGN, Padrones vol. 51, exp. 133.

48. AGN, Padrones vol. 49, exp. 227.

49. Laura Shelton, "Like a Servant or Like a Son? Circulating Children in Northwestern Mexico (1790–1850)," in *Raising an Empire: Children in Early Modern Iberia and Colonial Latin America*, ed. Ondina E. González and Bianca Premo (Albuquerque: University of New Mexico Press, 2007), 219.

50. AGN, Indiferente Virreinal c. 5555, exp. 31.

51. Bianca Premo, "Thinking beyond Lineage and across Race in Spanish Atlantic Family History," *William and Mary Quarterly* 70, no. 2, Centering Families in Atlantic Histories (2013): 299.

52. Araceli Reynoso Medina, "Aquí somos todos libres . . . La población de Igualapa, 1650–1750," in *De la libertad y la abolición: Africanos y afrodescendientes en Iberoamérica*, ed. Juan Manuel de la Serna (Mexico City: Consejo Nacional para la Cultura y las Artes, 2010), 166.

53. Part of the area of the *parcialidades* may also have been included in the *cuarteles* of the city, possibly resulting in an exaggeration of the population. See Sonia Pérez Toledo and Herbert S. Klein, *Población y estructura social de la Ciudad de México, 1790–1842* (Mexico City: Universidad Autónoma Metropolitana, 2005), 55.

54. Luis Fernando Granados, "Cosmopolitan Indians and Mesoamerican Barrios in

Bourbon Mexico City: Tribute, Community, Family, and Work in 1800" (PhD diss., Georgetown University, 2008), 30.

55. AGN, Tierras vol. 1550, exp. 1.

56. María Guevara Sangiés, "Vida cotidiana de castas en Guanajuato, siglo XVIII," in *Pardos, Mulatos y Libertos: Sexto Encuentro de Afromexicanistas*, ed. Adriana Naveda Chávez-Hita (Xalapa: Universidad Veracruzana, 2001), 149.

57. Vinson, "From Dawn 'til Dusk," 102; Miguel Marín Bosch, *Puebla neocolonial, 1777–1831: Casta, ocupación y matrimonio en la segunda ciudad de Nueva España* (Zapopan: Colegio de Jalisco, 1999), 156; and Patrick James Carroll, *Blacks in Colonial Veracruz: Race, Ethnicity, and Regional Development*, 2nd ed. (Austin: University of Texas Press, 2001), 115–16.

58. Enrique Florescano and Isabel Gil Sánchez, *Descripciones económicas regionales de Nueva España* (Mexico City: Instituto Nacional de Antropología e Historia, 1976), 25.

59. Catherine E. Doenges, "A Regional Society in Colonial Mexico: Eighteenth-Century Celaya, A Perspective from the Household" (PhD diss., Syracuse University, 1993), 73–74.

60. See Arrom, *Women of Mexico City*, 116; Cecilia Andrea Rabell, "Estructuras de la pobalción y características de los jefes de los grupos domésticos en la ciudad de Antequera (Oaxaca), 1777," in *Familias novohispanas: Siglos XVI al XIX*, ed. Gonzalbo Aizpuru (Mexico City: Colegio de México, 1991), 273–98; and Elizabeth Ann Kuznesof, "Gender Ideology, Race, and Female-Headed Households in Urban Mexico, 1750–1850," in *State and Society in Spanish America during the Age of Revolution*, ed. Victor M. Uribe-Uran (Wilmington, DE: Scholarly Resources, 2001), 160–61.

61. Marie Eileen Francois, *A Culture of Everyday Credit: Housekeeping, Pawnbroking, and Governance in Mexico City, 1750–1920* (Lincoln: University of Nebraska Press, 2006), 4–5.

62. Ixcateopan renters and farmers were male and female.

63. Susan Deans-Smith, *Bureaucrats, Planters, and Workers: The Making of the Tobacco Monopoly in Bourbon Mexico* (Austin: University of Texas Press, 1992), 191.

64. Lillian Estelle Fisher, *The Intendant System in Spanish America* (New York: Gordian Press, 1969), 288–89.

65. Vinson, "Racial Profile," 278–79.

66. AGN, Indiferente Virreinal c. 5555, exp. 31, f. 59.

67. Catherine E. Doenges, "Marriage Mobility in Late Colonial Celaya, Mexico," *Yearbook Conference of Latin Americanist Geographers* 22 (1996): 72.

68. AGN, Padrones vol. 50, exp. 203, f. 204.

69. James C. Scott, *Seeing Like a State: How Certain Schemes to Improve the Human Condition Have Failed* (New Haven, CT: Yale University Press, 1998), 66.

70. BNAH, Puebla, rollo 43.

71. AGN, Padrones vol. 51, exp 133, f. 133v.

72. AGN, Padrones vol. 51, exp. 133.

73. AGN, Indiferente Virreinal c. 4038, exp. 13, f. 28.

74. These were not uncommon in the sample, totaling more than five hundred records.

75. AGN, Tributos vol. 51, exp. 5, f. 111.

76. AGN, Indiferente Virreinal c. 3367, exp. 27.

77. AGN, Tributos vol. 8, exp. 1, ff. 58v–59.

78. AGN, Indiferente Virreinal c. 5555, exp. 31, f. 82v.

79. AGN, Indiferente Virreinal c. 5555, exp. 31, f. 24.

80. AGN, Tierras vol. 1550, exp. 1, f. 29v.

81. AGN, Tributos vol. 8, exp 1, ff. 79v–80.

82. AGN, Tributos vol. 60, exp. 9, f. 249.

83. AGN, Padrones vol. 49, exp. 227, f. 241v.

84. AGN, Tributos vol. 8, exp. 1, f. 80v.

85. AGN, Indiferente Virreinal c. 5555, exp. 31.

86. Cecilia Rabell Romero, "Trayectoria de vida familiar, raza y género en Oaxaca colonial," in *Familia y vida privada en la historia de Iberoamérica: Seminario de Historia de la Familia*, ed. Pilar Gonzalbo Aizpuru and Cecilia Rabell Romero (Mexico City: Colegio de México and UNAM, 1996), 112.

87. Peter Gerhard, *A Guide to the Historical Geography of New Spain* (Cambridge: Cambridge University Press, 1972), 272.

88. Cynthia Milton and Ben Vinson III, "Counting Heads: Race and Non-native Tribute Policy in Colonial Spanish America," *Journal of Colonialism and Colonial History* 3, no. 3 (2002): 22.

89. Ramírez Meza, "Matrícula y retasa," 195.

90. Miguel Ángel Cuenya, *Puebla de los Ángeles en tiempos de una peste colonial: Una mirada en torno al matlazahuatl de 1737* (Zamora: El Colegio de Michoacán, 1999), 59.

91. Guy P. C. Thomson, *Puebla de los Angeles: Industry and Society in a Mexican City, 1700–1850* (Boulder, CO: Westview Press, 1989), 63. The jurisdiction also had 18,369 residents of Spanish descent; 24,039 Indians; 10,942 mestizos; 2,416 *castizos*; and 12,670 belonging to other *castas*.

92. Rafael García Pérez, *Reforma y resistencia: Manuel de Flon y la intendencia de Puebla* (Mexico City: Editorial Porrúa, 2000), 111.

93. The Real Hacienda received 79,326 pesos in tribute monies between 1780 and 1789, which rose to 186,859 in 1790–1800. See Herbert S. Klein, *The American Finances of the Spanish Empire: Royal Income and Expenditures in Colonial Mexico, Peru, and Bolivia, 1680–1809* (Albuquerque: University of New Mexico Press, 1998), 88.

94. Klein, *American Finances of the Spanish Empire*, 75.

95. Thomson, *Puebla de los Angeles*, 21.

96. Thomson, *Puebla de los Angeles*, 33–34.

97. See Pablo Sierra, "Urban Slavery in Colonial Puebla de los Ángeles, 1536–1708" (PhD diss., University of California, Los Angeles, 2013); and Carlos Paredes Martínez and Blanca Lara Tenorio, "Los Trabajadores negros en el inicio del desarrollo económico poblano," *Antropología: Revista Interdisciplinaria del INAH* 78 (2005): 23–28.

98. Vinson, *Bearing Arms*, 111.

99. AGN, General de Parte vol. 65, exp. 180.

100. BNAH, Puebla, rollo 43.

101. Miguel Marín Bosch, *Puebla neocolonial, 1777–1831: Casta, ocupación y matrimonio en la segunda ciudad de Nueva España* (Zapopan: Colegio de Jalisco, 1999), 127.

102. In 1777, a slight majority (55.7 percent) of the *mulato* men registered in all of Puebla's parish records were married. Marín Bosch, *Puebla neocolonial*, 43.

103. BNAH, Puebla, rollo 44.

104. BNAH, Puebla, rollo 43.

105. BNAH, Puebla, rollo 44.

106. Marín Bosch, *Puebla neocolonial*, 114.

107. AGN, Tributos vol. 40, exp. 11, f. 222.

108. Ramírez Meza, "Matrícula y retasa," 167–97.

109. AGN, Tierras vol. 1550, exp. 1, f. 37v.

110. See the "Lista de tributarios que produce el quartel menor no. 8 sacada del Padrón" in Manuel Miño Grijalva, *Censo de la población de la Ciudad de México, 1790 censo de Revillagigedo* (CD-ROM) (Mexico City: El Colegio de México, 2002).

111. Scott, *Seeing Like a State*, 77.

Chapter 6

1. José Miranda, *El tributo indígena en la Nueva España durante el siglo XVI*, 2nd ed. (Mexico City: El Colegio de México, 2005), 161.

2. Laura E. Matthew, *Memories of Conquest: Becoming Mexicano in Colonial Guatemala* (Chapel Hill: University of North Carolina Press, 2012), 116.

3. Sean F. McEnroe, *From Colony to Nationhood in Mexico* (Cambridge: Cambridge University Press, 2012), 8. For the establishment of these privileges among Tlaxcalans as a group, see Charles Gibson, *Tlaxcala in the Sixteenth Century* (Stanford, CA: Stanford University Press, 1967), 160–61. In the context of tribute exemption, claims of Tlaxcalan ancestry can be found in northern New Spain throughout the eighteenth century. A few of these cases included *mulatos* and involved discussions of privileges granted to settlers on lands previously occupied by Chichimec peoples.

4. AGN, Indios vol. 69, exp. 189, f. 68v.

5. Yanna Yannakakis, *The Art of Being In-Between: Native Intermediaries, Indian Identity, and Local Rule in Colonial Oaxaca* (Durham, NC: Duke University Press, 2008), 194.

6. AGN, Indios vol. 69, exp. 189, fol. 68.

7. Peter B. Villella, "'Pure and Noble Indians, Untainted by Inferior Idolatrous Races': Native Elites and the Discourse of Blood Purity in Late Colonial Mexico," *Hispanic American Historical Review* 91, no. 4 (2011): 642.

8. Fabricio González-Soriano, "Herencia patológica en la medicina mexicana de la segunda mitad del siglo XIX," *Boletín Mexicano de Historia y Filosofía de la Medicina* 11, no. 1 (2008): 10–15.

9. This self-fashioning reworked scientific notions, principally from France, about the fitness of American peoples to present them as worthy and pure. For more on creole patriotism in historical and scientific thought, see D. A. Brading, *The First America: The Spanish Monarchy, Creole Patriots, and the Liberal State, 1492–1867* (Cambridge: Cambridge University Press, 1991), 422–46; and Jorge Cañizares-Esguerra, *How to Write the History of the New World: Histories, Epistemologies, and Identities in the Eighteenth-Century Atlantic World* (Stanford, CA: Stanford University Press, 2001).

10. AGN, Indios vol. 69, exp. 189, f. 68.

11. David Nirenberg, "Mass Conversion and Genealogical Mentalities: Jews and Christians in Fifteenth-Century Spain," *Past and Present* 174, no. 1 (2002): 3–41.

12. María Elena Martínez, *Genealogical Fictions: Limpieza de Sangre, Religion, and Gender in Colonial Mexico* (Stanford, CA: Stanford University Press, 2008), 201.

13. Administrative summaries destined for Spain grouped Apan with Tepeapulco, recording 942.5 Indian tributaries and 62.5 *negro* and *mulato* tributaries in 1781. By 1788 there were 849.5 Indian tributaries and 123 Afromexican tributaries. See "Cuentas del ramo de tributos," in AGI, Audiencia de México legs. 2105 and 2106. Gonzalo Aguirre Beltrán finds 1,059 *pardos* in Apan alone by 1793, though this figure is based on total population rather than tributary units. See Aguirre Beltrán, *La población negra de México,*

1519–1810: Estudio etno-histórico, 2nd ed. (Mexico City: Fondo de Cultura Económica, 1972), 226.

14. AGN, Tributos vol. 43, exp. 9, f. 277.

15. AGN, Indios vol. 69, exp. 226, f. 105.

16. McEnroe, *From Colony to Nationhood*, 210.

17. AGN, Indios vol. 69, exp. 226, ff. 105v–106.

18. Ann Twinam, *Purchasing Whiteness: Pardos, Mulattos, and the Quest for Social Mobility in the Spanish Indies* (Stanford, CA: Stanford University Press, 2015), 48.

19. Martínez, *Genealogical Fictions*, 87.

20. See Robert C. Schwaller, "'For Honor and Defence': Race and the Right to Bear Arms in Early Colonial Mexico," *Colonial Latin American Review* 21, no. 2 (2012): 247; and Ben Vinson III, *Bearing Arms for His Majesty: The Free-Colored Militia in Colonial Mexico* (Stanford, CA: Stanford University Press, 2001), 146–47.

21. Vinson, *Bearing Arms*, 4.

22. Karen B. Graubart, "The Creolization of the New World: Local Forms of Identification in Urban Colonial Peru, 1560–1640," *Hispanic American Historical Review* 89, no. 3 (2009): 474.

23. Other scholarship has treated the meanings of tribute for *pardo* militias and their families. See Paul Lokken, "Useful Enemies: Seventeenth-Century Piracy and the Rise of *Pardo* Militias in Spanish Central America," *Journal of Colonialism and Colonial History* 5, no. 2 (2004): 1–18; Vinson, *Bearing Arms*, 145–72; and Ben Vinson III and Matthew Restall, "Black Soldiers, Native Soldiers: Meanings of Military Service in the Spanish American Colonies," in *Beyond Black and Red: African-Native Relations in Colonial Latin America*, ed. Matthew Restall (Albuquerque: University of New Mexico Press, 2005), 15–52.

24. Richard L. Kagan, *Lawsuits and Litigants in Castile, 1500–1700* (Chapel Hill: University of North Carolina Press, 1981), 11.

25. Luis Jáuregui, *La Real Hacienda de Nueva España: Su administración en la época de los intendentes, 1786–1821* (Mexico City: Universidad Autónoma de México, 1999), 95.

26. See Article 133 published in Marina Mantilla Trolle, Rafael Diego-Fernández Sotelo, and Agustín Moreno, *Real Ordenanza para el establecimiento e instrucción de intendentes de ejército y provincial en el reino de la Nueva España: Edición anotada de la Audiencia de la Nueva Galicia* (Guadalajara: Universidad de Guadalajara, 2008), 288.

27. AGN, Indiferente Virreinal c. 3367, exp. 27, f. 14v.

28. AGN, Tributos vol. 60, exp. 9, f. 236.

29. AGN, Tributos vol. 13, exp. 2, f. 6.

30. AGN, Tributos vol. 13, exp. 2, f. 28.

31. María Elena Martínez, "The Language, Genealogy, and Classification of 'Race' in Colonial Mexico," in *Race and Classification: The Case of Mexican America*, ed. Ilona Katzew and Susan Deans-Smith (Stanford, CA: Stanford University Press, 2009), 41.

32. AGN, General de Parte vol. 77, exp. 133, f. 182v.

33. Michael T. Ducey, *A Nation of Villages: Riot and Rebellion in the Mexican Huasteca, 1750–1850* (Tucson: University of Arizona Press, 2004), 15–18.

34. Wayne S. Osborn, "Indian Land Retention in Colonial Metztitlán," *Hispanic American Historical Review* 53, no. 2 (1973): 217–38.

35. Ducey, *Nation of Villages*, 63.

36. The precise figure is 14,329 pesos, one real, and nine *tomines*. See "Cuentas del ramo de tributos" for 1788 in AGI, Audiencia de México leg. 2106.

37. AGN, Tributos vol. 12, exp. 2, f. 263v.

38. Juan Zapata y Sandoval, *Discertación sobre justicia distributiva y sobre la acepción de personas a ella opuesta*, ed. Arturo Ramírez Trejo and Paula López Cruz (Mexico City: Universidad Nacional Autónoma de México, 1994), 109.

39. AGN, Tributos vol. 12, exp. 2, f. 329.

40. AGN, Tributos vol. 12, exp. 2, ff. 87–89.

41. AGN, General de Parte vol. 78, exp. 14, f. 11v.

42. M. E. Galaviz de Capdevielle, "Descripción y pacificación de la Sierra Gorda," *Estudios de Historia Novohispana* 4 (1971): 28–31.

43. AGN, General de Parte vol. 78, exp. 14, f. 11v.

44. AGN, General de Parte vol. 78, exp. 14, f. 13v.

45. Richard Konetzke, *Colección de documentos para la historia de la formación social de Hispanoamérica*, vol. 3, pt. 2 (Madrid: Consejo Superior de Investigaciones Científicas, 1953–62), 439.

46. Patricia Seed observes that complaints based on "racial heritage" alone were in the minority. More petitioners interpreted the Pragmatic in broader terms, including honor and economic status. See *To Love, Honor, and Obey in Colonial Mexico: Conflicts over Marriage Choice, 1574–1821* (Stanford, CA: Stanford University Press, 1988), 207.

47. Steinar A. Sæther, "Bourbon Absolutism and Marriage Reform in Late Colonial Spanish America" *The Americas* 59, no. 4 (2003): 476.

48. AGN, Tributos vol. 60, exp. 9, f. 247v.

49. Diligencias practicadas a pedimento de Agustín González Muñiz, BNAH, Puebla, rollo 43, f. 1v.

50. María Elisa Velázquez Gutiérrez, *Mujeres de origen africano en la capital novohispana, siglos XVII y XVIII* (Mexico City: Universidad Nacional Autónoma de México, 2006), 233.

51. See Cynthia Milton, *The Many Meanings of Poverty: Colonialism, Social Compacts, and Assistance in Eighteenth-Century Ecuador* (Stanford, CA: Stanford University Press, 2007), 144–45; and, for obtaining ecclesiastical posts, see Richard Konetzke, *Colección de documentos*, vol. 3, pt. 1, 391–93.

52. BNAH, Diligencias, f. 5.

53. BNAH, Diligencias, ff. 1v–2. The document is damaged here, but it is clear that the petitioner attributes the confusion of *calidad* to the adoption.

54. Ann Twinam, *Public Lives, Private Secrets: Gender, Honor, Sexuality, and Illegitimacy in Colonial Spanish America* (Stanford, CA: Stanford University Press, 1999), 256.

55. See the case of Manuel Yllanes, a master blacksmith from Antequera, who attempted to avoid tribute by providing false information about his wife. The marriage record of their daughter confirmed that Manuel and his wife were *pardos*, but the tribute collector could not come to a decision regarding their registration. See John K. Chance, *Race and Class in Colonial Oaxaca* (Stanford, CA: Stanford University Press, 1978), 177–78.

56. Herman L. Bennett, *Colonial Blackness: A History of Afro-Mexico* (Bloomington: Indiana University Press, 2009), 78.

57. BNAH, Diligencias, f. 11.

58. BNAH, Diligencias, ff. 19–19v.

59. BNAH, Diligencias, f. 20.

60. BNAH, Diligencias, f. 26.

61. BNAH, Diligencias, f. 33v.

62. Joanne Rappaport, "'Asi Lo Paresçe Por Su Aspeto': Physiognomy and the Construction of Difference in Colonial Bogotá," *Hispanic American Historical Review* 91, no. 4 (2011): 612.

63. AGN, General de Parte vol. 77, exp. 130, ff. 181v–182.

64. Karen B. Graubart, *With Our Labor and Sweat: Indigenous Women and the Formation of Colonial Society in Peru, 1550–1700* (Stanford, CA: Stanford University Press, 2007), 121–55.

65. Norma Angélica Castillo, "La pérdida de la población de origen africano en la región de Puebla," in *Poblaciones y culturas de origen africano en México*, ed. María Elisa Velázquez and Ethel Correa (Mexico City: Instituto de Antropología e Historia, 2005), 315–16.

66. Carlos López-Beltrán, "The Medical Origins of Heredity," in *Heredity Produced: At the Crossroads of Biology, Politics, and Culture, 1500–1870*, ed. Staffan Müller-Wille and Hans-Jörg Rheinberger (Cambridge, MA: MIT Press, 2007), 106.

67. Verena Martinez-Alier, *Marriage, Class, and Colour in Nineteenth-Century Cuba: A Study of Racial Attitudes and Sexual Values in a Slave Society* (Cambridge: Cambridge University Press, 1974), 72.

68. Chance, *Race and Class in Colonial Oaxaca*, 181.

69. AGN, Indiferente Virreinal c. 6610, exp. 20, f. 6 and f. 51.

70. Milton, *Many Meanings of Poverty*, 144–45.

71. Ann Twinam, "The Church, the State, and the Abandoned: *Expósitos* in Late Eighteenth-Century Havana," in *Raising an Empire: Children in Early Modern Iberia and Colonial Latin America*, ed. Ondina E. González and Bianca Premo (Albuquerque: University of New Mexico Press, 2007), 164.

72. AGN, Tributos vol. 55, exp. 12, ff. 340v–341.

73. AGN, Tributos vol. 55, exp. 12, ff. 344v–345.

74. José R. Jouve Martín, *The Black Doctors of Colonial Lima: Science, Race, and Writing in Colonial and Early Republican Peru* (Montreal: McGill-Queen's University Press, 2014), 8.

75. Konetzke, *Colección de documentos*, vol. 3, pt. 2, 789.

76. Norma Angélica Castillo Palma, "Informaciones y probanzas de limpieza de sangre: Teoría y realidad frente a la movilidad de la población novohispana producida por el mestizaje," in *El peso de la sangre: Limpios, mestizos y nobles en el mundo hispánico*, ed. Nikolaus Böttcher, Bernd Hausberger, and Max-Sebastián Hering Torres (Mexico City: El Colegio de México, 2011), 239.

77. AGN, Tributos vol. 55, exp. 11, f. 300v.

78. AGN, Tributos vol. 55, exp. 11, f. 302v.

79. Konetzke, *Colección de documentos*, vol. 3, pt. 2, 790.

80. Lorgio Cobá Noh, *El "indio ciudadano": La tributación y la contribución personal directa en Yucatán, 1786–1825* (Mérida: Universidad Autónoma de Yucatán, 2009), 78.

81. Konetzke, *Colección de documentos*, vol. 3, pt. 2, 791.

82. This was not the case for all types of petitions that sought to alter caste and *calidad*. In the context of the *gracias al sacar*, some free people of African descent in Venezuela used hierarchies of color and physical appearance to pursue individual advancement. Tribute exemption and *gracias al sacar* petitions did share common implications for loyalty and service on the part of free *pardos* who positioned themselves as worthy

subjects of their king. See Ann Twinam, *Purchasing Whiteness: Pardos, Mulatos, and the Quest for Social Mobility in the Spanish Indies* (Stanford, CA: Stanford University Press, 2015), 245–46, for an example.

83. Rebecca Earle, *The Body of the Conquistador: Food, Race, and the Colonial Experience in Spanish America, 1492–1700* (Cambridge: Cambridge University Press, 2012), 6.

Conclusion

1. D. A. Brading, *The First America: The Spanish Monarchy, Creole Patriots, and the Liberal State, 1492–1867* (Cambridge: Cambridge University Press, 1991), 568.

2. See Document 261, "Representación sobre la inmunidad personal del clero, reducida por las leyes, por el Sr. Abad y Queipo," in *Colección de documentos para la historia de la guerra de independencia de México de 1808 a 1821*, ed. Juan E. Hernández y Dávalos, vol. 2 (Mexico City: José María Sandoval, 1878), 846.

3. See chapter 6 herein and AGN, Tributos vol. 55, exp. 11, f. 300v.

4. Brian Owensby has argued that this was the case of tributary Indians who sought justice within the colonial regime. See *Empire of Law and Indian Justice* (Stanford, CA: Stanford University Press, 2008), 299.

5. Ann Twinam, *Purchasing Whiteness: Pardos, Mulatos, and the Quest for Social Mobility in the Spanish Indies* (Stanford, CA: Stanford University Press, 2015), 412.

6. Marta Terán, "Geografía de los partidos tributarios de la Nueva España: Los subdelegados como recaudadores de los tributos, 1805–1810," in *De reinos y subdelegaciones: Nuevos escenarios para un nuevo orden en la América borbónica*, ed. Rafael Diego-Fernández Sotelo, María Pilar Gutiérrez Lorenzo, and Luis Alberto Arrioja Díaz Viruell (Zamora: El Colegio de Michoacán, 2014), 78–79. This chapter contains excellent maps and data visualizations based on the last years of widespread collection.

7. Aaron Pollack, "Hacia una historia social del tributo de indios y castas en Hispanoamérica: Notas en torno a su creación, desarrollo y abolición," *Historia Mexicana* 66, no. 1 (2016): 112.

8. Document 90, "Bando de don José María Ansorena publicado en Valladolid, aboliendo la esclavitud, el pago de tributo y otras gabelas," in *Colección de documentos para la historia de la guerra de independencia de México de 1808 a 1821*, ed. Juan E. Hernández y Dávalos, vol. 2 (Mexico City: José María Sandoval, 1878).

9. John Tutino, *From Insurrection to Revolution in Mexico: Social Bases of Agrarian Violence, 1750–1940* (Princeton, NJ: Princeton University Press, 1986), 134–35.

10. Reproduced in Fernando Serrano Migallón, *La vida constitucional de México*, vol. 2, pt. 3 (Mexico City: Fondo de Cultura Económica, 2009), 181.

11. Ernest Sánchez Santiró, *La imperiosa necesidad: Crisis y colapso del erario de Nueva España (1808–1821)* (Mexico City: Instituto Mora, 2016), 266–68.

12. This was especially true of the Indian category in the nineteenth century, which retained community and religious significance beyond caste. See Matthew O'Hara, *A Flock Divided: Race, Religion, and Politics in México, 1749–1857* (Durham, NC: Duke University Press, 2010), 198–203.

13. Norma Angélica Castillo Palma, "Probanzas y acusaciones sobre la limpieza de sangre antes y después de la Independencia: La lucha por los privilegios," in *1750–1850: La independencia de México a la luz de cien años; Problemáticas y desenlaces de una larga transición*, ed. Brian C. Connaughton (Mexico City: Universidad Autónoma Metropolitana, 2010), 373–81.

14. Robert H. Jackson has argued this for the case of *indios* in Cochabamba. See *Race, Caste, and Status: Indians in Colonial Spanish America* (Albuquerque: University of New Mexico Press, 1999), 22.

15. Patrick James Carroll, *Blacks in Colonial Veracruz: Race, Ethnicity, and Regional Development*, 2nd ed. (Austin: University of Texas Press, 2001), 143 and 153.

16. Mariana L. R. Dantas, *Black Townsmen: Urban Slavery and Freedom in the Eighteenth-Century Americas* (New York: Palgrave Macmillan, 2008), 7.

17. See the class-based arguments of accountant Juan Ordóñez in AGN, Tributos vol. 55, exp. 12, f. 341. A further discussion is found in Luis Fernando Granados, "Cosmopolitan Indians and Mesoamerican Barrios in Bourbon Mexico City: Tribute, Community, Family, and Work in 1800" (PhD diss., Georgetown University, 2008), 144.

18. Granados, "Cosmopolitan Indians," 128.

19. AGN, Tributos vol. 60, exp. 9, f. 232v.

20. Thomas E. Skidmore, "Racial Ideas and Social Policy in Brazil, 1870–1940," in *The Idea of Race in Latin America, 1870–1940*, ed. Richard Graham (Austin: University of Texas Press, 1990), 10. On the legacies of caste in nineteenth-century Mexican politics, see Ben Vinson III, *Before Mestizaje: The Frontiers of Race and Caste in Colonial Mexico* (Cambridge: Cambridge University Press, 2017), 184–201.

21. See Gonzalo Aguirre Beltrán, *La población negra de México, 1519–1810: Estudio etno-histórico*, 2nd ed. (Mexico City: Fondo de Cultura Económica, 1972), 279; and Laura Lewis, *Hall of Mirrors: Power, Witchcraft, and Caste in Colonial Mexico* (Durham, NC: Duke University Press, 2003), 182.

22. Christina A. Sue, *Land of the Cosmic Race: Race Mixture, Racism, and Blackness in Mexico* (New York: Oxford University Press, 2013), 49–50.

23. Laura Lewis, "Between 'Casta' and 'Raza': The Example of Colonial Mexico," in *Race and Blood in the Iberian World*, ed. María Elena Martínez, David Nirenberg, and Max-Sebastián Hering Torres (Zurich: LIT Verlag, 2012), 117.

24. Peter Wade, *Degrees of Mixture, Degrees of Freedom: Genomics, Multiculturalism, and Race in Latin America* (Durham, NC: Duke University Press, 2017), 259.

25. Patricia Seed, *To Love, Honor, and Obey in Colonial Mexico: Conflicts over Marriage Choice, 1574–1821* (Stanford, CA: Stanford University Press, 1988), 148.

26. Christine Hünefeldt, *Paying the Price of Freedom: Family and Labor among Lima's Slaves, 1800–1854* (Berkeley: University of California Press, 1994), 201.

27. María Elena Martínez, "The Language, Genealogy, and Classification of 'Race' in Colonial Mexico," in *Race and Classification: The Case of Mexican America*, ed. Ilona Katzew and Susan Deans-Smith (Stanford, CA: Stanford University Press, 2009), 41.

28. Carlos López Beltrán, "Sangre y temperamento: Pureza y mestizajes en las sociedades de castas americanas," in *Saberes locales: Ensayos sobre historia de la ciencia en América Latina*, ed. Frida Gorbach and Carlos López Beltrán (Zamora: El Colegio de Michoacán, 2008), 322–23.

29. Magali Carrera, *Imagining Identity in New Spain: Race, Lineage, and the Colonial Body in Portraiture and Casta Paintings* (Austin: University of Texas Press, 2003), 13.

30. Cynthia García Martínez, "Debates en torno a la población de origen africano y ascendencia africana en las Cortes Generales Extraordinarias de Cádiz," in *Negros y morenos en iberoamérica: Adaptación y conflicto*, ed. Juan Manuel de la Serna (Mexico City: Universidad Nacional Autónoma de México, 2015), 233–34.

31. See Ann Twinam's discussion of the delegates from New Spain to the Cortes in *Purchasing Whiteness*, 368–70.

32. María Camila Díaz Casas, "¿De esclavos a ciudadanos? Matices sobre la 'integración' y 'asimilación' de la población de origen africano en la sociedad nacional mexicana, 1810–1850," in *Negros y morenos en iberoamérica: Adaptación y conflicto*, ed. Juan Manuel de la Serna (Mexico City: Universidad Nacional Autónoma de México, 2015), 286–87.

33. Twinam, *Purchasing Whiteness*, 401.

34. Michele Reid-Vazquez, *The Year of the Lash: Free People of Color in Cuba and the Nineteenth-Century Atlantic World* (Athens: University of Georgia Press, 2011), 29–30. Alex Borucki similarly observes that "white acquaintances frequently lampooned" writer Jacinto Molina (1766–1841) as a result of their discomfort with "the idea of a black writer in a white world of letters." See *From Shipmates to Soldiers: Emerging Black Identities in the Río de La Plata* (Albuquerque: University of New Mexico Press, 2015), 185.

35. Herman L. Bennett, *Colonial Blackness: A History of Afro-Mexico* (Bloomington: Indiana University Press, 2009), 117.

36. Ben Vinson III, *Bearing Arms for His Majesty: The Free-Colored Militia in Colonial Mexico* (Stanford, CA: Stanford University Press, 2001), 151.

37. Vinson, *Bearing Arms*, 199–219.

Glossary

a cargo de. Phrase used to link dependents to a head of household on a tribute register.

agentes fiscales. Legal assistants to a *fiscal*, or crown attorney.

agregado. Added to a family unit on a register.

alcabala. Sales tax.

alcalde mayor. District judge comparable to a *corregidor*.

alcalde ordinario. Judge and town council member sometimes referred to simply as alcalde.

almojarifazgo. Customs duty.

amos. Masters or labor bosses.

arrimado. Term used on tribute registers to describe people living in improvised settlements or in the same household.

aspecto. Appearance, aspect.

audiencias. Regional high courts or areas of the court's jurisdiction.

ausente. Term used to designate those absent during tribute registration.

bando. Proclamation.

barrios. Neighborhoods or subdivisions within a town or city.

caballero. Gentleman.

cabecera. Head town or seat of administration.

cacique. Member of a family of status whose members held offices in local Indian governments.

calidad. Used to describe status and "qualities" of personhood based on occupation, physical appearance, family, lineage, economic standing, and language.

calidad de por ahora. Temporary tribute relief granted while authorities reviewed a case.

calidad tributaria. Tributary quality.

cargo y data. Charge and discharge system of accounting.

carta de pago. Receipt.

cartas de hidalguía. Recognition of nobility, available for purchase by commoners who had proven their worth and loyalty.
casados de edad. Married couples of legal majority.
casados sin edad. Married couples under eighteen years of age.
casta. Term referring to either lineage or a person of mixed ancestry.
castizo/a. Child of mestizo and Spanish parentage.
catastro. Census, register.
chino. Person of African descent, though also used to describe a person of East Asian ancestry.
clase. Class.
cofradías. Lay Catholic brotherhoods.
color quebrado. People of mixed ancestry, literally "broken color."
comisarios. Representatives or delegates.
condición. Status, often describing the "condition" of being enslaved or free.
congregaciones. Rural settlements and hamlets, population concentration.
contador. Accountant.
contador de retasas. Accountant in charge of reassessing accounts.
contaduría. Accounting section.
contribuyentes. Taxpayers.
corregidor. District judge charged with managing jurisdictions with non-Indian populations. Similar to the *alcalde mayor*. *Corregidores de indios* were assigned to Indian districts.
coyote. Uncommon caste usually referring to a person of Afro-Indigenous ancestry.
criollo. Born in or native to the Americas.
cuadrillas. Areas designated for workers' family dwellings.
cuartel. Town district or quarter.
cuates. Twins.
cuenta. Population calculation; account.
curato. Parochial jurisdiction.
de estado suelto. Unmarried.
degeneración. Degeneration.
depósito. Custody and confinement, often in a home.
diezmo. Tithe.
divorciado. Divorced.
doncella. Unmarried woman or young woman.
encomendero. Holder of an *encomienda*.
encomienda. Grant of Indian labor and tribute to Spaniards.
esclavo. Slave.
españoles. Spaniards and their descendants in the Americas, also translated as creoles.

estadística. Statistics, or that which is related to the state.
estados. States of accounts.
estancia. Small, private agricultural or cattle estate.
exento/a. Exempt.
expósito. Foundling or abandoned child.
fanega. Unit of measurement equal to around one and one-half bushels.
fiador. Guarantor.
fiscal. Crown attorney.
forastero. Outsider or migrant.
gemelos. Twins.
géneros de gente. Sixteenth-century description of different types of people.
gracias al sacar. Official whitening petition available for purchase.
hacendado. Owner of a hacienda.
haciendas. Large landed estates.
hermana. Sister.
hermano. Brother.
hidalgos. Spanish nobles.
hija/hijo de. Daughter of/son of.
hijo del anterior. Term used on tribute registers to designate a taxpayer as the child of the family from the preceding entry.
hijo natural. Illegitimate status, natural son.
huérfano. Orphan.
huipiles. Blouses or cloaks worn by Indian women.
indio. Legal, fiscal, and social category applied to Indians.
indio de reduccíon. Indian living in a forced settlement.
indios de pueblo. Indians who lived in legally defined towns.
indios laboríos. Indians who worked for wages on estates.
indios vagos. Temporary male workers unaffiliated with a specific Indian town.
Junta Superior de Real Hacienda. Superior board of the exchequer.
justicia. Magistrate.
labradores. Farmers.
limpieza de sangre. Purity of blood.
linaje. Lineage.
lobos. People of mixed Indian and African ancestry.
mapas. Maps or charts.
matlazahuatl. Epidemic disease, typhus.
matrícula. List or census sometimes referred to as a *padrón*.
mestizaje. Process of "mixing" racial or caste groups together.
mestizos. Children of Spaniards and Indians.
ministros. One-half real charge applied to Indian tributes to provide legal insurance.

morenos. People of African descent. Similar to *pardo*.
morisco. Person of mixed African descent, often also of European ancestry.
mulata/o. Person of African descent who also had European or Indian ancestry.
mulata/o libre. Free *mulato* person.
mulatillos. Children of African descent.
natural. Native of a place or interchangeable with *indio*.
negro libre. Free black person.
obrajes. Workshops, especially for textiles.
oficio. Trade.
oidores. Judges from an audiencia.
operarios de minas. Mine workers.
padrón. Register or census, similar to a *matrícula*.
padrón de pardos. Tribute register, list of *pardos*.
parajes. Rural settlements and hamlets.
parcialidad. District.
pardo. Somewhat euphemistic term for a person of African descent.
parroquia. Parish.
partido. Jurisdiction, district.
patria potestad. Authority of parents over children.
pecheros. Castilian commoners.
pechos reales. Royal taxes paid by commoners.
plebeyo. Plebeian.
pleito. Lawsuit, legal complaint.
pleitos de hidalguía. Lawsuits on behalf of an individual or family seeking noble status.
pobladores. Colonizers or settlers.
principal. Noble or elite Indians.
probanza. Proof.
procurador de pobres. Court-appointed representative for the poor.
próximos a tributar. Minors nearing tributary age who were next in line to pay tribute.
pueblo. Town.
puesto. Rural settlement or hamlet.
pulquería. Tavern serving the fermented drink *pulque*.
quinto. Royal mining tax totalling one-fifth.
rancho. Ranch or small town.
raza. Race or lineage.
real. One-eighth of a peso.
real cédula. Royal decree.
Real Hacienda. Royal Treasury.
reales cajas. Regional treasuries.

reales de minas. Jurisdictions containing a mine.
relaciones. Reports.
reserva. Temporary tribute relief.
reservado. Person temporarily excused from paying tributes.
sanguinidad. Lineage.
servicio personal. Indian labor and services, often rendered to colonists.
servicio real. Additional royal taxes charged of tributaries.
servicios. Supplemental taxes of variable amounts paid by *pecheros*.
sin hijos. Without biological children.
solteras. Unmarried women.
solteros. Unmarried men.
tanteos. Estimated levels of collection.
tasa. Rate of taxation.
tasación. Survey or assessment of a tributary community.
tercio. Four-month cycle customary in Castilian debt payments.
tianguis. Markets.
tomín. One-eighth of a *peso*.
tostón. Four reales, or half of one peso.
traje. Mode of dress.
tributario. Tributary.
tributo. Tribute.
vagos. Vagabonds.
vasallaje. Alternate name for royal tribute.
vecinos. Citizen of a local community.
visita. In-person inspection and evaluation by a *visitador*.
visitador. Royal inspector.
viudo/a. Widower or widow.
zambaigo. Person of mixed African and Indian ancestry.

Bibliography

Published Primary Sources and Contemporary Works

Acuña, René. *Relaciones geográficas del siglo XVI*. 10 vols. Mexico City: Universidad Nacional Autónoma de México, Instituto de Investigaciones Antropológicas, 1982.

Campillo y Cossío, José del. *Nuevo sistema de gobierno económico para la América*. Madrid: Imprenta de Benito Cano, 1789.

Canga Argüelles, José. *Diccionario de hacienda*. 5 vols. London: Imprenta Española de M. Calero, 1826–27.

Covarrubias Orozco, Sebastián de. *Tesoro de la lengua castellana o española*. Madrid: L. Sánchez, 1611.

Cowans, Jon. *Early Modern Spain: A Documentary History*. Philadelphia: University of Pennsylvania Press, 2003.

Diego-Fernández Sotelo, Rafael. *El proyecto de José de Gálvez de 1774 en las ordenanzas de intendentes de Río de la Plata y Nueva España*. Zamora: El Colegio de Michoacán, 2016.

Fonseca, Fabián de, and Carlos de Urrutia. *Historia general de Real Hacienda*. 6 vols. Mexico City: V. G. Torres, 1845–53.

García Acosta, Virginia, Juan Manuel Pérez Zevallos, and América Molina del Villar. *Desastres agrícolas en México: Catálogo histórico, tomo I: Epocas prehispánica y colonial (958–1822)*. Mexico City: Centro de Investigaciones y Estudios Superiores en Antropología Social, 2003.

García Icazbalceta, Joaquín. *Colección de documentos para la historia de México: Versión actualizada*. Alicante: Biblioteca Virtual Miguel de Cervantes, 1999. Available online at http://www.cervantesvirtual.com/nd/ark:/59851/bmc4b2z9.

Hernández y Dávalos, Juan E. *Colección de documentos para la historia de la guerra de independencia de México de 1808 a 1821*. 6 vols. Mexico City: José María Sandoval, 1877–82.

Humboldt, Alexander von. *Ensayo político sobre Nueva España*. Translated by Vicente González Arnao. 4 vols. Paris: Librería de Lecointe, 1836.

Klein, Herbert S., and John J. TePaske. *Las cartas cuentas de la Real Hacienda de la América española, siglo XVI a principios del siglo XIX* (CD-ROM). Mexico City: Colegio de México, 2004.

Konetzke, Richard. *Colección de documentos para la historia de la formación social de Hispanoamerica*. 4 vols. Madrid: Consejo Superior de Investigaciones Científicas, 1953–62.

Mantilla Trolle, Marina, Rafael Diego-Fernández Sotelo, and Agustín Moreno. *Real Or-*

denanza para el establecimiento e instrucción de intendentes de ejército y provincial en el reino de la Nueva España: Edición anotada de la Audiencia de la Nueva Galicia. Guadalajara: Universidad de Guadalajara, 2008.

Miño Grijalva, Manuel. *Censo de la población de la Ciudad de México, 1790 censo de Revillagigedo* (CD-ROM). Mexico City: El Colegio de México, 2002.

Ramírez Meza, Benito. "Matrícula y retasa de tributarios del Real de Nuestra Señora del Rosario: Real del Rosario, abril de 1774." *Clío* 6, no. 22 (1998): 161–97.

Real Academia Española. *Diccionario de Autoridades*. 6 vols. Madrid: Francisco del Hierro, 1729–39.

———. *Diccionario de la lengua castellana*. 1st ed. Madrid: D. Joaquín Ibarra, 1780.

Recopilación de leyes de los reynos de las Indias. 4 vols. Madrid: Julián de Paredes, 1681. Facsimile reprint, Madrid: Ediciones Cultura Hispánica, 1973.

Romero de Solís, José Miguel. *Padrón de negros en Colima de la Nueva España (siglo XVI)*. Colima: Archivo Histórico del Municipio de Colima, 2007.

Sánchez Santiró, Ernest. *Padrón del Arzobispado de México, 1777*. Mexico City: Archivo General de la Nación, 2003.

Sandoval, Alonso de. *Treatise on Slavery: Selections from De Instauranda Aethiopum Salute*. Translated by Nicole von Germeten. Indianapolis: Hackett Publishing, 2008.

Serrano Migallón, Fernando. *La vida constitucional de México*. 2 vols. Mexico City: Fondo de Cultura Económica, 2007–9.

Solano, Francisco de, ed. *Relaciones geográficas del Arzobispado de México, 1743*. 2 vols. Madrid: Consejo Superior de Investigaciones Científicas, 1988.

Solórzano Pereira, Juan de. *Política Indiana*. 2 vols. Madrid: Diego Díaz de la Carrera, 1648.

TePaske, John J., and Herbert S. Klein. *Ingresos y egresos de la Real Hacienda de Nueva España*. 2 vols. Mexico City: Instituto Nacional de Antropología e Historia, 1986–88.

Terreros y Pando, Esteban. *Diccionario Castellano con las voces de ciencias y artes y sus correspondientes en las tres lenguas: Francesca, Latina é Italiana*. 2 vols. Madrid: Ibarra, Hijos, 1787.

Torre Villar, Ernesto de la, ed. *Instrucciones y memorias de los Virreyes Novohispanos*. 2 vols. Mexico City: Editorial Porrua, 1991.

Villaseñor y Sánchez, José Antonio de. *Theatro americano: Descripción general de los reynos y provincias de la Nueva España y sus jurisdicciones*. Edited by María del Carmen Velázquez. Mexico City: Editorial Trillas, 1992.

Zapata y Sandoval, Juan. *Discertación sobre justicia distributiva y sobre la acepción de personas a ella opuesta (1609)*. Edited by Arturo Ramírez Trejo. Mexico City: Universidad Nacional Autónoma de México, 1994.

Zavala, Silvio. *Ordenanzas del trabajo, siglos XVI y XVII*. Mexico City: Editorial Elede, 1947.

Zavala, Silvio Arturo, and María Castelo. *Fuentes para la historia del trabajo en la Nueva España*. 8 vols. Mexico City: Fondo de Cultura Económica, 1939–46.

Secondary Sources

Adams, Maeve E. "Numbers and Narratives: Epistemologies of Aggregation in British Statistics and Social Realism, c. 1790–1880." In *Statistics and the Public Sphere: Numbers and the People in Modern Britain, c. 1800–2000*, edited by Tom Crook and Glen O'Hara, 103–20. New York: Routledge, 2011.

Aguirre Beltrán, Gonzalo. *El negro esclavo en Nueva España: La formación colonial, la medicina popular y otros ensayos*. Mexico City: Fondo de Cultura Económica, 1994.

———. *La población negra de México, 1519–1810: Estudio etno-histórico*. 2nd ed. Mexico City: Fondo de Cultura Económica, 1972.

Althouse, Aaron P. "Contested Mestizos, Alleged Mulattos: Racial Identity and Caste Hierarchy in Eighteenth Century Pátzcuaro, Mexico." *The Americas* 62, no. 2 (2005): 151–75.

Álvarez, Silvia G., and Cecilia Mejía de Rubira. *Parentesco, política y prestigio social en los pueblos de indios del partido de Santa Elena: Padrón de 1803*. Guayaquil: Archivo Histórico del Guayas, 2011.

Andrews, George Reid. *Afro-Latin America: Black Lives, 1600–2000*. Cambridge, MA: Harvard University Press, 2016.

———. *Afro-Latin America, 1800–2000*. Oxford: Oxford University Press, 2004.

Andrien, Kenneth J. *The Kingdom of Quito, 1690–1830: The State and Regional Development*. Cambridge: Cambridge University Press, 1995.

Ángel Cuenya, Miguel. *Puebla de los Ángeles en tiempos de una peste colonial: Una mirada en torno al matlazahuatl de 1737*. Puebla: Benemérita Universidad Autónoma de Puebla, 1999.

Arnold, Linda. *Bureaucracy and Bureaucrats in Mexico City, 1742–1835*. Tucson: University of Arizona Press, 1988.

Arrom, Silvia. *The Women of Mexico City, 1790–1857*. Stanford, CA: Stanford University Press, 1985.

Artola, Miguel. *La hacienda del Antiguo Régimen*. Madrid: Alianza, 1982.

Bakewell, P. J. *Silver Mining and Society in Colonial Mexico: Zacatecas, 1546–1700*. Cambridge: Cambridge University Press, 1971.

Barbier, Jacques A. "The Culmination of the Bourbon Reforms, 1787–1792." *Hispanic American Historical Review* 57, no. 1 (1977): 51–68.

Barrera-Osorio, Antonio. "Empiricism in the Spanish Atlantic World." In *Science and Empire in the Atlantic World*, edited by James Delbourgo and Nicholas Dew, 177–202. New York: Routledge, 2008.

Beneyto Pérez, Juan. *Historia social de España y de Hispanoamérica*. Madrid: Aguilar, 1961.

Bennett, Herman L. *Africans in Colonial Mexico: Absolutism, Christianity, and Afro-Creole Consciousness, 1570–1640*. Bloomington: Indiana University Press, 2003.

———. *Colonial Blackness: A History of Afro-Mexico*. Bloomington: Indiana University Press, 2009.

Benton, Lauren A. *Law and Colonial Cultures: Legal Regimes in World History, 1400–1900*. Cambridge: Cambridge University Press, 2002.

Berco, Cristian. "Perception and the Mulatto Body in Inquisitorial Spain: A Neurohistory." *Past and Present* 231, no. 1 (2016): 33–60.

Berquist, Emily Soule. *The Bishop's Utopia: Envisioning Improvement in Colonial Peru*. Philadelphia: University of Pennsylvania Press, 2014.

Bleichmar, Daniela. *Visible Empire: Botanical Expeditions and Visual Culture in the Hispanic Enlightenment*. Chicago: University of Chicago Press, 2012.

Blumenthal, Debra. *Enemies and Familiars: Slavery and Mastery in Fifteenth-Century Valencia*. Ithaca, NY: Cornell University Press, 2009.

Bolaños, Marta Vera. "La composición de la familia en la ciudad de México en 1790: Una reconstrucción demográfica." In *La población de la ciudad de México en 1790: Estructura social, alimentación y vivienda*, edited by Manuel Miño Grijalva and Sonia

Pérez Toledo, 115–46. Mexico City: Universidad Autónoma Metropolitana, Unidad Iztapalapa, 2004.

Bonil Gómez, Katherine. *Gobierno y calidad en el orden colonial: Las categorías del mestizaje en la provincia de Mariquita en la segunda mitad del siglo XVIII*. Bogotá: Universidad de los Andes, 2011.

Borah, Woodrow. "Un gobierno provincial de frontera en San Luis Potosí (1612–1620)." *Historia Mexicana* 13, no. 4 (1964): 532–50.

Borah, Woodrow Wilson. *Justice by Insurance: The General Indian Court of Colonial Mexico and the Legal Aides of the Half-Real*. Berkeley: University of California Press, 1983.

———. *Price Trends of Royal Tribute Commodities in Nueva Galicia, 1557–1598*. Berkeley: University of California Press, 1992.

Borucki, Alex. "Across Imperial Boundaries: Black Social Networks across the Iberian South Atlantic, 1760–1810." *Atlantic Studies* 14, no. 1 (2017): 11–36.

———. *From Shipmates to Soldiers: Emerging Black Identities in the Río de la Plata*. Albuquerque: University of New Mexico Press, 2015.

Bowser, Frederick P. *The African Slave in Colonial Peru, 1524–1650*. Stanford, CA: Stanford University Press, 1974.

———. "Colonial Spanish America." In *Neither Slave nor Free: The Freedmen of African Descent in the Slave Societies of the New World*, edited by David William Cohen and Jack P. Greene, 19–58. Baltimore: Johns Hopkins University Press, 1972.

Boyer, Richard E. "Honor among Plebeains: Mala Sangre and Social Reputation." In *The Faces of Honor: Sex, Shame, and Violence in Colonial Latin America*, edited by Lyman L. Johnson and Sonya Lipsett-Rivera, 152–78. Albuquerque: University of New Mexico Press, 1998.

———. *Lives of the Bigamists: Marriage, Family, and Community in Colonial Mexico*. Albuquerque: University of New Mexico Press, 2001.

———. "Negotiating Calidad: The Everyday Struggle for Status in Mexico." *Historical Archaeology* 31, no. 1 (1997): 64–73.

———. "Women, *La Mala Vida*, and the Politics of Marriage." In *Sexuality and Marriage in Colonial Latin America*, edited by Asunción Lavrin, 209–87. Lincoln: University of Nebraska Press, 1989.

Brading, D. A. *The First America: The Spanish Monarchy, Creole Patriots, and the Liberal State, 1492–1867*. Cambridge: Cambridge University Press, 1991.

———. *Miners and Merchants in Bourbon Mexico, 1763–1810*. Cambridge: Cambridge University Press, 1971.

Bristol, Joan. *Christians, Blasphemers, and Witches: Afro-Mexican Ritual Practice in the Seventeenth Century*. Albuquerque: University of New Mexico Press, 2007.

———. "From Curing to Witchcraft: Afro-Mexicans and the Mediation of Authority." *Journal of Colonialism and Colonial History* 7, no. 1 (2006): 1–37.

———. "Patriarchs, Petitions, and Prayers: Intersections of Gender and *Calidad* in Colonial Mexico." In *Women, Religion, and the Atlantic World, 1600–1800*, edited by Daniella Kostroun and Lisa Vollendorf, 180–204. Toronto: University of Toronto Press, 2009.

Brockington, Lolita Gutiérrez. *Blacks, Indians, and Spaniards in the Eastern Andes: Reclaiming the Forgotten in Colonial Mizque, 1550–1782*. Lincoln: University of Nebraska Press, 2006.

Brown, Kendall. *A History of Mining in Latin America*. Albuquerque: University of New Mexico Press, 2012.

Brown, Vincent. *The Reaper's Garden: Death and Power in the World of Atlantic Slavery*. Cambridge, MA: Harvard University Press, 2008.

Bryant, Christopher J. "Without Representation, No Taxation: Free Blacks, Taxes, and Tax Exemptions between the Revolutionary and Civil Wars." *Michigan Journal of Race and Law* 21, no. 1 (2015): 91–123.

Bryant, Sherwin K. *Rivers of Gold, Lives of Bondage: Governing through Slavery in Colonial Quito*. Chapel Hill: University of North Carolina Press, 2014.

Burns, Kathryn. "Unfixing Race." In *Histories of Race and Racism: The Andes and Mesoamerica from Colonial Times to the Present*, edited by Laura Gotkowitz, 57–71. Durham, NC: Duke University Press, 2014.

Cahill, David. "Colour by Numbers: Racial and Ethnic Categories in the Viceroyalty of Peru, 1532–1824." *Journal of Latin American Studies* 26, no. 2 (1994): 325–46.

Camarero Bullón, Concepción. "Averiguarlo todo de todos: El catastro de Ensenada." *Estudios Geográficos* 63, no. 248/49 (2002): 493–531.

Camba Ludlow, Ursula. *Imaginarios ambiguos, realidades contradictorias: Conductas y representaciones de los negros y mulatos novohispanos, siglos XVI y XVII*. Mexico City: El Colegio de México, 2008.

Campbell, Leon G. "Black Power in Colonial Peru: The 1779 Tax Rebellion of Lambayeque." *Phylon* 33, no. 2 (1972): 140–52.

Cañeque, Alejandro. *The King's Living Image: The Culture and Politics of Viceregal Power in Colonial Mexico*. New York: Routledge, 2004.

Cañizares-Esguerra, Jorge. *How to Write the History of the New World: Histories, Epistemologies, and Identities in the Eighteenth-Century Atlantic World*. Cultural Sitings. Stanford, CA: Stanford University Press, 2001.

———. *Nature, Empire, and Nation: Explorations of the History of Science in the Iberian World*. Stanford, CA: Stanford University Press, 2006.

———. "New World, New Stars: Patriotic Astrology and the Invention of Indian and Creole Bodies in Colonial Spanish America, 1600–1650." *American Historical Review* 104, no. 1 (1999): 33–68.

Carrera, Magali. *Imagining Identity in New Spain: Race, Lineage, and the Colonial Body in Portraiture and Casta Paintings*. Austin: University of Texas Press, 2003.

Carroll, Patrick J. "Black Aliens and Black Natives in New Spain's Indigenous Communities." In *Black Mexico: Race and Society from Colonial to Modern Times*, edited by Ben Vinson III and Matthew Restall, 72–95. Albuquerque: University of New Mexico Press, 2009.

———. "Black-Native Relations and the Historical Record in Colonial Mexico." In *Beyond Black and Red: African-Native Relations in Colonial Latin America*, edited by Matthew Restall, 245–67. Albuquerque: University of New Mexico Press, 2005.

Carroll, Patrick James. *Blacks in Colonial Veracruz: Race, Ethnicity, and Regional Development*. 2nd ed. Austin: University of Texas Press, 2001.

Castañeda García, Rafael. "Hacia una sociología fiscal: El tributo de la población de color libre de la Nueva España." *Fronteras de la Historia* 19, no. 1 (2014): 152–73.

Castillo, Norma Angélica. "La pérdida de la población de origen africano en la región de Puebla." In *Poblaciones y culturas de origen africano en México*, edited by María Elisa Velázquez and Ethel Correa, 299–325. Mexico City: Instituto Nacional de Antropología e Historia, 2005.

Castillo Palma, Norma Angélica. *Cholula, sociedad mestiza en ciudad india: Un análisis de las consecuencias demográficas, económicas y sociales del mestizaje en una ciudad novohispana (1649–1796)*. Mexico City: Plaza y Valdés Editores, 2001.

———. "Cohabitación y conflictividad entre afromestizos y nahuas en el México Colonial." In *Pautas de convivencia étnica en la América Latina colonial (Indios, negros, mulatos, pardos y esclavos)*, edited by Juan Manuel de la Serna Herrera, 163–86. Mexico City: Universidad Nacional Autónoma de México, 2005.

———. "Informaciones y probanzas de limpieza de sangre: Teoría y realidad frente a la movilidad de la población novohispana producida por el mestizaje." In *El peso de la sangre: Limpios, mestizos y nobles en el mundo hispánico*, edited by Nikolaus Böttcher, Bernd Hausberger, and Max-Sebastián Hering Torres, 219–50. Mexico City: El Colegio de México, 2011.

———. "Probanzas y acusaciones sobre la limpieza de sangre antes y después de la Independencia: La lucha por los privilegios." In *1750–1850: La independencia de México a la luz de cien años; Problemáticas y desenlaces de una larga transición*, edited by Brian C. Connaughton, 347–83. Mexico City: Universidad Autónoma Metropolitana, 2010.

Castro Gutiérrez, Felipe. *Nueva ley y nuevo rey: Reformas borbónicas y rebelión popular en Nueva España*. Zamora: El Colegio de Michoacán, 1996.

Celaya Nández, Yovana. *Alcabalas y Situados: Puebla en el sistema fiscal imperial, 1638–1742*. Mexico City: El Colegio de México, 2010.

———. "José de Gálvez: Pensamiento, evaluaciones y proyectos en la Hacienda novohispana, 1765–1786." In *Pensar la Hacienda pública: Personajes, proyectos y contextos en torno al pensamiento fiscal en Nueva España y México (Siglos XVIII–XX)*, edited by Ernest Sánchez Santiró, 45–72. Mexico City: Instituto Mora, 2014.

Chalhoub, Sidney, "Illegal Enslavement and the Precariousness of Freedom in Nineteenth-Century Brazil." In *Assumed Identities: The Meanings of Race in the Atlantic World*, edited by John D. Garrigus and Christopher Morris, 88–115. College Station: Texas A&M University Press, 2010.

Chamberlain, Robert S. *The Pre-Conquest Tribute and Service System of the Maya as Preparation for the Spanish Repartimiento-Encomienda in Yucatán*. Coral Gables, FL: University of Miami Press, 1951.

Chambers, Sarah C. *From Subjects to Citizens: Honor, Gender, and Politics in Arequipa, Peru, 1780–1854*. University Park: Pennsylvania State University Press, 1999.

Chance, John K. *Race and Class in Colonial Oaxaca*. Stanford, CA: Stanford University Press, 1978.

Chaves, María Eugenia. "Slave Women's Strategies for Freedom and the Late Spanish Colonial State." In *Hidden Histories of Gender and the State in Latin America*, edited by Elizabeth Dore and Maxine Molyneux, 108–26. Durham, NC: Duke University Press, 2000.

Coatsworth, John H. "The Limits of Colonial Absolutism: Mexico in the Eighteenth Century." In *Essays in the Political, Economic, and Social History of Colonial Latin America*, edited by Karen Spalding, 25–51. Newark: University of Delaware, Latin American Studies Program, Occasional Papers and Monographs No. 3, 1982.

———. "Political Economy and Economic Organization." In *The Cambridge Economic History of Latin America*. 2 vols. Edited by V. Bulmer-Thomas, John H. Coatsworth, and Roberto Cortés Conde, 235–74. Cambridge: Cambridge University Press, 2006.

Cobá Noh, Lorgio. *El "indio ciudadano": La tributación y la contribución personal directa en Yucatán, 1786–1825*. Mérida: Universidad Autónoma de Yucatán, 2009.

Commons, Aurea. "La población de Nueva España en 1790." *Tempus: Revista de Historia de Facultad de Filosofía y Letras* 3 (1995): 7–111.

Cook, Sherburne Friend, and Woodrow Wilson Borah. *Essays in Population History*. Vol. 1, *Mexico and the Caribbean*. Berkeley: University of California Press, 1971.

Cooper, Frederick. *Colonialism in Question: Theory, Knowledge, History*. Berkeley: University of California Press, 2005.

Cope, R. Douglas. *The Limits of Racial Domination: Plebeian Society in Colonial Mexico City, 1660–1720*. Madison: University of Wisconsin Press, 1994.

Corbeil, Laurent. "Identities in Motion: The Formation of a Plural Indio Society in Early San Luis Potosí, New Spain, 1591–1630." PhD diss., McGill University, 2014.

Córdova Aguilar, Maira Cristina. "Procesos de convivencia de negros, mulatos y pardos en la sociedad de Oaxaca: Siglos XVII y XVIII." PhD diss., Universidad Nacional Autónoma de México, 2017.

Cuenya, Miguel Ángel. *Puebla de los Ángeles en tiempos de una peste colonial: Una mirada en torno al matlazahuatl de 1737*. Zamora: El Colegio de Michoacán, 1999.

Dantas, Mariana L. R. *Black Townsmen: Urban Slavery and Freedom in the Eighteenth-Century Americas*. New York: Palgrave Macmillan, 2008.

———. "Humble Slaves and Loyal Vassals: Free Africans and Their Descendants in Eighteenth-Century Minas Gerais, Brazil." In *Imperial Subjects: Race and Identity in Colonial Spanish America*, edited by Andrew B. Fisher and Matthew D. O'Hara, 115–40. Durham, NC: Duke University Press, 2009.

Díaz, María Elena. *The Virgin, the King, and the Royal Slaves of El Cobre: Negotiating Freedom in Colonial Cuba, 1670–1780*. Stanford, CA: Stanford University Press, 2000.

Díaz Casas, María Camila. "¿De esclavos a ciudadanos? Matices sobre la 'integración' y 'asimilación' de la población de origen africano en la sociedad nacional mexicana, 1810–1850." In *Negros y morenos en iberoamérica: Adaptación y conflicto*, edited by Juan Manuel de la Serna, 273–304. Mexico City: Universidad Nacional Autónoma de México, 2015.

———. "Integration and Assimilation? Afro-Mexicans in the Birth of the Mexican Nation, 1810–1850." In *Slavery, Memory, Citizenship*, edited by Paul E. Lovejoy and Vanessa S. Oliveira, 267–83. Trenton, NJ: Africa World Press, 2016.

Díaz Rementería, Carlos J. "En torno a un aspecto de la política reformista de Carlos III: Las matrículas de tributarios en los virreinatos de Perú y Río de la Plata." *Revista de Indias*, no. 37 (1977): 51–139.

———. "El régimen jurídico del ramo de tributos en Nueva España y las reformas peruanas de Carlos III." *Historia Mexicana* 28, no. 3 (1979): 401–38.

Doenges, Catherine E. "Marriage Mobility in Late Colonial Celaya, Mexico." *Yearbook Conference of Latin Americanist Geographers* 22 (1996): 65–76.

———. "A Regional Society in Colonial Mexico: Eighteenth-Century Celaya, a Perspective from the Household." PhD diss., Syracuse University, 1993.

Ducey, Michael T. *A Nation of Villages: Riot and Rebellion in the Mexican Huasteca, 1750–1850*. Tucson: University of Arizona Press, 2004.

Durán Sandoval, Felipe. "Las condiciones para la utilización del trabajo de negros y afrodescendientes en la minería en San Luis Potosí durante la primera mitad del siglo XVII." In *Interculturalidad y relaciones interétnicas en afroindoamérica*, edited by J. Jesús Serna Moreno and Israel Pineda Ángeles, 173–89. Mexico City: Universidad Nacional Autónoma de México, 2015.

———. "Pueblos de indios y acceso a la tierra en San Luis Potosí, 1591–1767." *Revista Historia y Justicia* 5 (2015): 6–36.

Dym, Jordana. *From Sovereign Villages to National States: City, State, and Federation in Central America, 1759–1839*. Albuquerque: University of New Mexico Press, 2006.

Earle, Rebecca. *The Body of the Conquistador: Food, Race, and the Colonial Experience in Spanish America, 1492–1700*. Cambridge: Cambridge University Press, 2012.

———. "The Pleasures of Taxonomy: Casta Paintings, Classification, and Colonialism." *William and Mary Quarterly* 73, no. 3 (2016): 427–66.

Elisabeth, Léo. "The French Antilles." In *Neither Slave nor Free: The Freedmen of African Descent in the Slave Societies of the New World*, edited by David William Cohen and Jack P. Greene, 134–71. Baltimore: Johns Hopkins University Press, 1972.

Elliott, J. H. *Empires of the Atlantic World: Britain and Spain in America, 1492–1830*. New Haven, CT: Yale University Press, 2006.

———. *Imperial Spain, 1469–1716*. 2nd ed. London: Penguin Books, 2002.

Escobedo Mansilla, Ronald. *El tributo indígena en el Perú: Siglos XVI y XVII*. Pamplona: Ediciones Universidad de Navarra, 1979.

———. "El tributo de los zambaigos, negros y mulatos en el virreinato peruano." *Revista de Indias* 41, no. 163 (1981): 43–54.

Ewald, Ursula. *La industria salinera de México, 1560–1994*. Mexico City: Fondo de Cultura Económica, 1997.

Farriss, Nancy. *Maya Society under Colonial Rule: The Collective Enterprise of Survival*. Princeton, NJ: Princeton University Press, 1984.

Fisher, Andrew B. "Creating and Contesting Community: Indians and Afromestizos in the Late-Colonial Tierra Caliente of Guerrero, Mexico." *Journal of Colonialism and Colonial History* 7, no. 1 (2006): 1–32.

———. "Negotiating Two Worlds: The Free-Black Experience in Guerrero's Tierra Caliente." In *Black Mexico: Race and Society from Colonial to Modern Times*, edited by Ben Vinson III and Matthew Restall, 51–71. Albuquerque: University of New Mexico Press, 2009.

Fisher, Andrew B., and Matthew D. O'Hara. "Introduction: Racial Identites and Their Interpreters." In *Imperial Subjects: Race and Identity in Colonial Latin America*, edited by Andrew B. Fisher and Matthew D. O'Hara, 1–38. Durham, NC: Duke University Press, 2009.

Fisher, Lillian Estelle. *The Intendant System in Spanish America*. New York: Gordian Press, 1969.

Florescano, Enrique, and Isabel Gil Sánchez. *Descripciones económicas regionales de Nueva España*. Mexico City: Instituto Nacional de Antropología e Historia, 1976.

Francois, Marie Eileen. *A Culture of Everyday Credit: Housekeeping, Pawnbroking, and Governance in Mexico City, 1750–1920*. Lincoln: University of Nebraska Press, 2006.

Frederick, Jake. "Without Impediment: Crossing Racial Boundaries in Colonial Mexico." *The Americas* 67, no. 4 (2011): 495–515.

Fuentes, Marisa J. *Dispossessed Lives: Enslaved Women, Violence, and the Archive*. Philadelphia: University of Pennsylvania Press, 2016.

Galaviz de Capdevielle, María Elena. "Descripción y pacificación de la Sierra Gorda." *Estudios de historia novohispana* 4 (1971): 113–49.

García Bernal, Manuela Cristina. *La Sociedad de Yucatán, 1700–1750*. Seville: Escuela de Estudios Hispano-Americanos, 1972.

García García, Carmen. *La crisis de las haciendas locales: De la reforma administrativa a la reforma fiscal (1743–1845)*. Valladolid: Junta de Castilla y León, Consejería de Educación y Cultura, 1996.

García Martínez, Cynthia. "Debates en torno a la población de origen africano y ascendencia africana en las Cortes Generales Extraordinarias de Cádiz." In *Negros y morenos en iberoamérica: Adaptación y conflicto*, edited by Juan Manuel de la Serna, 213–45. Mexico City: Universidad Nacional Autónoma de México, 2015.

García Pérez, Rafael D. *Reforma y resistencia: Manuel de Flon y la intendencia de Puebla.* Mexico City: Editorial Porrúa, 2000.

———. "El régimen tributario en las intendencias novohispanas: La ordenanza para la formación de los autos de vistas, padrones, y matrículas de Revillagigedo II." *Anuario Mexicano de Historia del Derecho* 11/12 (2000): 279–307.

Garner, Richard L., and Spiro E. Stefanou. *Economic Growth and Change in Bourbon Mexico.* Gainesville: University Press of Florida, 1993.

Gauderman, Kimberly. *Women's Lives in Colonial Quito: Gender, Law, and Economy in Spanish America.* Austin: University of Texas Press, 2003.

Gerhard, Peter. *A Guide to the Historical Geography of New Spain.* Cambridge: Cambridge University Press, 1972.

———. *The North Frontier of New Spain.* Princeton, NJ: Princeton University Press, 1982.

Gibson, Charles. *The Aztecs under Spanish Rule: A History of the Indians of the Valley of Mexico.* Stanford, CA: Stanford University Press, 1964.

Gómez, Luis Ramos, and Carmen Ruigómez Gómez. "Una propuesta a la corona para extender la mita y el tributo a negros, mestizos y mulatos (Ecuador, 1735–1748)." *Revista Complutense de Historia de América* 25 (1999): 99–110.

Gómez Gómez, Amalia. *Las visitas de la real hacienda novohispana en el reinado de Felipe V: 1710–1733.* Seville: Editorial CSIC, 1979.

Góngora, Mario. *Studies in the Colonial History of Spanish America.* Cambridge: Cambridge University Press, 1975.

González, Ondina E. "Down and Out in Havana: Foundlings in Eighteenth-Century Cuba." In *Minor Omissions: Children in Latin American History and Society*, edited by Tobias Hecht, 102–13. Madison: University of Wisconsin Press, 2002.

González Undurraga, Carolina. "De la casta a la raza: El concepto de raza; Un singular colectivo de la modernidad, México, 1750–1850." *Historia Mexicana* 60, no. 3 (2011): 1491–525.

———. *Esclavos y esclavas demandando justicia: Chile, 1740–1823; Documentación judicial por carta de libertad y papel de venta.* Santiago de Chile: Editorial Universitaria, 2014.

González-Soriano, Fabricio. "Herencia patológica en la medicina mexicana de la segunda mitad del siglo XIX." *El Boletín Mexicano de Historia y Filosofía de la Medicina* 11, no. 1 (2008): 10–15.

Gonzalbo Aizpuru, Pilar. *Las mujeres en la Nueva España, educación y vida cotidiana.* Mexico City: El Colegio de México, 1987.

Grafe, Regina, and Maria Alejandra Irigoin. "The Spanish Empire and Its Legacy: Fiscal Re-distribution and Political Conflict in Colonial and Post-Colonial Spanish America." *Journal of Global History* 1, no. 2 (2006): 241–67.

———. "A Stakeholder Empire: The Political Economy of Spanish Imperial Rule in America." *Economic History Review* 65, no. 2 (2012): 609–51.

Granados, Luis Fernando. "Cosmopolitan Indians and Mesoamerican Barrios in Bourbon Mexico City: Tribute, Community, Family, and Work in 1800." PhD diss., Georgetown University, 2008.

Graubart, Karen B. "The Creolization of the New World: Local Forms of Identification in Urban Colonial Peru, 1560–1640." *Hispanic American Historical Review* 89, no. 3 (2009): 471–99.

———. *With Our Labor and Sweat: Indigenous Women and the Formation of Colonial Society in Peru, 1550–1700.* Stanford, CA: Stanford University Press, 2007.

Guardino, Peter F. *The Time of Liberty: Popular Political Culture in Oaxaca, 1750–1850*. Durham, NC: Duke University Press, 2005.

Gudmundson, Lowell, and Justin Wolfe. Introduction to *Blacks and Blackness in Central America: Between Race and Place*, edited by Lowell Gudmundson and Justin Wolfe, 1–23. Durham, NC: Duke University Press, 2010.

Guevara Sangiés, María. "Vida cotidiana de castas en Guanajuato, siglo XVIII." In *Pardos, Mulatos y Libertos: Sexto Encuentro de Afromexicanistas*, edited by Adriana Naveda Chávez-Hita, 139–61. Xalapa: Universidad Veracruzana, 2001.

Hämäläinen, Pekka. *The Comanche Empire*. New Haven, CT: Yale University Press, 2008.

Hamnett, Brian. *Politics and Trade in Southern Mexico, 1750–1821*. Cambridge: Cambridge University Press, 1971.

Haring, C. H. "The Early Spanish Colonial Exchequer." *American Historical Review* 23, no. 4 (1918): 779–96.

———. *The Spanish Empire in America*. New York: Harcourt, Brace and World, 1963.

Hassig, Ross. *Trade, Tribute, and Transportation: The Sixteenth-Century Political Economy of the Valley of Mexico*. Norman: University of Oklahoma Press, 1985.

Helg, Aline. *Liberty and Equality in Caribbean Colombia, 1770–1835*. Chapel Hill: University of North Carolina Press, 2004.

Hering Torres, M. "Colores de piel: Una revisión histórica de larga duración." In *Debates sobre ciudadanía y políticas raciales en las Américas Negras*, edited by C. Mosquera, 113–60. Bogotá: Universidad Nacional de Colombia, 2010.

Hering Torres, Max S. "Purity of Blood: Problems of Interpretation." In *Race and Blood in the Iberian World*, edited by María Elena Martínez, David Nirenberg, and Max-Sebastián Hering Torres, 11–38. Zurich: LIT Verlag, 2012.

Hernández Esteve, Esteban. "Reflexiones sobre la naturaleza y los orígenes de la contabilidad por partida doble." *Pecvnia*, no. 1 (2005): 93–124.

Herrera, Robinson A. *Natives, Europeans, and Africans in Sixteenth-Century Santiago de Guatemala*. Austin: University of Texas Press, 2003.

Herzog, Tamar. *Defining Nations: Immigrants and Citizens in Early Modern Spain and Spanish America*. New Haven, CT: Yale University Press, 2003.

Higgins, Kathleen J. *"Licentious Liberty" in a Brazilian Gold-Mining Region: Slavery, Gender, and Social Control in Eighteenth-Century Sabará, Minas Gerais*. University Park: Pennsylvania State University Press, 1999.

Hill, Ruth. *Hierarchy, Commerce, and Fraud in Bourbon Spanish America: A Postal Inspector's Exposé*. Nashville: Vanderbilt University Press, 2005.

Hünefeldt, Christine. *Paying the Price of Freedom: Family and Labor among Lima's Slaves, 1800–1854*. Berkeley: University of California Press, 1994.

Isenmann, Eberhard. "Medieval and Renaissance Theories of State Finance." In *Economic Systems and State Finance*, edited by Richard Bonney, 21–52. Oxford: Oxford University Press, 1995.

Jackson, Robert H. *Race, Caste, and Status: Indians in Colonial Spanish America*. Albuquerque: University of New Mexico Press, 1999.

Jarquín Ortega, María Teresa. *Formación y desarrollo de un pueblo novohispano: Metepec en el Valle de Toluca*. Metepec: Colegio Mexiquense, 1990.

Jáuregui, Luis. *La Real Hacienda de Nueva España: Su administración en la época de los intendentes, 1786–1821*. Mexico City: Universidad Autónoma de México, 1999.

Jouve Martín, José R. *The Black Doctors of Colonial Lima: Science, Race, and Writing in Colonial and Early Republican Peru*. Montreal: McGill-Queen's University Press, 2014.

Kagan, Richard L. *Lawsuits and Litigants in Castile, 1500–1700*. Chapel Hill: University of North Carolina Press, 1981.

Kanter, Deborah E. *Hijos del Pueblo: Gender, Family, and Community in Rural Mexico, 1730–1850*. Austin: University of Texas Press, 2008.

Katzew, Ilona. *Casta Painting: Images of Race in Eighteenth-Century Mexico*. New Haven, CT: Yale University Press, 2004.

Kellogg, Susan. "From Parallel Equivalent to Separate but Unequal: Tenocha Mexica Women, 1500–1700." In *Indian Women of Early Mexico*, edited by Susan Schroeder, Stephanie Gail Wood, and Robert Stephen Haskett, 123–44. Norman: University of Oklahoma Press, 1997.

———. *Weaving the Past: A History of Latin America's Indigenous Women from the Prehispanic Period to the Present*. New York: Oxford University Press, 2005.

Kinsbruner, Jay. *Not of Pure Blood: The Free People of Color and Racial Prejudice in Nineteenth-Century Puerto Rico*. Durham, NC: Duke University Press, 1996.

Klein, Herbert S. *The American Finances of the Spanish Empire: Royal Income and Expenditures in Colonial Mexico, Peru, and Bolivia, 1680–1809*. Albuquerque: University of New Mexico Press, 1998.

———. *Haciendas and Ayllus: Rural Society in the Bolivian Andes in the Eighteenth and Nineteenth Centuries*. Stanford, CA: Stanford University Press, 1993.

Klein, Herbert S., and Jacques A. Barbier. "Recent Trends in the Study of Spanish American Colonial Public Finance." *Latin American Research Review* 23, no. 1 (1988): 35–62.

Klein, Herbert S., and Ben Vinson III. *African Slavery in Latin America and the Caribbean*. 2nd ed. Oxford: Oxford University Press, 2007.

Kuethe, Alan J., and Kenneth J. Andrien. *The Spanish Atlantic World in the Eighteenth Century: War and the Bourbon Reforms, 1713–1796*. Cambridge: Cambridge University Press, 2014.

Kuznesof, Elizabeth Ann. "Gender Ideology, Race, and Female-Headed Households in Urban Mexico, 1750–1850." In *State and Society in Spanish America during the Age of Revolution*, edited by Victor M. Uribe-Uran, 149–70. Wilmington, DE: Scholarly Resources, 2001.

Ladero Quesada, Miguel Ángel. *Fiscalidad y poder real en Castilla (1252–1369)*. 2nd ed. Madrid: Real Academia de la Historia, 2011.

Lafuente, Antonio, and Nuria Valverde. "Making Scientific Objects and Setting Standards: Values, Technology, Government and the Enlightenment." *EMPIRIA: Revista de Metodología de Ciencias Sociales* 18 (2009): 115–46.

Landers, Jane. *Black Society in Spanish Florida*. Urbana: University of Illinois Press, 1999.

Landers, Jane G. "Cimarrón and Citizen: African Ethnicity, Corporate Identity, and the Evolution of Free Black Towns in the Spanish Circum-Caribbean." In *Slaves, Subjects, and Subversives: Blacks in Colonial Latin America*, edited by Jane G. Landers and Barry M. Robinson, 111–45. Albuquerque: University of New Mexico Press, 2006.

Lavrin, Asunción. "In Search of the Colonial Woman in Mexico: The Seventeenth and Eighteenth Centuries." In *Latin American Women: Historical Perspectives*, edited by Asunción Lavrin, 3–22. Westport, CT: Greenwood Publishing, 1978.

Lavrin, Asunción, and Edith Courturier. "Dowries and Wills: A View of Women's Socioeconomic Role in Colonial Guadalajara and Puebla, 1640–1790." *Hispanic American Historical Review* 59, no. 2 (1979): 280–304.

Lewis, Laura. "Between 'Casta' and 'Raza': The Example of Colonial Mexico." In *Race and Blood in the Iberian World*, edited by María Elena Martínez, David Nirenberg, and Max-Sebastián Hering Torres, 99–124. Zurich: LIT Verlag, 2012.

———. *Hall of Mirrors: Power, Witchcraft, and Caste in Colonial Mexico*. Durham, NC: Duke University Press, 2003.

Lipsett-Rivera, Sonya. *Gender and the Negotiation of Daily Life in Mexico, 1750–1856*. Lincoln: University of Nebraska Press, 2012.

Lockhart, James. *The Nahuas after the Conquest: A Social and Cultural History of the Indians of Central Mexico, Sixteenth through Eighteenth Centuries*. Stanford, CA: Stanford University Press, 1991.

Lokken, Paul. "Angolans in Amatitlán: Sugar, African Migrants, and *Gente Ladina* in Colonial Guatemala." In *Blacks and Blackness in Central America: Between Race and Place*, edited by Lowell Gudmundson and Justin Wolfe, 27–56. Durham, NC: Duke University Press, 2010.

———. "La recaudación del tributo de laborío y la formación burocrática de identidades sociales en la provincia de Guatemala, 1608–1644." *Boletín de la Asociación para el Fomento de los Estudios Históricos en Centroamérica* 51, no. 1 (2011): 1–49.

———. "Useful Enemies: Seventeenth-Century Piracy and the Rise of Pardo Militias in Spanish Central America." *Journal of Colonialism and Colonial History* 5, no. 2 (2004): 1–24.

López Valdés, Rafael L., and Ricardo E. Alegría. *Pardos y morenos esclavos y libres en Cuba y sus instituciones en el Caribe hispano*. San Juan, PR: Centro de Estudios Avanzados de Puerto Rico y el Caribe, 2007.

López-Beltrán, Carlos. "The Medical Origins of Heredity." In *Heredity Produced: At the Crossroads of Biology, Politics, and Culture, 1500–1870*, edited by Staffan Müller-Wille and Hans-Jörg Rheinberger, 105–32. Cambridge, MA: MIT Press, 2007.

———. "Sangre y temperamento: Pureza y mestizajes en las sociedades de castas americanas." In *Saberes locales: Ensayos sobre historia de la ciencia en América Latina*, edited by Frida Gorbach and Carlos López-Beltrán, 289–342. Zamora: El Colegio de Michoacán, 2008.

Love, Edgar F. "Marriage Patterns of Persons of African Descent in a Colonial Mexico City Parish." *Hispanic American Historical Review* 51, no. 1 (1971): 79–91.

Lutz, Christopher. *Santiago de Guatemala, 1541–1773: City, Caste, and the Colonial Experience*. Norman: University of Oklahoma Press, 1994.

Lynch, John. *Bourbon Spain, 1700–1808*. History of Spain. Oxford: Basil Blackwell, 1989.

MacLachlan, Colin M. *Spain's Empire in the New World: The Role of Ideas in Institutional and Social Change*. Berkeley: University of California Press, 1991.

Madeira Santos, Catarina. "Administrative Knowledge in a Colonial Context: Angola in the Eighteenth Century." *British Journal for the History of Science* 43, no. 4 (2010): 539–56.

Mangan, Jane E. "A Market of Identities: Women, Trade, and Ethnic Labels in Colonial Potosí." In *Imperial Subjects: Race and Identity in Colonial Spanish America*, edited by Andrew B. Fisher and Matthew D. O'Hara, 61–80. Durham, NC: Duke University Press, 2009.

———. *Trading Roles: Gender, Ethnicity, and the Urban Economy in Colonial Potosí*. Durham, NC: Duke University Press, 2005.

Marichal, Carlos. *Bankruptcy of Empire: Mexican Silver and the Wars between Spain, Britain, and France, 1760–1810*. Cambridge: Cambridge University Press, 2007.

———. "Beneficios y costes fiscales del colonialismo: Las remesas americanas a España, 1760–1814." *Revista de Historia Económica* 15, no. 3 (1997): 475–505.

———. "Una difícil transición fiscal: Del régimen colonial al México independiente,

1750–1850." In *De colonia a nación: Impuestos y política en México, 1750–1860*, edited by Carlos Marichal and Daniela Marino, 19–58. Mexico City: El Colegio de México, 2001.

———. "Money, Taxes, and Finance." In *The Cambridge Economic History of Latin America*. 2 vols. Edited by V. Bulmer-Thomas, John H. Coatsworth, and Roberto Cortés Conde, 423–60. Cambridge: Cambridge University Press, 2006.

Marichal, Carlos, and Matilde Souto Mantecón. "Silver and Situados: New Spain and the Financing of the Spanish Empire in the Caribbean in the Eighteenth Century." *Hispanic American Historical Review* 74, no. 4 (1994): 587–613.

Mariluz Urquijo, José María. *El agente de la administración pública en Indias*. Buenos Aires: Instituto Internacional de Historia del Derecho Indiano, 1998.

Marín Bosch, Miguel. *Puebla neocolonial, 1777–1831: Casta, ocupación y matrimonio en la segunda ciudad de Nueva España*. Zapopan: Colegio de Jalisco, 1999.

Marino, Daniela. "El afán de recaudar y la dificultad de reformar: El tributo indígena en la Nueva España tardocolonial." In *De colonia a nación: Impuestos y política en México, 1750–1860*, edited by Carlos Marichal and Daniela Marino, 61–83. Mexico City: El Colegio de México, 2001.

———. "Visitas, padrones y tributo: Una lectura política de la demografía indígena y la fiscalidad borbónica en Charcas," *Anuario IEHS: Instituto de Estudios histórico sociales* 12 (1997): 307–23.

Martin, Cheryl English. *Governance and Society in Colonial Mexico: Chihuahua in the Eighteenth Century*. Stanford, CA: Stanford University Press, 1996.

Martínez, María Elena. *Genealogical Fictions: Limpieza de Sangre, Religion, and Gender in Colonial Mexico*. Stanford, CA: Stanford University Press, 2008.

———. "The Language, Genealogy, and Classification of 'Race' in Colonial Mexico." In *Race and Classification: The Case of Mexican America*, edited by Ilona Katzew and Susan Deans-Smith, 25–42. Stanford, CA: Stanford University Press, 2009.

———. "Space, Order, and Group Identities in a Spanish Colonial Town: Puebla de los Angeles." In *The Collective and the Public in Latin America: Cultural Identities and Political Order*, edited by Luis Roniger and Tamar Herzog, 13–36. Brighton: Sussex Academic Press, 2014.

Martínez Aldana, Tania Itzel. "Amor y matrimonio: Familia, mestizaje y movilidad social; En un estudio de caso del Querétaro de finales del siglo XVIII." *Dos Puntas* 12 (2015): 137–56.

Martínez Santos, Pedro. "Reforma de la contabilidad colonial en el siglo XVIII." *Anuario de Estudios Americanos* 17 (1960): 253–536.

Martinez-Alier, Verena. *Marriage, Class, and Colour in Nineteenth-Century Cuba: A Study of Racial Attitudes and Sexual Values in a Slave Society*. London: Cambridge University Press, 1974.

Masferrer León, Cristina. *Muleke, negritas y mulatillos: Niñez, familia y redes sociales de los esclavos de origen africano en la ciudad de México, siglo XVII*. Mexico City: Instituto Nacional de Antropología e Historia, 2013.

Matthew, Laura E. *Memories of Conquest: Becoming Mexicano in Colonial Guatemala*. Chapel Hill: University of North Carolina Press, 2012.

McCaa, Robert. "Calidad, Clase, and Marriage in Colonial Mexico: The Case of Parral, 1788–90." *Hispanic American Historical Review* 64, no. 3 (1984): 477–501.

McEnroe, Sean F. *From Colony to Nationhood in Mexico*. Cambridge: Cambridge University Press, 2012.

McKinley, Michelle A. *Fractional Freedoms: Slavery, Intimacy, and Legal Mobilization in Colonial Lima, 1600–1700*. New York: Cambridge University Press, 2016.

Mecham, J. Lloyd. "The Real de Minas as a Political Institution: A Study of a Frontier Institution in Spanish Colonial America." *Hispanic American Historical Review* 7, no. 1 (1927): 45–83.

Milton, Cynthia. *The Many Meanings of Poverty: Colonialism, Social Compacts, and Assistance in Eighteenth-Century Ecuador*. Stanford, CA: Stanford University Press, 2007.

Milton, Cynthia E., and Ben Vinson III. "Counting Heads: Race and Non-native Tribute Policy in Colonial Spanish America." *Journal of Colonialism and Colonial History* 3, no. 3 (2002): 1–49.

Miranda, José. *El tributo indígena en la Nueva España durante el siglo XVI*. 2nd ed. Mexico City: El Colegio de México, 2005.

Miranda Nava, Luis Enrique. *La esclavitud en el Valle de Toluca, 1558–1630*. Toluca de Lerdo: Gobierno del Estado de México, 2010.

Molina del Villar, América. "Las prácticas sanitarias y médicas en la Ciudad de México, 1736–1739." *Estudios del hombre* 20 (2005): 39–58.

———. "Tributos y calamidades en el centro de la Nueva España, 1727–1762: Los límites del impuesto justo." *Historia Mexicana* 54, no. 1 (2004): 15–57.

Montoya, Alejandro. *San Luis Potosí Novohispano: Origen y evolución sociodemográfica de un real de minas*. San Luis Potosí: Universidad Autónoma de San Luis Potosí, 2009.

Morgan, Jennifer. *Laboring Women: Reproduction and Gender in New World Slavery*. Philadelphia: University of Pennsylvania Press, 2004.

Morgan, Philip D. "British Encounters with Africans and African-Americans, circa 1600–1780." In *Strangers within the Realm: Cultural Margins of the First British Empire*, edited by Bernard Bailyn and Philip D. Morgan, 157–219. Chapel Hill: University of North Carolina Press, 1991.

Mörner, Magnus. *Race Mixture in the History of Latin America*. Boston: Little, Brown, 1967.

Navarro García, Luis. "La crisis del reformismo borbónico bajo Carlos IV." *Temas Americanistas* 13 (1997): 1–22.

Naveda Chávez-Hita, Adriana. "Denominaciones raciales en archivos locales." In *Pardos, Mulatos y Libertos: Sexto Encuentro de Afromexicanistas*, edited by Adriana Naveda Chávez-Hita, 195–206. Xalapa: Universidad Veracruzana, 2001.

Nessler, Graham T. *An Islandwide Struggle for Freedom: Revolution, Emancipation, and Reenslavement in Hispaniola, 1789–1809*. Chapel Hill: University of North Carolina Press, 2016.

Nirenberg, David. "Mass Conversion and Genealogical Mentalities: Jews and Christians in Fifteenth-Century Spain." *Past and Present* 174, no. 1 (2002): 3–41.

O'Hara, Matthew. *A Flock Divided: Race, Religion, and Politics in México, 1749–1857*. Durham, NC: Duke University Press, 2010.

O'Phelan Godoy, Scarlett. *Rebellions and Revolts in Eighteenth Century Peru and Upper Peru*. Cologne: Bohlau Verlag, 1985.

O'Toole, Rachel Sarah. *Bound Lives: Africans, Indians, and the Making of Race in Colonial Peru*. Pittsburgh: University of Pittsburgh Press, 2012.

———. "Mobilizing Muleteer Indigeneity in the Markets of Colonial Peru." In *To Be Indio in Colonial Spanish America*, edited by Mónica Díaz, 95–121. Albuquerque: University of New Mexico Press, 2006.

———. "To Be Free and Lucumí: Ana de la Calle and Making African Diaspora Identities in Colonial Peru." In *Africans to Spanish America: Expanding the Diaspora*, edited by Sherwin K. Bryant, Ben Vinson III, and Rachel Sarah O'Toole, 73–92. Urbana: University of Illinois Press, 2012.

Osborn, Wayne S. "Indian Land Retention in Colonial Metztitlan." *Hispanic American Historical Review* 53, no. 2 (1973): 217–38.

Owensby, Brian. *Empire of Law and Indian Justice*. Stanford, CA: Stanford University Press, 2008.

Pagden, Anthony. "Identity Formation in Spanish America." In *Colonial Identity in the Atlantic World, 1500–1800*, edited by Nicolas P. Canny and Anthony Pagden, 51–94. Princeton, NJ: Princeton University Press, 1989.

Palmer, Colin A. *Slaves of the White God: Blacks in Mexico, 1570–1650*. Cambridge, MA: Harvard University Press, 1976.

Paquette, Gabriel B. *Enlightenment, Governance, and Reform in Spain and Its Empire, 1759–1808*. Basingstoke: Palgrave Macmillan, 2008.

———. "Introduction: Enlightened Reform in Southern Europe and Its Atlantic Colonies in the Long Eighteenth Century." In *Enlightened Reform in Southern Europe and its Atlantic Colonies, c. 1750–1830*, edited by Gabriel B. Paquette, 1–20. Burlington, VT: Ashgate, 2009.

Paredes Martínez, Carlos, and Blanca Lara Tenorio. "Los trabajadores negros en el inicio del desarrollo económico poblano." *Antropología: Revista Interdisciplinaria del INAH* 78 (2005): 23–28.

Patch, Robert. *Maya Revolt and Revolution in the Eighteenth Century*. Armonk, NY: M. E. Sharpe, 2002.

Pearce, Adrian J. *The Origins of Bourbon Reform in Spanish South America, 1700–1763*. Studies of the Americas. New York: Palgrave Macmillan, 2014.

Pérez Rosales, Laura. *Minería y sociedad en Taxco durante el siglo XVIII*. Mexico City: Universidad Iberoamericana, 1996.

Pérez Toledo, Sonia, and Herbert S. Klein. *Población y estructura social de la Ciudad de México, 1790–1842*. Mexico City: Universidad Autónoma Metropolitana, 2005.

Pescador, Juan Javier. *De bautizados a fieles difuntos: Familia y mentalidades en una parroquia urbana, Santa Catarina de México, 1568–1820*. Mexico City: Colegio de México, Centro de Estudios Demográficos y de Desarrollo Urbano, 1992.

Phelan, John Leddy. "Authority and Flexibility in the Spanish Imperial Bureaucracy." *Administrative Science Quarterly* 5, no. 1 (1960): 47–65.

———. *The People and the King: The Comunero Revolution in Colombia, 1781*. Madison: University of Wisconsin Press, 1978.

Phillips, William D. *Slavery in Medieval and Early Modern Iberia*. Philadelphia: University of Pennsylvania Press, 2014.

Pietschmann, Horst. *Las reformas borbónicas y el sistema de intendencias en Nueva España: Un estudio político administrativo*. Translated by Rolf Roland Meyer Misteli. Mexico City: Fondo de Cultura Económica, 1996.

Pollack, Aaron. "Hacia una historia social del tributo de indios y castas en Hispanoamérica: Notas en torno a su creación, desarrollo y abolición." *Historia Mexicana* 66, no. 1 (2016): 65–160.

Portillo Valdés, José M. *Fuero indio: Tlaxcala y la identidad territorial entre la monarquía imperial y la república nacional, 1787–1824*. Mexico City: El Colegio de México, 2015.

Poska, Allyson M. "Babies on Board: Women, Children, and Imperial Policy in the Spanish Empire." *Gender and History* 22, no. 2 (2010): 269–83.

Powell, Philip Wayne. *Soldiers, Indians, and Silver: The Northward Advance of New Spain, 1550–1600*. Berkeley: University of California Press, 1952.

Premo, Bianca. *Children of the Father King: Youth, Authority, and Legal Minority in Colonial Lima*. Chapel Hill: University of North Carolina Press, 2005.

———. *The Enlightenment on Trial: Ordinary Litigants and Colonialism in the Spanish Empire*. New York: Oxford University Press, 2017.

———. "Familiar: Thinking beyond Lineage and across Race in Spanish Atlantic Family History." *William and Mary Quarterly* 70, no. 2 (2013): 295–316.

———. "From the Pockets of Women: The Gendering of the Mita, Migration, and Tribute in Colonial Chucuito, Peru." *The Americas* 57, no. 1 (2000): 63–93.

Priestley, Herbert I. *José de Gálvez: Visitor-General of New Spain (1765–1771)*. Berkeley: University of California Press, 1916.

Proctor, Frank T. "Afro-Mexican Slave Labor in the Obrajes de Paños of New Spain, Seventeenth and Eighteenth Centuries." *The Americas* 60, no. 1 (2003): 33–58.

———. *Damned Notions of Liberty: Slavery, Culture, and Power in Colonial Mexico, 1640–1769*. Albuquerque: University of New Mexico Press, 2010.

———. "La familia y la comunidad esclava en San Luis Potosí y Guanajuato: 1640–1750." In *Rutas de la esclavitud en África y América Latina*, edited by Rina Cáceres Gómez, 223–50. San José: Editorial de la Universidad de Costa Rica, 2001.

Rabell Romero, Cecilia. "Trayectoria de vida familiar, raza y género en Oaxaca colonial." In *Familia y vida privada en la historia de Iberoamérica: Seminario de Historia de la Familia*, edited by Pilar Gonzalbo Aizpuru and Cecilia Rabell Romero, 75–118. Mexico City: Colegio de México and Universidad Nacional Autónoma de México, 1996.

Rabushka, Alvin. *Taxation in Colonial America*. Princeton, NJ: Princeton University Press, 2008.

Rafael, Vicente L. *Contracting Colonialism: Translation and Christian Conversion in Tagalog Society under Early Spanish Rule*. Durham, NC: Duke University Press, 1993.

Ramos, Donald. "Gossip, Scandal, and Popular Culture in Golden Age Brazil." *Journal of Social History* 33, no. 4 (2000): 887–912.

Ramos, Frances L. *Identity, Ritual, and Power in Colonial Puebla*. Tucson: University of Arizona Press, 2012.

Rappaport, Joanne. "'Asi Lo Paresçe Por Su Aspeto': Physiognomy and the Construction of Difference in Colonial Bogotá." *Hispanic American Historical Review* 91, no. 4 (2011): 601–31.

———. *The Disappearing Mestizo: Configuring Difference in the Colonial Kingdom of New Granada*. Durham, NC: Duke University Press, 2014.

Reid-Vazquez, Michele. *The Year of the Lash: Free People of Color in Cuba and the Nineteenth-Century Atlantic World*. Athens: University of Georgia Press, 2011.

Restall, Matthew. *The Black Middle: Africans, Mayas, and Spaniards in Colonial Yucatán*. Stanford, CA: Stanford University Press, 2009.

Reynoso Medina, Araceli. "Aquí somos todos libres . . . La población de Igualapa, 1650–1750." In *De la libertad y la abolición: Africanos y afrodescendientes en Iberoamérica*, edited by Juan Manuel de la Serna, 161–78. Mexico City: Consejo Nacional para la Cultura y las Artes, 2010.

Río, Ignacio del. *La aplicación regional de las reformas Borbónicas en Nueva España: Sonora y Sinaloa, 1768–1787*. 1st ed. Mexico City: Universidad Nacional Autónoma de México, 1995.

Rodríguez O., Jaime E. *The Independence of Spanish America*. Cambridge: Cambridge University Press, 1998.

Romero de Solís, José Miguel. *Negros y mulatos en Colima de la Nueva España (siglo XVI)*. Colima: Archivo Histórico del Municipio de Colima, 2007.

Rubio Mañé, José Ignacio. *El Virreinato: Orígenes y jurisdicciones y dinámica social de los virreyes*. Vol. 1. Mexico City: Instituto de Investigaciones Históricas, Universidad Autónoma de México, 1983.

Sæther, Steinar A. "Bourbon Absolutism and Marriage Reform in Late Colonial Spanish America." *The Americas* 59, no. 4 (2003): 475–509.

Safier, Neil. *Measuring the New World: Enlightenment Science and South America*. Chicago: University of Chicago Press, 2008.

Sánchez-Albornoz, Nicolás. *Indios y tributos en el Alto Perú*. Lima: Instituto de Estudios Peruanos, 1978.

Sánchez Bella, Ismael. *La organización financiera de las Indias, siglo XVI*. Seville: Escuela de Estudios Hispano-Americanos, 1968.

Sánchez Bella, Ismael, Alberto de la Hera, and Carlos J. Díaz Rementería. *Historia del Derecho Indiano*. Madrid: Editorial MAPFRE, 1992.

Sánchez Santiró, Ernest. *Azúcar y poder: Estructura socioeconómica de las alcaldías mayores de Cuernavaca y Cuautla Amilpas, 1730–1821*. Mexico City: Editorial Praxis, 2001.

———. *Corte de caja: La Real Hacienda de Nueva España y el primer reformismo fiscal de los Borbones (1720–1755)*. Mexico City: Instituto de Investigaciones Dr. José María Luis Mora, 2014.

———. *La imperiosa necesidad: Crisis y colapso del erario de Nueva España (1808–1821)*. Mexico City: Instituto de Investigaciones Dr. José María Luis Mora, 2016.

———. "El orden jurídico de la fiscalidad en la Real Hacienda de Nueva España: Un análisis a partir de la calidad, el estado y la clase de los contribuyentes." *Espacio, Tiempo y Forma* 4, no. 27 (2014): 85–107.

———. "Plata y privilegios: El Real de minas de Huautla, 1709–1821." *Estudios de Historia Novohispana* 26, no. 26 (2002): 85–123.

Sartorius, David A. *Ever Faithful: Race, Loyalty, and the Ends of Empire in Spanish Cuba*. Knowledge Unlatched Pilot Collection. Durham, NC: Duke University Press, 2013.

Saunders, A. C. de C. M. *A Social History of Black Slaves and Freedmen in Portugal, 1441–1555*. Cambridge: Cambridge University Press, 1982.

Schwaller, Robert C. "'For Honor and Defence': Race and the Right to Bear Arms in Early Colonial Mexico." *Colonial Latin American Review* 21, no. 2 (2012): 239–66.

———. *Géneros de Gente in Early Colonial Mexico: Defining Racial Difference*. Norman: University of Oklahoma Press, 2016.

———. "'Mulata, Hija de Negro y India': Afro-Indigenous Mulatos in Early Colonial Mexico." *Journal of Social History* 44, no. 3 (2011): 889–914.

Schwartz, Stuart B., and Hal Langfur. "Tapanhuns, Negros de Terra, and Curibocas: Common Cause and Confrontation between Blacks and Natives in Colonial Brazil." In *Beyond Black and Red: African-Native Relations in Colonial Latin America*, edited by Matthew Restall, 81–114. Albuquerque: University of New Mexico Press, 2005.

Scott, James C. *Seeing Like a State: How Certain Schemes to Improve the Human Condition Have Failed*. New Haven, CT: Yale University Press, 1998.

Scott, Rebecca J. "Social Facts, Legal Fictions, and the Attribution of Slave Status: The Puzzle of Prescription." *Law and History Review* 35, no. 1 (2017): 9–30.

Scott, Rebecca J., and Jean M. Hébrard. *Freedom Papers: An Atlantic Odyssey in the Age of Emancipation*. Cambridge, MA: Harvard University Press, 2012.

Seed, Patricia. "Social Dimensions of Race: Mexico City, 1753." *Hispanic American Historical Review* 62, no. 4 (1982): 569–606.

———. *To Love, Honor, and Obey in Colonial Mexico: Conflicts over Marriage Choice, 1574–1821*. Stanford, CA: Stanford University Press, 1988.

Seijas, Tatiana. *Asian Slaves in Colonial Mexico: From Chinos to Indians*. Cambridge: Cambridge University Press, 2014.

———. "Indios Chinos in Eighteenth-Century Mexico." In *To Be Indio in Colonial Spanish America*, edited by Mónica Díaz, 123–41. Albuquerque: University of New Mexico Press, 2006.

Shelton, Laura. "Like a Servant or Like a Son? Circulating Children in Northwestern Mexico (1790–1850)." In *Raising an Empire: Children in Early Modern Iberia and Colonial Latin America*, edited by Ondina E. González and Bianca Premo, 219–37. Albuquerque: University of New Mexico Press, 2007.

Sheridan, Thomas E. *Empire of Sand: The Seri Indians and the Struggle for Spanish Sonora, 1645–1803*. Tucson: University of Arizona Press, 1999.

Sierra, Pablo. "Urban Slavery in Colonial Puebla de los Ángeles, 1536–1708." PhD diss., University of California, Los Angeles, 2013.

Simpson, Lesley Byrd. *Studies in the Administration of the Indians in New Spain*. 3 vols. Berkeley: University of California Press, 1934.

Stein, Stanley J., and Barbara H. Stein. *Apogee of Empire: Spain and New Spain in the Age of Charles III, 1759–1789*. Baltimore: Johns Hopkins University Press, 2003.

———. *Silver, Trade, and War: Spain and America in the Making of Early Modern Europe*. Baltimore: Johns Hopkins University Press, 2000.

Stoler, Ann Laura. *Carnal Knowledge and Imperial Power: Race and the Intimate in Colonial Rule*. Berkeley: University of California Press, 2010.

Storrs, Christopher. "Felipe V: Caesura or Continuity?" In *Early Bourbon Spanish America: Politics and Society in a Forgotten Era (1700–1759)*, edited by Francisco A. Eissa-Barroso and Ainara Vázquez Varela, 9–22. Leiden: Brill, 2013.

Sue, Christina A. *Land of the Cosmic Race: Race Mixture, Racism, and Blackness in Mexico*. New York: Oxford University Press, 2013.

Sweet, James H. "The Iberian Roots of American Racist Thought." *William and Mary Quarterly* 54, no. 1 (1997): 143–66.

Tardieu, Jean-Pierre. *Resistencia de los negros en el Virreinato de México, siglos XVI–XVII*. Madrid: Iberoamericana, 2017.

Tavárez, David. "Legally Indian: Inquisitorial Readings of Indigenous Identity in New Spain." In *Imperial Subjects: Race and Identity in Colonial Spanish America*, edited by Andrew B. Fisher and Matthew D. O'Hara, 81–100. Durham, NC: Duke University Press, 2009.

Taylor, William B. *Drinking, Homicide, and Rebellion in Colonial Mexican Villages*. Stanford, CA: Stanford University Press, 1979.

Telesca, Ignacio. "Sociedad y afrodescendientes en el proceso de independencia del Paraguay." In *"Negros de la patria": Los afrodescendientes en las luchas por la independencia en el antiguo Virreinato del Río de la Plata*, edited by Silvia Mallo and Ignacio Telesca, 149–70. Buenos Aires: Editorial SB, 2010.

TePaske, John J. "Integral to Empire: The Vital Peripheries of Colonial Spanish America." In *Negotiated Empires: Centers and Peripheries in the Americas, 1500–1820*, edited by Christine Daniels and Michael V. Kennedy, 29–41. New York: Routledge, 2002.

———. *A New World of Gold and Silver*. Edited by Kendall W. Brown. Leiden: Brill, 2010.

Terán, Marta. "El movimiento de los indios, las castas y la plebe de Valladolid de Michoacán en el inicio de la guerra por la independencia, 1809–1810." In *Las guerras de inde-*

pendencia en la América española, edited by Marta Terán and José Antonio Serrano Ortega, 273–294. Zamora: El Colegio de Michoacán, 2010.

———. "Geografía de los partidos tributarios de la Nueva España: Los subdelegados como recaudadores de los tributos, 1805–1810." In *De reinos y subdelegaciones: Nuevos escenarios para un nuevo orden en la América borbónica*, edited by Rafael Diego-Fernández Sotelo, María Pilar Gutiérrez Lorenzo, and Luis Alberto Arrioja Díaz Viruell, 73–116. Zamora: El Colegio de Michoacán, 2014.

Terraciano, Kevin. *The Mixtecs of Colonial Oaxaca: Ñudzahui History, Sixteenth through Eighteenth Centuries*. Stanford, CA: Stanford University Press, 2001.

Terrazas, Danielle. "Capitalizing Subjects: Free African-Descended Women of Means in Xalapa, Veracruz, during the Long Seventeenth Century." PhD diss., Duke University, 2012.

Thomson, Guy P. C. *Puebla de los Angeles: Industry and Society in a Mexican City, 1700–1850*. Boulder, CO: Westview Press, 1989.

Thurner, Mark. *From Two Republics to One Divided: Contradictions of Postcolonial Nation-making in Andean Peru*. Durham, NC: Duke University Press, 1997.

Torales Pacheco, María Cristina. *Ilustrados en la Nueva España: Los socios de la Real Sociedad Bascongada de Amigos del País*. Mexico City: Universidad Iberoamericana, 2001.

Tutino, John. *From Insurrection to Revolution in Mexico: Social Bases of Agrarian Violence, 1750–1940*. Princeton, NJ: Princeton University Press, 1986.

———. *Making a New World: Founding Capitalism in the Bajío and Spanish North America*. Durham, NC: Duke University Press, 2011.

Twinam, Ann. "The Church, the State, and the Abandoned: *Expósitos* in Late Eighteenth-Century Havana." In *Raising an Empire: Children in Early Modern Iberia and Colonial Latin America*, edited by Ondina E. González and Bianca Premo, 163–86. Albuquerque: University of New Mexico Press, 2007.

———. "Honor, Sexuality, and Illegitimacy in Colonial Spanish America." In *Sexuality and Marriage in Colonial Latin America*, edited by Asunción Lavrin, 118–55. Lincoln: University of Nebraska Press, 1989.

———. *Public Lives, Private Secrets: Gender, Honor, Sexuality, and Illegitimacy in Colonial Spanish America*. Stanford, CA: Stanford University Press, 1999.

———. *Purchasing Whiteness: Pardos, Mulatos, and the Quest for Social Mobility in the Spanish Indies*. Stanford, CA: Stanford University Press, 2015.

Undurraga, Carolina González. "'De la casta a la raza': El concepto de raza; Un singular colectivo de la modernidad, México, 1750–1850." *Historia Mexicana* 60, no. 3 (2011): 1491–525.

Van Deusen, Nancy E. *Global Indios: The Indigenous Struggle for Justice in Sixteenth-Century Spain*. Narrating Native Histories. Durham, NC: Duke University Press, 2015.

Van Young, Eric. "Etnia, política local e insurgencia en México, 1810–1821." In *Los colores de las independencias americanas: Liberalismo, etnia y raza*, edited by Manuel Chust Calero and Ivana Frasquet, 143–70. Madrid: Consejo Superior de Investigaciones Científicas, 2009.

———. *Hacienda and Market in Eighteenth-Century Mexico: The Rural Economy of the Guadalajara Region, 1675–1820*. Berkeley: University of California Press, 1981.

Velasco Murillo, Dana. *Urban Indians in a Silver City: Zacatecas, Mexico, 1546–1810*. Stanford, CA: Stanford University Press, 2016.

Velázquez, María Elisa, and Carolina González Undurraga, eds. *Mujeres africanas y af-*

rodescendientes: Experiencias de esclavitud y libertad en América Latina y África, Siglos XVI al XIX. Mexico City: Secretaría de Cultura, Instituto Nacional de Antropología e Historia, 2016.

Velázquez Gutiérrez, María Elisa. "Juntos y revueltos: Oficios, espacios y comunidades domésticas de origen africano en la capital novohispana según el censo de 1753." In *Pautas de convivencia étnica en la América Latina colonial (Indios, negros, mulatos, pardos, y esclavos)*, edited by Juan Manuel de la Serna Herrera, 331–46. Mexico City: Universidad Nacional Autónoma de México, 2005.

———. *Mujeres de origen africano en la capital novohispana, siglos XVII y XVIII*. Mexico City: Universidad Nacional Autónoma de México, 2006.

Velázquez Gutiérrez, María Elisa, and Gabriela Iturralde. *Afrodescendientes en México: Una historia de silencio y discriminación*. 2nd ed. Mexico City: Instituto Nacional de Antropología e Historia, 2016.

Villella, Peter B. *Indigenous Elites and Creole Identity in Colonial Mexico, 1500–1800*. Cambridge Latin American Studies 101. New York: Cambridge University Press, 2016.

———. "'Pure and Noble Indians, Untainted by Inferior Idolatrous Races': Native Elites and the Discourse of Blood Purity in Late Colonial Mexico." *Hispanic American Historical Review* 91, no. 4 (2011): 633–63.

Vinson, Ben, III. *Bearing Arms for His Majesty: The Free-Colored Militia in Colonial Mexico*. Stanford, CA: Stanford University Press, 2001.

———. *Before Mestizaje: The Frontiers of Race and Caste in Colonial Mexico*. Cambridge: Cambridge University Press, 2017.

———. "Facetas del concepto de castas: Observaciones sobre la interpretación y el significado de "*casta*" en la Nueva España." In *Vicisitudes Negro Africanas en Iberoamerica: Experiencias de Investigación*, edited by Juan Manuel de la Serna, 357–83. Mexico City: Universidad Autónoma de México, 2012.

———. "From Dawn 'til Dusk: Black Labor in Late Colonial Mexico." In *Black Mexico: Race and Society from Colonial to Modern Times*, edited by Ben Vinson III and Matthew Restall, 96–135. Albuquerque: University of New Mexico Press, 2009.

———. "The Racial Profile of a Rural Mexican Province in the 'Costa Chica': Igualapa in 1791." *The Americas* 57, no. 2 (2000): 269–82.

Vinson, Ben, III, and Matthew Restall. "Black Soldiers, Native Soldiers: Meanings of Military Service in the Spanish American Colonies." In *Beyond Black and Red: African-Native Relations in Colonial Latin America*, edited by Matthew Restall, 15–52. Albuquerque: University of New Mexico Press, 2005.

Von Germeten, Nicole. *Black Blood Brothers: Confraternities and Social Mobility for Afro-Mexicans*. Gainesville: University Press of Florida, 2006.

———. *Violent Delights, Violent Ends: Sex, Race, and Honor in Colonial Cartagena de Indias*. Albuquerque: University of New Mexico Press, 2013.

Von Mentz, Brígida. "Esclavitud en centros mineros y azucareros novohispanos: Algunas propuestas para el estudio de la multietnicidad en el centro de México." In *Poblaciones y culturas de origen africano en México*, edited by María Elisa Velázquez Gutiérrez and Ethel Correa Duró, 259–80. Mexico City: Instituto Nacional de Antropología e Historia, 2005.

Von Vacano, Diego A. *The Color of Citizenship: Race, Modernity, and Latin American/Hispanic Political Thought*. New York: Oxford University Press, 2012.

Vos, Paula de. "The Rare, the Singular, and the Extraordinary: Natural History and the Collection of Curiosities in the Spanish Empire." In *Science in the Spanish and Portu-*

guese Empires, 1500–1800, edited by Daniela Bleichmar, 271–89. Stanford, CA: Stanford University Press, 2009.

Wade, Peter. *Degrees of Mixture, Degrees of Freedom: Genomics, Multiculturalism, and Race in Latin America*. Durham, NC: Duke University Press, 2017.

———. *Race and Ethnicity in Latin America*. 2nd ed. London: Pluto Press, 2010.

Walker, Charles F. *The Tupac Amaru Rebellion*. Cambridge, MA: Belknap Press of Harvard University Press, 2014.

Wanderley, Marcelo da Rocha. "Mulatos libres, redes personales y cogniciones en la Nueva España (siglos XVII–XVIII)." In *Esclavitud, mestizaje y abolicionismo en los mundos hispánicos*, edited by Aurelia Martín Casares, 129–50. Granada: Universidad de Granada, 2015.

Weber, David. *Bárbaros: Spaniards and Their Savages in the Age of Enlightenment*. New Haven, CA: Yale University Press, 2005.

Wheat, David. *Atlantic Africa and the Spanish Caribbean, 1570–1640*. Chapel Hill: University of North Carolina Press, 2016.

Wightman, Ann M. *Indigenous Migration and Social Change: The Forasteros of Cuzco, 1570–1720*. Durham, NC: Duke University Press, 1990.

Wulf, Karin A. *Not All Wives: Women of Colonial Philadelphia*. Ithaca, NY: Cornell University Press, 2000.

Yacher, Leon. "Marriage Migration and Racial Mixing in Colonial Tlazazalca, 1750–1800." Syracuse University Department of Geography, Discussion Paper Series, no. 32 (1977): 1–38.

Yannakakis, Yanna. *The Art of Being In-Between: Native Intermediaries, Indian Identity, and Local Rule in Colonial Oaxaca*. Durham, NC: Duke University Press, 2008.

———. "Costumbre: A Language of Negotiation in Eighteenth-Century Oaxaca." In *Negotiation within Domination: New Spain's Indian Pueblos Confront the Spanish State*, edited by Ethelia Ruiz Medrano and Susan Kellogg, 137–71. Boulder: University Press of Colorado, 2010.

Zavala, Silvio. *Los esclavos indios en Nueva España*. 2nd ed. Mexico City: Colegio Nacional, 1981.

———. *Las instituciones jurídicas en la conquista de América*. 2nd ed. Mexico City: Editorial Porrúa: 1971.

———. *El servicio personal de los indios en la Nueva España*. 7 vols. Mexico City: Colegio de México, 1984.

Zúñiga, Jean-Paul. "Visible Signs of Belonging: The Spanish Empire and the Rise of Racial Logics in the Early Modern Period." In *Polycentric Monarchies: How Did Early Modern Spain and Portugal Achieve and Maintain a Global Hegemony?*, edited by Pedro Cardim, Tamar Herzog, José Javier Ruiz Ibáñez, and Gaetano Sabatini, 125–46. Brighton: Sussex Academic Press, 2012.

Index

Page numbers in italics refer to illustrations.